GEO-SOCIAL REGIONS
OF MEXICO

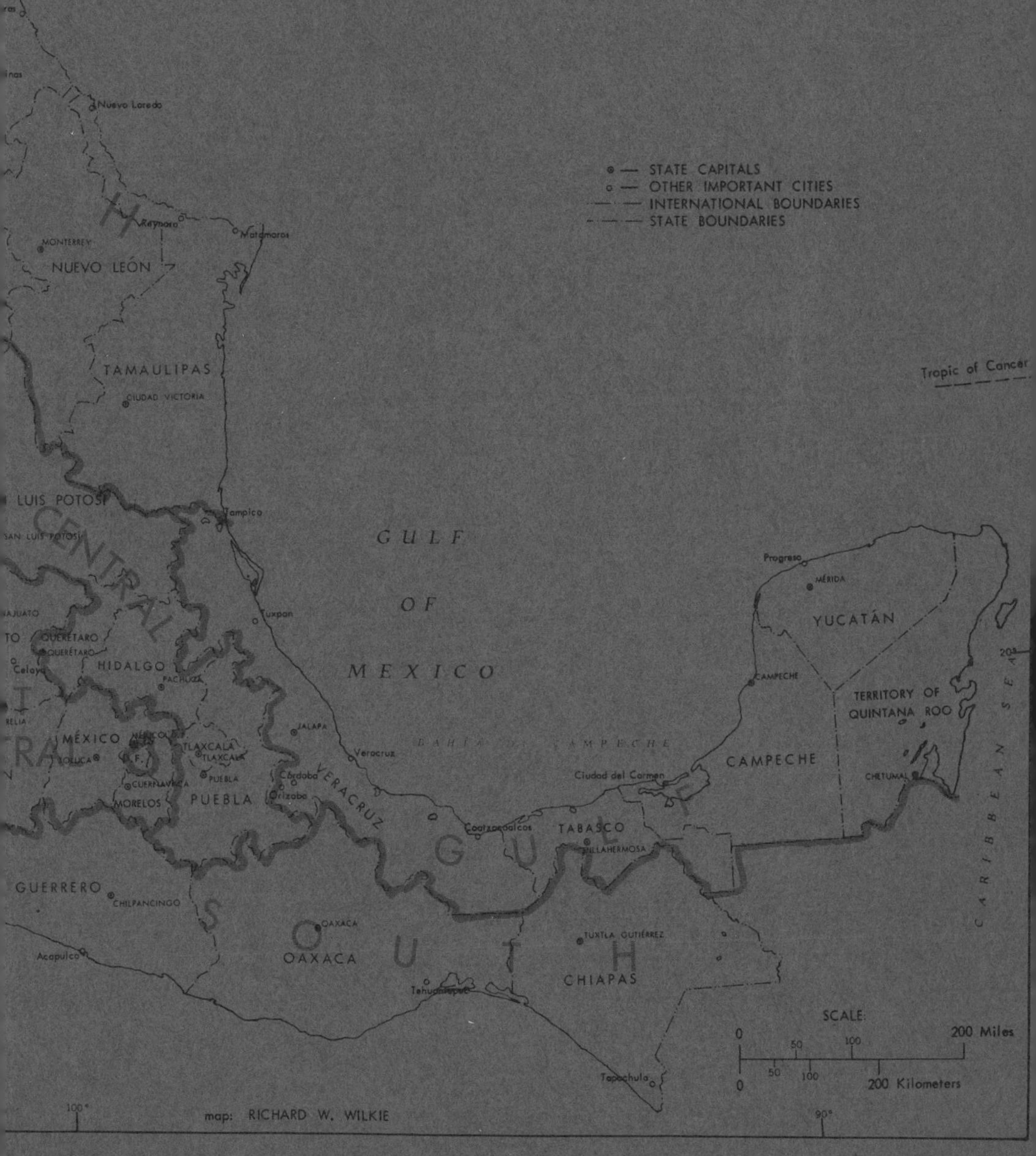

● — STATE CAPITALS
○ — OTHER IMPORTANT CITIES
— — INTERNATIONAL BOUNDARIES
—·— STATE BOUNDARIES

Tropic of Cancer

Nuevo Laredo

Reynosa   Matamoros

MONTERREY
NUEVO LEÓN

TAMAULIPAS

CIUDAD VICTORIA

LUIS POTOSÍ   Tampico

SAN LUIS POTOSÍ

G U L F

O F

M E X I C O

Progreso
MÉRIDA

YUCATÁN

CENTRAL   Tuxpan

CAMPECHE

TERRITORY OF
QUINTANA ROO

QUERÉTARO   HIDALGO
QUERÉTARO   PACHUCA

Celaya

JALAPA

Veracruz   *B A H I A   D E   C A M P E C H E*   CAMPECHE

MÉXICO
TOLUCA   TLAXCALA
TLAXCALA
D.F.   Córdoba   VERACRUZ   Ciudad del Carmen
CUERNAVACA   PUEBLA   Orizaba
MORELOS   PUEBLA   *G   U   L*   TABASCO   CHETUMAL
Coatzacoalcos   VILLAHERMOSA

GUERRERO   CHILPANCINGO   *S*

OAXACA   *O   U   T   H*
Acapulco   OAXACA
TUXTLA GUTIÉRREZ
CHIAPAS
Tehuantepec

C A R I B B E A N   S E A

SCALE:
0   50   100   200 Miles

0   50   100   200 Kilometers

Tapachula

map: RICHARD W. WILKIE

The Mexican Revolution:

FEDERAL EXPENDITURE AND SOCIAL CHANGE SINCE 1910

The Mexican Revolution:

FEDERAL EXPENDITURE
AND SOCIAL CHANGE
SINCE 1910

by James W. Wilkie

WITH A FOREWORD BY HOWARD F. CLINE

SECOND EDITION, REVISED

University of California Press

BERKELEY AND LOS ANGELES 1970

UNIVERSITY OF CALIFORNIA PRESS
BERKELEY AND LOS ANGELES, CALIFORNIA

UNIVERSITY OF CALIFORNIA PRESS, LTD.
LONDON, ENGLAND

SECOND EDITION, REVISED, 1970

DEDICATION

This book is dedicated to my parents, Lucile and Waldo Wilkie, who have studied Spanish, traveled to Mexico, and personally supported Latin American studies in their own way for the last dozen years.

Foreword

The Mexican Revolution, now past its fiftieth year, is an established historical fact. It has had many successes, despite frustrating obstacles to the attainment of the broad goals its leaders have set. A remarkable political system has achieved stability and an economic system has been painfully devised to produce an increasing volume of goods and services for a rapidly expanding population. The Mexican nation has made notable contributions in artistic and intellectual realms. In short, Mexico has achieved many of the aspirations common to what now are termed "newly emergent" countries, whose present is not unlike the Mexican past.

In this study of Mexico's recent history, James Wilkie separates social development from economic, and asks how successive presidents have allotted federal revenues to achieve change in different ideological phases of the Revolution. He analyzes the rate and direction of social change, using as measures the stated national goals: elimination of poverty, illiteracy, and malnutrition. Wilkie's methods, I think, are adaptable to the analysis of other emergent countries in their course toward similar goals.

The first problem that Wilkie set for himself was an analysis of Mexican national budgets as indicators of the actual, rather than the projected, amounts spent to alleviate poverty. As one who some years ago attempted the same thing, I can attest to the difficulties the author has faced and the unseen amount of drudgery that lies behind his revealing tables.[1] Merely to glean actual expenditures from scattered sources, much less to reduce them to a common measure (as Wilkie has done) is a tremendous task.

[1] Howard F. Cline, *Mexico: Revolution to Evolution, 1940–1960* (New York, Oxford University Press, 1962), pp. 237–241.

Equally impressive is his analysis of these figures as allotted to various fields by each president. Here the "style" of the various presidents emerges, as does the fact that, until Lázaro Cárdenas, negligible sums were apportioned for the social benefits long promised by the Constitution of 1917. Quite striking is the rate at which Cárdenas's successors exceeded his pioneering efforts, both relatively and in the aggregate. It may come as a shock to the detractors of Miguel Alemán, for example, to note the remarkable results his policies achieved in the social field.

The second part of this volume charts the heartbreakingly slow process of upgrading a whole society, virtually decapitated during the violent phases of the Revolution (1910–1917). Wilkie's main device—a Poverty Index—is an innovation. He explains it sufficiently to obviate summary here. The Index can be extended and its trajectories statistically gauged as later figures become available, especially at decennial census intervals. Whatever its limitations, the Index does give us one measure of how the national investment in social improvement has produced net gains in welfare, even in the face of a population explosion.

To the historical elements treated in Part I, Wilkie adds geographical elements in Part II by applying the Poverty Index to the regions of Mexico. In common with other investigators (like myself), he found that the statistical regions into which Mexican officials traditionally have divided the Republic are inadequate for socio-historical research; hence he had to devise subdivisions that are historically more coherent and likely to yield more valid findings.[2]

The application of the Poverty Index to regional units (again a massive and arduous series of calculations) reveals not only the general gains but the depth of penetration of the Mexican Revolution's social aspects in various parts of the Republic. Important inferences can immediately be drawn from his summary Table 9–11: all regions have improved since 1940, and a majority have accelerated their rates of such improvement over the decade 1950–1960. The same table provides an interesting statistic for the

[2] Howard F. Cline, *The United States and Mexico* (Cambridge: Harvard University Press, 1953), pp. 88–111; Cline, *Mexico,* pp. 49–59. Wilkie's scheme provides more regional units, especially in the North and Central portions.

students of urbanization: the Federal District, the recipient of the bulk of internal migrants, remained static.

Wilkie's data and conclusions have wide-ranging implications. What will be the future policy for expenditures on social change? Wilkie has indicated that substantial outlays of funds now over a relatively extended period are making visible if still only modest progress. But, as he stresses, the widespread feeling that their government continues to strive to achieve the goals of the Revolution satisfies most Mexicans.

Beyond the statistical matters I have stressed here, readers will find much that is new and exciting in this study. In the course of his research, the author interviewed many participants in the Revolution and its governments. Their frank and often revealing remarks about how Mexico is governed form a contribution in themselves.

Anyone interested in present-day Mexico and documented social change can profitably read and enjoy this work.

Howard F. Cline

Arlington, Virginia
August, 1966

Preface to the Second Edition

Revisions in this second edition present new data regarding "indirect measurement" of Mexico's Revolution, especially in the area of land reform. Since the first revision of statistics on land reform, recently prepared by the Mexican government, needs to be disseminated widely, it is important to include a full summary for analysis in this work. Other changes, for example, involve inclusion of statistics on the land policy of Francisco I. Madero for the year 1912-1913 as well as revision of figures to account for changes in definition of the economically active population since 1910. Because complete data on federal expenditure and social modernization for the entire decade of the 1960's will not be in existence until the 1970's, no new or revised analyses of state policy or "direct measurement" of social conditions have been undertaken. Thus, excepting a minor adjustment in an aspect of the Poverty Index for 1910 to account for new data on the Baja Californians, the basis of this book remains the same.

Changes in this new edition in no way affect my original interpretations; rather, they strengthen the work and make new series available to the student of Mexico.

J.W.W.

San José, Costa Rica
July, 1969

Acknowledgments

Grants to carry out this study came from the Inter-American Cultural Convention (1960–1961), the Modern Foreign Language Fellowship Program (1962–1963), the William Harrison Mills Traveling Fellowship Program in International Relations (1963–1964), and the Foreign Area Fellowship Program of the American Council of Learned Societies and the Social Science Research Council (1964–1965). This generous assistance permitted full-time research in Mexico for three years as well as almost a year in which to write. While expressing gratitude for these grants, it is also important to note that the interpretations expressed in this work do not necessarily represent views of the above fellowship programs.

Indebtedness to several scholars is acknowledged for their counsel and support. Woodrow W. Borah suggested presentation of this unified study of federal expenditure and social change as a separate part of my studies of the Mexican Revolution. Clark W. Reynolds not only advised on statistical method and organization of the material but patiently criticized the formulation and reformulation of the ideas presented here. James F. King pointed out that interviews with historical figures of Mexico would be doubly valuable if tape recorded. A long and careful critical evaluation of the manuscript by Stanley R. Ross aided greatly in revising the work, toning down exaggerations, and filling in logical gaps between some concepts. Oscar Lewis generously offered his time to discuss the concept of poverty developed in this work, and Robert H. Bremner suggested the definition of social deprivation which deals with characteristics of poverty. Howard F. Cline gave encouragement and consulted on the method of presenting poverty statistics. Robert E. Scott drew upon his experi-

ence in Mexico to suggest some changes in presentation of the
study; and Lyle C. Brown spent two days discussing editorial
changes, clarifying concepts, and developing writing style. Others
who carefully read the manuscript and made many helpful comments were Arturo Torres-Ríoseco, Robert R. Miller, Albert
Michaels, and John J. TePaske. Special thanks goes to Dauril
Alden for his continued help. It is also necessary to note that
without the tireless research and editorial assistance of my wife,
Edna Monzón Wilkie, this study would not have been possible.
Richard W. Wilkie supplied the cartographic assistance and
spent two weeks carefully checking tables for logic in presentation
and for errors. The Bancroft Library of the University of California, under the direction of George P. Hammond and Robert
H. Becker, graciously facilitated transcription of the oral history
materials; and the Computer Center at the Ohio State University,
under advisers Earl Raley and Clinton Foulk, speeded necessary
mathematical calculations. Statistical questions raised by Albert
Fishlow assisted in sharpening the focus of this study immensely;
and the content of Chapter 10, especially, is directly related to his
critical analysis. Of course, valuable aid and criticism from these
counselors does not in any way make them responsible for the
final results presented here.

   Probably there is no adequate way in which to thank the many
Mexican citizens who participated in oral history interviews or
granted access to documents and statistics. Their kindness has
made investigation in Mexico a great pleasure. Since expressions
of gratitude to individual Mexicans would include most of the
living leaders of the Revolution and its opponents, gratitude is
here acknowledged in a collective manner. The presidency of
Mexico was especially helpful in permitting and encouraging research in the official records of the nation.

Contents

Contents   xvii

TABLES

GRAPHS

MAPS

Introduction

This study is primarily intended for three different groups of readers. Mexicanists will find the history of the Mexican Revolution, 1910 to the early 1960's, examined from the point of view of federal expenditure and social change. Students of social change in underdeveloped areas will find an attempt to measure decrease in poverty and to link it with the politics of modernization. Political analysts will find an attempt to assess outcomes of ideology. Since readers interested in each of these themes may approach this study from their own particular vantage points in history or social science, it is hoped that they will understand from the outset that there are many difficulties in linking analyses which fall into the purview of several academic disciplines.

Through an examination of carefully delineated statistical data, it is possible to assess the Mexican Revolution in two new ways. The Mexican federal budget may be tested against actual expenditures in order to determine to what extent the official party of the Revolution has carried out its projections to raise the standard of living for the poverty-stricken masses. By investigating and organizing budgetary figures in relation to social, economic, and administrative expenditure, we may characterize varying presidential programs from 1910 to 1963 and concretely test the ideology of each leader's program as it works out in practice. Analysis of social statistics gathered in the decennial censuses from 1910 to 1960 permits the preparation of an index of poverty or social deprivation which allows us to examine levels of characteristics of poverty in order to measure the effectiveness of government programs in bringing about social change.

The Mexican Revolution was begun in 1910 to protest the lack of democratic elections, but it could not be contained. As civil war ravaged the country for the next six years, ideas about the reconstruction of society on a new basis gradually came to the fore. In 1916 Manuel Gamio, one of Mexico's most famous anthropologists, suggested that Mexico's national well-being depended upon integration of the huge mass of poverty-stricken, isolated, illiterate, and non-Spanish-speaking population into Mexican society. This population had no loyalty to the *patria* because the federal government had done nothing for it except perhaps to sanction the seizure of its ancient land holdings, levy taxes, and search its villages for military conscripts. Gamio's call was one of many for the integration of the Mexican nation, and a new constitution, which was written in 1916–1917, offered a program of action. The Constitution of 1917 postulated active state intervention in social and economic life to favor the masses: the state represents the interests of all classes of society and collective interest is vital for the fulfillment of individual rights. In contrast, the nineteenth-century Mexican state was conceived in the Liberal mold: governmental action with few exceptions meant administrative maintenance of the status quo. In Liberal philosophy, poverty was seen to be inevitable, and the state was not allowed to upset the operation of natural laws. Thus seventy-nine years of nationhood prior to 1910 did not result in national strength, but in national weakness.

The Revolution's program of state-directed integration of Mexican social and economic life has always been justified on the basis that it has given the poor classes a better standard of living. However, creation of a common national interest and a myth of the fatherland which bind people into nations has been a long process. Fifty years is a short period for the task of eliminating a high level of poverty in a country where relatively little social improvement took place prior to 1910. The Revolution has taken different approaches to developing an integrated nation.

In the Mexican debate over the nature of government policy and its results since 1910, several stereotypes about the Revolution have emerged. Advocates of violence as a solution to continued problems have urged a new violent political upheaval on the grounds that mass social change only occurs with the explosive overthrow of government, as in the decade from 1910 to 1920.

Critics of government intervention in social and economic spheres of life have maintained that a change in laws is quite adequate to bring about social advance, as during the latter 1920's when "statesmanship" was considered more important than "demagogy." A decade of proletarian organization and strikes in the 1930's has resulted in the criticism that government-sponsored social action kills private investment and brings a halt to economic growth. This stereotype has been countered with another which claims that the greatest social benefits for the masses come during times of social tension and proletarian self-assertion. According to this view, immediate, direct benefits for the people are justified on the grounds that the masses have waited long years to see the promise of the Mexican Revolution fulfilled. Land distribution, agricultural credit, educational outlay, public welfare expenditure, an adequate minimum wage, and the right to strike are deemed absolutely necessary for national integration, even if economic laws and the economic order must be sacrificed to achieve social justice.

Since Mexico entered into a period of economic development during World War II, a new set of stereotypes has emerged to compete with the old ones. Proponents of industrialization have argued that healthy national integration requires development of economic infrastructure which will allow Mexico to keep up with twentieth-century modernization. In this view, direct governmental intervention in favor of the masses is not necessary, for in the long-run the common man will gain jobs and opportunities from economic development. Nonintervention in favor of the masses has been further justified on the basis that capital formation, vitally necessary for industrialization, has always been achieved at the temporary expense of the worker. To counter such arguments, critics have insisted that the masses have been sacrificed for unrealistic and unattainable goals. The Revolution, it is claimed, came to an end after 1940.

Since only a small band of vocal Communists and some disaffected intellectuals see violent revolution on the horizon, and since Mexico is committed to an active role for the state, the locus of debate has centered upon the programs of Lázaro Cárdenas and Miguel Alemán. These two presidents are the respective advocates of social and economic revolution. On one hand, during the period from 1934 to 1940 Cárdenas is said to have set back Mexico's economy, and on the other, Alemán supposedly sacrificed the masses in order to industrialize the country from 1946 to 1952. To ease tensions in the Revolutionary Family (the group which rules Mexico) developing over what course government action should take, Adolfo López Mateos propounded a "balanced revolution" during his presidency from 1960 to 1964. This formula calls for balanced political, social, and economic change under the sponsorship of the revolutionary regime.

Scholars have previously identified these periods of different ideological emphasis within the Revolution in which Mexico's presidents have taken a political, social, economic, or balanced approach to make Mexico a better place in which to live.[1] However, no one has attempted to gauge the real difference in governmental programs or to assess directly the social change which has resulted. Since economic change is much easier to evaluate than social change, students of Mexican history have examined the former and inferred that the latter develops at the same rate. Thus the present study is one of the first attempts to balance economic analysis of the results of the Revolution with an assessment of change in the level of poverty for the half century from 1910 to 1960. It is also one of the first attempts to measure pragmatically the ideology of the Mexican Revolution. Fortunately, the first three ideological periods of the Revolution begin and end with census years, and the task of analyzing social results of government programs is greatly simplified. The fourth period has only recently begun, and though outcomes of government spending can not be evaluated, we can assess policy. It would be folly, of course, to predict that balanced revolution launched by López Mateos will or will not continue under new presidents. If a balanced ideological program continues, its results may be measured in the 1970 census.

Part I examines governmental expenditure in several aspects. Projected budgets are contrasted with actual expenditures in order to show how each president wanted to spend the federal purse

[1] See, for example, works by Howard F. Cline: "Mexico: A Matured Latin American Revolution," *Annals of the American Academy of Political and Social Science* 334 (1961) 84–94: *Mexico: Revolution to Evolution, 1940–1960* (London: Oxford University Press, 1962); *The United States and Mexico* (Cambridge: Harvard University Press, 1963. Rev. ed.).

and how he actually spent it. Theoretically, presidents may wish to give a certain emphasis to their expenditure, but the domestic and foreign political context may preclude independent action. Also, since the budget circulates freely and the account of actual expenditure does not, the budget may be used as a propaganda device which leaves the president free to go ahead with whatever programs he actually desires. More often, however, neither government officials nor the public are aware in quantitative terms of executive policy and its results. However, politicans and the citizenry in general *are* aware of contraction or expansion of agricultural credit, investment in public works, budgetary emphasis on certain government agencies over others, and the general tone of expenditure which give a style to each president. This style is felt throughout Mexico. Analysis of yearly gross federal expenditure yields a pragmatic measure of presidential style and the analysis is summarized in the share of funds spent for social, economic, or administrative activity. Since there is no complete record of where total federal funds have been expended geographically, it is impossible to link directly expenditure and regional social change.

Part II develops an index of social characteristics which may be denominated an Index of Poverty. This index is based upon census items which portray the number of people who actually responded that they lived in conditions of deprivation or traditionalism in 1910, 1921, 1930, 1940, 1950, and 1960. The index is analyzed by federal entity and by region. Mexico's total Poverty Index is linked indirectly to presidential policy by a discussion of decrease in the level of characteristics of poverty during each decade. Analysis is based on the assumption that it is the style of each ideological period which contributes to social advances, for example, and not social expenditure per se which brings about a decrease in the level of poverty. The index or scale of poverty is to some degree associated with traditional Indian culture and it reflects the type of characteristics from which the Mexican Revolutionists have consciously sought to escape in order to build an integrated nation. The Revolution has tried to ameliorate these conditions of poverty while maintaining the best values of Indian culture.

Eleven notations on the limits and nature of this study are in order. *First,* summaries of method and generalizations about budgetary policy are presented in Chapters 1 and 2, respectively, in order that the argument of the thesis in Part I may be clearly followed. Since these résumés are not linked to historical circumstance until Chapters 3 and 4, and since the internal movement of funds behind the generalizations is not presented until Chapters 5, 6, and 7, the reader is advised to suspend judgment until each aspect of the case has been examined. In addition, budgetary analysis is presented in percentage terms as well as in terms of expenditure of standard pesos per capita. Expansion of federal funds since the 1930's has given each president a great deal more money with which to work, but the test of ideology still remains with the percentage of allocation for different types of expenditure. Ramifications and relations of these two kinds of analysis will be made clear, in turn, and further suspension of judgment is required until this has been accomplished.

Second, this work is not developed with the usual approach taken by students of public finance. Since political programs and social results in historical context are the themes which follow, orthodox analysis of federal finances is not included. This study does not take up such types of economic classification and monetary analysis as capital and current expenses, direct (exhaustive) and indirect (non-exhaustive) expenditure, and virtual, cash, and net outlay. In contrast to economic analysis which considers, for example, only interest payments on the federal debt, this study of gross federal expenditure also includes analysis of the percentage of the budget devoted to redemption of the debt. Thus, for the purpose of our investigation, the term "debt payment" refers to payment of interest as well as retirement of the debt. Readers interested in economic analysis of Mexico's public finances should look elsewhere for such data.[2] It should be noted that the figures

[2] See, for example, Roberto Santillán López and Aniceto Rosas Figueroa, *Teoría General de las Fianzas Públicas y el Caso de México* (México, D. F.: Universidad Nacional Autónoma de México, 1962); Combined Mexican Working Party, *The Economic Development of Mexico* (Baltimore: International Bank for Reconstruction and Johns Hopkins Press, 1953); Ernest O. Moore, *Evolución de las Instituciones Financieras de México* (México, D. F.: Centro de Estudios Monetarios Latinoamericanos, 1963); Henry J. Gumpel and Hugo B. Margaín, *Taxation in Mexico* (Boston: Little, Brown, for Harvard University, 1957); Ernesto Flores Zavala, *Elementos de Fianzas Públicas Mexicanas, Los Impuestos* (México, D. F.: Editorial Porrúa, 1963); Ramón Beteta, *Tres Años de Política Hacendaria, (1947–1948–1949), Perspectiva y Acción* (México, D. F.: Secretaría de Hacienda y Crédito Público, 1951);

prepared by the United Nations are generally based upon net federal expenditure and will usually not agree with projected and actual figures given here. It is important to note also that the Mexican government has traditionally presented its own budgetary analysis to the public almost exclusively in terms of gross federal expenditure.

Third, in line with the above qualification on economic analysis, federal income is not discussed except tangentially, for we are interested in types of expenditure and not detailed taxation policies. The latter study would, of course, be extremely useful; but it requires complex historical analysis in itself and must be left for another scholar to develop as fully as is required.

Early governments of the Revolution received limited amounts of income, but at that time this often was not conceived as a great problem. In spite of Mexico's Constitution of 1917, until the 1930's the Mexican Government's role was limited by the Western world's apparent return to the normalcy of nineteenth-century Liberalism after the Great War. Only since the world depression of the 1930's gave rise to the active state has a large income been necessary in order for the state to fulfill its expanded role.[3]

Fourth, the budget does not represent the entire impact of federal policy, as Chapter 1 points out. This factor is no problem, however, because public expenditure by governmental decentralized agencies and mixed public and private enterprises has been autonomous and excluded from direct presidential control.

We do not know the historical extent of decentralized expenditure, and there is a great need for a study which makes such an investigation. Also, since decentralized agencies are mixed public and private organs, it is difficult to assess their effect in terms of either public or private expenditure. Certainly this relationship needs to be explored but to date we have no such scholarship.

Ricardo Torres Gaitán, *Política Monetaria Mexicana* (México, D. F.: Distribuidora Librería Ariel, 1944); Manuel Yáñez Ruiz, *El Problema Fiscal en las Distintas Etapas de Nuestra Organización Política* (México, D. F.: Estampillas y Valores, 1958–1961. 6 vols.). R. L. Bennett, *The Financial Sector and Economic Development; The Mexican Case* (Baltimore: Johns Hopkins Press, 1965).

[3] For a cogent discussion of the Western world's concept of the state after 1929, see Karl Polanyi, *The Great Transformation; the Political and Economic Origins of Our Time* (Boston: Beacon Press, 1963).

We can not then judge the activeness of the state in relation to its total impact upon society, but we can examine the percentage allocations of the federal income to characterize the government's concept of its role and measure the rise of its active policies.

Fifth, it must be acknowledged that the government is not solely responsible for social change. The private sector plays a key role in national integration. However, the government creates the climate within which private enterprise operates. The government sets policy, consciously or unconsciously, which is a major determinant of what role the private sector will be able to play. Therefore, when this study asserts that any federal policy has resulted in a given amount of social and economic change, it intends to say not that the change came from government policy itself, but that it came from the over-all climate which the attitude of the government engendered. Also, since no direct link between federal expenditure and social changes can be established, we may suggest the results of each governmental period of ideology by evaluating the decrease in poverty in relation to economic change. Recent writings of other investigators may be consulted for specific contributions of the private sector to the process of change in Mexico.[4]

Sixth, analysis of per-capita social change and vital statistics does not fit into the framework of direct examination which is offered here. As stated in Part II, per-capita analysis is not very revealing in underdeveloped areas. Figures may well show that there is one automobile per capita, but in reality a small percentage of the population may own most of the vehicles. The postulate of this study is that we must attempt to find out what has happened to people, and we can do this by examining data which directly offer measures of social standards. Vital statistics are not examined because the Mexican government has not systematically compiled them with historical consistency. In contrast to the census data which have been gathered according to a

[4] Consult Frank R. Brandenburg, "A Contribution to the Theory of Entrepreneurship and Economic Development: The Case of Mexico," *Inter-American Economic Affairs* 16:3 (1962) 3–23, and *The Making of Modern Mexico* (Englewood Cliffs: Prentice-Hall, 1964); see also Raymond Vernon, *The Dilemma of Mexico's Development, the Roles of the Private and Public Sectors* (Cambridge: Harvard University Press, 1963); and Raymond Vernon (ed.), *Public Policy and Private Enterprise in Mexico* (Cambridge: Harvard University Press, 1964).

concerted plan, vital statistics are volunteered by the populace. There has been no organized coverage and the available vital statistics show strange patterns generally related to campaigns which attempt to convince people that they should report, for example, birth, sickness, and death to the authorities.

Seventh, construction of the Poverty Index in Chapter 9 is based upon a relatively small sample. This problem is difficult to overcome because only the readily identifiable census items have been utilized which cover six censuses with any consistency. Even with this statistical limitation, however, the Poverty Index offers a method for examination of social change in a developing area. Though Mexican statistics often have been criticized for incompleteness or for containing errors, they provide the best sample available and do reveal a remarkably logical view in most cases. Where obvious errors or omissions have been encountered, some adjustments have been made with full explanation. Items included in the Index are actually quite broad in scope.

Eighth, this study does not undertake an examination of social change in the middle sectors of society or even in all ranges of the lower sector. The role of the middle class in sponsoring social change is not considered since we are interested in examining the ideology of elite political leaders and its effect on the masses. Chapter 8 contains a brief discussion of existing literature on social class change which is based upon indirect analysis. Exclusion of the middle sectors from our discussion does not mean that they have not been of major import in stimulating social and economic change in Mexico. In order to develop an investigation, however, of the lowest level of society as carefully defined with a series of measurable characteristics, it has been necessary to leave other strata of society out of the discussion. Indeed, this analysis does not delve into the several layers of poverty which exist at the very bottom of the social scale. Different indices are needed to explore the nature of these other levels.

Ninth, the definition of poverty which is developed here does not necessarily deal with individual poverty. Persons included in the index may exhibit several characteristics of poverty and yet have a relatively high income. Nevertheless, collectively speaking, the integration of the Mexican nation is greatly impeded by the persistence of a high level in characteristics of poverty. Social modernization, along with economic development, is required in order to raise general standards of living. The Poverty Index seeks to measure decrease in the collective level of social deprivation in Mexico at different historical times.

Tenth, many students of the Mexican Revolution have claimed that each period within the movement has built upon the preceding one in order to obtain ever-mounting social and economic change. If this were true, theoretically, indices of economic growth and decreases in the characteristics of poverty should have changed with greater rapidity in each decade, yet this has not happened. It is true that many government programs may take years to phase into operation and there is a lag in the consequence of decisions and programs developed at an early stage of the Revolution; but it is probably impossible to take this into account given our present state of knowledge about Mexico and the state of methodology in general. There is little lag in the consequence, however, between changes in political ideology. Given the power of the president in Mexico, fixed costs of budgetary policy are few and the great flexibility of the budget allows the chief executive largely to mold federal expenditure in his own particular manner, as will be explained in some detail in Part I. Also, characteristics of poverty chosen for this study do not represent items which require long periods of time to reflect a change in living standards. In other words, a person who simply stops going barefoot and buys a pair of shoes immediately has changed his position in relation to an aspect of the poverty scale. He has not engaged in a social investment that will require years to show up in the censuses. Likewise, given the elementary criteria of literacy in the Mexican census, persons who have received several months of instruction in one of the many government campaigns to extend education to the masses will qualify for moving out of the poverty level in relation to this item. In sum, the politics of the budget and the poverty index stand as quite accurate reflectors of immediate changes within each period. We do not have to allow specifically for great lag in consequence in discussion of the effect of the budget on the index of poverty, though we must bear in mind that in general the Mexican Revolution has been successful precisely because each president has had a more solid social, economic, and political base with which to work. What we have done here is to isolate several factors that are largely more related to current policy than other long term programs which would not show up as distinctly belonging to one era or another.

Eleventh, the following study attempts to solve some new problems which historians face as social scientists. It is hoped that the reader will accept the spirit in which the work has been developed and will look upon the analysis as a point of departure for discussion and further research. Mexican statistics are sometimes incomplete or need adjustment, but we are looking for trends, not exact data. If the work presented here stimulates more thought and research about the problems of measuring social and economic change in relation to governmental programs, then the rather primitive quantitative analysis presented here may well have served a useful purpose. Because some readers may not agree with all of our methods and conclusions, full data has been provided so that other scholars may make use of it in relation to their own research. Obviously this study can not be definitive; as we fit together more and more pieces in the Mexican puzzle, conclusions tentatively reached here will have to be modified.

Though this study was prepared for publication in 1966, it was written basically in 1965 with data gathered through 1964. As a historical work, it can never be up-to-date, but it can bring together historical data which allow fresh perspectives of the Mexican Revolution. Many prior analyses offer a statistical view of a certain period or a given moment in time. The present study is intended to present statistical patterns in which numbers take on a historical relevance.

The nature of a study such as this requires citation of sources. Full citation for a source is given in the footnotes only once and subsequently a shortened form of reference is used. The bibliography serves as a ready key to shortened citations and is organized alphabetically rather than topically.

J.W.W.

La Paz, Bolivia
August, 1966

LIST OF SYMBOLS

Three dots (. . .) indicate that data are *not available*.

Three dashes (– – –) indicate that the magnitude is *zero or negligible* (less than .05).

Two dashes (– –) indicate that the item or category *does not apply*.

A minus sign (–) before a figure indicates a *deficit or a decrease in magnitude*.

An asterisk (*) is used to indicate *partially estimated figures*.

PART I

THE FEDERAL BUDGET

The following seven chapters characterize the policies of each president since 1910 and present a comparative view of four different periods of ideology within the Mexican Revolution. Chapter 1 discusses the method used in breaking down budgetary expenditures. Chapter 2 offers a summary view of executive policy by examining the average actual expenditure of each president. Since governmental financial policy is not made in a vacuum, Chapters 3 and 4 examine presidential programs in the light of Mexico's political history since 1910. Chapters 5, 6, and 7 take a thematic approach to the federal budget: administrative, economic, and social expenditure are analyzed respectively. This latter approach delves into the Revolution to examine, for example, educational expenses from 1910 to 1963. In contrast to a general examination of all expenditure within given periods, a thematic scrutiny of expenditure allows compact presentation of statistical data for each important organizational category in the Mexican budget. This arrangement of statistics into tables by type of expenditure facilitates interpretation of specific aspects of government policy which range over fifty years of history.

There is no intent in this study to offer a history of Mexico or to duplicate the interpretations of other investigators. The Mexican Revolution is examined in the light of ideology as expressed in pragmatic action.

1

Problem and Method

The federal budget has always been the most important governmental expenditure in Mexico because state and local authorities have had little access to sources of income. Table 1-1 shows the relationship of federal income to all governmental income in

TABLE 1-1

Income in Mexico: Federal, State, and Local Shares
in Selected Years, 1900–1960

Year	Total[a]	Per Cent	Federal	State	Local
1900	63	100.0	63.0	24.1	12.9
1923	84	100.0	72.6	14.5	12.9
1929	101	100.0	71.1	21.2	7.7
1932	86	100.0	64.0	27.1	8.9
1940	122	100.0	71.4	23.3	5.3
1950	180	100.0	78.3	18.4	3.3
1960	369	100.0	71.1	26.3	2.6

[a] In pesos per capita of 1950.

SOURCE: México, Dirección General de Estadística, *Anuario Estadístico* (cited as *Anuario Estadístico*) *1906*, 222–224; *1923–1924*, II, 285; *1926*, 285; *1940*, 741, 745, 747–748; *1942*, 1245; *1954*, 695, 697–698; *1960–1961*, 585, 587, 592.

Mexico in selected years. Though real income has increased at all levels, local government has received a progressively smaller share of total national revenues, and the federal and state governments have competed unequally for the rest of the income; federal income has been about 70 per cent of all receipts.

THE PROBLEM

Given the importance of the federal government as an organized body with the resources and the desire to effect social change, the question which faces us is how to analyze policy as it is reflected in actual expenditure of the federal purse. How can the style of each president and period be pinned down? A special problem has always plagued analysis of ideology in Mexico, for personalism has been a major point at issue. Are policies undertaken at the whim of the president or strongman behind the presidency? Or has the Revolutionary Family, represented by an official party which monopolizes election victory, responded to the changing demands of different interest groups?[1] We know that Mexican politicians have a love of rhetoric which obfuscates the ideological terminology that Western society has developed to such a fine degree. Also, since each president has promised everything to everybody at one time or another, the problem of determining actual presidential policy is compounded. By determining concrete actions in a manner that makes presidential programs easily comparable, however, we can resolve the problem. If the personal whim of the leader really takes precedence over actions which form a consistent way of resolving social and economic problems, there should be little difference in expenditure from one executive to another. Further, there would be no correlation between presidential leadership and periods of ideology in the Mexican Revolution.

Several investigators have attempted to treat the Mexican budget, but they have not been able to get very far with their analyses. Gustavo F. Aguilar of the Mexican Treasury Department has published an unofficial account of Mexican projected budgets since colonial times, but his work suffers from two seri-

---

[1] Cf. Robert E. Scott, *Mexican Government in Transition* (Urbana: University of Illinois Press, 1959), who sees a relatively democratic official party, in which interest groups *can* influence the president of Mexico; he also develops the role of interest groups outside the official party. Whereas Brandenburg, *The Making of Modern Mexico* (Englewood Cliffs: Prentice Hall, 1964) sees Mexico as ruled by an elite, Scott postulates a more sophisticated approach to understanding why the Mexican Revolutionary Family has been able to maintain power. We take the view that both writers are essentially correct but will show that personalism and pragmatic ideology have interacted (see Chapters 3 and 4).

ous problems.[2] First, the projected budgets which he presents have almost no relation to actual expenditures since 1910, as we shall see. Second, Aguilar presents only the total amounts for each agency; he does not examine the changing functions of agencies in order to separate the budget into meaningful categories which have historical continuity and validity.

Other investigators have run into the problem of sources. Whereas the projected budget is given wide publicity, the real budget is printed in a limited edition which is not readily available in Mexico, let alone outside the country. Actual figures are almost never summarized or commented upon in the press. As noted above, analysis in Mexico has almost exclusively treated projected budgets.[3] It is no wonder that investigators have not been aware of the problem which the Mexican budget presents. Such talented investigators as Howard F. Cline and Oscar Lewis have compared projected budgets of one year to actual budgets of another.[4] Without the ready availability of budgetary publications, they have been unable to decipher the budgetary category entitled *erogaciones adicionales* (unclassified expenditures). The Mexican budget has been confused since the creation of this category in 1947, for it cuts across agency lines, and it has expended 15 to 23 per cent of actual funds. Scholars have, in general, tended to treat this category as a lump sum "general expenditure," which prevents any real understanding of policy behind the Mexican budget.

Signs that the Mexican budget handling is to improve somewhat are evidenced by the new law which beginning in 1965 brought decentralized and mixed public and private agencies under the control of projected and actual accounting by the Mexican Treasury Department. Projections for 1965 indicated that regular governmental expenses were to be about equal to autonomous expenditure by 52 decentralized agencies and 96 mixed cor-

[2] Gustavo F. Aguilar, *Los Presupuestos Mexicanos desde los Tiempos de la Colonia hasta Nuestros Días* (México, D. F.; n.p., 1947).

[3] For an exception see *El Día*, Oct. 30–31, 1964, which printed the results of the actual expenditure for 1963. The *Anuario Estadístico* presents total budgets and results without analysis, except for education and irrigation in recent years.

[4] Cline, *Mexico; Revolution to Evolution, 1940–1960*, Chapter 25; Oscar Lewis, "México desde 1940," *Investigación Económica* 18:70 (1958) 185–256.

porations.[5] The latter expenditures are classified as "indirect" budgetary considerations, and therefore the direct analysis of the Mexican budget presented here can be carried forward with no difficulty. Apparently, presidential control over indirect expenditure of the public sector had diminished to such an extent that abuse of autonomous authority by members of the Revolutionary Family was growing steadily. Executive action was necessary to bring all federal expenditure under control.[6] Not until after the election of 1964, however, was this budgetary reform announced. Presidents prudently often have chosen to reform the government at the beginning of their term instead of the end in order that they might have time to regain the confidence of the Revolutionary Family and the general public well before elections and the transfer of power.

Since total expenditure of decentralized agencies and mixed corporations is not known, we can only indirectly gauge the activeness of the state in relation to society, as was pointed out in the fourth qualification of this study. Table 1-2 reveals the growth

TABLE 1-2

The Public Sector's Capital Investment Expenditure as a Per Cent of Gross National Product, Selected Years, 1925–1961

Year	Per Cent	Year	Per Cent
1925	2.1	1940	4.3
1928	2.3	1946	3.9
1930	2.6	1952	5.8
1932	2.6	1958	5.8
1934	2.6	1961	7.8

SOURCE: México, Secretaría de la Presidencia, *México Inversión Pública Federal, 1925–1963* (México, D. F.: Talleres Gráficos de la Federación, 1964). GNP is from México, [Secretaría de la] Presidencia and Nacional Financiera, S. A., *50 Años de Revolución en Cifras* (México, D. F.: Editorial Cultura, 1963), 32 (cited as *50 Años en Cifras*).

[5] For the number of decentralized agencies and mixed public and private enterprises see *El Día*, Jan. 4, 1965; for projected budget, 1965, see *El Universal*, Dec. 16, 1964.

[6] Vernon, *The Dilemma of Mexico's Development*, 118–119, comments on the president's lack of control over the decentralized agencies at the beginning of the López Mateos term.

in importance of the public sector, but it is incomplete for the early years. Appendix J shows the relationship of capital investment by the public sector to investments by the private sector, but no data are available prior to 1939. For the purposes of this study, Table 1-3 theoretically should be quite revealing as it presents direct federal expenditure as a percentage of the Gross National Product. Since no method for the formation of the GNP is presented in the source for comparison, and no method for conversion of the GNP to prices of 1950 is given, however, it is not really possible to judge the impact of federal expenditure upon

TABLE 1-3

Actual Federal Expenditure as a Per Cent of Gross National Product in Selected Years, 1925–1961

Year	Per Cent	Year	Per Cent
1925	6.3	1940	8.6
1928	6.1	1946	6.6
1930	6.4	1952	10.8
1932	7.0	1958	11.1
1934	6.7	1961	13.7

SOURCES: Table 1-8, and *50 Años en Cifras*, 32.

society; therefore our analysis concentrates on characterizing the government's concept of its role. We mainly attempt to measure the rise of the active state through analysis of direct federal projected and actual expenditure of federal income.

After the investigator has located and defined the appropriate sources, can he be sure that the data have been presented accurately? In making the myriad calculations necessary for the presentation of statistical tables in the following chapters, we found no error in the government's presentation. Of course, one may question the reliability of the Mexican accounts themselves. Since the House of Deputies conducts only a superficial audit of expenditure, a question of possible falsification of accounts is raised. Here we may note that Mexican politics have always been more sophisticated than foreigners have tended to point out. If accounts were falsified by the government, actual expenditure would agree

with projected figures, and this is not the case. Also, falsification
of accounts is a clumsy method of taking a share of the federal
purse for private use. The general manner in which money is
allotted to the faithful in the Revolutionary Family is through
the granting of contracts for public works. Work is generally per-
formed; however, the result may be very costly. The point is,
however, that the work is completed, and funds are generally
spent for what the accounting office says they are spent to obtain.
As in the United States, kickbacks and high profits from substi-
tution of shoddy material and substandard workmanship yield the
same result as pilfering from the till. Also, no one knows when
he will lose favor with the government. If he has been a simple
thief, he is doomed; but if he has merely contracted with the government, he is fairly safe—the government does not like to in-
criminate itself and adverse propaganda is taboo.

Ramón Beteta, Minister of the Treasury Department under
President Miguel Alemán, 1946–1952, has summed up his cogent
view of dishonesty in government:

Corruption in the Mexican Government, unfortunately, is a fact.
It is not, as people are apt to believe, that the minister of the treasury
or the president of the republic or some other minister can one day
say, "Well, from such and such appropriations of the budget, send one
half to my home." There are some people who believe this, mind
you. . . . [Upon resigning as treasury minister in 1952], I personally
was accused, for example, of having taken the gold reserves of the Bank
of Mexico with me to Europe when I went there as ambassador [to
Italy from 1952 to 1958]. I say it is absurd, but there are people who
believe it. As you say, that is not necessarily the only way to take advantage of the government. There are many less vulgar ways, unethical
but legal, in which a public official can acquire wealth.

Let us say that a public official knows that a highway is to be constructed, and that he also knows the person in charge of building or
directing the work. He can buy, directly or indirectly, the land that will
be affected by such a highway and thus obtain an advantageous position. This is not ethically right, but legally it is not a crime. And this
kind of thing is quite common, much more so than people think.

A public official has innumerable means of acquiring advantages
from his position, without there necessarily being corruption, in the
sense that he need not collude to receive money as happens in the very
inferior [governmental] levels. . . . [For example], fiscal inspectors do
take what in Mexico is called a *mordida,* that is a bribe or a tip, in
order to do or not do a certain thing. This has several degrees. There

is the mordida paid to have something done rapidly which one has a right to have done—that is really a tip. Then there is the *mordida* paid in order to have something done slowly which one does not wish done quickly—this is going much further. The third step is to have something done to which one does not have a right, for example to smuggle merchandise into Mexico. This, unfortunately, does exist, but Mexico is not the only country where it does, and it does not happen at the ministerial level. That is to say, there has not been any president or minister of, let us say, the last five or six terms who has ever gained a significant advantage for himself through really illegal means.

The treasury minister receives a relatively low salary—in my time it was 5,000 pesos [a month]—, but he also receives expenses for representation . . . let us say 3,000 or 4,000 pesos a month. But besides, he is a member of the board of directors of Nacional Financiera, [the government development corporation], the Bank of Mexico, the railroads, Petróleos, [the national oil industry], and of, well, many of the decentralized organizations which frequently practice the custom of paying a share in profits earned during the year. One can receive about 100,000 or 150,000 pesos in a year from one of these agencies as participation in profit sharing. This is perfectly legitimate for all concerned, and it is one of the ways in which a public official receives a higher income than that which his salary indicates.[7]

This is one of the most candid, authoritative views on governmental dishonesty in Mexico ever presented.

In sum, the efficiency of Mexican government expenditure is not an issue in determining governmental policy. We may say, in fact, that there is an undetermined overhead cost in maintaining any bureaucracy. This does not mean that policy cannot be determined, it means that policy may be overly expensive in all realms of government. This seems to be an especially necessary aspect of government in countries which are dominated by one political party. Some observers have maintained that this extra cost of government contributes to capital formation in less-developed countries, but, since the recipients of this unorthodox governmental subsidy usually prefer to invest in luxury items and real estate instead of capital goods, this view is difficult to substantiate.

Final historical considerations regard the Mexican president's transfer of funds marked for one category in the budget to another category, and the expenditure of funds not authorized in the

[7] Ramón Beteta, Oral History Interviews with James and Edna Wilkie, Dec. 17, 1964, Mexico City.

budget. If we were to examine only the projected budgets, this factor would present a problem. Any discrepancies, however, in the amount allocated and the amount actually allotted for all expenditures show up in the final accounts, and this helps explain why actual expenditure has little relation to projected budgets.[8]

THE METHOD

In order to determine the amount of federal expenditure in economic, social, and administrative activity, projected budgets and actual expenditures of each budgetary category are analyzed according to emphasis. It is assumed, for example, that all expenditure for education serves a social purpose, and that the costs of administering education contribute to social development. Educational expenditure includes salaries, construction, books, equipment, and all the expenses which make a governmental agency function. Social expenditure is classified differently from economic expenditure, for the former is long term and its results are hard to measure. A dam may take ten years to build, but specialized education of a youth may take twice that long, and even then there is no concrete result. Administrative expenditure includes only expenses devoted to governing society. This expenditure does not build the nation; it only maintains an orderly atmosphere in which development can take place. Since the government acts as a transfer agent for many funds, transfer expenditures are included in federal expenditure, for they provide development that might otherwise not take place. However, as Table 1-4 shows, transfer payments are separated by function. To locate government transfer payments for economic development from 1937 to 1946, it has been necessary to go beyond the projected and actual account books of the Mexican government, and to consult Treasury Department files (*auxiliares por ramo*) for investment records.

As noted above, the Mexican federal budget is constructed on

[8] Robert E. Scott, "Budget Making in Mexico," *Inter-American Economic Affairs* 9:2 (1955) 3–20, especially 4–5. The projected budget is the key to actual accounts which are listed only by number. When new items are added to the expenditure during the year there is thus no key to the actual accounts readily available. In 1956 there were 32 items under unclassified expenditure in the projected budget, and 12 more items were added during the year; none were added in 1951. Classification is usually clear, but improvement is needed to show exactly what the expenditures were.

agency lines, except that many different types of expenditure are included in an unclassified category called *erogaciones adicionales*. In order to overcome the problem of what this item means and to present a clear picture of the nature of all federal expenditure, this category is broken down into administrative, economic, and social shares according to each item's function. To develop analysis of federal expenditure it also has been necessary to separate some budgetary items from their category in order to form divisions not included in the Mexican budget. For example, agricultural credit has its own category under our classification. It was included in the "investments" item within the funds assigned to the Treasury Department from 1931 to 1932, after which investments became a separate budgetary category. Agricultural credit, however, was included in investments only from 1935 to 1948 (no agricultural credit was provided 1933–1934). Since the category *erogaciones adicionales* was established in the budget, it has included agricultural credit. Thus when agricultural credit was separated from Treasury funds, 1931–1932, investments, 1935–1948, and unclassified expenditures since 1949, organizational units have been modified considerably in order that they functionally have historical consistency and validity.

Other modifications of the Mexican budget have been necessary. Government pensions have been separated into a new category. They were included in the Treasury Department expenditure until 1923 when they were reclassified as part of the public debt, and in 1948 they were transferred to the unclassified expenditure category. The public debt itself was included as an item in the Treasury Department division until it became a separate category of the budget in 1923. These shifts are indicated in Appendix D in order to show changes which have been made here in official budgetary organization.

For clarity, many of the categories in the Mexican budget have been combined. The Ministry of Development, for example, became the Ministry of Commerce and Industry (including an inadequate labor department) after the Revolution, and during the 1930's its name and functions were changed to the ministry of National Economy. It has since become the Ministry of Commerce and Industry once again. As we shall see in Chapters 6 and 7, the change of name of this ministry in the 1930's and the crea-

tion of an autonomous labor department marked the full emergence of the active state in Mexico.

With regard to classification by type of expenditure in Table
1-4, a few comments are in order. First, government pensions are
treated as an administrative expense following the budgetary classification of the United States. Though the Mexican government
classifies pensions as a social expenditure, the bureaucracy is notably inefficient and overstaffed, and government employees have
long been looked upon as an arm of the official party's power resource. In any case, since pensions were included as an expense
of the Treasury Department prior to 1922, and were not separated
from general public-debt figures in 1928, 1929, and 1931, it has
seemed clearer to consider them as an administrative cost in order
to establish consistency in the global percentages for administrative expense. Medical payments and insurance for public employees, however, clearly support social needs and are easily identifiable for classification as social expenditures.

Second, expenditure on the public debt is classified as an administrative expense since the government must manage its redemption, interest, and cost payments in relation to social and
economic expenditure. Also, debt payment does not contribute
directly to national development. Whereas debt redemption is
excluded from budgets analyzed by economists, especially in developed nations, it must be included for underdeveloped areas
which are dependent on foreign capital and which are required
to pay their debts in order to enjoy good standing among credi-
tor nations and investors of the world. In Mexico, the debt has
been linked with political policy, and political policy is the subject of this work.

Finally, the Agrarian Department is classified under economic
expenditure, since its purpose has been to shift Mexico's land
tenure system to a stronger economic base for national development than the hacienda system provided.

Classification of Mexican expenditures set forth in Table 1-4
presents a pragmatic test of ideology in the Mexican Revolution.
Surprisingly, or not surprisingly, it is very close to the functional
budget prepared by the Ministry of the Treasury since the mid-
1950's. A functional analysis supposes an item-by-item grouping

TABLE I-4

*Classification of Mexican Federal Government Budgetary
Expenditure by Type of Emphasis*

ECONOMIC EXPENDITURE:
  Commerce and Industry (including National Economy and Statistics)
  Communications and Public Works
  Agriculture, Livestock, and Forestry (Fomento)
  Agricultural Credit
  Agrarian Department
  Hydraulic Resources and Irrigation
  Tourism
  Investments in trust funds, stocks, bonds, railways, electrical industry, etc.
  Economic Share of Unclassified Category:
    Transfers to industry and commerce, price supports (Compañía Nacional
      de Subsistencias Populares, etc.), subsidies to decentralized agencies
      (Puertos Libres Mexicanos, Comisión Nacional de Valores, railways, etc.)
SOCIAL EXPENDITURE:
  Education and Physical Education
  Indian Affairs
  Public Health, Welfare, and Assistance
  Potable Water and Sewage Disposal
  Labor
  Social Share of Unclassified Category:
    National Housing Institute and Social Security Institute
    Social and Cultural Aids (including agricultural insurance, Banco Nacional
      Hipotecario Urbano y de Obras Públicas, S.A., and Patrimonio Indígena
      del Valle del Mezquital).
    Payments to governmental employee medical services
    Military and Civilian Insurance Programs
ADMINISTRATIVE EXPENDITURE:
  Public Debt (including redemption, interest, and costs)
  Military (including army, navy, and military industry)
  Legislative
  Executive
  Judicial
  Foreign Relations
  Interior (Gobernación)
  Attorney General
  Treasury (including Accounting Department)
  General Expenses:
    Department of General Supply (1919–1924)
    Department of Press and Publicity (1937–1939)
    National Resources (1947–present)
  Administrative Share of Unclassified Category:
    General Services (including interest and contingency funds)
    Transfers (including subsidies to states and territories), government pensions
      and administration of pensions.

SOURCE: México, Secretaría de Hacienda y Crédito Público, *Presupuesto General de
Egresos de la Federación* (cited as *Presupuesto*) and *Cuenta Pública* by year. For the Leyes
de Secretarías y Departamentos de Estado, from 1821 to the present, consult the
Revista de Administración Pública (Mexico City) 10 (1958), 49–165 and 11–40.

TABLE 1-5

A Budgetary Comparison of (A) the Mexican Government's Functional Analysis and (B) Classification by Type of Emphasis, 1954–1963 (in percentage shares)

I

Projected Expenditure	1954	1955	1956	1957	1958	1959	1960	1961	1962	1963
Economic (A)	45.9	45.9	49.2	47.3	48.1	42.1	42.6	41.3	38.6	38.9
(B)	43.1	44.2	46.6	45.6	45.4	40.9	40.1	39.2	36.8	37.2
Diff. B to A	−2.8	−1.7	−2.6	−1.7	−2.7	−1.2	−2.5	−2.1	−1.8	−1.7
Social (A)	20.7	22.6	22.3	23.9	24.1	27.4	30.5	31.4	34.7	35.0
(B)	19.4	19.7	20.0	21.6	23.2	26.1	29.9	30.7	33.6	33.7
Diff. B to A	−1.3	−2.9	−2.3	−2.3	−.9	−1.3	−.6	−.7	−1.1	−1.3
Administrative (A)	33.4	31.5	28.5	28.8	27.8	30.5	26.9	27.3	26.7	26.1
(B)	37.5	36.1	33.4	32.8	31.4	33.0	30.0	30.1	29.6	29.1
Diff. B to A	4.1	4.6	4.9	4.0	3.6	2.5	3.1	2.8	2.9	3.0

II

Actual Expenditure	1954	1955	1956	1957	1958	1959	1960	1961	1962	1963
Economic (A)	...	49.8	50.6	50.8	52.2	46.1	43.1	32.1	37.1	42.0
(B)	...	50.5	52.4	50.5	51.0	44.8	42.1	31.8	35.1	41.3
Diff. B to A	...	.7	1.8	−.3	−1.2	−1.3	−1.0	−.3	−2.0	−.7
Social (A)	...	14.8	15.4	16.3	16.7	18.1	17.0	18.0	21.1	24.2
(B)	...	12.8	15.5	15.2	16.4	17.4	16.4	18.7	20.9	22.6
Diff. B to A	...	−2.0	.1	−1.1	−.3	−.7	−.6	.7	−.2	−1.6
Administrative (A)	...	35.4	34.0	32.9	31.1	35.8	39.9	49.9	41.8	33.8
(B)	...	36.7	32.1	34.3	32.6	37.8	41.5	49.5	44.0	36.1
Diff. B to A	...	1.3	−1.9	1.4	1.5	2.0	1.6	−.4	2.2	2.3

SOURCE: *Presupuesto* and *Cuenta Pública, 1954–1964. See also* Appendix B.

which cuts across organizational lines to reorganize expenditure in regard to function. The Mexican government breaks its budget down in the following functional expenditure groups: (1) communication and transportation; (2) agriculture, livestock, conservation, and forestry; (3) industry and commerce; (4) education and culture; (5) health, assistance, and hospital programs; (6) welfare and social security; (7) military; (8) administration; and (9) public debt.[9] If we consider these groups as serving economic (1–3), social (4–6), and administrative (7–9) roles, we can compare the government's analysis of percentage of expenditure to our form of analysis. Table 1-5 shows a résumé of governmental functional analysis and our analysis of percentage shares for projected and actual expenditure.

Our analysis of projected expenditure, 1954–1964, summarized in Table 1-5, is in all cases very close to the government's functional analysis, extreme differences being no more than 4.9 to —2.8 per cent. This treatment is even closer to governmental analysis of actual expenditure, and the extreme difference is negligible, ranging from 2.3 to —2.0. In fact, the slight difference between the Mexican government's functional analysis and our analysis of social and administrative expenditure can largely be explained by the classification of pensions as an administrative expenditure instead of as a social expenditure. Table 1-6 reveals the difference if pensions are counted as a social expenditure.

In all except a few cases differences have been reduced to as little disagreement as could be expected. *Therefore we can say with some certitude that the method of budgetary analysis used here for the entire Revolution is probably quite accurate, within the tolerances suggested above.* In any case, consistency in analysis is more important than differences about whether such an item as pensions is categorized as a social or administrative expenditure. Presumably the method of budgetary analysis by category presented here is simpler and easier to apply than the Mexican government's complex method of item-by-item analysis; and, in any case, we may question the Mexican system of classification which defines payments for administration of governmental social

[9] See Appendix A for a complete breakdown of the Mexican government's functional classification.

TABLE 1-6

Pensions Calculated as a Social Expenditure to Account for Differences in Table 1-5

Diff. B to A	1954	1955	1956	1957	1958	1959	1960	1961	1962	1963
I. Projected Expenditure										
Social	.6	−1.1	−.5	−.5	1.6	1.4	1.9	.7	.1	.5
Administrative	2.2	2.8	3.1	2.2	1.1	−.2	.6	1.4	1.7	1.2
II. Actual Expenditure										
Social	...	−.8	1.3	.6	1.3	.8	.4	2.0	1.8	.8
Administrative	...	.1	−3.1	−.3	−.1	.5	.6	−1.7	.2	−.1

SOURCE: Tables 1-5 and 5-5.

security programs, for example, as a social rather than as an administrative function.

Two types of projected budgets can be used. The president sends an initiative budget to the House of Deputies for its debate and approval. The approved congressional budget is theoretically the real guide for governmental action. In practice, the presidential budget is rarely modified to any extent, and it is frequently not changed at all. Table 1-7 presents a comparison of these two budgets. It is obvious that since the Revolution of 1910 began Congress has had little authority to change the presidential budget. President Benito Juárez had the least control over the House of Deputies, for his initiative was reduced by 28.5 per cent. President Porfirio Díaz's budgets were changed only slightly, usually from 1 to 2 per cent. Francisco Madero followed in the Díaz tradition, but Victoriano Huerta had some trouble with the Deputies, for his budgets were modified by 7.7 and 9.2 per cent.

Presidents since Carranza have exercised absolute authority over the House of Deputies. From 1918 to 1928 there was only one change in the budget submitted by the president and approved by the House, and this amounted to only .1 per cent. This kind of control was possible since the president could ignore the House and decree his budget in case of an emergency, as was done in 1919, 1920, 1921, 1922, and 1924. The 1930's witnessed the last congressional budgetary modifications of any extent in Mexico. In 1932 and 1937 the president's initiative was changed by about 1 per cent, and in 1934 it was revised by 6 per cent, the high during the whole Revolution. Only very slight modifications of .1 to .2 per cent were made in the presidential budget from 1939 to 1953. Congress has abandoned its role as overseer of expenditure since 1954, except for a moment of daring in 1960 when it upped projections .1 per cent, and this exception may have been authorized by the executive in order to bring his budget up to date.

The president and the House really need not worry about projected budgets except as a statement of the government's ideology translated into practical terms, for two systems of the budgetary process make change of the actual expenditure a simple matter. First, many of the presidential budgetary items are approved by the House for automatic amplification should more funds become available. The president, of course, is free to determine the

TABLE I-7

Presidential Budget Compared to Congressional Budget

Year	President	(A) Presidential Budget[a]	(B) Congressional Budget[a]	Percentage Difference B to A
1869–1870	Juárez	25,637	18,324	−28.5
1900–1901	Díaz	58,009	58,941	1.6
1910–1911	Díaz	100,306	102,294	2.0
1911–1912	Madero	103,602	105,432	1.8
1912–1913	Madero	109,246	111,370	1.9
1913–1914	Huerta	129,413	141,356	9.2
1914–1915	Huerta	152,205	140,466	−7.7
1917	Carranza	178,524	176,942	− .9
1918	Carranza	187,138	187,138[c]	− − −
1919	Carranza	203,482	b	− − −
1920	Carranza	213,250	b	− − −
1921	Obregón	250,803	b	− − −
1922	Obregón	383,659	b	− − −
1923	Obregón	348,487	b	− − −
1924	Obregón	297,982	b	− − −
1925	Calles	291,634	291,864	.1
1926	Calles	304,405	b	− − −
1927	Calles	318,721	b	− − −
1928	Calles	291,118	b	− − −
1929	Portes Gil	288,283	288,373	− − −
1930	Portes Gil	293,774	b	− − −
1931	Ortiz Rubio	298,489	299,490	.3
1932	Ortiz Rubio	212,987	215,217	1.0
1933	Rodríguez	215,015	215,542	.2
1934	Rodríguez	243,062	257,698	6.0
1935	Cárdenas	275,795	b	− − −
1936	Cárdenas	286,000	287,199	.4
1937	Cárdenas	330,593	333,226	.8
1938	Cárdenas	418,555	431,110	3.0
1939	Cárdenas	445,266	445,876	.1
1940	Cárdenas	447,800	448,769	.2
1941	Avila Camacho	492,000	492,931	.2
1942	Avila Camacho	554,747	555,227	.1
1943	Avila Camacho	707,332	707,845	.1
1944	Avila Camacho	1,101,000	1,101,816	.1
1945	Avila Camacho	1,004,250	1,006,631	.2
1946	Avila Camacho	1,200,000	1,201,427	.1
1947	Alemán	1,665,000	1,667,041	.1

TABLE 1-7 (continued)

Presidential Budget Compared to Congressional Budget

Year	President	(A) Presidential Budget[a]	(B) Congressional Budget[a]	Percentage Difference B to A
1948	Alemán	2,300,000	2,302,617	.1
1949	Alemán	2,550,000	2,551,258	.1
1950	Alemán	2,746,057	2,746,549	– – –
1951	Alemán	3,101,713	3,102,902	– – –
1952	Alemán	3,995,949	3,999,203	.1
1953	Ruiz Cortines	4,158,057	4,160,382	.1
1954	Ruiz Cortines	4,827,681	b	– – –
1955	Ruiz Cortines	5,681,399	b	– – –
1956	Ruiz Cortines	6,696,374	b	– – –
1957	Ruiz Cortines	7,577,874	b	– – –
1958	Ruiz Cortines	8,402,552	b	– – –
1959	López Mateos	9,385,756	b	– – –
1960	López Mateos	10,251,341	10,256,341	.1
1961	López Mateos	11,041,481	b	– – –
1962	López Mateos	12,319,783	b	– – –
1963	López Mateos	13,801,440	b	– – –

[a] In thousands of current pesos (rounded-off).
[b] Congressional budget is the same as presidential budget.
[c] *Cuenta Pública* corrects printing error in *Presupuesto*.
SOURCES: Aguilar, *Los Presupuestos Mexicanos*, table facing p. 172; Santillán López and Rosas Figueroa, *Teoría General*, 222; Flores Zavala, *Elementos*, 393; *El Popular*, Dec. 15, 1959; *El Universal*, Nov. 19, 1955; *El Día*, Dec. 16, 1964; México, Secretaría de Hacienda y Crédito Público, *Boletín de Informaciones*, Nov., 1929. *See also* Appendix B.

amount of amplification in each case. Second, if the president wishes to use new funds for items not covered by automatic amplification or to change budgetary allocations, he sends initiatives to the House for modification of the budget already approved for the fiscal year. Congress complies, changes in the budget are made, legality is followed, and presidential flexibility to disburse federal funds is maximum. Since the original presidential and congressional budgets will be completely changed by the end of the fiscal year, there is no need to fight over budgetary policy at the beginning of the fiscal year. In any case, if a Deputy wishes to modify the budget, he must not upset the budgetary balance of income and outgo submitted by the executive unless he provides a new source of income to meet new expense. Since this is virtually impossible for deputies to do every time they wish to make a change, and since income is strictly controlled by the Ministry of the Treasury, modification of the budget is virtually impossible.

The president's power over Congress stems from his political power. As head of the official party he literally appoints congressmen and senators or else delegates his power to appoint several legislators to an important personage in return for political support—elections are controlled by the president and his Minister of the Interior. Thus legislators are not in a position to question the president, and in fact there is no reason to do so. They do not really represent any district or state, and therefore do not have any constituents to satisfy with a money bill. The fact that they can not be re-elected for a succeeding term means that they have little drive to win public approval for taking a stand against the president. Once a politician leaves Congress, he is dependent upon the official party of the Revolutionary Family for a new post; hence loyalty is to the party and not to the people. Electoral reforms (discussed in Chapter 4) have introduced significant opposition-party representation to the House of Deputies since 1964; and though the caliber of debate and prestige of the House has increased immeasurably, the official party still controls the legislative process and no change can be predicted at this time.[10]

Since there is little, if any, difference between presidential and congressional budgets, and since the president is responsible for both budgets, budgetary analysis in this work utilizes either type. It has not been possible to locate all the original or all the ap-

[10] Aguilar, in *Los Presupuestos Mexicanos*, 146–151, discusses presidential decrees of the budget. Scott, "Budget Making in Mexico," 4, notes that presidential decrees were necessary as congress often failed to enact the budget until after the beginning of the fiscal year as in 1919, 1923, 1929, and 1936. Scott discusses the process of formulating the budget as does William P. Tucker, *The Mexican Government Today* (Minneapolis: University of Minnesota Press, 1957), Chapter 11. Examples of complaints about the budget-making process by the opposition parties may be consulted in México, Cámara de Diputados, *Diario de los Debates*, Oct. 11, 1961, 9–10, and *El Día*, Nov. 28, 1964. A proposal by the *Partido de Acción Nacional* to modify the budget by increasing salaries of the Supreme Court Justices to those of cabinet ministers is presented in full in *El Día*, Dec. 28, 1964—the modification was for a small amount which would not "affect the budget balance."

proved budgets. Table 1-8 contains a note about which type of projected budget is used for each year.

In order to assess the emphasis of a presidential program, all budgets are presented in percentage terms. Administrative, economic, and social expenditure are calculated as percentages of yearly total budgets. (Chapters 5, 6, and 7 further break down percentage expenditure for specific categories.) Detailed statistics are presented in order that they may be rearranged if the reader does not agree with the organization presented here. It should be noted that in order to shorten the calculation process, many numbers have been rounded and that the figures in this study may differ slightly from figures prepared by other scholars.

Projected and actual budgets are also calculated in real pesos per capita to facilitate comprehension of the meaning of expenditure in historical analysis. Table 1-8 shows how yearly total budgets are converted to real pesos. The price index used for conversion of per-capita budgets to real pesos is the wholesale price index for Mexico City, based upon 1929 price levels, prepared by the Ministry of National Economy in 1943.[11] It has since been carried forward by the Ministry of Industry and Commerce, and for the purposes of this study it is converted to pesos of 1950. The wholesale price index includes 33 articles prior to 1929 and 50 articles thereafter.

One may question whether the wholesale price index for Mexico City is representative of prices in all Mexico, but since there is no other index which covers Mexico's history from 1900 to 1963, we have no choice but to use it. In any case, Mexico City is the key producer and distributor of manufactured goods in Mexico. Goods purchased in or distributed throughout Mexico are based upon price levels in the capital. In addition, high trans-

[11] Federico Bach and Margarita Reyna, "El Nuevo Indice de Precios al Mayoreo en la Cuidad de México de la Secretaría de la Economía Nacional," *El Trimestre Económico* 10 (1943) 1–63. There is an alternative wholesale price index available for Mexico City since 1939 which is prepared by the Bank of Mexico. Though this index is quite complete, it is not usable for analysis here as it has 210 items which appear to understate the impact of inflation on the masses and overstate the cost of social and economic change, 1910–1960. The great number of items included make it incomparable with the price index prepared by the Ministry of National Economy for the period 1900–1963. Santillán López and Rosas Figueroa, *Teoría General,* 247, present the Bank of Mexico index. Sanford A. Mosk, *Industrial Revolution in Mexico* (Berkeley: University of California Press, 1950), 274, uses the same price index as we do.

TABLE 1-8

Projected and Actual Expenditure Since 1900 in Pesos of 1950

Year	Thousands of Current Pesos		Price Index (1950 = 100)	Thousands of Pesos of 1950	
	Projected Budget	Actual Budget		Projected Budget	Actual Budget
1900–1901	58,941[a]	59,832	14.7	400,959	407,020
1910–1911	102,294[a]	101,237	19.6	521,908	516,515
1911–1912	105,432[a]	97,293	19.4	543,464	501,510
1912–1913	111,370[a]	111,272	19.2	580,052	579,542
1913–1914	141,356[a]	...	...	...	...
1914–1915	140,466[a]	...	...	...	...
1917	178,524	73,024	...	...	...
1918	187,138[a]	109,717	43.3	432,189	253,388
1919	203,482[a]	59,167	34.6	588,098	171,003
1920	213,250[a]	131,966	36.3	587,466	363,543
1921	250,803[a]	226,353	33.1	757,713	683,846
1922	383,659[a]	228,093	27.8	1,380,068	820,478
1923	348,487[a]	235,354	29.8	1,169,419	789,779
1924	297,982[a]	276,570	28.5	1,045,551	970,421
1925	291,864[a]	302,164	30.0	972,880	1,007,213
1926	304,405[a]	324,938	29.4	1,035,391	1,105,231
1927	318,721[a]	310,082	28.7	1,110,526	1,080,425
1928	291,118[a]	287,946	27.6	1,054,775	1,043,283
1929	288,283	275,541	27.5	1,048,302	1,001,967
1930	293,774[a]	279,122	28.0	1,049,193	996,864
1931	298,489	226,478	24.7	1,208,457	916,915
1932	212,987	211,625	22.5	946,609	940,556
1933	215,015	245,951	23.9	899,644	1,029,084
1934	243,062	264,740	24.7	984,057	1,071,822
1935	275,795[a]	300,822	24.9	1,107,610	1,208,120
1936	286,000	406,098	26.4	1,083,333	1,538,250
1937	333,226[a]	478,756	31.3	1,064,620	1,529,572
1938	418,555	503,765	32.7	1,279,985	1,540,566
1939	445,266	582,228	33.6	1,325,196	1,732,821
1940	447,800	603,818	33.8	1,324,852	1,786,444
1941	492,000	681,869	35.9	1,370,474	1,899,357
1942	554,747	836,848	39.7	1,397,348	2,107,929
1943	707,332	1,075,539	47.5	1,489,120	2,264,293
1944	1,101,000	1,453,335	60.9	1,807,882	2,386,429
1945	1,004,250	1,572,804	67.0	1,498,881	2,347,469
1946	1,200,000	1,770,544	78.5	1,528,662	2,255,470

TABLE 1-8 (continued)

Projected and Actual Expenditure Since 1900 in Pesos of 1950

| Year | Thousands of Current Pesos | | Price Index (1950 = 100) | Thousands of Pesos of 1950 | |
	Projected Budget	Actual Budget		Projected Budget	Actual Budget
1947	1,665,000	2,142,961	80.1	2,078,652	2,675,357
1948	2,300,000	2,773,365	85.0	2,705,882	3,262,782
1949	2,550,000	3,740,587	90.0	2,833,333	4,156,208
1950	2,746,057	3,463,290	100.0	2,746,057	3,463,290
1951	3,101,713	4,670,088	120.6	2,571,901	3,872,378
1952	3,995,949	6,464,230	132.5	3,015,811	4,878,664
1953	4,158,057	5,490,402	135.2	3,075,486	4,060,948
1954	4,827,681[a]	7,916,807	145.6	3,315,715	5,437,367
1955	5,681,399[a]	8,883,121	168.0	3,381,785	5,287,572
1956	6,696,374[a]	10,270,112	178.3	3,755,678	5,760,018
1957	7,577,874[a]	11,303,248	189.3	4,003,103	5,971,077
1958	8,402,552[a]	13,287,707	198.0	4,243,713	6,710,963
1959	9,385,756[a]	14,157,742	200.8	4,674,181	7,050,668
1960	10,251,341	20,150,330	212.3	4,828,705	9,491,441
1961	11,041,481[a]	20,362,040	214.2	5,154,753	9,506,088
1962	[b]12,320,000[a]	20,219,156	217.2	5,672,192	9,309,005
1963	13,801,440[a]	20,294,906	221.2	6,239,349	9,174,912

[a] Presidential budget approved by Congress with minor (if any) modifications.
[b] 12,319,783 rounded to 12,320,000.
SOURCES: Price index sources: 1900–1947: *Trimestre de Barómetros Económicos* 2:8 (1948) 71; 1948–1957: México, Dirección General de Estadística, *Compendio Estadístico 1956–1957*, 382 (cited as *Compendio Estadístico*); 1958–1962: *ibid., 1962*, 177; 1963: México, Dirección General de Estadística, *Revista de Estadística* 27:8 (1964) 911. *See also* Appendix B.

portation costs, including the traditional "toll" for the highway police, raise prices in much of the country. If a price index is intended to measure the level at which rural Mexico can subsist, then the wholesale price index for Mexico City is obviously not adequate for all Mexico. If, however, we are looking at social modernization in Mexico, price levels of Mexico City are our best indicator for analytical purposes. Mexico City dominates the nation. It is the urban center of the country, and it is the hub of

TABLE 1-9

Projected and Actual Expenditure Since 1900 in Pesos of 1950 Per Capita

Year	Estimated Population	Projected Expenditure[a]	Actual Expenditure[a]	Year	Estimated Population	Projected Expenditure[a]	Actual Expenditure[a]
1900–1901	13,755,137	29.1	29.6	1938	19,071,222	67.1	80.8
1910–1911	15,160,369[b]	34.4	34.1	1939	19,413,095	68.3	89.3
1911–1912	*15,000,000	36.2	33.4	1940	19,653,552[b]	67.4	90.9
1912–1913	*15,000,000	38.7	38.6	1941	20,208,163	67.8	94.0
1913–1914	...	...	...	1942	20,656,807	67.6	102.0
1914–1915	...	...	...	1943	21,164,788	70.4	107.0
1917	...	...	...	1944	21,674,111	83.4	110.1
1918	*14,000,000	30.9	18.1	1945	22,233,243	67.4	105.6
1919	*14,150,000	41.6	12.1	1946	22,778,814	67.1	99.0
1920	*14,150,000	41.5	25.7	1947	23,439,813	88.7	114.1
1921	14,334,780[b]	52.9	47.7	1948	24,128,596	112.1	135.2
1922	14,444,434	95.5	56.8	1949	24,824,995	114.1	167.4
1923	14,692,554	79.6	53.8	1950	25,791,017[b]	106.5	134.3
1924	14,945,233	70.0	64.9	1951	25,585,000	100.5	151.4
1925	15,203,787	64.0	66.3	1952	27,403,000	110.1	178.0
1926	15,467,979	66.9	71.5	1953	28,246,000	108.9	143.8
1927	15,737,956	70.6	68.7	1954	29,115,000	113.9	186.8
1928	16,011,879	65.9	65.2	1955	30,011,000	112.7	176.2
1929	16,295,918	64.3	61.5	1956	30,935,000	121.4	186.2
1930	16,552,722[b]	63.4	60.2	1957	31,877,000	125.5	187.3
1931	16,875,976	71.6	54.3	1958	32,868,000	129.1	204.2
1932	17,169,635	55.1	54.8	1959	33,880,000	138.0	208.1
1933	17,469,659	51.5	58.9	1960	34,923,129[b]	138.3	271.8
1934	17,776,212	55.4	60.3	1961	36,075,000	142.9	263.5
1935	18,089,465	61.2	66.8	1962	37,265,000	152.2	249.8
1936	18,409,596	58.8	83.6	1963	39,238,000	159.0	233.8
1937	18,763,786	56.8	81.6				

a Calculated from Table 1-8.

b Census figures, see Appendix K.

SOURCES: Population estimates: 1900–1950 are given by the Combined Mexican Working Party, *Economic Development*, 180; 1951–1962 are from *50 Años en Cifras*, 42; 1963 is from the *Revista de Estadística*, 27:8 (1964) 860.

CENSUS: México, Dirección General de Estadística, *Censos Generales de la Población; Resumen, 1910, 1921, 1930, 1940, 1950, 1960* (cited as *Resumen del Censo*).

financial enterprise without par in Mexico. Government expenditure is directed from the Federal District, and is related to the outlook of the vast federal bureaucracy in the central valley of Mexico.

To provide the statistics for budgetary analysis, projected and actual expenditures for all years since 1917 are presented, and the years 1910–1916 are included where available. Civil war disrupted record keeping of actual expenses in the fiscal years from 1913 to 1915, but projected figures give an idea concerning what Mexico's leaders might have spent had conditions been normal. No data are available for 1916. Two years of the Díaz government are included for contrast to the Revolutionary period, and it is important to note that during the Díaz period, after 1900, projections and actual expenditure percentages did not vary much. It was difficult to locate comparative data for President Benito Juárez, the outstanding figure of mid-nineteenth-century politics, as he governed for many years from the carriage that took him back and forth across war-torn Mexico. The year 1869–1870 has been chosen as a fair year to represent Juárez's budgetary policy, for stability had been restored somewhat after the French were driven out of Mexico in 1867, and military expenses were less, so that Juárez could think of more creative uses for the federal purse. Since our price index does not extend back to 1869–1870, Juárez's budget is not converted to pesos of 1950.

Population figures play an important role in determining how far projected and actual expenditure will stretch. Since Part II attempts directly to measure the cost of social change, real budgets in Table 1-8 are reduced to per-capita terms in Table 1-9. Population estimates between census years are taken from calculations by the Mexican Statistical Agency for the years 1901–1949 and 1963–1964, and from calculations by Nacional Financiera for the period 1951–1962.

There is a pattern in the difference between projected and actual expenditure in pesos per capita of 1950 (Table 1-9) which must be explained. Let us take educational outlay as an example. In 1961 López Mateos projected 19.1 per cent of the federal budget, or 27.3 pesos, for the Ministry of Education (Table 7-2). By the end of the year, however, total budgetary expenditure increased 84.4 per cent over the projected amount. Thus total per-capita expenditure in Table 1-9 went up from 142.9 to 263.5 in actual amount. The Ministry of Education received 28.5 pesos, slightly more than were projected, but due to the increased budget, it actually received only 10.8 per cent of the federal purse. If it had received the 19.1 per cent projected, it would have spent 50.3 pesos. Ironically, education lost in percentage emphasis, but gained in monetary affluence. This pattern often holds true in the post-1936 period and even in some years prior to that time for many budgetary items. Table 1-10 shows the yearly increase in actual budgets over projected budgets which causes this phenomenon. The increase is the same for current pesos, pesos of 1950, and pesos of 1950 per capita.

TABLE I-IO

Increase in Actual over Projected Total Expenditures Since 1933

Year	Per Cent	Year	Per Cent	Year	Per Cent
1933	14.4	1944	32.0	1954	64.0
1934	8.9	1945	56.6	1955	56.4
1935	9.1	1946	47.5	1956	53.4
1936	42.0	1947	28.7	1957	49.2
1937	43.7	1948	20.6	1958	58.1
1938	20.4	1949	46.7	1959	50.8
1939	30.8	1950	26.1	1960	96.6
1940	34.8	1951	50.6	1961	84.4
1941	38.6	1952	61.8	1962	64.1
1942	50.9	1953	32.0	1963	47.0
1943	52.1				

Source: Tables 1-8 and 1-9.

Since 1935, Cárdenas's first year of presidency, actual expenditures per capita have exceeded projected expenditures per capita. During the years after 1942 this discrepancy became astounding, especially in 1952 and 1960. Indeed during the presidencies of Adolfo Ruiz Cortines and López Mateos the difference between projected budgets per capita and actual expenditures was so consistently disparate as to suggest that Mexico's executives had refused to take into account the growth rate of federal expenditure.

Of course, if this were the case, it would have left the president great freedom in determining how new income should be distributed, but it also meant that for all practical purposes the projected budget was next to useless. In 1960, for example, the government underestimated real expenditure, in 1950 terms, by 4,662,736,000 pesos. This amount was nearly half of all federal expenditure (49.1 per cent). Changes and authorization for the chief executive to use increased income as he sees fit are automatically forthcoming from Congress, and the president directly enjoys increasingly more power than he did in the years in which the government lived in relative poverty.

The practice of deficit spending by the Mexican government has only become a significant factor in budgetary policy since the Cárdenas era. Since 1936, deficit spending has become commonplace. The analysis of deficit spending presents a different problem from that of analysis of actual budgets. In the latter case it has been necessary to use the unrevised account books for each year in order to examine the total impact of each budget. It has not been possible to bring these account books up to date as revisions are often not published for ten years. Since these changes are generally small, usually presenting amounts which had not yet been paid in the original account books, and since juggling such figures would necessitate a giant bookkeeping arrangement which the Mexican government has never even attempted, revision of actual expenditure totals has not been attempted. In the former case, the *Anuario Estadistico* presents revised total income and actual expenditure by year. Although this is without analysis, it is suitable for our purposes to summarize the amount of deficit spending. Table 1-11 offers this data.

The largest percentage of deficit spending in relation to income came in 1911–1912, Madero's first year in office. The confusion of taking office after violent revolution and the problems caused by several major rebellions in 1911 necessitated unorthodox monetary policy. Other years of violent upheaval did not cause much deficit spending. Rebellion did coincide with deficit spending in 1918 and 1926, but the deficits were not large. Deficit spending apparently carried over to 1927 in the latter case. Under Cárdenas actual expenditure exceeded income regularly, reaching 15.1 per cent in 1938, the year of oil expropriation. The Second World

TABLE I-II

Deficit Spending

Years	Deficits[a]	Per Cent of Income
1910–1911	10	9.1
1911–1912	27	21.4
1918	9	5.7
1926	16	5.2
1927	15	5.1
1933	23	10.3
1936	21	5.5
1937	28	6.2
1938	66	15.1
1939	46	8.6
1940	55	9.5
1941	17	2.6
1942	91	12.2
1944	158	12.2
1945	169	12.0
1947	88	4.3
1948	118	4.4
1952	126	2.0
1953	467	9.3
1954	203	2.6
1956	76	.8
1957	433	4.0
1958	105	.8
1960	693	3.6
1961	421	2.1
1963[b]	591	3.0

[a] In millions of pesos.

[b] Cf. *Anuario Estadístico 1962–1963*, 527, where totals do not agree with actual expenditure in the *Cuenta Pública* due to the *Anuario Estadístico's* strange method of presentation of the debt payments. For example, the debt payment for 1963 is given as 3,472 million pesos in the former and 12,459 million in the latter—a difference of 8,987 million which is attributed to gross "operations of the revolving debt" which are considered neither as "income nor expenditure." These figures are corrected in *Anuario Estadístico 1964–1965*, 559.

SOURCE: *Anuario Estadístico 1940*, 741, *1955–1956*, 728, *1964–1965*, 559. Totals are revised and may not agree with Table 1-8.

War years witnessed a high level of deficits. Since 1947 deficits have remained relatively minor, except for 1953, as a percentage of income.

Prior to 1947, extraordinary expenditures are excluded from total figures of deficits in Table 1-11 and in examinations of actual expenditure throughout this study. This exclusion follows Mexican government policy. The amount of extraordinary expenditure has usually been minimal. For example, in 1920 it totaled 1.0 per cent more than actual expenditure and its purpose was to amortize civil war paper money. Disaster funds in 1918 and 1919 amounted to .2 and .3 per cent more than the actual budget. In 1944 extra funds totaled .7 per cent to cover Treasury Department loans to the Defense Ministry and to a decentralized agency. Extraordinary expenditure seems to have reached a marked high in 1940, for such funds were 9.0 per cent more than the actual budget. About half of this went for a Treasury loan to the Ministry of Communications and Public Works for road construction and the rest covered expenditure in excess of or without budgetary allocation. Apparently all extraordinary expenditures have been included in *erogaciones adicionales* since 1947 to eliminate the problem of direct federal expenditure outside of the regular budget.

2

A Résumé of Comparative
Presidential Budgetary Policies

This chapter summarizes presidential policy by comparing the average expenditure of each executive during the last half century. The purpose here is to fix limits on historical periods and to demonstrate quantitatively the nature of ideological actions of the Mexican government since 1910.

A QUANTITATIVE SUMMARY SINCE 1910

We have seen that the federal budget in Mexico is a very personal arm of presidential power. It is important to note that though theoretically the Mexican federal system is close to its model in the United States, in practice there is little similarity of action. Whereas the budget of the United States is not greatly flexible due to the extensive number of long-range commitments, the Mexican budget has not achieved such complexity. Even more important, the budget in the United States is drawn up by the executive of a huge bureaucracy, debated by the public, and scrutinized by Congress. If any bureaucratic agency feels that the executive has not asked Congress for enough funds, it can subtly appeal to Congress to restore or increase its appropriation.[1] In Mexico the president and his treasury minister are the all-powerful figures, and their financial decisions are rarely seriously de-

[1] Aaron Wildavsky, *The Politics of the Budgetry Process* (Boston: Little, Brown, 1964).

bated in public.[2] Certainly there may be inside pressure from an agency or a friend, but in the end, the executive's program is final. In the process of balancing the nation's needs with the ideological drive of the moment, the executive has flexibility in determining what budgetary items shall be emphasized or de-emphasized.[3]

Table 2-1 summarizes the course of presidential action during the Revolution. The variations in executive programs stand out in the type of budgetary emphasis which each leader manifested. The averages for each presidential administration summarize detailed yearly analysis which is presented in later chapters. It should be noted that the averages are meaningless in themselves and serve only for comparative purposes. They reduce to a few figures data that are very comprehensive. A caution is in order, for the averages may tend to hide short-term policy, especially after 1935 when presidential terms became longer.

It is important to note that the years and presidents in parts A and B are not the same, 1911–1920 and 1928–1934, owing to political disruption. In 1920, for example, the projected budget was prepared by Carranza but actually administered by Adolfo de la Huerta. Since De la Huerta's interim presidency, executives have served until November 30 of the year in which their term ends. Therefore, since presidential terms begin in a year which has only one month left, budgetary policy continues to be that of the preceding president. Table 2-1 reflects this aspect of the budget, and presidential averages are computed from each executive's first entire year in office. For example, Calles took office in 1924, but his four-year average covers 1925–1928. A one-month discrepancy is negligible here. The exceptions to the above occurred in the period 1930–1932. Interim President Emilio Portes Gil turned over his office to Pascual Ortiz Rubio on February 4, 1930, and Ortiz Rubio resigned office prematurely on September 1, 1932. There is no analytical problem here, for Portes Gil is credited with the budget projection of 1930, and Ortiz Rubio is credited with actual expenditures 1930–1932. President Abe-

---

[2] Gustavo Díaz Ordaz's prolonged wage controversy with the medical students and much of the medical profession upon taking office in late 1964 and early 1965 seems to be a precedent for public debate which directly challenges the president's fiscal policy.

[3] Cf. Lewis H. Kimmel, *Federal Budget and Fiscal Policy, 1789–1958* (Washington, D. C.: Brookings Institution, 1959), for a discussion of United States policy.

TABLE. 2-I

Average Per Cent of Federal Budgetary Expenditure by Type
of Emphasis and Presidential Term

A. Projected Expenditure

Years	President	No. of Years in Avg.	Per Cent			
			Total	Economic	Social	Admin.
1869–1870	Juárez	(1)	100.0	19.1	2.7	78.2
1900–1911	Díaz	(2)ᵃ	100.0	16.7	6.4	76.9
1911–1913	Madero	(2)	100.0	17.4	9.3	73.3
1913–1915	Huerta	(2)	100.0	15.4	10.1	74.5
1917–1920	Carranza	(4)	100.0	15.0	2.3	82.7
1921–1924	Obregón	(4)	100.0	18.7	12.0	69.3
1925–1929	Calles	(4)	100.0	21.4	10.4	68.2
1929–1930	Portes Gil	(2)	100.0	25.7	13.2	61.1
1931–1932	Ortiz Rubio	(2)	100.0	28.7	15.2	56.1
1933–1934	Rodríguez	(2)	100.0	22.0	17.0	61.0
1935–1940	Cárdenas	(6)	100.0	30.5	23.0	46.5
1941–1946	Avila Camacho	(6)	100.0	30.7	23.5	45.8
1947–1952	Alemán	(6)	100.0	39.2	18.6	42.2
1953–1958	Ruiz Cortines	(6)	100.0	43.8	20.4	35.8
1959–1963	López Mateos	(5)ᵇ	100.0	38.8	30.8	30.4

B. Actual Expenditure

1869–1870	Juárez	(1)	100.0	5.0	1.6	93.4
1900–1911	Díaz	(2)ᵃ	100.0	16.0	6.6	77.4
1911–1912	Madero	(1)	100.0	17.6	9.9	72.5
1912–1913	Huerta	(1)	100.0	15.2	8.9	75.9
1917–1919	Carranza	(3)	100.0	16.3	2.0	81.7
1920	De la Huerta	(1)	100.0	17.2	2.3	80.5
1921–1924	Obregón	(4)	100.0	17.9	9.7	72.4
1925–1928	Calles	(4)	100.0	24.8	10.1	65.1
1929	Portes Gil	(1)	100.0	23.2	12.9	63.9
1930–1932	Ortiz Rubio	(3)	100.0	28.1	15.8	56.1
1933–1934	Rodríguez	(2)	100.0	21.7	15.4	62.9
1935–1940	Cárdenas	(6)	100.0	37.6	18.3	44.1
1941–1946	Avila Camacho	(6)	100.0	39.2	16.5	44.3
1947–1952	Alemán	(6)	100.0	51.9	13.3	34.8
1953–1958	Ruiz Cortines	(6)	100.0	52.7	14.4	32.9
1959–1963	López Mateos	(5)ᶜ	100.0	39.0	19.2	41.8

ᵃ 1900–1901 and 1910–1911.

ᵇ Data for 1964 not included.

ᶜ Data for 1964 not available.

SOURCE: *Presupuesto* and *Cuenta Pública* by year. *See also* Appendix B.

lardo Rodríguez took office with the difficult task of filling out
Ortiz Rubio's term, and he probably did not change the nature
of actual expenditure which was already mostly committed by
September 1. Appendix C presents a chronological list of periods
in which each president of the twentieth century has held office.

Table 2-1 reveals some interesting conclusions. Juárez's economic and administrative expenditures were projected at about
the same rate as those of Porfirio Díaz, but actual economic disbursement was sacrificed for general administrative expense that
can not be assigned to one agency or to the military. By the twentieth century, Díaz was allocating a larger share of the budget to
social expenditure than had previous presidents, but the percentage was not high. Beginning with Alvaro Obregón, social expenditure gained steadily until it hit a peak under Cárdenas. It fell
off under Alemán and Ruiz Cortines, but rose again under López
Mateos. Until Cárdenas, economic expenditure in the Revolution
did not actually begin its upward climb. Under Plutarco Elías
Calles some gain was made; and under Ortiz Rubio economic dis-

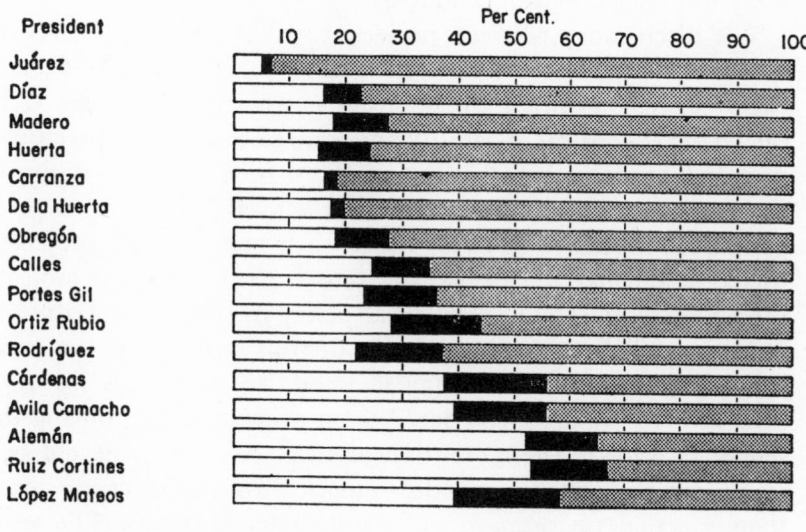

FIG. 1. Average Actual Per Cent of Federal Budgetary Expenditure by Type
of Emphasis and Presidential Term.

bursement leaped as a byproduct of a cutback in administrative expenses in order to balance the budget during the depression. To be fair to Ortiz Rubio, it must be pointed out that he entered office with a desire to emphasize economic expenditure. He made a noble attempt to supply agricultural credit to the countryside during the height of the depression in 1932 while he was attempting to minimize governmental expenditures, but, as we shall see in Chapter 6, the 4.1 per cent he actually expended was a unique event before and after, until Cárdenas came into the presidency. In the matter of economic expenditure, it is clear that Ruiz Cortines slightly outdid his mentor Miguel Alemán.

It is obvious that percentage emphasis in the average projected budget has very little to do with actual expenditure. From Cárdenas to Ruiz Cortines, for example, average social expenditure actually ran about 6 per cent behind projected figures; the disparity increased to 11.6 per cent during López Mateos's first five years. In contrast, economic expenditure ran way ahead of projections during the terms from Cárdenas to Ruiz Cortines; it has since been sacrificed for administrative costs, such as payments on the public debt, by López Mateos.

The discrepancy between projected and actual budgets has occurred for two reasons. First, in recent years federal budgetary resources have grown tremendously, as we saw in Chapter 1. In earlier years political instability and limited funds often precluded presidential action based upon any factor other than the desire to stay in power. Table 2-2 summarizes the average amount of pesos per capita (in prices of 1950) which each president has projected to spend and has actually spent. This is the companion table to the above summary of presidential policy in percentage terms.

The overthrow of Díaz did not disrupt government expenditure, for actual federal outlay increased to 33.4 pesos (in 1950 prices) under Madero, compared to an average of 31.9 during the ten years prior to the revolution of 1910. Average projected per-capita expenditure continued to mount through Obregón's term, though actual performance collapsed under Carranza. The years of civil war and inflation which engulfed Mexico from 1913 to 1917 severely limited governmental expenditures. Treasury records were not kept and the lack of measurement of inflation in prices prevents us from any examination of those years.[4] Where these records are available for the Carranza Epoch we find that, though the price level was stabilized, government expenditure was limited by Carranza's inability to control the nation and to raise funds. Recovery was partial under De la Huerta, and complete under Obregón, who brought average actual expenditure per capita to a high point in Mexican history. Calles had further expanded funds to work with, but Portes Gil and Ortiz Rubio presided over decreasing totals, which they recognized in their projections of expenditure per capita. Rodríguez governed in times of renewed budgetary vigor, and Cárdenas spent more than his projected expenditures by a great deal. Since that time, the budget per capita in constant pesos has grown tremendously.

Whereas Cárdenas placed 18.3 per cent of his actual budget in social expenditures, Alemán spent only 13.3 per cent; yet, in the amount of real pesos per capita expended, Alemán exceeded Cárdenas's effort by 4.5 pesos. López Mateos, whose average percentage emphasis in social expenditure slightly exceeded that of Cárdenas, spent 47.0 pesos per capita compared to Cárdenas's 15.0 pesos per capita. Thus it is obvious that increasing budgetary amounts have meant greater expenditure per capita even though percentage emphasis from president to president has varied greatly. Therefore, while the amount of funds spent is considered in the following analysis, the real test of ideology of each president is in how he has allocated federal expenditure in percentage terms.

FOUR IDEOLOGICAL PERIODS

The quantitative summaries of expenditure in the Mexican Revolution reveal four periods of ideological action. Francisco I. Madero, apostle of the Mexican Revolution of 1910, took over the presidency in 1911 with a wide base of support among the politically aware population, but he did not make a sharp break with Porfirio Díaz's budgetary policies. Madero's average projected and actual expenditures differed only slightly in percentage terms from those of the dictator he had overthrown. The man who

[4] See Edwin Walter Kemmerer, *Inflation and Revolution, Mexico's Experience of 1912–1917* (Princeton: Princeton University Press, 1940).

TABLE 2-2

*Average Amount of Budgetary Expenditure by Type
of Emphasis and Presidential Term*

A. Projected Expenditure

Years	President	No. of Years in Avg.	Pesos of 1950 per Capita			
			Total	Economic	Social	Admin.
1900–1911	Díaz	(2)[a]	31.8	5.3	2.0	24.5
1911–1913	Madero	(2)	37.5	6.5	3.5	27.5
1917–1920	Carranza	(4)	38.0	5.7	.9	31.4
1921–1924	Obregón	(4)	74.5	13.9	9.0	51.6
1925–1929	Calles	(4)	66.9	14.4	6.9	45.6
1929–1930	Portes Gil	(4)	63.9	16.4	8.4	39.1
1931–1932	Ortiz Rubio	(2)	63.4	18.2	9.6	35.6
1933–1934	Rodríguez	(2)	53.5	11.8	9.1	32.6
1935–1940	Cárdenas	(6)	63.3	19.3	14.6	29.4
1941–1946	Avila Camacho	(6)	70.6	21.7	16.6	32.3
1947–1952	Alemán	(6)	105.3	41.3	19.6	44.4
1953–1958	Ruiz Cortines	(6)	118.6	51.9	24.2	42.5
1959–1963	López Mateos	(5)[b]	146.1	56.5	45.2	44.4

B. Actual Expenditure

1900–1911	Díaz	(2)[a]	31.9	5.1	2.1	24.7
1911–1912	Madero	(1)	33.4	5.9	3.3	24.2
1912–1913	Huerta	(1)	38.6	5.9	3.4	29.3
1917–1919	Carranza	(3)	15.1	2.5	.3	12.3
1920	De la Huerta	(1)	25.3	4.3	.6	20.4
1921–1924	Obregón	(4)	55.8	10.0	5.4	40.4
1925–1928	Calles	(4)	67.9	16.8	6.9	44.2
1929	Portes Gil	(1)	61.5	14.3	7.9	39.3
1930–1932	Ortiz Rubio	(3)	56.4	15.9	8.9	31.6
1933–1934	Rodríguez	(2)	59.6	12.9	9.2	37.5
1935–1940	Cárdenas	(6)	82.2	30.9	15.0	36.3
1941–1946	Avila Camacho	(6)	103.0	40.4	17.0	45.6
1947–1952	Alemán	(6)	146.7	76.1	19.5	51.1
1953–1958	Ruiz Cortines	(6)	180.8	95.3	26.0	59.5
1959–1963	López Mateos	(5)[c]	245.4	95.2	47.0	103.2

[a] 1900–1901 and 1910–1911.
[b] Data for 1964 not included.
[c] Data for 1964 not available.
SOURCE: Calculated from data in Tables 1-9 and 2-1.

might have reoriented drastically the role of the state set a conservative precedent of governmental action. Succeeding governments during the period from 1913 to 1920 held to this concept of government. Though there was much radical talk of aiding the masses, especially in the early 1920's, there was only a gradual shift away from a passive role for the state in social and economic affairs.

The first actual dramatic presidential action which rejected the old concept of the administrative state came under Lázaro Cárdenas, 1934–1940. Cárdenas, who predicated his program on achieving social justice, sought and found greater funds for state action, and he used them. He increased social expenditure to a new high. This action and Cárdenas's expenditure of an average of 37.6 per cent of the federal purse in the economic sphere of national life marked the turning point of Mexico's Revolution.

Though subsequent presidents would often balk at using the resources of the state to intervene in social affairs, as Chapter 7 specifically shows, the active state was firmly established. The implementation of the Constitution of 1917 could finally be under-

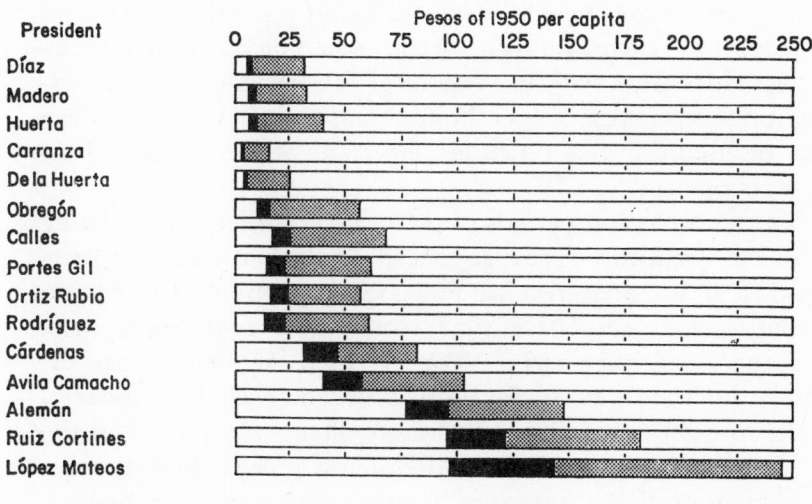

FIG. 2. Average Actual Amount of Federal Budgetary Expenditure by Type of Emphasis and Presidential Term.

taken. As we shall see, Cárdenas's program was rooted in a consensus for state action after 1930. Ortiz Rubio, caught up in the ideological swirl of how to cope with the depression, made halting moves to achieve economic recovery and social well-being. Cárdenas became a presidential candidate in the trough of a depression, but as Table 4-2 shows, basically the economy had recovered by the time he took office. With actual pesos per capita at their predepression level in 1934, Cárdenas could effectively call upon the country's resources for radical new experiments in statecraft.

The wartime presidency of Manuel Avila Camacho projected almost exactly the same average percentage expenditure as Cárdenas had projected, but an actual shift away from social expenditure to greater economic expenditure became evident. The ideology of emphasis on economic development won a startling percentage increase under Miguel Alemán in the postwar period. Alemán projected an average economic expenditure of almost 40 per cent of the budget, but he spent 51.9 per cent of the expanded federal purse for economic development. This emphasis in the revolution lasted until López Mateos de-emphasized economic expenditure in favor of renewed social goals. López Mateos projected the ideology of a balanced revolution, and nowhere is this clearer than in his budgets which offered to spend a relatively balanced percentage of federal funds on social, economic, and administrative activities. However, in years of greatly expanding actual expenditure per capita, López Mateos emphasized the percentage share of administrative functions, especially at the expense of social development.

In sum, ideological periods of political revolution (emphasizing administrative forms of change), social revolution, economic revolution, and balanced revolution may be quantitatively seen to encompass four respective time spans: 1910–1930, 1930–1940, 1940–1959, and 1959–1963. Naturally there are many crosscurrents within these periods, for no analysis can be wholly consistent. At best the periods of ideological drive offer a way to look at the spirit of the times in Mexico. All interest groups do not necessarily approve of the trajectory of any given period, but they do operate within each period's context, and they may actively seek to change the direction of their times. Unless such dissident groups offer a plausible program which can be carried out through a consensus of society, however, they will have to resort to rebellion and rule by sheer force.

Since President Venustiano Carranza's attempt to rule by military control of Mexico from 1915 to 1920, Mexico's Revolutionary Family has based its appeal on social and economic gains in society. Ideology of Revolution has been the banner for continued power, though until the 1930's the official party did not undertake a really active role of national integration. Thus, for example, dissident Catholic and Communist groups have not appealed to enough persons to shift directly the historical path of Mexico in any given period. Certainly they have never been able to build upon any general dissatisfactions or tensions in society to overthrow the Revolutionary Family. But let us turn to the political context of budgetary policy.

3

*The Political Context
of Budgetary Policy*

Since budgetary policy is part of political policy, this chapter traces the political problems and social and economic considerations which impinged on governmental action of the early revolutionary regimes.

The idea that "ideology" is important in Mexico may bother some who see Mexico as a prime example of a country where the person is the determinant factor in politics, not the idea. However, ideology and personalistic government are interacting forces. As a noted work on the authoritarian personality has stated, ideology is "an organization of opinions, attitudes, and values—a way of thinking about man and society. . . . Ideologies have an existence independent of any single individual; and those which exist at a particular time are results of both historical process and of contemporary social events." [1] Another authority adds that "a political philosophy is in itself a social reality; it is an ideology in terms of which certain institutions and practices are justified and others attacked; it provides the phrases in which demands are raised, criticisms made, exhortations delivered, proclamations formulated, and at times policies are determined." [2] In regard to ideology in the developing nations one investigator has noted, "The dictionary defines 'ideology' as a 'systematic scheme or coordinated body of ideas about human life or culture'—a definition that seems to equate ideology with philosophy or social theory.

[1] T. W. Adorno *et al. The Authoritarian Personality* (New York: Harper, 1950), 2.
[2] C. Wright Mills, *The Marxists* (New York: Dell, 1962), 12.

In common usage, however, the word has additional connotations —of commitment (both emotional and intellectual), of action-orientation (the maintenance of the *status quo,* which may be the goal of conservative ideologies, is itself an action), and even of conscious or unconscious distortion of the facts to fit a pre-established doctrine." The investigator adds that "the doctrines of modernizing nationalism do not have the all-encompassing quality of the great ideological world-systems of Marxism, Christianity, or utilitarian liberalism, although they may coincide in some respects with one or another element in these ideologies. They are held by leaders with a wide variety of religious and philosophical outlooks, or with no particular metaphysical presuppositions." [3]

Mexican history shows that the Mexican leaders have acted with certain conceptions of society and the role of the state even if they could not or have not expressed their beliefs.

It is important to note, however, that ideas have never come to dominate Mexico entirely, and even today the president of Mexico is the all-powerful master of political life.[4] Yet, if he wishes to maintain the party's position, he and his advisers must remain receptive to change. Cárdenas, who insisted that the weakness of Mexican politics has been in its base of strong personalistic leaders, was and remains a powerful influence in national affairs. He is still the regional strongman from the state of Michoacán, yet he has always remained faithful to his ideology, or way of looking at society. Though he has headed economic development of the Río Balsas and its headwaters in eight states, social development has been a primary concern, and in his international politics he has continued to be Marxist. Let us go back to the beginnings of ideology in Mexican Revolutionary leadership.

THE IDEOLOGY OF POLITICAL REVOLUTION

Francisco I. Madero was a reluctant revolutionary. All he wanted was a free election in 1910 as Porfirio Díaz had promised in his

[3] Paul E. Sigmund, Jr., *The Ideologies of the Developing Nations* (New York: Praeger, 1963), 3-4. Víctor Alba attempts a first examination of *Las Ideas Sociales Contemporáneas en México* (México, D. F.: Fondo de Cultura Económica, 1960).

[4] See Frank Tannenbaum, "Personal Government in Mexico," *Foreign Affairs* 27 (1948) 44–57, and his "The Political Dilemma in Latin America," *Foreign Affairs* 38 (1960) 497–515.

interview in 1908 with an American newsman, James Creelman of *Pearson's Magazine*.[5] However, in the Mexico of 1910, a free election was too much to ask for, and Madero was forced into revolution to bring Díaz's long reign of power to end. Díaz resigned May 25, 1911, and immediately left for Europe. But his resignation contained a trap, for it was contingent upon transactions made at Ciudad Juárez, on the Texas border, which from the very first compromised Madero's revolution; the Díaz group had won several concessions that would contribute to Madero's fall. Madero agreed to disband his army and leave the governmental bureaucracy intact. The Revolution which came to power, then, did not propose to shake up the old system, and in fact, political change on a grand scale was not contemplated.

From the very first of the Revolution, however, Emiliano Zapata led the attack against Díaz in the South on the assumption that the great haciendas, which had existed since colonial times, would be broken up. Díaz had encouraged the concentration of the Mexican land ownership into the hands of an elite which ruled society. By the time of political revolution, one investigator has estimated that between 82.4 and 96.9 per cent of the heads of rural families were without agricultural property.[6] Agricultural wages had collapsed during the period from 1792 to 1908, especially after 1891 when the rural laborer was exploited to make land monopolization yield even bigger profits. While the wage level remained fixed, the price of corn rose 197 per cent, beans 565 per cent, chili 123 per cent, rice 75 per cent, wheat 465 per cent, and flour 711 per cent. All this spelled trouble in a country where 71.2 per cent of the labor force was occupied in agriculture in 1910.[7] Once authoritarian government which had kept the masses in subjugation was overthrown, participants in battle, as well as non-participants, wanted more change in society, and in-

[5] Stanley R. Ross, *Francisco I. Madero, Apostle of Mexican Democracy* (New York: Columbia University Press, 1955), 57–64.

[6] [Moisés González Navarro], *Estadísticas Sociales del Porfiriato, 1887–1910* (México, D. F.: Dirección General de Estadística, 1956), 40–41 and 217–219; changes in census classifications make the estimate subject to an undetermined amount of error.

[7] Eyler N. Simpson, *The Ejido, Mexico's Way Out* (Chapel Hill: University of North Carolina Press, 1937), 37–38; Jesús Silva Herzog, *El Agrarismo Mexicano y la Reforma Agraria; Exposición y Crítica* (Mexico, D. F.: Fondo de Cultura Económica, 1959), 127. The figure on the population occupied agriculturally is from *50 Años en Cifras*, 29.

deed they were becoming insistent upon it. Zapata refused to lay down his arms until his people received land. But Madero insisted upon an orderly consideration of the land problem after the upheaval had quieted down, and thus he tried to ignore a problem which would not go away.

Since Madero allowed a very conservative, inflexible government to rule Mexico from May 25 to November 6, 1911, when he took the presidency, and since Madero's conservative uncle, Ernesto Madero, and his reactionary cousin, Rafael Hernández, took over the important posts of Treasury and Justice in the interim government, we must judge Madero as responsible for the character of government during the entire first fiscal year of revolutionary rule, 1911–1912.[8] In February of 1912 Madero announced, "I have always advocated the creation of the small property, but that does not mean that any landowner should be despoiled of his properties."[9] Madero was deceiving the public, however, for he was a late nineteenth-century Liberal and he acted with a Díaz-like flair when he appointed Rafael Hernández to be his Minister of Development and thus to handle agrarian policy. Hernández was not only reputed to be a reactionary, he had been Díaz's emissary in the transactions at Ciudad Juárez. Now Hernández published a circular which calmed the nerves of hacendados who feared the loss of their lands, and he checked the arbitrary seizing of haciendas by revolutionists.[10]

With such policies permitted and sanctioned by Madero during the first year of revolutionary government, it is understandable, then, that the Díaz program of legal alienation of public lands into latifundia was continued at a rapid rate. During 1911–1912 some 434,532 hectares passed into private hands, an average of 36,211 hectares a month. These grants included some large amounts, all given in the last two months of 1911 and the first

---

[8] Charles C. Cumberland, *Mexican Revolution: Genesis Under Madero* (Austin: University of Texas Press, 1952), 152–153, and Ross, *Francisco I. Madero*, 177–178, take up the conservative nature of the interim government.

[9] *El Imparcial*, June 27, 1912, quoted by Ross, *Francisco I. Madero*, 241. Madero had previously emphasized: "It has been claimed that the Revolution . . . was to resolve the agrarian problem; that is inexact; the Revolution was to conquer our liberty, because liberty alone will resolve the rest of the problems by itself." *El Imparcial*, June 26, 1912, cited by Alba, *Las Ideas Sociales Contemporáneas*, 299.

[10] Helen Phipps, *Some Aspects of the Agrarian Question in Mexico—A Historical Study* (Austin: University of Texas Press, 1925), 134.

six months of 1912 when Madero was directly accountable for the administration of federal government. The United States and Mexico Realty Company claimed 14,389 hectares of land in the municipality of Durango, capital of the state of Durango, and three persons in Durango received 48,900 hectares; Rafael Dorantes was sold 122,932 hectares in several parts of Tabasco, but 103,760 was in one lump; José Irigoyen and successors were allowed 33,347 hectares in Tacámbaro, Michoacán, under the laws of composition; Tirso Sáenz received 16,346 hectares of lands declared not to be public in Uruapan, Michoacán; and the Mexican Land, Lumber and Fuel Company was granted 26,881 hectares in Oaxaca under the same provision of the law.[11] In sum, the manner in which Madero alienated public lands was not calculated to change the traditional pattern of great land holdings, and indeed it may be compared to Díaz's policies. The average extent of land which each president gave away during the first years of this century in the majority of cases created new latifundia, as Table 3-1 shows. The "average" here is meaningless, of course, and it is only presented to show the relative policy of the two presidents.

These figures hardly show any intent by Madero to create a nation of small landholders. Also, Madero continued to grant communal lands (*ejidos*) in severalty to the members of the commune—an old Liberal policy to create a nation of small landholders—in spite of the discrediting of such a policy under Díaz. Díaz used the policy to throw choice communal (*ejidal*) land open to the market, for once lands owned in common lost the protection of the village, individuals who received the grants were vulnerable to pressure to sell to speculators or monopolists.[12]

[11] Mexico, Secretaría de Fomento, *Memoria 1911–1912*, LXXXII, and 379–389.

[12] Madero was aware of the problem of crooked dealings in Grants in Severalty, and he sent out a circular to all state governors dated Feb. 17, 1912, asking them to survey communal lands and examine titles so that continual problems of ownership could be solved and communal holdings definitively divided (*ibid.*, 394). During the period July 1, 1911–January 31, 1913, Madero alienated 510,810 hectares into private holdings, an average of 26,885 hectares per month (*ibid.*, 1912–1913, 452–470). It is interesting to contrast Madero's grant of 2 hectares of land to 23 poor laborers in Quintana Roo with his allowance of 10,142 hectares to Domingo Diego Sucessores in Campeche and 15,793 hectares of land to A. F. Krohn in Sinaloa. Sale of public lands, however, came to an effective end after July 1, 1912 (*ibid.*, 1912–1913, 452–470). Cf. Manuel González Ramírez, *Las Ideas—La Violencia*, Vol. I of *La Revolución Social de México* (México, D. F.: Fondo de Cultura Económica, 1960), Chapter 16, for a defense of Madero based upon Madero's land program in the state of Chihuahua which led to the Orozco Rebellion.

TABLE 3-I

*Average Legal Alienation of Public Lands into Private Holdings,
by Method, 1901–1911 and 1911–1913*

	Díaz[a]			Madero[b]		
Method[c]	Titles	Hectares[d]	Avg. Per Title	Titles	Hectares[d]	Avg. Per Title
Compensation	172	1,003,418	5,834	– – –	– – –	– – –
Sale	1,285	4,360,075	3,393	34	167,516	4,927
Claimed	880	889,431	1,101	44	113,417	2,578
Declared Not Public	58	612,749	10,565	23	127,627	5,549
Composition	155	711,025	4,587	13	82,192	6,322
Grants in Severalty	14,415	202,045	14	1,003	15,577	16
Colonization	633	6,373	10	25	156	6
Poor Laborers	520	38,660	74	45	814	18
Railroads	. . .	117,870	. . .	– – –	– – –	– – –
Other	9	15,841	1,760	1	3,511	3,511

[a] Through June 30, 1911.

[b] From July 1, 1911 to January 31, 1913.

[c] Compensation—lands awarded to survey companies locating unclaimed public lands;

Sale—sale of public lands;

Claimed—grants of untitled public land (*baldíos*) to claimants;

Declared Not Public—lands determined to be private in the first instance;

Composition—grants of land held without legal title;

Grants in Severalty—grants of communal land holdings to individual members of the commune (*ejido*);

Colonization—lands granted to individual colonists;

Poor Laborer Grants—grants of land held without title and worth less than 200 pesos;

Railroads—right of way grants.

[d] One hectare equals 2.471 acres.

SOURCE: México, Secretaría de Fomento, *Memoria, 1901–1904*, vii; *1905–1907*, 7; *1907–1908*, xi; *1908–1909*, 10–20; *1909–1910*, 3; *1910–1911*, 201; *1911–1912*, lxxxii and 379–389; *1912–1913*, 452–470.

Francisco I. Madero was a mystic who did not understand that Mexico had entered the twentieth century as a backward nation. In 1910 more than 70 per cent of the population lived in scattered rural communities with fewer than 2500 inhabitants. At

TABLE 3-2

Per Cent of Federal Budgetary Expenditure by Type of Emphasis, 1910–1911 to 1912–1913

President	Fiscal Year	Economic		Social		Administrative	
		Projected	Actual	Projected	Actual	Projected	Actual
Díaz	1910–1911	19.1	16.7	9.0	9.2	71.9	74.1
Madero	1911–1912	19.1	17.6	9.4	9.9	71.5	72.5
Madero[a]	1912–1913	15.8	– –	9.2	– –	75.0	– –

[a] Madero was overthrown in February, 1913. See also Appendix C.
SOURCE: Presupuesto and Cuenta Pública, see Appendix B.

least 87 per cent of the populace could neither read nor write. The Indian, defined in terms of language, could not participate in the national way of life; some 1,617,994 persons, or about 13 per cent of the population, spoke only an Indian tongue and were thus excluded from modern markets, jobs, and civil rights.[13] Laborers who had worked for long hours under dangerous conditions at very low pay had begun to protest, but their inchoate uprisings against Díaz at Córdoba, in Veracruz, and Cananea, in Sonora, during the first decade of the new century, did not improve their lot. Madero set up several commissions to study such problems, but no changes were implemented as he felt that the problems of Mexico could only be solved over a long period of time.[14] This was neither a realistic nor a revolutionary approach; Mexico's problems would indeed require years of action, but Madero did not see that the successful revolutionist must undertake some immediate and decisive action before the initiative passes and the counterrevolution of tradition regains prestige.

Madero's use of federal funds during his first year in office and his projections for the second year, which were eclipsed with his fall from power, reveal that he was as conservative in this regard as he was in land reform. In 1911–1912 he and his uncle Ernesto, Minister of the Treasury during the whole fiscal year, planned to emulate Díaz's expenditures in economic, social, and administrative investment. It is clear that in his first year Madero actually emphasized economic and social spheres of national life in his expenditure little more than Díaz had in his last year of office; and Madero planned to decrease the percentage of the budget devoted to economic and social costs during the year 1912–1913. He was in fact no more radical than Porfirio Díaz, and he did not change the structure of government. In all due fairness, administrative expenses, including military costs, might have demanded more funds for Madero's second year in office. However, since military expenses did not go up during Madero's first year in office, a period in which three serious rebellions had been suppressed, it is hard to justify the planning for 1912–1913, especially

---

[13] See Chapter 9 below.
[14] Cf. Ross, *Francisco I. Madero*, Chapter 15, for a view which places Madero in a more favorable light. Cumberland, *Mexican Revolution*, Chapter 12, also takes a milder view of Madero's action than is presented here.

since federal expenditure per capita had increased since 1910. Perhaps Madero felt that by increasing the military's share from 18.6 to 26.7 per cent of the federal budget he could pacify Mexico and open the way for a true political democracy. While he did not demobilize Díaz's army, he added his own soldiers to the payroll. Madero was not actually backing away from a revolution of society which was so desperately needed, because such a program had never been promised. He emphasized only what he had always preached when calling for the "reestablishment" of democratic political practices.[15] However, the public could not help feeling the effects of Madero's expenditure and plans which did not even project, for example, reconstruction of national communications.

It was urgent that Madero reconstruct war-damaged national communications and forge new systems in order to unite the country. With his uncle Ernesto at the helm of the Finance Ministry during the interim government as well as after he came to the presidency, Madero had an early opportunity to act. His expenditures in communications (Table 3-3) show without doubt that he never did conceive of his role as an active one.

TABLE 3-3

Per Cent of Federal Budgetary Expenditure in Communications and Public Works, 1910–1911 to 1912–1913

President	Year	Projected	Actual
Díaz	1910–1911	15.3	13.4
Madero	1911–1912	15.2	14.1
Madero[a]	1912–1913	12.1	– –

[a] Madero was overthrown in February, 1913.
SOURCE: *Presupuesto* and *Cuenta Pública*, see Appendix B.

Madero's approach to the public debt also clearly shows that he did not want to change the basic nature of society; he was content with the nineteenth-century Liberal philosophy which limited the role of the state to administration of the nation, and he used the

[15] Quoted by Ross, *Francisco I. Madero*, 241.

budget to do so, spending one quarter of it to pay off the internal and external public debt in 1911–1912. He planned to spend almost the same percentage the following year in time of national crisis when funds were needed for national development! Some may argue that Madero had no choice except to service the debt or face foreign intervention, but a real revolutionist would not have been deterred by such logic.

Despite Madero's caution, and because of it, terrible problems arose for the new democratic regime. First, for example, Madero antagonized United States Ambassador Henry Lane Wilson. Though, like Díaz, Madero emphasized debt payments as a large share of his administrative expenditure and treated American land companies with friendliness, it was evident that the day of diplomatic interference in judicial cases was over.[16] Second, political unrest unnerved business interests. Third, cries for immediate distribution of land from Zapata in Morelos and the Yaqui Indians in Sonora frightened property owners. Fourth, the press took advantage of the new democracy to print inflammatory editorials which had been prohibited for years. Fifth, the clergy was worried that the Church-State truce of the Díaz period had come to an end and that the dreaded Constitution of 1857, which had occasioned war for ten years, might once again be enforced with its limitations on Church prerogatives. And, sixth, the generals stirred uneasily, for the nation was seething and the leader who had kept order among Mexicans so long, the Great God Porfirio, was gone. Madero did not have the personal strength or the program to keep from sinking in the Ten Tragic Days of February, 1913, which shook Mexico. General Victoriano Huerta abandoned Madero, his commander-in-chief, and assumed the presidency with the expressed approval of Henry Lane Wilson. Madero was shot to death while trying to "escape." [17]

In the ensuing years of civil war to avenge the murder of Madero, Mexico degenerated into internal chaos that often had no purpose but plunder and bloodshed. Madero's Revolution had

---

[16] Cumberland, *Mexican Revolution*, 250–251.

[17] Cumberland, *Mexican Revolution*, 250–253, and Ross, *Francisco I. Madero*, 322. Mrs. Madero's sworn statement of April 29, 1927, concerning her interview with Henry Lane Wilson in an attempt to save her husband's life is very damaging to Wilson; statement in full is in Ernest Gruening, *Mexico and Its Heritage* (New York: Century, 1928), 570–572.

started out with limited goals; his death stimulated the intellectuals to think about what the Revolution should become. Madero's martyrdom disrupted life patterns of all people as armies were mobilized to settle the matter of leadership. Once Huerta was beaten, the victorious avengers Venustiano Carranza, Alvaro Obregón, Francisco Villa, and Emiliano Zapata quarreled over the issue of presidential succession. This story is ably told and shown elsewhere in its diplomatic and ideological aspects, as well as in its political and military problems.[18] It is only necessary to note here that in the end President Woodrow Wilson's continued attempts to teach Mexico democratic methods alienated all factions of the Revolution. The seizure of Veracruz to prevent delivery of arms to Huerta, and the sending of American forces to Mexico in search of Pancho Villa, whose troops had raided a New Mexican town, contributed to an ever-growing list of Mexican complaints against American foreign policy. Wilson would not recognize Carranza, the new president, without guarantees of American rights in Mexico. Despite these problems, Carranza and Obregón were able to defeat Villa in 1915 and to attempt to restore order to Mexico.

Carranza called a Constitutional Convention in 1916–1917 in which delegates elected by the backers of the Revolution planned a new order. It is rare in Mexico's history that a convention writes its own plan, for the chieftain who calls the gathering generally submits his plan for ratification. Five major articles in Carranza's nineteenth-century Liberal plan, which only modified the Constitution of 1857, were rejected in 1917 by radical delegates. These delegates, fired by the spirit of the French Revolution, called themselves "Jacobins." They were led in their assault against the "classical Liberals" at the convention by Francisco J. Múgica.[19] Múgica, a thirty-two-year-old representative from Michoacán, felt that the conception of the state which Carranza offered to the convention was outmoded. The state must no longer stand aside

[18] Robert E. Quirk, *The Mexican Revolution 1914–1915; The Convention of Aguascalientes* (Bloomington: Indiana University Press, 1960).

[19] See the "Manifesto to the Nation" signed by the "Jacobins" against the "Classical Liberals." The manifesto charged the liberals with attempting to disrupt the work of the Convention, according to Juan de Dios Bojórquez (pseud. Djed Bórquez), *Crónica del Constituyente* (México, D. F.: Botas, 1938), 555–562; Múgica's role is summarized 699–704.

and let the economy run freely, nor must it watch idly while the underprivileged of the society are exploited. Múgica announced that Liberalism was dead and that the state must educate its citizens to be loyal to the nation instead of to the Church. He asked for a document which would chart the course of new nation-building, a positive course directed in all spheres by the government. By and large his fellow delegates agreed with him. After spirited debates with the conservative Carranza wing of the Revolutionary Family, leftists and rightists attempted to outdo each other in proposing radical departures for the state.[20] There was perhaps one delegate influenced by Marxism in the gathering, Professor Luis G. Monzón of San Luis Potosí, but at the time he was not an avowed Communist—the Russian Revolution had not yet taken place to provide the influence it later had in Mexico. Delegate Juan de Dios Bojórquez captured the spirit of the Constitutional Convention:

In the broadest sense of the word, revolutionary tendencies can not have limitations. For the revolutionist conscious of his mission, the world has no frontiers and therefore the glorious revolution of 1789 did not write in its annals the rights of Frenchmen, but it proclaimed the rights of man.

Therefore universal socialists are united across all beliefs and all nations. Suffering is one; the clamour that is raised in Mexico for improvement is the same that stirs all nations. . . . [Although] man never can arrive at the perfectability of social institutions. . . . [since] our ideals march at the same speed as our desires . . . , nevertheless it is necessary to fight. While we are revolutionists, we always have to be moved by universal misery.[21]

The resulting Constitution of 1917 is based upon many socialist precepts, but it was calculated to solve the problems of Mexico's colonial and Liberal tradition. A strong state would forge a new Mexican society based upon controlled private rights.

Radicalism was set down in Articles 3, 5, 27, 123 and 130, which will be taken up topically rather than in numerical order.

Article 5, patterned on the Constitution of 1857, dealt with prohibiting what the Constitutionalists felt were sophisticated

[20] Victor E. Niemeyer, Jr., "The Mexican Constitutional Convention of 1916–1917: The Constitutionalizing of a Revolutionary Ideology," unpublished M.A. thesis in history, Austin, University of Texas, 1951.

[21] Bojórquez, *Crónica*, 240.

forms of slavery. Accordingly, they decided that no one should be compelled to sign contracts, covenants, or agreements which involve the abridgment, loss, or irrevocable sacrifice of the liberty of man, whether by reason of labor, education, or religious vows. "The law, therefore, does not permit the establishment of monastic orders. . . ." Furthermore, no one shall be compelled to render personal service without his consent and without receiving due compensation, except as specified in the Constitution.[22]

Article 123 was specifically related to the above precepts, for a maximum eight-hour work day was fixed, seven if the work shift be at night, and nightwork and unhealthy or dangerous work was forbidden to women and to children under sixteen years of age. Other clauses required that employers grant one day's rest for every six days' work. Women shall not be required to exert themselves in any physical labor during the three months immediately preceding childbirth and shall enjoy special privileges of rest during and after parturition. Workers shall have the right to a decent minimum wage and a share in profits from their employer, the amounts to be determined by the several states of the union. Wages shall be paid in legal tender only, and shall not be paid in merchandise, and overtime shall be paid at double time rates. Employers are liable for occupational diseases and accidents and shall be bound to maintain hygenic and sanitary working conditions. In addition, workers have the right to organize and strike while employers can utilize lockouts only to maintain prices reasonably above the cost of production and when excess of production may cause prices to fall. Conciliation and arbitration are required, the government acting as final judge. Any employee who is discharged has the right to three months' indemnity, but if he be fired for participation in a strike, he may require his employer to fulfill the labor contract. To ensure the elimination of debt peonage, a workman may not contract debts with his employers which are collectable from his family or from the taking of more than his entire wages for any one month. This article of "labor and social welfare" also provided that the state shall determine what property constitutes the unalienable and unmortgagable

[22] H. N. Branch, comp., *The Mexican Constitution of 1917 Compared with the Constitution of 1857* (Philadelphia: American Academy of Political and Social Science, 1917), 3.

family patrimony. And it required that agricultural, industrial, and mining concerns furnish healthful dwelling places, schools, dispensaries, and land for the establishment of community centers where the population exceeds 2500 persons, no saloon or gambling houses being permitted in such labor centers.[23]

Article 27 asserted state ownership of all lands and waters and the rights to transmit titles to private persons. Particularly, the nation was vested with direct ownership of all minerals or subsoil wealth. Since "the ownership of the Nation is inalienable and may not be lost by prescription," concessions shall be granted by the federal government to private parties or civil and commercial corporations on condition that the resources be regularly developed and laws observed. Foreigners may own land if they agree to subject themselves to Mexican laws and not to invoke the protection of their government. They may not directly own lands or waters within 100 kilometers from the border or 50 kilometers from the coast.

Regarding Mexico's land and resources, the Constitution says:

The Nation shall have at all times the right to impose on private property such limitations as the public interest may demand as well as the right to regulate natural resources, which are susceptible of appropriation, in order to conserve them and equitably to distribute the public wealth. For this purpose necessary measures shall be taken to divide large landed estates; to develop small landed holdings; to establish new centers of rural population with such lands and waters as may be indispensable to them; to encourage agriculture and to prevent the destruction of natural resources, and to protect property from damage detrimental to society. Settlements, hamlets situated on private property and communes which lack lands or water or do not possess them in sufficient quantities for their needs shall have the right to be provided with them from the adjoining properties, always having due regard for small landed holdings. Wherefore, all grants of lands made up to the present time under the decree of January 6, 1915, are confirmed.[24]

Carranza had issued the decree of January 6, 1915, to win support of groups demanding land distribution. Though the decree allowed the restoration of land to villages, and the outright grant of land to villages without title, *acasillado* communities, settle-

[23] *Ibid.*, 94–103.
[24] *Ibid.*, 15–24; quote is on p. 16.

ments of resident hacienda laborers, were not included and these made up a very large percentage of the agricultural villages. Emphasis was placed on creation of individual rather than communal holdings. The burden of initiative and proof fell upon the villages, and judicial injunction could be obtained by the large landholder to stop restoration or bestowal of lands, including the definitive grant by the president of Mexico himself. Constitutionalists took a slightly broader view of the problem by providing that bestowal of lands would automatically be considered if restitution proceedings failed. The Federal Congress and the state legislatures were empowered to limit the size of land holdings which any one individual or legally organized corporation could own. The right of communal villages to own land, abolished in 1857, was expressly provided. Still, however, problems laid by the decree of January 6, 1915, persisted. Múgica later complained to Frank Tannenbaum that the soldiers of the Constitutional Convention wanted to socialize property, but they were frightened by their own courage and by their own ideas, for they found all of the learned men of the assembly opposed to them.[25] Thus private property constituted the basis of Article 27.[26]

Article 27 was related in part to Article 130, for both regulated the rights of the Church. The former article stipulated that religious institutions of any kind may in no case acquire, hold, or administer real property and that such property, even held indirectly, reverts to the nation, and can be denounced by and sold to private persons. Further, all places of public worship are the property of the nation which has the right to determine which of them may continue to be devoted to their present purposes. Episcopal residences, rectories, seminaries, orphanages, and collegiate establishments of religious institutions, convents, or other buildings used for religious instruction belong to the nation to be used for public services.[27]

Article 130 gave the federal government regulative control over all matters of religious worship, but did not allow the state the right to establish or forbid any religion. The Church is denied juridical personality and clergymen are considered under the law

[25] Frank Tannenbaum, *Peace by Revolution, an Interpretation of Mexico* (New York: Columbia University Press, 1933), 166–167.

[26] Simpson, *The Ejido*, Chapter 5.

[27] Branch, *The Mexican Constitution*, 19.

as persons exercising a profession. The legislatures of the states have the exclusive power of determining the maximum number of clergymen of each religious creed according to the needs of each locality, only Mexicans by birth being allowed to function as clergymen. Clergymen are excluded from any political action and may not vote, hold office, or criticize the government. The Constitution required that clergymen register with the government. Finally, clergymen are not permitted to inherit any real property unless related to the testator by blood within the fourth degree.[28] General Múgica's radicalism helped to sway passage of this anti-clerical article. Múgica noted that he did not feel that Article 130 would offend the Mexican people, for, he said,

I have seen them with delirious enjoyment in Michoacán, in Tamaulipas, and on the northern frontier attend the burning of the images which in days before they had worshipped on the altars. This is consoling; it shows you that effectively the religious problem does not exist in Mexico. . . .[29]

Article 3 provided for governmental supervision of education as follows:

Instruction is free; that given in public institutions of learning shall be secular. Primary instruction, whether higher or lower, given in private institutions shall likewise be secular.
No religious corporation nor minister of any religious creed shall establish or direct schools of primary instruction.
Private primary schools may be established only subject to official supervision.
Primary instruction in public institutions shall be gratuitous.[30]

Much debate had surrounded this article, for Francisco J. Múgica led the radical spearhead to establish "scientific education." Many have since claimed that the redrafting of Article 3 in 1934 to provide for Socialistic Education was out of line with the original constitutional precept of 1917, but this was not wholly the case. The First Commission of Reforms, which was chaired by Múgica and was charged by the convention with reporting on the projected Constitution, rejected Carranza's proposed Article 3 and suggested one of its own. In doing so Múgica's group also decided

[28] *Ibid.*, 103–107.
[29] *Diario de los Debates del Congreso Constituyente, 1916–1917* (México, D. F.: Talleres Gráficos de la Nación, 1960, 2 vols.), II, 1058.
[30] Branch, *The Mexican Constitution*, 2.

against Luis G. Monzón's motion specifically to require "rational" education, for it noted:

The Commission understands secular education to mean education outside of all religious belief, education inspired in a rigourously scientific criteria which transmits truth and combats error; the Commission does not find another word which expresses this idea, except that of secular, and thus it is used, with the reservation that it carries no neutral meaning. . . .[31]

With mounting confusion over the meaning of "secular education" during the 1920's, however, Luis G. Monzón would find his dissent vindicated when Article 3 was reformed.

Carranza accepted the Constitution that was written against his wishes, but he did not like it and he did not implement it. Without regulatory laws the Constitution had only the moral force of a guide to action, for there was no means to enforce it or to penalize those who disobeyed it. Certainly there were many groups who refused to recognize the Constitution of 1917, for they had not been allowed to vote for the convention delegates, nor had the citizenry in general ever approved of the document. Catholic leaders and other enemies of the Revolution were thus not consulted about the law under which they had to live. At the time this made little difference, for Carranza was not disposed to challenge their defiance of the new government.

Don Venustiano had been a perennial Porfirian senator, and when he took up the leadership to restore Constitutional government to Mexico and to punish Huerta for his coup d'état, he put off the entreaties of his assistant, Francisco J. Múgica, that the Revolution act in a revolutionary manner. Carranza insisted that the Revolution must triumph before it could afford to risk antagonizing large sectors of public opinion.[32] Once victory was his, however, he made Madero's mistake all over again, for he failed to assume a revolutionary posture after years, not months, of violence, and he decided that the only way to peace was to create a military force which could impose it forcibly. Thus he ignored the Constitution, did not distribute the land, and emphasized expenditure of the federal budget in such a way virtually as to ignore

[31] *Diario de los Debates del Congreso Constituyente, 1916–1917,* I. 639.
[32] Armando de María y Campos, *Múgica, Crónica Biográfica* (México, D. F.: Compañía de Ediciones Populares, 1939), 29–30.

the social and economic reconstruction of the nation. Table 3-4 shows why Carranza could not long command the respect of a republic which had been shaken by years of war and which had a radical constitution which articulated the desires of the masses.

TABLE 3-4

Average Federal Expenditure by Type of Emphasis, 1917–1919

Analysis	Economic		Social		Administrative	
	Projected	Actual	Projected	Actual	Projected	Actual
Per Cent	15.0	16.3	2.3	2.0	82.7	81.7
Pesos[a]	5.7	2.5	.9	.3	31.4	12.3

[a] In pesos of 1950 per capita.
SOURCE: Tables 2-1 and 2-2.

Though a collapse in average actual expenditure per capita in 1950 pesos necessitated that Carranza devote 81.7 per cent of his budget for administration, projected figures had not collapsed, and they also emphasized an administrative approach to national affairs. Indeed, Table 2-2 shows that projected budgets had risen from 31.8 to 38.0 pesos per capita since the Díaz period. Given an administrative attitude, Carranza probably failed to pacify Mexico because he offered the whip without a meaningful social program behind which dissident elements could rally. When Carranza tried to impose his own candidate on Mexico in the 1920 presidential election, the army forced him out of Mexico City and he was murdered on his way to Veracruz where he had planned to defend his government.

THE IDEOLOGY OF PEACEFUL POLITICAL REVOLUTION

General Obregón inherited the mantle of president after an interim government under Adolfo de la Huerta had presided over the elections of 1920. Obregón realized that military force alone could not pacify Mexico, and he set out to unify the Revolution-

ary Family. Carranza had imperiously refused to listen to the
wishes of the Revolutionary Family, and indeed had practically
branded as a traitor anyone such as his old aide, Múgica, who
asked him to reconsider his dictatorial policies.[33] Obregón sent
his representatives to dissident leaders such as General Juan Andreu Almazán, and asked for their co-operation in governing
Mexico. General Almazán, who served as a major leader under
Madero, Zapata, and Huerta, had fought as a guerrilla against Carranza, whom he considered to be an intransigent senator of the
old regime. As Almazán has explained, he was willing to join
Obregón in 1920, for Obregón offered unification of the military
to bring peace to Mexico.[34]

Obregón enjoyed a certain amount of prestige for having backed
the Jacobins at the Constitutional Convention in 1916–1917, and
he had expedited one of the first minimum wage laws in 1915.[35]
Now, as president, with peace established and actual expenditure
per capita (in pesos of 1950) at its highest point in Mexican history, he promised to revitalize the revolution by beginning land
distribution in earnest and emphasizing state direction of the society. Obregón's projected budget for 1922, his first opportunity
to plan, postulated an increase in agricultural development funds
from 2.9 per cent of the budget during Carranza's last year in
office to 10.1 per cent. He desired to restore the importance of
educational expenditures, and he indeed increased them to a new
high of 13 per cent of the budget, but the realities of office limited his average for four years. Though he had higher hopes than
Madero, his actual percentage emphasis of expenditure approxi-
mated Madero's benchmark with close similarity (Table 3-5).
Obregón had to worry a great deal about United States recognition, for President Coolidge took the opportunity of Carranza's
death to withhold diplomatic ties until Mexico promised not to
enforce troublesome provisions of the new Mexican Constitution
which threatened foreign subsoil rights in minerals and oil. Obregón also faced a major military rebellion in 1923 over his choice

[33] *Ibid.*, 68–69.
[34] Juan Andreu Almazán, Oral History Interviews with James and Edna Wilkie,
July 4, 1964, Acapulco.
[35] Bojórquez, *Crónica*, 88–91.

TABLE 3-5

*Per Cent of Federal Budgetary Expenditure by
Type of Emphasis, 1921–1924*

	Economic		Social		Administrative	
Year	Projected	Actual	Projected	Actual	Projected	Actual
1921	14.5	16.9	6.1	5.9	79.4	77.2
1922	25.9	18.0	14.9	10.9	59.2	71.2
1923	20.1	18.3	16.8	11.1	63.1	70.6
1924	14.3	18.4	10.2	11.0	75.5	70.6

SOURCE: *Presupuesto* and *Cuenta Pública*, see Appendix B.

of fellow Sonoran General Plutarco Elías Calles to succeed him, 1924–1928.[36]

Calles was in a strange position, for he was seen as something of a two-headed monster when he came into office. On the one hand he was combated by José Vasconcelos, who had organized a first national attempt at federal public education under Obregón. Vasconcelos, who had grown up on the northern frontier facing the United States, feared that Calles was a representative of *pochismo*, a blend of United States and Mexican border culture in which confusion of language and custom predominates. According to Vasconcelos, *pochismo* culture would corrupt Mexico's tradition, language, and religion.[37] On the other hand, domestic and foreign capitalists, and the United States Department of State did not look upon Calles as the harbinger of Yankee culture insidiously working its way into Mexican tradition, for they saw him as the next thing to a Bolshevik. Calles sought support from organized labor as the standard-bearer of the proletariat, and he talked in highly nationalistic tones about the solution to Mexico's problems.[38] In effect, Calles was nationalistic and hostile to the United States during the first half of his presidency, but after

[36] John W. F. Dulles, *Yesterday in Mexico, A Chronicle of the Revolution, 1919–1936* (Austin: University of Texas Press, 1961), 88–264.

[37] José Vasconcelos, *El Desastre; Tercera Parte de Ulises Criollo* (México, D. F.: Botas, 1938).

[38] Plutarco Elías Calles, *Mexico Before the World; Public Documents and Addresses of . . .* , tr. by R. H. Murray (New York: Academy Press, 1927), 14–16, for example.

several sobering years, and especially after having experienced a major military revolt in 1927, his attitude appeared to change.

Actually, Calles had never been so radical as the United States Department of State thought. Upon entering office, for example, he sponsored a law in 1925 which changed the form of land distribution from a collectivistic orientation to an individualistic one in which the recipient of land was guaranteed his plot. Previously the land had been granted to villages for complete control of assignments of plots.[39] Of course, if the recipient of land did not live up to the requirements of the law, the land could be taken from the peasant and redistributed to another villager, but provisions were now in force to protect the patrimony of those who received land under the Revolution.

Calles had become enmeshed in the tangle of diplomatic relations inherited from Obregón. Obregón had agreed to pay off the pre- and post-1910 debt in a series of complicated meetings and agreements after 1922 with the International Committee of Bankers on Mexico. Calles accepted these agreements but was in constant difficulty trying to determine how they could be honored at a time when Mexico's own development and promises of the Revolution demanded fulfillment. The thicket of high, international finance of the late 1920's in which he found himself threatened to obscure the goals of the Revolution. Caught in this predicament, Calles was forced into a position of having to defend Mexico's national honor which was impugned by the arrogant actions of United States Ambassador James R. Sheffield. This diplomat insisted that the Mexican government was attempting to confiscate the oil holdings of United States citizens through legal subterfuges.[40]

Calles was rescued by the arrival of a new ambassador from the United States in 1927. President Calvin Coolidge, realizing that a hard line with Mexico was leading nowhere, sent Dwight W. Morrow to "keep us out of war." Morrow immediately saw that Calles was not a Bolshevik, and he treated him with the respect due the president of a sovereign state.[41] Calles responded to Mor-

[39] Simpson, *The Ejido*, 88–90.

[40] L. Ethan Ellis, *Frank B. Kellogg and American Foreign Relations, 1925–1929* (New Brunswick: Rutgers University Press, 1961), 24–40.

[41] For a discussion of Morrow's technique in winning Calles to his viewpoint see Stanley R. Ross, "Dwight Morrow, Ambassador to Mexico," *Americas* 14 (1958)

row's friendship by describing his troubles with the oil companies. Morrow wrote Secretary of State Frank B. Kellogg his account of the interview on November 8, 1927:

[Calles] said that the Government of Mexico had never wanted to confiscate any property. Least of all did they want to confiscate the oil properties; that they needed the revenues, and obviously "they did not want to commit suicide;" that the act of 1925 was a most necessary piece of legislation at the time because the country was in considerable disorder and there was an extreme radical wing whose wishes had to be met in that legislation; that he had thought the grant of the 50-year right as good as a perpetual right to take out the oil, and that such a grant would satisfy every practical purpose, but that the oil companies had not co-operated with him at all, but in fact their representatives had boasted all over Mexico that they did not need to obey the laws of Mexico.[42]

At a time when Morrow's old company, J. P. Morgan, was doing very well on Wall Street, and Wall Street appeared to have the solution to prosperous economic development, Calles was anxious to listen to Morrow for some tips on how to solve Mexico's problems. This is not surprising, for Calles had never attacked capital very strongly when appealing to the proletariat, and even the archcritics of capitalism were quieted throughout the world as the stock market in the United States spiraled higher and higher —Thorstein Veblen, for example, yielded to the lure of Wall Street by investing in oil stock in the late 1920's.[43]

Calles had been an exponent of economic normalcy during his first year in office, and having promoted a sound peso and monetary control under the centralized Bank of Mexico, it was easy for him to call for the development of national infrastructure. Thus he began the building of roads that Mexico so lacked, and he pumped the first money into irrigation works.

Though Calles instituted the first permanent, effective income tax in Mexico and firmly established taxes on industry as an important share of revenue (as Appendix F shows), analysis of his budgetary expenditure reveals that he did not conceive of a larger role for the state in economic affairs than had Obregón (Table

272–290, and his "Dwight Morrow and the Mexican Revolution," *Hispanic American Historical Review* 38 (1958) 506–528.

[42] United States, Department of State, *Foreign Relations, 1927*, III, 191.

[43] Robert L. Heilbroner, *The Worldly Philosophers; The Lives, Times, and Ideas of the Great Economic Thinkers* (New York: Simon and Schuster, 1961), 214.

3-6). True, when Calles founded the Bank of Mexico in 1925 he gave great emphasis to economic expenditure, but actual figures never again approached his first year's action. Calles's attitude toward the role of the government is best summarized by the fact that he tried to make government pay its own way through public service taxes; these taxes contributed 19 per cent of federal income by the time he left office.

TABLE 3-6

Per Cent of Federal Budgetary Expenditure by
Type of Emphasis, 1925–1928

	Economic		Social		Administrative	
Year	Projected	Actual	Projected	Actual	Projected	Actual
1925	14.4	32.5	8.5	8.7	77.1	58.8
1926	20.0	21.5	10.2	9.7	69.8	68.8
1927	25.1	22.2	10.9	10.3	64.0	67.5
1928	26.3	23.1	11.9	11.7	61.8	65.2

SOURCE: *Presupuesto* and *Cuenta Pública*, see Appendix B.

Calles based his presidency on organization of the Mexican government along efficient lines, and he insisted over and over again in his speeches that the role of individualism was primary in Mexico. His government was postulated on somewhat the same lines as Herbert Hoover's in the United States. Hoover was willing to use the state for limited intervention in national problems, but basically he believed that the state must remain passive. Calles announced in November, 1927:

There is in Mexico a pronounced trend in favor of individualism, and this can only be satisfied within the limits set up by the present so-called capitalist system. For this reason the Government will do everything in its power to safeguard the interests of foreign capitalists who invest in Mexico.[44]

When Obregón decided that he was the only one who could keep the peace in Mexico after Calles left office, he had to over-

[44] Calles, *Mexico Before the World*, 194. See also a work by his ideologist Luis L. León, *La Doctrina, la Táctica y la Política de la Revolución* (México, D. F.: El Nacional Revolucionario, 1930?).

come vocal opposition to his re-election, for the banner of Mexican politicians since the nineteenth century has been that re-election must be prohibited. He toured the country during his campaign even though he had no opposition, and by the sheer force of his personality convinced the Revolutionary Family that he should succeed Calles. Ironically, he phrased his campaign in Madero's terms of political revolution, except he did not use Madero's slogan of "effective suffrage and no re-election." His speeches were filled with fond memories of military battle and he played down the social struggle of classes which had provided the heat for controversy in the early 1920's. Speaking of the middle class, he said:

> It is necessary that everyone know that for us the middle class is but an integral part of the working classes, because it is to its personal effort that it owes the daily income with which it provides for the daily needs of its home. For us, a worker is he who realizes a constant effort to solve the financial problems of his home, to solve the educational problems of his children, and to cooperate in making his Fatherland great; and so when we have occupied ourselves in formulating a law which may resolve the problems of the working class in a particular manner, we have declared that for us there only exist two classes in society: those who work and those who pay; and workers are those who realize a muscular or mental effort to solve everyday domestic problems. It is for this reason that we . . . have always looked for the support of all the classes which belong to the working family. . . .[45]

This was a far cry from the Mexican political tone of the 1930's which was shortly to be ushered in by the world depression.

Economic disruption caused by the collapse of the world market system and the contraction of investment capital was preceded in Mexico by a political crisis of first magnitude. On July 17, 1928, President-elect Alvaro Obregón was assassinated by a Catholic zealot. Obregón's followers, however, were sure that the president-elect had been shot by Calles and his group in order not to lose control of their lucrative hold over government. Calles prevented general civil war by announcing that he was through with politics. Calling for the foundation of an official National Revolutionary Party (PNR), he finished his term and left the presidency to his Minister of the Interior.

[45] Alvaro Obregón, *Discursos* . . . (México, D. F.: Biblioteca de la Dirección General de Educación Militar, 1932, 2 vols.), II, 453–455, speech of July 15, 1928.

Emilio Portes Gil came into the interim presidency November 30, 1928, with a zeal to reintroduce class struggle and land reform into national politics, and his program yielded rich dividends, for, as he has explained, he was able to defeat a military revolt, with the aid of Calles, by calling upon the peasants to back the government.[46] Considering the multiple problems which Portes Gil faced in his fourteen months in office, he worked wonders without changing budgetary patterns. The religious strife which resulted in Obregón's death had complicated the Mexican scene since 1926 as lay Catholics rebelled against government regulations implementing constitutional limitations on clerical functions. A full-scale guerrilla war was in progress in western Mexico from 1926 to 1929, but in 1929 Portes Gil played an important role in bringing about a Church-State truce in which the Church gave up warfare as a means to achieve its goals.[47] This was no mean accomplishment, for Portes Gil was distributing land at a rate greater than that of any revolutionary president, and he attempted to reform the federal labor code in order to strengthen labor's position in regard to capital. At the same time he organized an election to fill out Obregón's term, 1928–1934.

Pascual Ortiz Rubio defeated José Vasconcelos in the presidential election of 1929, and took over the presidency at a difficult time, for whereas Portes Gil had only a political crisis to face, severe economic problems and deflation now set in to compound a very difficult situation.

The passive state enjoyed almost unchallenged authority from 1910 to 1930. True, the constitutionalists of 1917 had offered an alternative type of state, but their plan largely was ignored as Mexican presidents became involved with concern over recognition and financial backing from abroad. New agencies were created to stimulate national integration, but by and large this approach only obliquely attacked social problems. A decade of civil war demanded a decade of peace, it seems, and ideology of violent political revolution turned to ideology of peaceful political revolution. This latter program did not mean free elections; it meant a reorganization of political forms to permit the orderly develop-

[46] Emilio Portes Gil, Oral History Interviews with James and Edna Wilkie, May 7, 1964, Mexico City.

[47] James W. Wilkie, "The Meaning of the Cristero Religious War against the Mexican Revolution," *A Journal of Church and State* 8 (1966) 214–233.

ment of society. The ideology expressed in the Constitution of 1917 that the masses must directly benefit from the Mexican upheaval was gradually pushed aside during the 1920's. The old guard revolutionist generally came to enjoy thick carpets, fine food, easy women, and the lure of the gambling table. It was quite a change to deal with the world of legality and sophisticated business after years of battle, and perhaps in order to cast off the rough manners of the country, many of the politicians of the 1920's refused to recall the misery of their village background. They had earned the right to direct society, and they did so by phrasing their conception of the state and its role in political terms. The exhortation that the Revolution was doing something for the masses was still in evidence, but political power became the factor which extinguished governmental social conscience. Portes Gil made an effort to shake up the Revolutionary Family, but he was helpless, as Calles was the real boss of Mexico, and Portes fought a losing battle.[48]

[48] For a contemporary picture of corrupt politics from 1924 to 1928 see Gruening, *Mexico and Its Heritage,* 393–512, and 657–664.

4

The Rise of the Active State

The effects of the world depression of the 1930's discredited capitalism in the eyes of many Mexican leaders. Persons asked each other over and over again the same thing: Why should Mexico be dependent upon a capitalistic world market that is subject to cycles of prosperity and depression? Others wanted to know why the Russian experiment with an alternative to capitalism had not been more closely examined. As the Mexican economy contracted and the upper classes felt the pinch of an economy which suffered some three years of deflation, the poverty of the masses could no longer be ignored. Intellectuals pointed out that twenty years after the revolution of 1910, almost 67 per cent of the population was still illiterate. More than 8 per cent of the population could speak only an Indian language, and the 1,185,162 persons in this group did not include the large percentage of the population which spoke mainly Indian and some Spanish. Where was the national community of interest when 66.5 per cent of the population lived in scattered villages with less than 2500 persons who had no communications, educational opportunity, or health care? [1] The Mexican Revolution was essentially oriented toward the worker and the peasant, but the worker was bound into corrupt unions linked to the government by Luis Morones, and the peasant had received very little land by 1930.

TRANSITION: 1930–1933

President Portes Gil had entered office one year too soon for the type of program he tried to foster in Mexico, and Ortiz Rubio

[1] See Chapter 9, below.

became president one year too late. Whereas Portes Gil offered a land and labor program in harmony with the radical provisions of the Constitution of 1917, Ortiz Rubio represented Calles's conversion to the ideas of Dwight Morrow.

Calles had toured in Europe during the latter part of Portes Gil's term, and he became convinced that land distribution had to come to an end—reportedly he was worried that Mexico might develop *minifundios* such as those in France.[2] Calles's statement, published in Mexico on December 26, 1929, that land distribution should be terminated as soon as possible, and that remaining distribution should be included in the national debt, marked a full response to Dwight Morrow's earlier suggestions.[3] The uproar which followed gave Calles pause. One month later he claimed that his remarks had been made in a distracted moment and had been misinterpreted.[4] But misinterpretation seems highly unlikely, for the government propaganda newspaper, *El Nacional,* had printed the December 26 story in full, with a laudatory editorial following on December 27.

President-elect Ortiz Rubio took his cue in Washington, D. C., where he was wined and dined by President Hoover with elaborate honors heretofore reserved for presidents. He announced at the White House on December 27, 1929, that the land problem in Mexico was settled. In the future, he said, land expropriation would be paid in cash and earlier expropriations would be paid in bonds. He also agreed to refinance Mexico's debt with the foreign bankers.[5] Needless to say, during his one-month stay in the United States he was welcomed wherever he went. A reception for him at the New York Yacht Club was an especially successful occasion, for he was compared to Hoover by the president of the Union Pacific Railroad, Carl A. Bickel.[6]

Upon return to Mexico, Ortiz Rubio stopped issuing presidential resolutions to distribute further land, thereby creating a panic in agrarian circles. Though the actual rate of land distribution was halved, compared to Portes Gil's term, Ortiz Rubio pushed

[2] Simpson, *The Ejido,* 111–123.

[3] Antonio Galván Duque, "Declaraciones del General Calles Sobre Nuestro Problema Agrario," *El Universal,* Dec. 26, 1929.

[4] *El Universal,* Jan. 29, 1930.

[5] *Ibid.,* Dec. 27, 1929.

[6] *El Nacional,* Dec. 13, 1929.

agricultural credit and reformed the law to prevent juridical proceedings from interfering with land distribution. These latter two
positive acts, however, could not overcome the bad impression he
made in Mexico for failing to cope with the depression or to
worry about the misery of the masses. Like Herbert Hoover in
the United States, he soon became quite unpopular.

He was especially disliked by labor, which strenuously objected
to his new labor code. Earlier, Portes Gil's projected labor code,
which greatly favored unions, had not passed congress because of
strenuous objections from foreign and domestic manufacturing concerns. Now, however, many workers felt that the new law passed
in 1931 favored management by restricting labor's rights in order
to attract foreign capital to Mexico. Domestic manufacturers, however, also objected to the law, and Ortiz Rubio lost support on
all sides.[7]

Ortiz Rubio assumed office believing that Mexico could overcome the depression if the federal budget were balanced. He made
heroic cuts in administrative expenditure, as Table 4-1 shows,
thereby increasing social and economic outlay as a percentage
share of the national budget. In addition, his Minister of Communications and Public Works, General Juan Andreu Almazán,
pushed a program of road construction which was unhampered
by the depression until 1932 (see Appendix L).

Unrest in all sectors of Mexican life was stimulated by increasing propaganda from intellectuals, workers, peasants, and younger
members of the Revolutionary Family who favored a class struggle against what they called outdated capitalism. This criticism
required that Calles speak out. On October 30, 1931, he summed
up his philosophy of government to the state governors assembled
at the Chapultepec Restaurant in Mexico City:

We should not agitate, we should not augment disorder and anarchy.
The work of the revolutionaries should now tend towards a constructive era.

In the political order uncontainable ambitions are excited that
sometimes create situations of disorder and anarchy. That is what we
must correct. To discipline the forces of the revolution, to unify them

[7] *New York Times*, Aug. 18, 1931; *Excelsior*, July 29, 1931; Chicago *Daily Tribune*,
April 4, 1931. For background and analysis of labor in a limited political context
see the study by Marjorie Ruth Clark, *Organized Labor in Mexico* (Chapel Hill:
University of North Carolina Press, 1934).

TABLE 4-1

*Per Cent of Federal Budgetary Expenditure by
Type of Emphasis, 1929–1934*

	Economic		Social		Administrative	
Year	Projected	Actual	Projected	Actual	Projected	Actual
1929	24.8	23.2	12.1	12.9	63.1	63.9
1930	26.6	29.3	14.3	14.6	59.1	56.1
1931	27.1	26.7	14.7	17.0	58.2	56.3
1932	30.3	28.4	15.7	15.8	54.0	55.8
1933	21.1	20.3	17.7	15.7	61.2	64.0
1934	22.8	23.2	16.4	15.0	60.8	61.8

SOURCE: *Presupuesto* and *Cuenta Pública*, see Appendix B.

so that they support the Government is what we must do today more than ever in order that they serve to support the State.

We have not given opportunity to the youth, we have not prepared it to receive the legacy of the revolution and to carry it forward. Very few opportunities have we given to young men. . . .

In the States of the Republic we should sincerely undertake work to approach true democracy, in order that the vote be respected and true representatives of the majority of the people enter the house of deputies the same as in elections of governors. We must avoid the error of forming cliques which succeed each other in order to keep the same men in power.

We are passing through a difficult critical situation. It does not matter whether the measures taken by the Government are very wise to provide relief if we do not manage to establish a situation of confidence and tranquility. If we do not establish this situation, we shall not obtain private cooperation so necessary for the progress of all the economic activities of the country.

We need to establish political tranquility in order to achieve spiritual tranquility.[8]

Thus the ideology of Political Revolution could not cope with new forces of depression. Political Revolution begun by Madero reached bankruptcy along with the Mexican economy. Calles forced Ortiz Rubio to resign the presidency on September 1, 1932, scant months later, for he needed a new leader in the National

[8] *CROM; Organo de la Confederación Regional Obrera Mexicana*, Nov. 1, 1931, 41–42.

Palace to give Mexico confidence that economic problems would be resolved. General Abelardo Rodríguez took office to fill out Ortiz Rubio's term. Though he was one of Mexico's leading capitalists, and Baja California was considered to be his personal domain, he could not help sensing the need for a new type of action to cope with the apparent failure of capitalism.

The arrival of a new ambassador to Mexico, Josephus Daniels, marked a change in United States policy, which gave the new president freedom of action to attack the problems of depression.[9] Daniels did not come to talk of balanced budgets, payments on the debt, and economic development, as had previous representatives from Washington. He came to talk of social reform, education, and the welfare of the masses. He was a representative of Franklin Delano Roosevelt's New Deal, and he was sympathetic to social experiment.[10] The speech he gave at the presentation of his diplomatic credentials to the Mexican government in April, 1933, clearly set the tone for his stay in Mexico, and front-page coverage of his speech meant that Mexico recognized that a new element had been injected into Washington's relations with Mexico.[11] Mexico was free to develop an ideology of social revolution.

THE IDEOLOGY OF SOCIAL REVOLUTION

Abelardo Rodríguez presided over a period of ferment. Everyone had ideas about how Mexico could escape from the depression and build a national independence free from the cyclical fluctuations of the world market of capitalism. Calles offered a Six-Year Plan—it was the era of such plans and Calles was not to be caught short in his statesmanship—but it was rewritten by the radicals at the Convention of Querétaro in 1933.[12] This Convention chose General Lázaro Cárdenas to be the official party candidate on the basis of his social program in the state of Michoacán where he had been governor from 1928 to 1932. Cárdenas set about his campaign six months before the election of 1934, and he toured

---

[9] See E. David Cronon, *Josephus Daniels in Mexico* (Madison: University of Wisconsin Press, 1960) for discussion of Daniels's role in Mexico.

[10] *Ibid., passim.*

[11] *El Universal*, April 25, 1933.

[12] See Partido Nacional Revolucionario, *Memoria de la Segunda Convención Ordinaria* (México, D. F.: La Impresora, 1934).

the entire country carrying the message of land for the landless, the right to strike for the worker, and a rejuvenated Revolution.

The effects of the world depression in the early 1930's had a significant impact on Mexico, as Table 4-2 shows, but it is obvious that Mexico had emerged from the depression by the time Cárdenas took office in 1934. The depression was a blow to Mexican economic thought which believed that Mexico could remain an agricultural nation exchanging exports for imports. Exports and imports contracted by half between 1929 and 1932, the low point of the depression in Mexico, and a sharp change in Mexican intellectual views opened the way for Mexican industrialization. Exports hit a post-1913 low and imports fell to a post-1916 low. The Gross National Product, which had tended to go up after the violent phase of the Revolution, contracted to a post-1921 low in 1932. Thus the effects of the depression were no less economic than social. A public outcry to relieve the lot of the masses brought Cárdenas the nomination for the presidency in 1933. The Six-Year Plan which was projected for his term was a call for social revolution.

TABLE 4-2

Indices of Depression in Mexico, 1929–1935

| | (1932 = 100) | | |
| | Gross National Product | Value | |
Year		Exports	Imports
1929	124	194	211
1930	115	151	193
1931	119	131	120
1932	100	100	100
1933	110	120	135
1934	118	211	190
1935	126	246	224

SOURCE: *50 Años en Cifras*, 32, 139–140.

In response to the depression, President Rodríguez implemented much of the Six-Year Plan before Cárdenas took office. A minimum wage was fixed in the late summer of 1933—it was not the four pesos a day about which Rodríguez had talked, for the amount was developed on the theory that the government had to convince the entrepreneur that increased wages would yield increased output from the labor force.[13] Also in the summer of 1933 a Ministry of National Economy was projected to co-ordinate state planning in Mexico. A new agrarian code in 1934 revamped the method of land distribution and opened the way for resident hacienda peons to obtain land from the government.[14] Rodríguez endorsed other changes in the role of the state, but he refused to approve of Socialist Education on the grounds that it was too radical.

The transitional nature of Rodríguez's presidency is seen in Appendix F. Rodríguez chose tax reform as an indirect method of resolving Mexico's problems. He de-emphasized the regressive stamp tax which had provided about 12 to 13 per cent of federal revenue since Obregón's administration, and he also reflected the shift in the spirit of the Revolution by continuing Ortiz Rubio's policy of cutting taxes on public services. The state would henceforth provide most services rather than charge for them, as Calles had postulated.

Cárdenas assumed office November 30, 1934, and, in contrast to Rodríguez except in tax policies, he immediately postulated a direct social revolution. He believed that Mexico's traditional way of life had to be changed, otherwise the Mexican nation would never be integrated. His program called for immediate benefits for the masses. He adopted Socialist Education to teach the concept of class struggle and to limit the power of the Church. Setting out to make Mexico economically independent, he broke up the age-old latifundia which had dominated Mexican life. President Cárdenas took a Marxist tack and looked at class struggle as the primary fact of Mexico's history. Since Cárdenas had little formal education—six years of primary school—he never concretely defined his position while in office from 1934 to 1940, but has since expressed his way of looking at politics:

Capitalism represents an economic regime which is characterized by the growing concentration of wealth in the hands of a minority of so-

[13] *Excelsior,* Aug. 29, 1933.
[14] For a complete account of this period see Francisco Javier Gaxiola, Jr., *El Presidente Rodríguez* (México, D. F.: Editorial Cultura, 1938).

ciety, and this harms the integral improvement of popular sectors, thus causing capitalism to be a constant threat for peace in every country.

Socialism breaks with private property, which is transferred into the hands of society on the basis that the State plans and intervenes in a determinate form to direct the whole process of the country's economy in order to increase the welfare of the people.

Communism is a more advanced and mature stage than socialism. It facilitates the integral development of the individual, who enjoys the advancements of science and technology, whose needs are covered, as its motto says, "to each according to his capacities, to each according to his needs" [sic].[15]

It is clear from Cárdenas's own definitions that he thinks of social and economic organization in a Marxist pattern of stages, and that he favors the latter stage of development.

Cárdenas announced his presidential plan for labor May 1, 1934:

The Six-Year Plan of our Political Party—which establishes in several of its postulates the supremacy of the cooperative system, socially organizing the rural and urban laborers as producers and consumers —will eventually transform the economic system of production and distribute the wealth among those who directly produce it. But it is not a matter here of bourgeois pseudo-cooperation established among us since the dictatorship, but a genuine cooperativism constituted by laborers in which every working and consuming element, without any exceptions, . . . can collaborate to stamp out exploitation of man by man and the slavery of man to mechanization in order to substitute the idea of exploitation of the soil and factory for the benefit of the peasant and the laborer.[16]

As president, Cárdenas warned private industry on February 11, 1936, that:

The managing class should take great care that its agitations do not become a political cause, for that would lead us to an armed fight.

Entrepreneurs who feel fatigued by the social struggle can turn over their industries to the workers or the Government. That would be patriotic, the lockout would not.[17]

[15] Interview by author with Lázaro Cárdenas, Sept. 11, 1962, Pátzcuaro, Michoacán; Cárdenas provided this typed statement in response to a questionnaire given to him at an interview on Aug. 26, 1962.

[16] *Excelsior*, May 4, 1934.

[17] Speech of Feb. 11, 1936, in Lázaro Cárdenas, *Los Catorce Puntos de la Política Obrera Presidencial* (México, D. F.: P[artido] N[acional] R[evolucionario], 1936, 48; this speech was reiterated over national radio on March 11, 1936), and the text is found in Lázaro Cárdenas, *Cárdenas Habla* (México, D. F.: P[artido] R[evolucionaria] M[exicana] 1940), 59–65.

Cárdenas's idea of the role of the state clashed with Calles's view at a time when Calles felt his venerable concepts should be deeply respected. Cárdenas, of course, agreed to carry out Calles's suggestions about how to solve Mexico's problems, but he did not live up to his agreements. When the greatest number of strikes in Mexico's history was fostered by Cárdenas in 1935, Calles spoke out openly against his protégé. Between June 12, 1935, and April 10, 1936, the Cárdenas and Calles groups were locked in a struggle for the control of Mexican government. Cárdenas won and deported Calles from Mexico.[18] Cárdenas did not execute his opponents, he humiliated them with exile, and Calles's deportation marked a turning point in Mexican politics, for ex-presidents would never try overtly to control the political scene again.

Once Calles was out of the way, Cárdenas was free to develop social revolution. He was aided by his old friend Francisco J. Múgica, the radical constitutionalist, who became Minister of the National Economy and, later, Minister of Communications and Public Works. The social revolution that Cárdenas undertook was rooted in a Jacobin spirit. Parades took on a new flavor of excitement as workers marched for their rights and for fatherland. In a decade when marching demonstrations were frequent and athletes were exalted, it became the mode for the youth, athletically clad, to join in long parades past the presidential palace. Monuments went up and the *patria* got a new propaganda lift. Public welfare and the regulation of food prices became the concern of the government as the state attempted to organize the nation economically. The Indian was looked upon as a noble savage who had only to be integrated into national linguistic life and markets for redemption. As in Jacobin days of the French Revolution, churches were turned into schools at a fantastic rate.

Social revolution under Cárdenas also meant Socialist Education, for the masses were to be educated in a collectivist spirit calculated to overcome individual selfishness which the capitalistic ethic was seen to foster. In this view, if the masses were educated to have class solidarity, they could win rights from their

[18] James Wilkie, "Ideological Conflict in the Time of Lázaro Cárdenas," unpublished M.A. thesis in history, Berkeley University of California, 1959. The author treats the rise of Cárdenas to the presidency and the Calles-Cárdenas conflict in detail in a manuscript in preparation.

exploiters, whether in the private sector or the political sector of national life.[19]

Cárdenas insisted that the most effective way for the proletariat to defend itself was to join into unified, industry-wide groupings which would then unite in one vast labor organization under the wing of the government. Pragmatically, then, labor would be educated to win its rights and to act in concert to hold them.

And it was thus that Cárdenas came to institutionalize the Mexican Revolution. When the showdown came with Calles over who was to be the power in Mexico, Cárdenas mobilized labor, with the aid of Vicente Lombardo Toledano, into the Confederation of Mexican Workers (CTM) to gain a popular base from which he could combat the old interest groups. The state-based peasant leagues had already done their share in catapulting Cárdenas into the presidency in 1934, so that for the first time in Mexican history the masses were brought into national politics in an organized fashion. The army was no longer the sole arbiter of Mexico's destiny. The new balance of power in politics, of course, did not mean democracy, but it did mean that mass pressure groups had gained a position in politics and that if their support were to be counted on, concrete gains would have to be forthcoming.

Mexican governmental politics were becoming more sophisticated: leaders now acted less on individual whim than on limitations generated by public opinion. The position of the masses in national politics was formally recognized in 1938 when Cárdenas reorganized the National Revolutionary Party on sector lines as the Party of the Mexican Revolution (PRM) in order to give the workers, peasants, military, and popular (other) sectors equal voice in party councils. The new party has never generated policy from the bottom up, but the sectors have had a formal way of voicing their wishes or grievances. Since industrial, commercial banking, and transportation interests—in short, the capitalistic groups—were left out of the proletarian official party, they were required to join "corporations" of interest under government supervision, somewhat according to the Italian fascist style, which could act as pressure groups to articulate and defend their respective rights

[19] On Socialist Education and its context see Lyle C. Brown, "Mexican Church-State Relations, 1933–1940," *A Journal of Church and State* 6 (1964) 202–222, and Wilkie, "Idelogical Conflict in the Time of Lázaro Cárdenas," Chapter 3.

as well as to mobilize campaigns to gain new prerogatives. Virtually all groups in Mexico now had a mode of expression and influence, direct or indirect, on politics. Subsequently, in 1940 the military sector was abolished and military personnel were accorded representation as private persons in the popular sector; later (1946) the official party's name was changed from the Party of the Mexican Revolution (PRM) to the Party of Institutional Revolution (PRI).

Regarding the matter of land distribution, Cárdenas crushed the strength of *latifundia* by signing resolutions to break up 20,-136,936 hectares of land and to give it to the rural masses. This meant that in six years 10.2 per cent of the country's continental area was designated for eventual distribution, an average of 279,-680 hectares per month. This was rapid work, compared even to Porfirio Díaz's creation of the *latifundia*, for Díaz's average was only 132,139 hectares per month.[20] Cárdenas's activity was truly astounding, and it is no wonder that conservative elements raised active opposition to such a policy. When Cárdenas came into power previous presidential resolutions had pledged only about 6 per cent of Mexico's area for distribution, and when Cárdenas left office about 16.0 per cent had been marked for rearrangement into small holdings.[21] Resolutions do not tell the whole story, however, for they must be carried out. We will discuss this aspect of the problem of land when we assess, in Part II, the results of Revolution as a whole.

Land reform psychologically affected Mexican life. After Cárdenas, Mexico was definitively committed to land redistribution; investment in land, the traditional pattern, was no longer feasible, for land might be taken over at any time—paid off in government notes of questionable value. Even if land holdings were within the legal limits of small property protected by law, in the rush to distribute lands, legal formalities might be overlooked. Also, one could never tell when the maximum size of legal holdings might be reduced. On the one hand, investors had to look for new sources of investment, and industry and commerce gained as agricultural investment declined. On the other hand, the recipients of parcels

[20] James Wilkie, "Mexican Latifundia and Land Reform: A Statistical View from 1856 to 1964," manuscript in preparation.
[21] See source given in Table 8-4, page 188 below.

of land could take pride in owning their plot of ground. No longer were they required to work for someone else. If this meant subsistence agriculture based on *minifundio* in most cases, it also meant a change in the way the peasant comported himself. He was no longer an unequal, inferior being.

Cárdenas was able to shake the roots of the old order by budgetary policy. Though he largely worked within the traditional tax framework (his government was able to take advantage of economic recovery by increasing the taxes on exports), he injected federal government into the social and economic life of the nation by de-emphasizing the passive role of the state. Actual administrative investment fell below 50 per cent of the budget for the first time in Mexico's republican history. Cárdenas managed this feat without unduly trimming debt payments as a percentage of expenses. Administrative expenses would only rise above 50 per cent of the budget once again when President Manuel Avila Camacho paid out 22.5 per cent of the national budget in 1942 to reduce the national debt. The Mexican government, as well as the private sector, has always had to rely on foreign capital so heavily that unless the percentage of the budget devoted to the national debt remains relatively high, Mexico's image abroad suffers and a reduction of capital imports or even a flight of capital may result; hence presidents, worried about foreign relations, have tended to stress payment of the national debt to the detriment of Mexico's society which is heavily dependent upon government impetus. Cárdenas achieved a balance between payments on the debt and expenditure in Mexico's needs by avoiding undue stress on debt payments; he stayed within the usual 10 per cent of the budget slated for retirement of the debt and he economized in other realms of administrative expenses such as the enormous sums that had been lavished on the army. Indeed, since Cárdenas had a mass-based power support, he could afford to reduce the military share of federal expenses to as low as 16.7 per cent in 1938, the year the last military uprising against the government took place. The military relatively lost power which it never recovered; the good old days of the 1920's, when the generals received 30 to 40 per cent of national funds were over. Cárdenas had started the defense establishment on a downward spiral which would go as low as 5.4 per cent of actual budgetary outlay in 1960. Although military expenditure has gone down in percentage terms, it has tended to remain constant in pesos per capita since 1944. Certainly the military has done well in absolute monetary terms, but it began to lose its influence in national politics when it lost its great share of the national purse.

Cárdenas expended funds saved from administration in agricultural credit and social welfare. This latter expenditure covered education, public health and welfare, labor department affairs, and expenses to help the Indian adapt to modern life. Cárdenas's budgetary policy was a revolution in Mexican history in economic terms. Its achievement in social terms does not look so great, but we must remember that the shift he brought about here is obscured by the fact that decreasing government expenditure because of depression in the early 1930's left only the essential government functions, such as education and public welfare, unaffected by a cut in total allotments, and thus these items *apparently* received a greater emphasis than they *actually* did. It was Cárdenas who securely established the social sphere of governmental action, and he has remained the standard-bearer for governmental social action ever since.

TABLE 4-3

*Per Cent of Federal Budgetary Expenditure by
Type of Emphasis, 1935–1940*

	Economic		Social		Administrative	
Year	Projected	Actual	Projected	Actual	Projected	Actual
1935	28.9	31.6	20.5	17.3	50.6	51.1
1936	30.6	42.6	22.2	16.9	47.2	40.5
1937	26.9	41.9	23.2	17.4	49.9	40.7
1938	37.1	37.0	22.0	19.9	40.9	43.1
1939	31.8	38.2	24.4	18.4	43.8	43.4
1940	27.8	34.1	25.9	19.7	46.3	46.2

SOURCE: *Presupuesto* and *Cuenta Pública*, see Appendix B.

If one compares Tables 3-6 and 4-3 it is obvious that Calles had a different philosophy of the role of the state than Cárdenas.

Where Calles had seen the state's role somewhat as Herbert Hoover had seen it, Cárdenas set a precedent of expenditure in the economy which became standard, especially during the late 1940's and the 1950's under Presidents Miguel Alemán and Adolfo Ruiz Cortines. Thus not only did Cárdenas's presidential policies cause anxiety in social life as he emphasized social justice and rearranged the land tenure of the country, but his use of the budget worried private economic interests. In 1936 and 1937 the percentage of economic expenditure rose to more than 40 per cent of the budget.

The expropriation of the foreign-owned oil industry in 1938 was the high point of Cárdenas's economic nationalism. At one stroke Mexico's pride was protected, the foreigner put in his place, and Mexican national sovereignty assured. Of course Cárdenas had already completed nationalization of the railroads in 1937, but that did not involve the dramatic confrontation of world-wide business with a determined president of a weak country. The upshot of the oil expropriation was that Cárdenas had to abandon such programs as Socialist Education, strict regulation of the Church, and stimulation of labor against capital.[22] To carry off the oil expropriation successfully, he had to battle economic boycotts of Mexico's oil, as well as diplomatic pressure.[23] This was in addition to the usual strains of approaching elections in 1940. A turn to moderation was in order.

Since there were some Communists in Cárdenas's government, especially in the Ministry of Education, and since Lombardo Toledano, Cárdenas's labor adviser, was an avowed Marxist, if non-Communist, some observers considered the regime to be Communist-dominated. Cárdenas answered the charge as follows:

The cause of social agitation does not center in the existence of Communist nuclei. These form minorities without particular influence in the destiny of the country. The agitations come from the existence of just aspirations and needs of the laboring masses which are not satisfied, and from the lack of fulfillment of the labor laws, which gives the reason for agitation.

The presence of small groups of Communists is neither a new phenomenon nor exclusive of our country. These small minorities exist in Europe, the United States, and, in general, in all the countries of

[22] Wilkie, "Ideological Conflict in the Time of Lázaro Cárdenas," Chapters 4–5.
[23] Cronin, *Josephus Daniels in Mexico*, Chapter 9.

the earth. Their action neither compromises the stability of our institutions, nor alarms the government and it should not alarm the entrepreneur.

Fanatics who assassinate teachers and oppose the fulfillment of the law and the revolutionary program have damaged the Nation more than the Communists, and nevertheless, we have to tolerate them.[24]

Cárdenas was willing to work with the Communists, for as a Marxist he had much in common with them. He was not willing, however, to let them dominate his government, and he carefully relegated them to positions where they could not have much power. The struggle between Cárdenas and the Communists which ensued behind the scenes has generally been obscured and confused by charges that Cárdenas was a Communist or a Communist-dupe. The story of this bitter and difficult struggle for power, has been told in a study by Lyle C. Brown. Professor Brown's sophisticated examination of competing power groups in the Cárdenas years is a model analysis in political history of a misunderstood era.[25]

Cárdenas's Minister of Communications and Public Works, General Francisco J. Múgica, was the logical choice to succeed Cárdenas for the 1940–1946 presidential term, but he was considered too radical by many sectors of the Mexican public. There is a question whether Cárdenas wanted his intellectual mentor to follow him in office, for such a person would be hard to influence. Personalism may have had something to do with Cárdenas's rejection of Múgica, too, for a smart politician in Mexico does not antagonize the president's family. Múgica implicated Lázaro's brother, Dámaso, in a scandal of badly laid roads constructed for the Ministry of Communications and Public Works. Dámaso always claimed that he was not associated with the private firm which Múgica required to rebuild the main route through Michoacán, and Lázaro must have resented public questioning of his family's honesty.[26] Speculation aside, however, there was much

[24] Cárdenas, *Los Catorce Puntos de la Política Obrera Presidencial,* 47–48.

[25] Lyle C. Brown, "General Lázaro Cárdenas and Mexican Presidential Politics, 1933–1940; A Study in the Acquisition and Manipulation of Political Power," unpublished Ph.D. thesis in political science, Austin, University of Texas, 1964. See Karl M. Schmitt, *Communism in Mexico* (Austin: University of Texas Press, 1965) for a view since the 1940's.

[26] Cárdenas has long been plagued by charges that his family is corrupt, and recently, for example, his son Cuauhtémoc has had to defend himself against charges

opposition to Múgica, and Cárdenas, one of Mexico's most astute politicians, had too many years of army duty behind him to permit hard-won peace to degenerate into another civil war.

By 1939 times had changed, and the consensus that Cárdenas enjoyed when he entered the presidency in 1934 had vanished for three reasons. First, as groups won their limited demands from the government, they pulled up short to prevent any more basic changes which might threaten their newly won interests. Second, groups which received nothing began to protest en masse, such as the peasants who formed the *sinarquista* movement in the late 1930's. These groups demanded an end to the "anarchy" which their conservative leaders saw in Mexico, as social and economic traditions were upset. The anti-revolutionary public had never accepted attacks on religion which Calles and Cárdenas had both undertaken, and after 1938 they were even less ready to see the proletariat take over Mexico under the guise of a new official party of the Mexican Revolution.[27] Expropriation of oil won nearly unanimous approbation at the moment, but that was the last consensus that Cárdenas had as the enormity of what had been done began to filter into the minds of persons who, already, were dubious about radical uses of state power. And finally, the coming of World War II changed the Mexican intellectual mold which had sponsored social justice during the 1930's. Obviously capitalism was not dead and would make an effective ally against fascism. Also, as the war got under way, industrialization became the keynote of the times. The potential of industrialization soon became a panacea for bringing backward nations up to the level of more developed nations. Amid these pressures and currents, Cárdenas left the presidency to his old army chief of staff, General Manuel Avila Camacho.

---

of using family influence to gain lucrative contracts for governmental public works projects; see Cuauhtémoc's defense in "Aclaraciones," *Política*, Oct. 15, 1962, 44.

[27] *Sinarquismo* is discussed in Nathal L. Whetten, *Rural Mexico* (Chicago: University of Chicago Press, 1948), Chapter 20, and in Albert L. Michaels, "Fascism and Sinarquismo: Popular Nationalism Against the Mexican Revolution," *A Journal of Church and State* 8 (1966) 234–250.

THE IDEOLOGY OF ECONOMIC REVOLUTION

Avila Camacho acknowledged in his campaign the difficult transition of the 1940 election. Speaking in Tepic, Nayarit, on May 3, 1940, he said:

But the beneficiaries of the Reaction—active in this campaign behind all types of masks—cannot run up any flag for the people. Are they going to invite the masses to subvert a constitutional order which has given the land to those who work it, which has made the modest country homes of the peasant communities, previously overwhelmed with abandonment and spoliation, the central motive of the revolutionary Administration? Are they going to rise in arms because the Government of the Revolution has constantly preoccupied itself with extending credit to the ejido, with founding rural schools, with giving the waters to the people, with bettering the hygienic conditions of communities? Are they going to rise up because the program of the Revolutionary Party will continue in this struggle with the same spirit of liberation at the service of the people, purging the errors of progress? Perhaps because it is necessary to return to a regime of administrators of haciendas, of company stores, of iniquitous exploitation and of hard and silent submission to the tyranny of privileged and exploiting classes? [28]

Later in the same month Avila Camacho picked up this theme again when he noted in Hermosillo, Sonora:

We harvest the inheritance of the Revolution, with its conquests, with its beneficial achievements for the majority of the people; but we also harvest its inheritance of errors. We are not ashamed of the errors because they have been a consequence of the uncontrollable dynamic force of the redemptory struggle, and we harvest them in order to redeem them. . . . We know that the loyalty of the people shall be with us in order to purify the Revolution of its errors of action by means of the sensible and patient creation of a new economic horizon for Mexico. [29]

Between 1940 and 1958 Mexico moved into a period of economic development under the auspices of the government. Since Cárdenas presided over the shift in the presidency in 1940, and since he participated as Minister of Defense in the Avila Camacho administration from 1940 to 1946, there is not much doubt that

[28] *Avila Camacho y su Ideología* (México, D. F.: S. Turanzas del Valle, 1940), 125–126, speech of May 3, 1940, in Tepic, Nayarit.
[29] *Ibid.*, 151, speech of May 28, 1940, in Hermosillo, Sonora.

he was the precursor of change. But, like the man who had preceded him in the presidency, and like Calles for that matter, he
did not foresee to what extremes his new program would go after
1946. Certainly Cárdenas was backing away from social revolution
when he chose Avila Camacho over his old mentor, Francisco J.
Múgica. Despite Cárdenas's public protestations that he was leav-
ing his successor an absolutely free hand, he may have influenced
some key policy decisions during the early years of the Avila
Camacho period, for the shift from land distribution to economic
development during the early 1940's was managed by two staunch
supporters of Cárdenas. Silvano Barba González, Cárdenas's private secretary prior to 1934 and Minister of Labor and Minister
of Interior from 1934 to 1940, became Avila Camacho's chief of
the Agrarian Department. Eduardo Suárez, Cárdenas's Minister
of the Treasury, held the same important post in Avila Camacho's cabinet. Table 4-4 portrays the transition to economic

TABLE 4-4

*Per Cent of Federal Budgetary Expenditure by
Type of Emphasis, 1941–1946*

	Economic		Social		Administrative	
Year	Projected	Actual	Projected	Actual	Projected	Actual
1941	23.9	37.0	25.3	18.5	50.8	44.5
1942	22.8	29.4	26.2	17.4	51.0	53.2
1943	29.2	39.0	22.4	15.3	48.4	45.7
1944	32.2	43.2	16.9	14.5	50.9	42.3
1945	38.6	41.4	25.6	17.0	35.8	41.6
1946	37.7	45.4	24.3	16.0	38.0	38.6

SOURCE: *Presupuesto* and *Cuenta Pública*, see Appendix B.

revolution brought on by World War II. Appendix F shows the
shift of federal revenue from import taxes to income taxes. Economic revolution was originally predicated on taxing of income,
probably to prevent inflation during the war boom as much as to
give the government a significant new tax base. Income from ex-

port taxes rose briefly during the war, but then declined as a share of revenue.

Miguel Alemán, the first elected civilian president since Madero, gave economic revolution an ideological basis from 1946 to 1952. Alemán's New Group,[30] composed of university-educated leaders, dramatically spoke out for the development of industry and infrastructure: manufacturing, irrigation, dams, electrical power, roads and communications became the keys to create jobs and rescue the masses from poverty.[31] This approach was based upon the "trickle down" theory of economic development. The masses wait for their benefits while the country is developed to offer the jobs and economic climate in which social change can come about indirectly, but with a sound base. However, let Alemán himself explain his program:

The political constitution which rules us—magnificent concretion of the principles of the Mexican Revolution—guarantees with its norms individual rights, social conquests, and political liberties. It organizes the juridical life of the State and governs human relations on the principle of the dignity of man. Its essence is democracy, prized inheritance bequeathed to us by our elders, in which the Mexican people have placed their faith. Its practical purpose is the welfare of the people; its universal aspiration equality of nations. We feel the victory of the democracies in the world as the triumph of our own doctrine.

The next administration must count not only upon the support of the best popularly organized forces, but it must integrate itself with the representative elements of the progressive social forces of the nation in order to invigorate [national] unification. . . . The State must guarantee the liberty of entrepreneurs to open centers of production and to multiply the industries of the country, sure that their investments will be safe from the contingencies of injustice. National economic development must normally be based in the spirit of equity that animates factors indispensable for its realization.

The State must offer the most ample liberty to private investment, recognizing that general economic development is primordially the field of private enterprise. Those enterprises indispensable for the national economy which private initiative does not undertake will be

---

[30] The New Group was called "los licenciados" in Mexico.

[31] For discussion of the New Group see the following three works: Sanford A. Mosk, *Industrial Revolution in Mexico*, Chapters 2 and 3; Raymond Vernon, *The Dilemma of Mexico's Development; the Roles of the Private and Public Sectors*, Chapter 5; and Rafael Izquierdo, "Protectionism in Mexico," in Vernon (ed.), *Public Policy and Private Enterprise in Mexico*, 241–289.

developed by the state, which will make the necessary investments and will create the means for their function and development.[32]

Cárdenas had justified his government in collectivistic and socialistic terms; Alemán now posed an alternative: the state would encourage individualistic and capitalistic development of society. Alemán used the state as a means of capital formation by which contracts for public works could be provided to the Revolutionary Family. The Calles group came back into power along with Alemán, for it backed the ideological shift from collectivism to individualism. Thus social expenditure in the federal budget fell to its lowest average percentage since the pre-depression days of 1930. Educational expenditure collapsed as a significant percentage of federal investment, falling from a high of 13.6 per cent of actual expenditures in 1937 to a low of 7.1 in 1952 which was comparable to the Calles figure of 1925. Alemán placed his emphasis on less administrative investment and more economic impulse. In his sixth year of office, 1952, he pushed economic expenditure to a high point of 56.9 per cent, as Table 4-5 reveals.

TABLE 4-5

*Per Cent of Federal Budgetary Expenditure by
Type of Emphasis, 1947–1952*

	Economic		Social		Administrative	
Year	Projected	Actual	Projected	Actual	Projected	Actual
1947	40.6	45.8	21.5	15.9	37.9	38.3
1948	43.0	49.5	17.9	13.8	39.1	36.7
1949	36.9	56.7	18.3	11.9	44.8	31.4
1950	38.2	49.2	18.2	14.4	43.6	36.4
1951	37.4	53.3	18.5	12.5	44.1	34.2
1952	39.2	56.9	16.9	11.2	43.9	31.9

SOURCE: *Presupuesto* and *Cuenta Pública*, see Appendix B.

[32] Miguel Alemán, "Programa de Gobierno," *El Universal*, Sept. 30, 1945, reprinted in *Política*, Aug. 15, 1964, xxviii-xliv. For a study of regional economic production, see Manuel Germán Parra (ed.), *Conferencias de Mesa Redonda, 27 de Agosto de 1945–17 de Junio de 1946, Presididas Durante Su Campaña Electoral por el Licenciado Miguel Alemán* (México, D. F.: Cooperativa Talleres Gráficos de la Nación, 1949).

Alemán de-emphasized the agrarian problem of Mexico; land distribution hit the lowest monthly average since Ortiz Rubio's ill-fated attempt to bring the program to an end in 1930. Article 27 of the Constitution was reformed to provide legal protection for the small property holder. A holding of one hundred hectares of irrigated land was declared inalienable, the amount going up to 800 hectares for mountainous and dry land. Special provision was made for the granting of "certificates of inaffectability" to livestock ranchers; land needed to raise 500 head of cattle was declared exempt from distribution.[33]

Alemán's successor for the period from 1952 to 1958 was a colorless bureaucrat, Adolfo Ruiz Cortines, supposedly chosen as a compromise candidate by the Revolutionary Family after Cárdenas and Alemán deadlocked over the official party's standard-bearer.[34] The astounding corruption of the Alemán regime was a major campaign issue in 1952, and once in office Ruiz Cortines openly broke with Alemán over corruption in government and in the letting of contracts. However, Ruiz Cortines did not change his mentor's emphasis on development of the infrastructure. By further streamlining administrative expenses, he managed to shift a slightly higher per cent of actual national expenditure into state-fostered economic revolution; in 1954 economic expenditure reached an unprecedented high of 57.9 per cent. Juárez would have been astounded at the new Mexican "Liberalism." Neglect of the governmental bureaucracy could not long continue with a budget allotment of only 29.4 per cent, for it marked a new low percentage and it indicated a great reversal of Juárez's budgetary policy in which administration ate up over 90 per cent of federal funds. Nor could social expenditure remain as low as Alemán had dropped it in 1952, 11.2 per cent. Table 4-6 shows that Ruiz Cortines left office with the following actual budgetary

[33] Alejandro Rea Moguel, *México y su Reforma Agraria Integral* (México, D. F.: Antigua Librería Robredo, 1962), 106.

[34] Brandenburg, *The Making of Modern Mexico*, 106–107. Corruption under Miguel Alemán reached such startling proportions that protests from the intellectuals opened a floodgate of criticism about the Revolution's "turn to the right." See Jesús Silva Herzog, *La Revolución Mexicana en Crisis* (México, D. F.: Cuadernos Americanos, 1944) for an early view which criticized the trend. Consult Daniel Cosío Villegas, "Mexico's Crisis [1947]" in *American Extremes*, 3–27, tr. by Américo Paredes (Austin: University of Texas Press, 1964) for a criticism during Alemán's term.

TABLE 4-6

*Per Cent of Federal Budgetary Expenditure by
Type of Emphasis, 1953–1958*

Year	Economic		Social		Administrative	
	Projected	Actual	Projected	Actual	Projected	Actual
1953	37.9	54.0	18.5	14.1	43.6	31.9
1954	43.1	57.9	19.4	12.7	37.5	29.4
1955	44.2	50.5	19.7	12.8	36.1	36.7
1956	46.6	52.4	20.0	15.5	33.4	32.1
1957	45.6	50.5	21.6	15.2	32.8	34.3
1958	45.4	51.0	23.2	16.4	31.4	32.6

SOURCE: *Presupuesto* and *Cuenta Pública*, see Appendix B.

emphasis in 1958: economic expenditure, 51.0; social expenditure, 16.4; and administrative expenditure, 32.6 per cent.

Development of the economy in the post-1940 periods of Avila Camacho and Alemán, however, did indeed lend credence to the New Group's theory that the government could play a positive role in stimulating the growth of the Gross National Product. According to one source, whereas GNP had increased only 53.7 per cent from 13,524,000,000 pesos in 1910 (calculated in pesos of 1950) to 20,792,000,000 pesos by 1940, the GNP nearly trebled between 1940 and 1958 to 60,000,000,000 pesos, most of this gain coming since the end of World War II when the GNP stood at about 30,000,000,000 pesos.[35]

But the Revolution had not been undertaken for economic development—or so went the cry, as complaints began to be voiced about neo-Porfirian coteries. The echoes of Constitutional Delegate Alonzo Romero's words of 1917 haunted the proponents of economic revolution: "It has been said in this tribune that while the agrarian problem and the labor problem are not resolved, there will have been no revolutionary work done, and I add that unless the religious problem is resolved, much less will revolutionary labor have been done." [36] Manuel Avila Camacho termi-

[35] *50 Años en Cifras*, 32.
[36] *Diario de los Debates del Congreso Constituyente*, II, 1030–1031.

nated governmental anticlerical programs when he announced to Mexico, on the eve of taking office, "I am a believer." [37] Since that statement the age-old struggle between Church and State has come to an end and the Church has gradually regained strength, until in the 1960's religious holidays in the public schools are compulsory once again.[38] Avila Camacho also revised Article 3 of the Constitution to remove collectivism from the official educational policy. In 1942 Socialistic Education was replaced with a harmless campaign to stamp out illiteracy. Other strands of constitutional radicalism were broken by shifts in agrarian and labor policy. Alemán and Ruiz Cortines cut back distribution of land even further than Avila Camacho.

The labor problem appeared to be ignored as inflation ran far ahead of wage increases. One investigator concludes that between 1939 and 1957 real wages in reference to the cost of living declined in the Federal District to a low index of 65.3 in 1947 (1941 = 100); in the following ten years the index came up only to 84.8.[39] Since wages in the Federal District have always far outrun the rest of the nation, inflation also obviously took its toll outside of the Federal District. Another writer complains that real wages per capita were distributed so unequally during the period 1940–1950 that in the agricultural sector average income disparity between entrepreneur and salaried worker nearly trebled and in the nonagricultural sector the disparity increased almost by half. Further, in 1950 some 50 per cent of Mexican families received 19.1 per cent of personal income, but this income had fallen to 15.6 by 1957.[40] The government could not prevent a rash of strikes during the war, but Alemán and Ruiz Cortines saw to it that there were few strikes thereafter.

Ruiz Cortines told the nation before he took office:

It is indispensable that the State handle the delicate mechanism of labor legislation with the most balanced discretion, anticipating any conflict in the relations between employers and workers which may

[37] Wilkie, "Ideological Conflict in the Time of Lázaro Cárdenas," Chapter 5.

[38] Also, the Ministry of Education has suspended classes in private schools on Catholic religious holidays.

[39] E. Berdejo Alvarado, *Niveles de vida de la Población del Distrito Federal* (México, D. F.: n.p., 1960), 61.

[40] Ifigenia M. de Navarrete, *La Distribución del Ingreso y el Desarrollo Económico de México* (México, D. F.: Universidad Nacional Antónoma de México, 1960), 85, 95.

interrupt the process of improvement . . . [and waste] energies to the detriment of national production.[41]

Of course, the government could always argue that there was no need for strikes, since labor was a sector of the official party and the doors were always open for consultation; but the corrupt and degenerate position of union leaders acting in common interest with politicians (often one and the same person) gave this argument no weight. Ruiz Cortines's Labor Minister, Adolfo López Mateos, won fame for resolving hundreds of labor conflicts and keeping the number of strikers down to a post-1941 low. On the basis of this record he was chosen by the official party to be president from 1958 to 1964.

THE IDEOLOGY OF BALANCED REVOLUTION

In spite of López Mateos's reputation as a labor mediator, or perhaps because of it, a large number of strikes broke out as his presidential term got under way. After a shaky start in which the strikes were labeled "politically motivated," and dissident labor leaders were jailed with the use of large numbers of troops, López Mateos suffered only one more severe setback before he got complete control of the government. In 1961 when the United States sponsored an invasion of Cuba, Mexican Communists demonstrated in favor of Fidel Castro. These demonstrations not only challenged the authority of the Mexican government which, ironically, was friendly to Cuba, but frightened private domestic investors into fleeing the country at a rate which threatened disruption of the Mexican economy. López Mateos jailed the lot of Communists, including the famous painter David Alfaro Siqueiros, and settled down to bring about a balanced revolution. Conscious of pressure from the left and from the right as to what programs the government should emphasize in order to satisfy the growing tensions in Mexico, López Mateos chose aspects of both social and economic revolution to undertake the "integral" or balanced revolution which had been talked about since the 1920's, but which had never been achieved.

[41] Bernardo Ponce, *Adolfo Ruiz Cortines* (México, D. F.: Biografías Grandesa, 1952), 203, speech of Oct. 14, 1951.

López Mateos summarized the ideology of balanced revolution in his first State of the Union address to Congress:

The national development must be directed. In order to do it equitably and to extend it to all, we require that it be general, balanced, and that, without losing dynamism, it eliminate the privileges of minorities. . . . The work that our development requires can only be done within the balance of all productive factors, and the equitable distribution of its results. Both circumstances are correlatives of our progress; we have to be vigilant that they join and prevent that one sector impose its interests on the whole nation. We do not forget that in our Magna Carta property and wealth are included in the hierarchy of social function, and that they oblige great responsibilities to those who possess them.

The ideals of the Mexican Revolution permit us to fight today for social justice without sacrificing spiritual and political liberties. . . . With agrarian reform, labor rights, development and stimulation of production, and stabilization of prices we will elevate the purchasing power of our money and create better conditions of life for the people of Mexico.[42]

Ramón Beteta, "defender" of Cárdenas's social revolution during the 1930's[43] and Minister of the Treasury for Alemán's economic revolution in the late 1940's and early 1950's, has interpreted López Mateos's balanced revolution as follows:

The principal difference between the government of Cárdenas and the government of Alemán—I had occasion to work in both as you know and was very close to the two, Cárdenas as much as Alemán—[was that although] they had the same goal of improving the standard of living of the people, their method was different. As you have said, and it is true, Cárdenas believed in attacking the social problem, to better immediately the conditions of living of the people, to improve salaries, to permit labor pressure to gain the most benefits possible, to distribute land even though there would be a momentary diminution in production. . . . I believe that later prosperity would have been impossible without the social basis of greater justice which Cárdenas established.

But later Lic. Alemán, without ignoring nor minimizing the importance of social justice, thought that the important thing was that there be more [benefits] to distribute, and then as you say, we did put the most emphasis possible in augmenting production, in promoting

[42] Adolfo López Mateos, *5 Informes de Gobierno* (Naucalpan de Juárez, México: Novaro Editores-Impresores, 1964), 45–46.
[43] Ramón Beteta (ed.), *Social and Economic Program of Mexico* (México, D. F.: n.p., 1935).

agriculture and industrialization, and above all in something that is difficult to measure in money, that is, in giving the people self-confidence. The government of Lic. Alemán created an euphoria, created a security, created a state of animation that permitted the people to invest their money, to work, to take a chance, to undertake new enterprises, and that was what gave impulse to the country. Then came the epoch of Ruiz Cortines . . . which was destructive of precisely this [self-confidence] for the principal problem of Ruiz Cortines was that he ended the sense of security created by the previous government.

Then came the present regime which has tried to do at the same time the two things that Cárdenas and Alemán had done, that is to say, it has put emphasis in investments and has expanded the infrastructure of the country, but at the same time it has spent enormous quantities of money in the social security that it has extended to millions of people, it has spent greatly . . . [in] certain aspects such as student breakfasts, which went up from slightly over 100 thousand to three million, thus, in concrete things which are not investments, but an immediate improvement of the standards of living. Thus, the current president has tried to be a synthesis of the two theses, the thesis of Cárdenas and the thesis of Alemán.[44]

How did López Mateos specifically undertake balanced revolution? He offered to emphasize equal percentage shares of economic, social, and administrative expenditure in the budget. A shift toward social expenditure to balance the economic emphasis of previous periods was obvious, and social expenditure reached a high point in Mexican history in 1962 and 1963 in both absolute and percentage terms. However, actual social expenditure did not come anywhere near the projections of 33.6 and 33.7 per cent of total investment. Education was projected to rise from 15.8 per cent of the budget in 1959, López Mateos's first effective year of office, to 21.8 per cent in 1963; actual expenditures ran behind planning, however, and increased from only 10.6 to 14.2 per cent. The absolute gain in monetary terms for education has been considerable, but not as significant as projected. Table 4-7 reveals Lopez Mateos's hopes for balanced revolution and the discrepancy which has resulted from a skyrocketing increase of funds available for expenditure after the initial budget has been prepared. Though agencies of the federal government have usually received the absolute sum projected, percentage shares have changed as

[44] Ramón Beteta, Oral History Interviews with James and Edna Wilkie, Oct. 28, 1964, Mexico City.

TABLE 4-7

Per Cent of Federal Budgetary Expenditure by
Type of Emphasis, 1959–1963

	Economic		Social		Administrative	
Year	Projected	Actual	Projected	Actual	Projected	Actual
1959	40.9	44.8	26.1	17.4	33.0	37.8
1960	40.1	42.1	29.9	16.4	30.0	41.5
1961	39.2	31.8	30.7	18.7	30.1	49.5
1962	36.8	35.1	33.6	20.9	29.6	44.0
1963	37.2	41.3	33.7	22.6	29.1	36.1

SOURCE: *Presupuesto* and *Cuenta Pública*, see Appendix B.

extra money has been channeled into economic or administrative realms of expenditure.

López Mateos may have made one serious mistake with his allocation of public funds. Always worried about his government's image, in 1961 he determined to pay off domestic and foreign debts. To do this he shifted funds from economic expenditure to retirement of the national debt, thus eclipsing economic outlay and running the administrative portion of the actual budget up to 49.5 per cent at a time when domestic capital was fleeing Mexico due to the United States–Cuban situation. This shift in expenditure was felt, even if not identified, and one foreign analyst viewed balanced revolution as a "political strait jacket" which could prevent economic development.[45] By 1963, however, López Mateos avoided a policy of devoting 36.2 per cent of the entire federal expenditure to pay off the debt as he had done in 1961.

López Mateos's debt payment in 1961 was consistent with his tax program in 1960 which derived 33.2 per cent of federal income from borrowing, as Appendix F shows. The total federal

[45] For a view of the flight of capital and of the recession in the Mexican economy see Vernon, *The Dilemma of Mexico's Development*, 116–122, 177, 188. Vernon is overly pessimistic, for he fails to give emphasis to his own chart on page 4 which shows that though Mexico's economy has slowed in growth, it has not slowed as drastically as United States economic growth, and it is successful by Latin American standards; apparently world economic conditions may have as much to do with Mexico's growth as internal conditions, and thus Mexico faces no great dilemma other than that of adjusting her political ideology to the needs of new times.

debt soared in 1960 to over 12 billion pesos from about 8 billion pesos in 1958. Appendix M reveals the estimated debt structure of the federal government since 1950, excluding debts of autonomous state agencies and mixed public and private enterprises unless accepted as federal obligations by the Mexican congress. The Mexican Treasury Department has not prepared any figures concerning total debt before or since 1950 and other sources, including the *Cuenta Pública* and statistical year books, give contradictory information. Appendix M offers the most logical series of figures available, but it must be used with caution. The astounding rise in debt and payment in 1960 was never directly revealed to the Mexican people. Even ex-Treasury Minister Ramón Beteta, late general director of the newspaper *Novedades*, was greatly surprised to hear in 1964 that so much emphasis had been placed on payment of the debt.[46] Of course López Mateos's policy could be justified on the grounds that interest on the debt was being cut down, and that payment of the debt, largely to Mexican creditors, would win the confidence of private investors at home and abroad as well as facilitate more foreign loans to the Mexican government. Large federal borrowing in 1960 had interrelated purposes, no doubt, for it facilitated Mexico's purchase of the foreign-owned Mexican Light and Power Company and this in turn provided a propaganda weapon to advertise continuation of the Mexican economic revolution.

Projected budgetary figures alone propounded a balanced revolution but the actual results, especially as reflected in the averages in Chapter II, reveal that López Mateos's budgets were only slightly more balanced than either Cárdenas's or Avila Camacho's actual expenditures. Therefore, we must look for balanced revolution in more than budgetary intentions.

Where Avila Camacho slowed land distribution, López Mateos emulated the agrarian policy of 1934 to 1940 without upsetting

[46] See note 44. See also López Mateos, 5 *Informes de Gobierno*, pp. 79 and 147, for López Mateos's plans to pay off debts dating since Independence in order to show the reliability of Mexico and the Mexican government. Vernon, *The Dilemma of Mexico's Development*, 118–119, notes a sharp increase in expenditure of decentralized agencies during the period while López Mateos was still not in complete control of the government, but this is almost impossible to verify as total expenditure for the agencies is not available. The study of the public sector, México, Secretaría de la Presidencia, *México · Inversión Pública Federal, 1925–1963*, only shows increase in total investments by the public sector in 1960, 1961, 1963.

the nation as had Cárdenas. López Mateos signed fewer new resolutions than he executed, thus distributing land authorized by
previous presidential administrations. He placed great emphasis
on confirming titles to *ejido* lands held with *de facto* historical
rights. The new president, Díaz Ordaz, says that he will not grant
"certificates of inaffectability" to livestock ranchers, and will not
renew certificates which reach their twenty-year expiration date.[47]

López Mateos won praise for increasing the number of persons
covered by social security from 7.7 per cent of the total population
in 1958 to an estimated 15.9 per cent in 1964. This was a much
heralded gain of about 106 per cent in six years, for since the
social security system was established in 1943 increase in coverage
had been slow. The government made much propaganda about
bringing rural population under coverage because persons living
in isolated communities with less than 2500 inhabitants were most
in need of aid. In 1964, however, only about 11.6 per cent of all
those covered lived in rural areas of the republic, though this was
quite an increase from 3.9 per cent in 1958.[48]

To bring further social benefits into line with economic advances, Article 27 and the Federal Labor Law were reformed to
enable employees to share in company profits. Profit-sharing was
provided in the Constitution of 1917, but it did not become a
reality until 1962. In the spirit of balanced revolution, however,
this was not simply imposed upon capitalists; representatives of
capital, labor, and government formed a council to agree on the
method in which profit-sharing would be implemented.

The government also stressed subsidized sales of agricultural
products to the masses. Thus while it guaranteed agricultural
prices, the people were offered food at reasonable costs. To end
speculation in the price of tortillas and *masa* (the dough from
which the tortilla is made), the government acquired a factory in
1962 which processes corn flour of high quality for inexpensive
packaged sales distribution throughout the republic.[49]

[47] See *El Día,* May 4, 1965, for a policy speech given by Norberto Aguirre (Jefe
del Departamento Agrario for Díaz Ordaz) entitled "El Problema Ganadero de
Chihuahua," April 24, 1965, Chihuahua, Chihuahua.

[48] Table 1-9 above and Nacional Financiera, S. A., *La Economía Mexicana en
Cifras* (México, D. F.: n.p., 1965), 226. Cf. Telésforo Chapa, "Necesidad de Consolidar y Extender un Solo Sistema de Seguridad Social," *El Día,* Jan. 22, 1964.
The latter writer, a founder of the social security system, criticizes the present
operation.

[49] López Mateos, *5 Informes de Gobierno,* 214.

In regard to private business, López Mateos successfully nego-
tiated with foreign-owned electrical power companies to sell to
the government. The circumstances were different from 1938
when Cárdenas nationalized the oil industry, for the electrical
power companies were anxious to sell, and they bargained for an
acceptable price, whereas the oil companies did not. The "nationalization" of electrical power was billed as the first great step
forward since the oil expropriation. López Mateos also placed
heavy emphasis on state participation with private investment to
undertake and guarantee development of industry and resources
necessary for Mexico's economic growth.[50]

If the Revolution were to be truly balanced, social and economic programs of the post-1930 periods needed to be accompa-
nied by political reforms. The political terms of Madero dominated Mexican governmental thought until 1930; since that time
the official party always has maintained that Mexico is a democracy with free elections. At no time, however, has there been a
free election since Madero, and after 1930 even token opposition
was rarely tolerated. To balance the three earlier periods of political, social, and economic ideology in Mexico, López Mateos
offered a plan to permit opposition parties to enter the House of
Deputies in numbers large enough to be impressive but small
enough to be ineffective when threatening official party control
of legislation. This electoral reform not only was part of López
Mateos's ideology of balanced revolution, it was necessitated by
his jailing of large numbers of strikers early in his term. Such
a move had resulted in bad publicity for the Revolution, and
López Mateos desired to repair his public image. Electoral reform
did indeed allow the opposition to win seats in the 1964 elections
and to gain access to a public rostrum for debate, but the reform
was mainly a propaganda triumph. Members of the opposition
came into the House of Deputies as representatives of their party
and not of electoral districts. The official party could thus sweep
almost all districts, never sacrificing a man for the sake of opposition, and still have some opponents in Congress; López Mateos truly managed the proverbial eating of his cake and having
it too.

[50] See Miguel Wionczek, "Electrical Power: The Uneasy Partnership," in Vernon
(ed.), *Public Policy and Private Enterprise in Mexico*, 19–110, and Calvin P. Blair,
"Nacional Financiera: Entrepreneurship in a Mixed Economy," in *ibid.*, 191–240.

The balanced revolution has only recently gotten under way, and thus we are not in position to see as yet what its many changes mean, or whether it will continue under Gustavo Díaz Ordaz from 1964 to 1970. Díaz Ordaz campaigned on the concept of balanced revolution, and he brought together dissident wings within the Revolutionary Family in an unprecedented show of official party harmony. Since the 1964 presidential election was the least controversial and least violent election in Mexico's history, and because it was the first to thwart a crisis in the Mexican economy,[51] the relatively sophisticated appeal of balanced revolution would seem to be a well-tested program for action. López Mateos's Minister of the Treasury, Antonio Ortiz Mena, the man who budgeted balanced revolution, continued in the same post under the new president.

The active state has played an increasingly more important role in the integration of the Mexican nation since the first halting steps to expanded governmental action were taken during the years 1930–1933. With the rise of Cárdenas to the presidency in 1934, advocates of the active state joined battle with the Calles wing of the Revolutionary Family. The expulsion of Calles from Mexico in 1936 allowed fulfillment of the postulate of the Constitution of 1917 that the role of the state should become decisive in national affairs. Though the ideology of social revolution was transformed into economic revolution during World War II, the active state was not rejected. A sophisticated attempt by López Mateos to balance his actions by adapting the ideology of earlier periods to the needs of the 1960's has introduced a new element into the Mexican Revolution. The contrast of ideology in epochs of political, social, economic, and balanced revolution is clearly seen in the following three chapters which take up administrative, economic and social expenditure, respectively.

[51] "La Economía Mexicana en Tiempos de Elecciones," *El Día,* June 28, 1964.

5

Administrative Expenditure

We have examined the general context of budgetary policy in the Mexican Revolution, and now we may look at specific policy regarding the outlay of governmental funds. Administrative expenditure is taken up first because the concept of the passive state which prevailed in Mexico until the 1930's determined that funds to govern society were of primary importance. Since the 1930's administrative expenditure on the armed forces, public debt, judiciary, legislature, and other governing agencies has diminished as economic and social expenditures have gained. The story of this changing emphasis in administrative expenditure is told in Table 5-1.

The year-by-year view of administrative expense in Table 5-1, summarized in the averages of Table 2-1, reveals trends within presidential terms and allows us to pinpoint changing policies in crucial years. The first big change in administrative emphasis in the budget came in 1922 under Obregón who reduced projections to 59.2 per cent, 10 to 20 per cent lower than expenditures in all previous years. Actual change did not come until 1925 when 58.8 per cent was spent on administration. This rate did not become a pattern until 1930–1932. The lower percentage was disrupted under Rodríguez, and then reduced dramatically under Cárdenas. In 1936 administrative projections and actual percentages dipped below 50 per cent to 47.2 and 40.5 respectively. In Cárdenas's last year in office the totals were about 46 per cent. Avila Camacho raised the totals to more than 50 per cent for the last time in 1942 when actual expenditure for administration ran 53.2 per cent. By 1946, however, he had scaled down administration to about 38 per cent of the budget.

TABLE 5-1

*Administrative Expenditure: Percentage Share and
Pesos Per Capita Since 1910*

Year	President[a]	Per Cent Projected	Pesos[b]	Per Cent Actual	Pesos[b]
1869–1870	Juárez	78.2	...	93.4	...
1900–1901	Díaz	81.9	23.8	80.6	23.9
1910–1911	Díaz	71.9	24.7	74.1	25.3
1911–1912	Madero	71.5	25.9	72.5	24.2
1912–1913	Madero/Huerta	75.0	29.0	75.9	29.3
1913–1914	Huerta	74.7	...	...	...
1914–1915	Huerta	74.4	...	...	...
1917	Carranza	84.3	...	85.6	...
1918	Carranza	81.2	25.1	80.5	14.6
1919	Carranza	82.4	34.3	79.1	9.6
1920	Carranza/De la Huerta	82.8	34.4	80.5	20.7
1921	Obregón	79.4	42.0	77.2	36.8
1922	Obregón	59.2	56.5	71.1	40.4
1923	Obregón	63.1	50.2	70.6	38.0
1924	Obregón	75.5	52.9	70.6	45.8
1925	Calles	77.1	49.3	58.8	39.0
1926	Calles	69.8	46.7	68.8	49.2
1927	Calles	64.0	45.2	67.5	46.4
1928	Calles	61.8	40.7	65.2	42.5
1929	Portes Gil	63.1	40.6	63.9	39.3
1930	Portes Gil/Ortiz Rubio	59.1	37.5	56.1	33.8
1931	Ortiz Rubio	58.2	41.7	56.3	30.6
1932	Ortiz Rubio	54.0	29.8	55.8	30.6
1933	Rodríguez	61.2	31.5	64.0	37.8
1934	Rodríguez	60.8	33.7	61.8	37.3
1935	Cárdenas	50.6	31.0	51.1	34.1
1936	Cárdenas	47.2	27.8	40.5	33.9
1937	Cárdenas	49.9	28.3	40.7	33.2
1938	Cárdenas	40.9	27.4	43.1	34.8
1939	Cárdenas	43.8	29.9	43.4	38.8
1940	Cárdenas	46.3	31.2	46.2	42.0
1941	Avila Camacho	50.8	34.4	44.5	41.8
1942	Avila Camacho	51.0	34.5	53.2	54.3
1943	Avila Camacho	48.4	34.1	45.7	48.9
1944	Avila Camacho	50.9	42.5	42.3	46.6
1945	Avila Camacho	35.8	24.1	41.6	43.9

TABLE 5-1 (continued)

Administrative Expenditure: Percentage Share and Pesos Per Capita Since 1910

Year	President[a]	Per Cent Projected	Pesos[b]	Per Cent Actual	Pesos[b]
1946	Avila Camacho	38.0	25.5	38.6	38.2
1947	Alemán	37.9	33.6	38.3	43.7
1948	Alemán	39.1	43.8	36.7	49.6
1949	Alemán	44.8	51.1	31.4	52.6
1950	Alemán	43.6	46.4	36.4	48.9
1951	Alemán	44.1	44.3	34.2	51.8
1952	Alemán	43.9	48.3	31.9	56.8
1953	Ruiz Cortines	43.6	47.5	31.9	45.9
1954	Ruiz Cortines	37.5	42.7	29.4	54.9
1955	Ruiz Cortines	36.1	40.7	36.7	64.7
1956	Ruiz Cortines	33.4	40.5	32.1	59.8
1957	Ruiz Cortines	32.8	41.2	34.3	64.2
1958	Ruiz Cortines	31.4	40.5	32.6	66.6
1959	López Mateos	33.0	45.5	37.8	78.7
1960	López Mateos	30.0	41.5	41.5	112.8
1961	López Mateos	30.1	43.0	49.5	130.4
1962	López Mateos	29.6	45.1	44.0	109.9
1963	López Mateos	29.1	46.3	36.1	84.4

[a] Slash indicates latter person administered actual funds.
[b] In pesos per capita of 1950.
SOURCE: See Appendix B.

The last big decreases in administrative expenditure as a percentage of federal outlay came under Alemán and Ruiz Cortines. The former president planned to spend more than 40 per cent on administrative affairs, but he was generally at least 10 per cent under this amount after 1949. The latter president made the last dramatic reduction when he managed to reduce actual administrative influence to 29.4. After that low, administration increased under López Mateos. Ruiz Cortines also managed to spend the percentage on administration which he planned, but López Mateos channeled great percentages into administration which had not been projected. In 1961 he spent 19 per cent more on admin-

istration than budgeted. This was some 87 pesos per capita (in
1950 prices) above his projections. The 130.4 pesos per capita
which López Mateos spent on purely administrative agencies and
categories paralleled the 110-peso-per-capita totals he spent in 1960
and 1962. Prior to this time, administration had been affluent
when it almost reached 50 pesos per capita under Calles in 1926;
it went above 50 pesos in 1942 under Avila Camacho and in
1951–1952 under Alemán. Real gains came under Ruiz Cortines,
and relative wealth came under López Mateos. Since Cárdenas,
without exception the administrative categories have received
more pesos per capita, often many, many more, than projected.
Carranza is the only president who projected a great deal more
than he could spend for administration, because revenue contracted greatly during years of violence.

Let us look at the component parts of administrative expenditure in order to understand the above patterns. A note is in order
regarding presentation of these parts. The totals of all the following tables in this chapter add up to the totals each year of administrative expenditure in Table 5-1. Tables 5-1, 6-1, and 7-1 add
up to 100.0 per cent for each year presented. Expenditure per
capita (which is always treated in prices of 1950 in this work in
order that full comparison of years is possible) is offered for all
categories of the budget except the minor ones. It would be re-
petitive and space-consuming to offer this data for items which
have no great impact on budgetary policy. Expenditure per capita
for minor expenditure percentages may be calculated, however,
by using the yearly budgetary totals of pesos per capita presented
in Table 1-7. In calculation of pesos per capita, figures may not
add to totals because of rounding.

MILITARY OUTLAY

Ever since the generals came to the fore in Mexican society, when
Mexico won her independence from Spain in 1821, the military
has played a major role in government. The army was the only
organized force with power to ensure its importance, and its
swashbuckling generals strode romantically to the center of the
stage when they influenced Mexican politics and public policy for
more than a century. Few presidents of Mexico have been civilians

—Juárez was an outstanding exception during the nineteenth century—and it has not been until the post-World War II era that generals have yielded the presidency to nonmilitary men.

The process of de-emphasizing the role of the military in the Mexican Revolution has been long and arduous. An examination of how this came about cannot be undertaken in these pages, but the analysis of budgetary policy shown in Table 5-2 does shed new light on a story that is told elsewhere.[1]

Projected military expenditure, including army, industry, and navy, had decreased to slightly more than 20 per cent of the budget by 1910, and, projected emphasis increased to 72.2 per cent in 1917. Projections fell to less than 70 but never below 60 per cent until Obregón came into power and reduced military emphasis to as low as 36 per cent. Generals Ortiz Rubio and Rodríguez brought the military down to 28.5 and 25.1 per cent in 1932–1933 and 1934, but the real break came under Cárdenas. In 1938 Cárdenas cut the military to 20.2 per cent of the federal purse.

The role of the military in budgetary affairs was not ended however, and during World War II appropriations increased to around 25 per cent. In 1944 the military expenditure was reduced to a low for Mexican history—17.8 per cent; and after a brief increase for one year, following years have witnessed a gradual decrease in the military's share of federal funds. Though the generals' measure of influence decreased to about 12 and 14 per cent under presidents Alemán and Ruiz Cortines, the final reduction of the military's role to a less than 10 per cent voice in federal policy did not come until 1962.

Actual expenditures closely paralleled projections in percentage terms under Díaz and during the first years of the Revolution. Carranza spent less on military affairs than he had thought necessary, and he was able to hold the generals down to 55.5 per cent of the budget in 1918, 9 per cent less than projections. He did better than this in 1919 when actual expenditures were 18.5 per cent less than projections. Perhaps Carranza was able to achieve these savings by authorizing the military to forage for funds. Certainly the military was able to act with a high hand during these and earlier years. We have no account of federal funds during the

[1] See, for example, Edwin Lieuwen's *Arms and Politics in Latin America* (New York: Praeger, for Council on Foreign Relations, 1961), Chapter 4.

TABLE 5-2

Military Expenditure

Year	President[a]	Per Cent Projected	Pesos[b]	Per Cent Actual	Pesos[b]
1869–1870	Juárez	38.0	...	32.2	...
1900–1901	Díaz	23.1	6.7	23.5	7.0
1910–1911	Díaz	20.6	7.1	20.4	7.0
1911–1912	Madero	20.2	7.3	18.6	6.2
1912–1913	Madero/Huerta	26.7	10.3	25.8	10.0
1913–1914	Huerta	30.9	...	...	...
1914–1915	Huerta	30.8	...	...	...
1917	Carranza	72.2	...	69.6	...
1918	Carranza	64.5	19.9	55.5	10.0
1919	Carranza	65.9	27.4	47.4	5.7
1920	Carranza/De la Huerta	62.1	25.8	48.4	12.2
1921	Obregón	60.9	32.2	53.0	25.3
1922	Obregón	40.8	39.0	46.4	26.4
1923	Obregón	36.3	28.9	33.6	18.1
1924	Obregón	36.0	25.2	42.6	27.7
1925	Calles	31.7	20.3	30.9	20.5
1926	Calles	31.2	20.9	29.8	21.3
1927	Calles	28.2	19.9	31.9	21.9
1928	Calles	33.5	22.1	32.3	21.0
1929	Portes Gil	34.0	21.9	37.3	22.9
1930	Portes Gil/Ortiz Rubio	31.5	20.0	30.9	18.6
1931	Ortiz Rubio	27.3	19.5	29.9	16.2
1932	Ortiz Rubio	28.5	15.7	28.8	15.8
1933	Rodríguez	28.5	14.7	24.6	14.5
1934	Rodríguez	25.1	13.9	22.7	13.7
1935	Cárdenas	22.5	13.8	20.9	14.0
1936	Cárdenas	24.3	14.3	17.3	14.5
1937	Cárdenas	24.1	13.7	17.4	14.2
1938	Cárdenas	20.2	13.6	16.7	13.5
1939	Cárdenas	20.9	14.3	15.8	14.1
1940	Cárdenas	24.6	16.6	19.7	17.9
1941	Avila Camacho	26.4	17.9	19.1	18.0
1942	Avila Camacho	26.2	17.7	18.4	18.8
1943	Avila Camacho	25.2	17.7	18.1	19.4
1944	Avila Camacho	17.8	14.8	14.7	16.2
1945	Avila Camacho	20.7	14.0	15.0	15.8
1946	Avila Camacho	18.5	12.4	14.3	14.2

TABLE 5-2 (continued)

Military Expenditure

Year	President[a]	Per Cent Projected	Pesos[b]	Per Cent Actual	Pesos[b]
1947	Alemán	16.8	14.9	12.9	14.7
1948	Alemán	14.2	15.9	11.1	15.0
1949	Alemán	13.7	15.6	8.8	14.7
1950	Alemán	12.9	13.7	10.0	13.4
1951	Alemán	12.1	12.2	8.2	12.4
1952	Alemán	11.3	12.4	7.2	12.8
1953	Ruiz Cortines	12.2	13.3	9.3	13.4
1954	Ruiz Cortines	14.2	16.2	8.1	15.1
1955	Ruiz Cortines	12.6	14.2	8.0	14.1
1956	Ruiz Cortines	12.3	14.9	7.5	14.0
1957	Ruiz Cortines	12.1	15.2	8.0	15.0
1958	Ruiz Cortines	12.0	15.5	7.3	14.9
1959	López Mateos	10.6	14.6	6.5	13.5
1960	López Mateos	11.2	15.5	5.4	14.7
1961	López Mateos	10.6	15.1	5.5	14.5
1962	López Mateos	9.9	15.1	6.1	15.2
1963	López Mateos	10.3	16.4	6.5	15.2

[a] Slash indicates latter person administered actual funds.
[b] In pesos per capita of 1950.
SOURCE: See Appendix B.

turbulent years after Madero was assassinated, but Carranza has described how the military operated from 1913 to 1917. He noted, "As regards revenue and expenditure, the disbursements of the campaign . . . had been made, most of the time, by military chiefs, the funds for this purpose being procured wherever they could be found. . . ." [2] There is good reason to suppose that the generals continued to provide for themselves until the early 1920's.

Obregón promised to cut military expenditure drastically in 1922 and channel it into social and economic spheres of national

[2] Quoted by Guillermo Butler Sherwell, *Mexico's Capacity to Pay; A General Analysis of the Present Economic Position of Mexico* (Washington, D. C.: n.p., 1929), 90.

affairs, but he wound up approximating the actual percentage emphasis of Carranza's expenditure of 1919.

In 1923 Obregón achieved a breakthrough against the military system which had grown out of the upheaval of 1910; he reduced the actual budgetary percentage of the military to 33.6 per cent. Because of the rebellion of December, 1923, and the early months of 1924, however, military totals were raised to 42.6 per cent of the budget in 1924. In his last year of the presidency and in Calles's years as president, 30 to 32 per cent became standard. Military rebellion in 1929 brought the percentage of the military's share of the federal purse up to 37.3 per cent, an amount only 3.3 per cent more than projected for that year. Abelardo Rodríguez made an even greater cut of the generals' funds than he had thought possible, and a major shift downward was accomplished when the percentage for military affairs fell to 22.7 per cent in 1934. Thus Cárdenas assumed office with a good position to de-emphasize the military role in public policy, and by organizing labor and peasants he was able to create counter-forces to the military's age-old power.

The tangible benefits which Cárdenas offered the masses meant the military's percentage of the budget dropped below 20 per cent in 1936, 7 per cent below projections. In 1939 this total fell to 15.8 per cent. World War II brought about increased defense as social and economic gains were sacrificed for preparedness, but actual percentage of expenditure never did go above 20 per cent of the budget as it was projected. By 1944 Avila Camacho was able to reduce this actual percentage to 14.7 per cent, an even lower point for Mexican history than he had thought possible when he drew up the budget for that year. Percentage outlay fell below 10 per cent under Alemán, and it went as low as 7.2 per cent in 1952. The generals won an increase in 1953 to 9.3 per cent to compensate for their loss in 1952. From 1954 to 1958 their percentage share of actual expenditure ranged from 7.3 to 8.1. The regime of Adolfo López Mateos marked a further decrease in the influence of the military, for it was reduced to only 5.4 per cent of the budget in 1960.

Generals retained a major voice in public policy until the early 1930's. As late as 1933 they still received almost one quarter of all federal funds, and therefore they played the most influential role in governmental circles. Cárdenas broke the back of military power between 1935 and 1939. The final significant decline of military influence came under Miguel Alemán. The leaders of social revolution and economic revolution had finally ended the influence of the generals.

Of course, projected per-cent expenditure for the military has run higher than actual percentages, but we may surmise that this is the way the civilian government has effectively curtailed military prerogatives. As projected and actual budgets have differed due to increasing funds which were not projected, the military has received the promised amount of pesos in per-capita terms of 1950 but has lost in percentage terms. Thus, the military has been subtly reduced in influence in government circles as it receives a smaller and smaller share of federal expenditure.

The military received 6 to 7 pesos per capita (in 1950 prices) in projected and actual budgets between 1900–1911, but, ironically, Madero began the trend toward high budgets per capita for the politically ambitious generals in order to restore peace to the country. He projected 10 pesos per capita in 1912–1913, and, when he was overthrown, Huerta spent the amount allotted. The lack of a price index for the years 1913–1916 prevents analysis of the budgetary pattern in pesos per capita for those years, but the index for 1919 shows that Carranza raised per-capita projections to as high as 27.4 pesos per capita. Limited income allowed him to provide the military with only 5.7 pesos per capita. In 1922 Obregón raised the total projected to 39.0 pesos per capita, the high for Mexican history during the twentieth century, and he spent 26.4 pesos per capita, a very high actual amount. He did this while reducing the percentage expenditure on the military in projected and actual budgets, for increased federal revenues which came with unification of revolutionary forces allowed him to create the armed forces necessary to enforce the peace. Thus Obregón, by his political policy and his budgetary policy, discovered the key to stability in Mexico. Obregón is the man who found Mexico's manner of escaping the perpetual civil wars which seemed to have begun during the decade 1910–1920.

The relation of projected and actual expenditure per capita on military affairs was balanced in 1924 and has held fairly steady since then. An exception occurred in 1931 when the military was

promised 19.5 pesos per capita and received only 16.2 as Ortiz
Rubio shaved administrative expenses to balance the budget during the depression. The economy drive during the depression
brought the generals down to the amount which they have more
or less maintained until the present day, 14 to 15 pesos per capita.
This amount took a temporary upswing during World War II,
but returned to the usual amount thereafter. Avila Camacho managed to reduce the military to about 12 pesos per capita projected
and actual expenditure in 1946 and Alemán did the same thing
in 1951 and 1952. In sum, though the Ministry of National Defense has held its own since the early 1930's in monetary terms,
it has gradually lost out in percentage terms until it is no longer
the decisive factor in Mexican politics, it is only one of many.
The above budgetary figures offer perhaps the one tentative measure of military influence which we have, and students of the
soldiery may also be interested in examining nondeflated expenditure presented in Appendix E.

PAYMENT ON THE PUBLIC DEBT

The public debt of Mexico has been an administrative problem
second only to military outlay. The latter has been related to internal crises; the former, to crises in foreign relations. However,
the president who has chosen to emphasize debt payments may
find that he has solved external problems only to precipitate new
internal difficulties.

Discussion of payment of the debt requires several clarifications
before we can proceed. It might be argued that if the debt is pub-
licly held, Mexico owes the amount to herself; but as we have
pointed out in the Preface, the debt represents an important consideration in total outlays in a developing country which seeks to
attract foreign capital. True, loans may provide social and economic development, but loans are credited to these types of expenditure in budgetary analysis. They may provide change at one
moment in history, but they will have to be repaid at another
moment in time. Also, bond issues and borrowing may be infla-
tionary if they are over-extended. Mexico must consider at what
point debt repayment becomes such an important factor in expenditure that national integration is compromised. We cannot

answer this question here, but in analyzing the following data we should consider it.

Another factor which we should take into account concerns long-term fixed governmental debt payments which may well compromise presidents who do not contract them. Fixed costs, in general, limit the power of the presidents in the United States, but this has not yet happened to any significant degree in Mexico. Certainly development projects may overlap presidential administrations in Mexico, but presidential power over the budget is so great that sometimes old projects are throttled financially or even cancelled by a new president. There is a tradition in Mexico that most projects will be finished within the presidential term in which they are started in order that the appropriate chief executive receives credit for his work; consequently the number of dedications increases frantically toward the end of each president's term in office.

The outstanding fixed debt which the Mexican government faithfully redeemed was that which covered expropriation of the oil industries in 1938. The two years in which the debt payment for oil shows up significantly as a share of total public debt outlay were 1942 and 1948. In those years Mexico settled with the oil companies of the United States and England respectively, and outlay for this item may have been as much as one fifth of all payments on the debt. Subsequent annual payments until 1947 and 1962, when the respective debts were completely paid, did not amount to more than 1 to 2 per cent of actual federal expenditure and thus did not loom large in debt payments.[3]

One cost that citizens of the United States would generally consider fixed is payment on the agrarian debt for expropriation of land. Mexican leaders, however, paid this debt domestically with worthless bonds in order to maintain budgetary flexibility. Though Mexican citizens lost, citizens of the United States gained repayment for expropriated lands through the general claims settlement between the United States and Mexico in 1941. Annual payments, however, were rarely great enough to show up as more than 1 per cent in total actual federal expenditure.[4]

[3] Percentages are calculated from figures given by Howard F. Cline, *The United States and Mexico*, 249–251.
[4] *Ibid.*, 225, 248.

TABLE 5-3

Public Debt Outlay

Year	President[a]	Per Cent Projected	Pesos[b]	Per Cent Actual	Pesos[b]
1869–1870	Juárez	8.2	...	5.1	...
1900–1901	Díaz	33.3	9.7	32.3	9.6
1910–1911	Díaz	25.8	8.8	27.8	9.5
1911–1912	Madero	24.5	8.9	25.5	8.5
1912–1913	Madero/Huerta	23.2	9.0	23.8	9.2
1913–1914	Huerta	19.6	...	...	...
1914–1915	Huerta	21.5	...	...	...
1917	Carranza	.7	...	.2	...
1918	Carranza	1.7	.5	4.0	.7
1919	Carranza	1.6	.7	5.1	.6
1920	Carranza/De la Huerta	3.3	1.4	4.7	1.2
1921	Obregón	3.0	1.6	3.0	1.4
1922	Obregón	2.7	2.6	7.1	4.0
1923	Obregón	10.6	8.4	16.5	8.9
1924	Obregón	23.1	16.2	7.5	4.9
1925	Calles	26.7	17.1	6.9	4.6
1926	Calles	19.0	12.7	13.8	9.9
1927	Calles	16.9	11.9	16.7	11.5
1928	Calles	9.3	6.1	13.5	8.8
1929	Portes Gil	9.9	6.4	7.0	4.3
1930	Portes Gil/Ortiz Rubio	7.0	4.4	4.6	2.8
1931	Ortiz Rubio	11.4	8.2	3.6	2.0
1932	Ortiz Rubio	4.4	2.4	5.9	3.2
1933	Rodríguez	10.2	5.3	10.5	6.2
1934	Rodríguez	14.0	7.8	14.0	8.4
1935	Cárdenas	9.1	5.6	7.7	5.1
1936	Cárdenas	4.6	2.7	7.3	6.1
1937	Cárdenas	8.2	4.7	9.4	7.7
1938	Cárdenas	5.6	3.8	11.2	9.0
1939	Cárdenas	9.1	6.2	14.5	12.9
1940	Cárdenas	8.9	6.0	12.5	11.4
1941	Avila Camacho	9.4	6.4	12.1	11.4
1942	Avila Camacho	11.4	7.7	22.5	23.0
1943	Avila Camacho	13.1	9.2	16.6	17.8
1944	Avila Camacho	25.7	21.4	19.1	21.0
1945	Avila Camacho	6.2	4.2	16.9	17.8
1946	Avila Camacho	10.5	7.0	14.9	14.8

TABLE 5-3 (continued)

Public Debt Outlay

Year	President[a]	Per Cent Projected	Pesos[b]	Per Cent Actual	Pesos[b]
1947	Alemán	12.3	10.9	15.6	17.8
1948	Alemán	15.7	17.6	16.0	21.6
1949	Alemán	22.7	25.9	14.2	23.8
1950	Alemán	22.1	23.5	16.0	21.5
1951	Alemán	23.3	23.4	16.5	25.0
1952	Alemán	24.5	27.0	13.8	24.6
1953	Ruiz Cortines	22.9	24.9	14.7	21.1
1954	Ruiz Cortines	13.5	15.4	13.3	24.8
1955	Ruiz Cortines	14.1	15.9	20.1	35.4
1956	Ruiz Cortines	12.5	15.2	16.0	29.8
1957	Ruiz Cortines	11.9	14.9	17.6	33.0
1958	Ruiz Cortines	10.7	13.8	15.6	31.9
1959	López Mateos	12.6	17.4	22.0	45.8
1960	López Mateos	8.4	11.6	27.3	74.2
1961	López Mateos	9.5	13.6	36.2	95.4
1962	López Mateos	9.0	13.7	27.2	67.9
1963	López Mateos	7.3	11.6	17.1	40.0

[a] Slash indicates latter person administered actual funds.
[b] In pesos per capita of 1950.
SOURCE: See Appendix B.

Porfirio Díaz enjoyed success in international relations and with international capital largely because he not only created a stable atmosphere which welcomed investors, but he allocated and paid out from one fourth to one third of the national budget on the foreign and domestic public debt of Mexico. Madero's revolution in 1910 did not change this pattern. When Huerta overthrew Madero in 1913, he handled the debt as Madero had projected in his second year. Though we do not have the data to determine how Huerta did after that, at least he projected about 20 per cent of the budget to cover this category during the following two years. Table 5-3 reveals that, despite different platforms, the ideology of the passive state was paramount in the philosophy of these men, and national integration was sacrificed in favor of federal policy which emphasized public debt payments and military expenditures.

Carranza came to power at a time when absolute confusion in federal affairs had resulted in suspension of debt payments. He established a new federal government, renewed budgetary procedures in 1917, and talked about resuming debt payments, but the last was impossible in a time of chaos.[5] In 1917 only .7 per cent was projected for this category and only .2 per cent was paid. This was mainly because the army and basic governmental administration required all the funds that shrunken revenue could provide. Also, though relations with foreign nations were strained as Mexican nationalism began to assert itself, the world was at war so that Mexico was left in some peace in regard to debt payments in comparison to later years. Carranza won diplomatic recognition from the United States in February of 1916, but, when he was killed, the United States declined to continue relations with the new government of Obregón until American rights were secure and payments were resumed on the debt. Obregón refused to worry about debt obligations until he had gained diplomatic recognition from the power to the North, and most of his term was thus taken up in negotiations with United States representatives which culminated in the Bucareli Agreements of 1923. American land and subsoil rights were secured and Mexico was extended recognition in August. Resumption of debt payments as a significant share of the budget came in 1923 as Obregón paid out 16.5 per cent of actual expenditures for this purpose. He had promised only 10.6 per cent but apparently he wished to show the Mexican government's good faith in the Bucareli Agreements. Obregón promised to pay out 23.1 per cent of the budget in 1924, but the military rebellion in December, 1923, and early 1924 eclipsed this plan and only 7.5 per cent was paid out.

Calles came into the presidency in 1925 and upped projected debt payments to a high for revolutionary history to that date, 26.7 per cent, a figure which surpassed even Porfirio Díaz's last allocation. Given the amount of the budget compared to Díaz's days, the projected pesos per capita doubled the amount Díaz had

[5] Edgar Turlington, *Mexico and Her Foreign Creditors* (New York: Columbia University Press, 1930), 269, 278.

promised to pay. The turmoil of politics, however, limited Calles's ability to pay. Actual percentage share of the budget and actual pesos per capita were low in 1925. Calles promised a significantly smaller share of the budget for the debt as his term wore on, until in 1928 he offered only 9.3 per cent for this purpose, but per-capita expenditure reached a 1927 high of 11.5 pesos which was not to be exceeded until World War II.

The public debt was a key point of controversy during the late 1920's. Though Calles was willing to pay off the public debt, he was reluctant to assume responsibility for carrying out the Bucareli Agreements which had been ratified by neither the Mexican nor the United States congresses, because these Agreements in effect nullified Article 27 of the Constitution of 1917.[6] With Mexico's Bucareli commitments in doubt, foreign property was apparently threatened. United States Ambassador Morrow was able to talk these problems over successfully with Calles. Morrow tied all of Mexico's instability of government to a shaky financial situation in which foreign capitalists were discouraged from investing in Mexico. He specifically suggested to Calles that Mexico's financial problems were the result of an unbalanced budget, and that the problem of the public debt was at the heart of this imbalance. He wrote to Secretary of State Kellogg on November 9, 1928:

I have called [Calles's] attention to the great weakness in the Mexican budgetary situation arising from the present method of financing the Government's agrarian policy under which new obligations are being continuously created on account of lands taken for "ejidos" [communal land holdings]. The Minister of Hacienda [Treasury] has no control whatever over these new obligations or of the rate at which they are incurred. Under these conditions no budget can really be considered balanced. As long ago as April I had a long talk with President Calles about this situation and suggested the possibility of a reform in the method of financing agrarian programs. The following figures for the last five years show a rapidly decreasing rate of expropriation of land in pursuance of the government agrarian policy:

1923	1,272,260 hectares
1924	956,852
1925	911,738
1926	502,700
1927	289,933

[6] See Dulles, *Yesterday in Mexico*, Chapters 18, 36, and 37.

The Department of Agriculture estimated that a sum of from six to eight million pesos would be sufficient to pay for the lands which would probably be taken during 1928 and that during each year thereafter the amount would probably decrease. Since April I have frequently brought to the attention of responsible members of the Government the desirability of setting aside in the budget a definite sum to pay in cash for any additional lands taken. Such a course would aside from its beneficial effect on the budget have a two-fold influence. It would lead the Government to examine most carefully every application for additional "ejidos" as they would be weighing the desirability of that particular application of cash against the desirability of an equal expenditure for new roads, agricultural schools or other requirements. From the point of view of the land owner there would be the assurance that no more land would be taken from him unless it were paid for in cash. This would unquestionably lead to a more active utilization of present holdings for agricultural purposes. This would add not only to the general prosperity of the country, but also to increased government revenues. Such a policy would require changes in existing laws and therefore the action of Congress. President Calles and the heads of finance and agricultural departments have informally expressed their general approval of this proposal and of stopping the issue of additional agrarian bonds beyond those which the Government is already obligated. General Obregón did not feel that the time for such a reform was opportune; and it must be admitted that it would meet with opposition from some leaders of the Obregonista party.[7]

Though Morrow came to Mexico to talk about the debt, he did not come as a debt collector.[8] Morrow's point of view regarding Mexican problems was that the government could not resume payments of any important amount until her house had been put in order and until a sound financial situation had given national affairs a solid basis for growth.[9]

Obregón's assassination brought about a new political crisis which coincided with the economic crisis of depression, as we saw in the last two chapters; and as public revenues decreased under

[7] United States, Department of State, Decimal File Microfilm on Mexico, 812.51/1642, 7–8.

[8] Ross, "Dwight Morrow, Ambassador to Mexico," 278.

[9] See the interchange of letters between Morrow and T. W. Lamont (Lamont was Morrow's old partner in the House of Morgan and Chairman of the International Committee of Bankers on Mexico) in United States, Department of State, *Foreign Relations 1930*, III, 478–486. See also Harold Nicolson's *Dwight Morrow* (New York: Harcourt, Brace and Co., 1935).

Ortiz Rubio, the agrarian program was de-emphasized in order to include land distribution in the public debt. The public debt itself, however, could not be paid off in those trying times, and after projecting 11 per cent of the budget in 1931, little emphasis was placed on payments of the public debt until Rodríguez was able to plan and execute more than a 10 per cent payment in 1933 and a 14 per cent payment in 1934.

Cárdenas kept projections under 10 per cent of the budget during his entire six years, reducing them to as low as 5.6 in 1938, but in actuality he paid up to 14.5 per cent in 1939. After the oil expropriation in 1938 apparently he felt that his government was obliged to allot a larger real share of the federal purse for payment of the national debt than he had projected.

Avila Camacho followed Cárdenas's lead until 1942 when he increased actual debt payments to 22.5 per cent of expenditure, the highest figure since Madero and Huerta had held office in 1912–1913. Avila Camacho's projections did not catch up to actual expenditures until 1944 when he promised to spend one quarter of the budget on the debt, but actual expenditures amounted to only 20 per cent. This high percentage included oil expropriations payments, as we have seen. A high debt outlay at this time was undoubtedly due to the favorable financial position the Mexican government gained during the war when her dollar account rapidly expanded—payment under these conditions was easier for Mexico than at a time when dollars would be scarce. Also, inflation meant that amounts repaid at that time would pay off dollars borrowed in times of deflation.

Miguel Alemán maintained very high projections to pay off the debt, his percentage estimations reaching from 22.1 to 24.5 per cent during the years 1949 to 1952. The projections were promises which did not come true, for he never spent more than 16.5 per cent of the budget on the public debt. The high figure of actual per capita expenditure which Alemán made commonplace after 1948 stemmed from the impetus which Avila Camacho had begun in 1942. Avila Camacho twice spent over 20 pesos of 1950 per capita, and Alemán maintained that rate for five years. Projections of this rate did not catch up to actual expenditure until 1949.

President Ruiz Cortines began the policy of paying even higher amounts in per capita pesos on the foreign debt. He reached 35 pesos in 1955 though percentage and per-capita projections did not nearly begin to approach this figure. The rapid expansion of federal revenues allowed the government to allot a smaller percentage of the budget for the debt, yet maintain a high peso-per-capita rate of payment.

Adolfo López Mateos's projected payments of the debt had absolutely nothing to do with reality. He decreased the projected percentage to 8.4 in 1960 while upping the actual share to 27.3 per cent, a new high for the Revolution. He outdid himself in 1961 by projecting an allotment of 9.5 per cent while spending 36.2 per cent of the budget on the public debt—more than one third of the budget. Porfirio Díaz must have looked down—or up —with benign approval at this action. In 1962 López Mateos cut back this percentage to 27.2 per cent, but it was still high considering the level of poverty and national integration remaining to be accomplished. Payments on the debt in per-capita-pesos of 1950 zoomed to 74.2 in 1960, 95.4 in 1961, and then fell off to 40.0 in 1963, still higher than any other president's payments in Mexican history. As we saw in the last chapter, the payments of López Mateos have been linked directly to his desire to improve Mexico's image as well as reduce the newly expanded federal debt. The giant celebrations of Mexico's one hundred forty years of independence and fifty years of Revolution were important factors in the unprojected decision to pay off debts that were not due. Treasury Minister Antonio Ortiz Mena inadvertently revealed the contradiction in prematurely paying off loans in times of economic crisis when he paid off an Export Import Bank credit of 100 million dollars four years early in 1964. He noted that the loan was made to Mexico during the economic recession of 1959 to maintain the gold reserve of the Bank of Mexico and to satisfy imports of capital goods.[10] But perhaps Ortiz Mena found a way of utilizing loans to pay off debts which are not due in order to attract more investment capital to the country. Either he is a genius or he does not know what he is doing in seeking huge loans while paying out one third of the budget on the debt during a recession. A third alternative is that the pride of López Mateos and the Revo-

[10] *El Día*, May 21, 1964.

lutionary Family necessitated sacrifice of economic considerations in the face of propaganda needs.[11]

TREASURY DEPARTMENT EXPENDITURE

Projected and actual percentage of the budget expended by the Mexican Ministry of the Treasury has declined steadily though per-capita expenditure has generally been from 5 to 7 pesos (Table 5-4). The decreasing importance within government circles of the Treasury Department in percentage terms has not been followed by a decrease in the authority of this agency. The Minister of the Treasury is responsible for formulation of the budget and execution of all direct federal disbursements. Since he also works out the projected income upon which outlay is based, the budget he sends to Congress is generally final. The Department of the Treasury administers the investments category of the budget as well as many items within the category of unclassified expenditure. Therefore, the role of the minister is greater than it appears; and it has actually grown greatly since the 1930's. Investments and unclassified expenditure have been separated into economic categories in order to show consistency in the presentation of administrative and economic expenditure.

Cárdenas and Avila Camacho reduced the projected and actual percentage share of the budget dedicated to Treasury activities to a post-Madero-Huerta low. Alemán further reduced the Treasury's role in order to channel extra funds into economic development. López Mateos reduced the actual share still further to 2.3 per cent in 1960.

PENSIONS

Pensions were included in the Treasury Department's sphere of control until 1922 when they became part of the public debt.

---

[11] The debt which was paid was not projected for payment. Budget item 9202-01 was projected for 1,000,000 pesos, but 879,699,000 were actually spent for "debts from previous fiscal expenditure for categories other than personal services," *Presupuesto y Cuenta 1961*. Perhaps the Mexican government suddenly discovered that many of these debts were due, but this was never reflected in projections. Public discussion of government debt policy took place precisely because presidential style was felt even if the facts were not known. See the comments on debt policy which appeared in "Deuda Externa y Capacidad de Pago," *El Día*, Oct. 25, 1964, and López Mateos's response to such comments in the interview with the press on the La Paz Ferry, *El Día*, Nov. 11, 1964.

TABLE 5-4

Treasury Department Outlay

Year	President[a]	Per Cent Projected	Pesos[b]	Per Cent Actual	Pesos[b]
1869–1870	Juárez	12.1	...	4.0	...
1900–1901	Díaz	12.0	3.5	11.1	3.3
1910–1911	Díaz	8.0	2.7	8.3	2.8
1911–1912	Madero	7.9	2.9	8.7	2.9
1912–1913	Madero/Huerta	7.5	2.9	8.0	3.1
1913–1914	Huerta	6.1	...	...	...
1914–1915	Huerta	7.0	...	...	...
1917	Carranza	4.4	...	8.0	...
1918	Carranza	7.9	2.4	10.2	1.8
1919	Carranza	7.6	3.2	14.7	1.8
1920	Carranza/De la Huerta	9.0	3.7	13.5	3.4
1921	Obregón	7.4	3.9	10.3	4.9
1922	Obregón	7.3	7.0	6.5	3.7
1923	Obregón	6.9	5.5	9.5	5.1
1924	Obregón	7.5	5.3	9.9	6.4
1925	Calles	8.7	5.6	10.5	7.0
1926	Calles	8.8	5.9	15.4	11.0
1927	Calles	9.0	6.4	9.3	6.4
1928	Calles	9.5	6.3	9.5	6.2
1929	Portes Gil	9.8	6.3	10.0	6.2
1930	Portes Gil/Ortiz Rubio	10.0	6.3	10.9	6.6
1931	Ortiz Rubio	9.6	6.9	11.8	6.4
1932	Ortiz Rubio	10.4	5.7	9.6	5.3
1933	Rodríguez	11.6	6.0	17.5	10.3
1934	Rodríguez	11.4	6.3	15.4	9.3
1935	Cárdenas	10.3	6.3	13.9	9.3
1936	Cárdenas	9.8	5.8	8.6	7.2
1937	Cárdenas	8.8	5.0	7.3	6.0
1938	Cárdenas	6.9	4.6	8.6	6.9
1939	Cárdenas	6.5	4.4	6.1	5.4
1940	Cárdenas	6.5	4.4	7.9	7.2
1941	Avila Camacho	7.8	5.3	6.6	6.2
1942	Avila Camacho	6.9	4.7	6.6	6.7
1943	Avila Camacho	5.4	3.8	6.6	7.1
1944	Avila Camacho	4.0	3.3	4.9	5.4
1945	Avila Camacho	4.3	2.9	5.8	6.1
1946	Avila Camacho	4.6	3.1	5.1	5.0

TABLE 5-4 (continued)

Treasury Department Outlay

Year	President[a]	Per Cent Projected	Pesos[b]	Per Cent Actual	Pesos[b]
1947	Alemán	4.1	3.6	4.0	4.6
1948	Alemán	4.4	4.9	4.6	6.2
1949	Alemán	3.3	3.8	4.1	7.0
1950	Alemán	3.4	3.6	4.0	5.4
1951	Alemán	3.4	3.4	3.5	5.3
1952	Alemán	2.8	3.1	2.6	4.6
1953	Ruiz Cortines	2.9	3.2	3.1	4.5
1954	Ruiz Cortines	4.3	4.9	2.9	5.4
1955	Ruiz Cortines	3.8	4.3	2.8	4.9
1956	Ruiz Cortines	3.3	4.0	2.7	5.0
1957	Ruiz Cortines	3.4	4.3	2.7	5.1
1958	Ruiz Cortines	3.1	4.0	2.6	5.3
1959	López Mateos	4.1	5.7	2.6	5.4
1960	López Mateos	4.0	5.5	2.3	6.3
1961	López Mateos	3.8	5.4	2.4	6.3
1962	López Mateos	3.6	5.5	2.8	7.0
1963	López Mateos	3.9	6.2	3.4	7.9

[a] Slash indicates latter person administered actual funds.
[b] In pesos per capita of 1950.
SOURCE: See Appendix B.

Since 1948 they have been included in *erogaciones adicionales*. Pensions are presented here in Table 5-5 to offer a view of what the bureaucracy costs the official party which administers state finances. Adequate medical care is relatively new for the bureaucrats and it is separated here as a social cost of government. The new Institute of Security and Social Services of the State Workers (ISSSTE) is clearly divided in the budget to show what amount of money goes for pensions and what amount goes for medical services. The former amount of money is administered with enlarged scope by ISSSTE, which has replaced the old Dirección de Pensiones.

Pensions were a fairly important share of Juárez's budget of

TABLE 5-5

Pensions

Year	President[a]	Per Cent Projected	Pesos[b]	Per Cent Actual	Pesos[b]
1869–1870	Juárez	6.3	...	4.0	...
1900–1901	Díaz	1.3	.4	1.4	.4
1910–1911	Díaz	.9	.3	.8	.3
1911–1912	Madero	.8	.3	.9	.3
1912–1913	Madero/Huerta	.8	.3	.9	.3
1913–1914	Huerta	.7	...	...	...
1914–1915	Huerta	.7	...	...	...
1917	Carranza	1.2	...	2.1	...
1918	Carranza	1.2	.4	3.0	.5
1919	Carranza	1.1	.5	1.4	.2
1920	Carranza/De la Huerta	1.0	.4	2.7	.7
1921	Obregón	.9	.5	1.6	.8
1922	Obregón	.6	.6	2.0	1.1
1923	Obregón	1.3	1.0	1.7	.9
1924	Obregón	1.2	.8	1.7	1.1
1925	Calles	2.1	1.3	1.9	1.3
1926	Calles	1.8	1.2	1.6	1.1
1927	Calles	1.9	1.3	1.8	1.2
1928	Calles	1.9	1.3	2.1	1.4
1929	Portes Gil	1.9	1.2	2.1	1.3
1930	Portes Gil/Ortiz Rubio	1.9	1.2	2.3	1.4
1931	Ortiz Rubio	2.0	1.4	2.4	1.3
1932	Ortiz Rubio	3.1	1.7	3.5	1.9
1933	Rodríguez	3.0	1.5	3.5	2.1
1934	Rodríguez	2.7	1.5	2.5	1.5
1935	Cárdenas	2.4	1.5	2.2	1.5
1936	Cárdenas	1.2	.7	1.6	1.3
1937	Cárdenas	2.3	1.3	1.4	1.1
1938	Cárdenas	1.9	1.3	1.3	1.1
1939	Cárdenas	1.9	1.3	1.2	1.1
1940	Cárdenas	1.4	.9	1.2	1.1
1941	Avila Camacho	2.2	1.5	1.3	1.2
1942	Avila Camacho	1.2	.8	.8	.8
1943	Avila Camacho	.4	.3	.9	1.0
1944	Avila Camacho	.1	.1	.8	.9
1945	Avila Camacho	.9	.6	.6	.6
1946	Avila Camacho	.8	.5	.9	.9

TABLE 5-5 (continued)

Pensions

Year	President[a]	Per Cent Pro- jected	Pesos[b]	Per Cent Actual	Pesos[b]
1947	Alemán	.6	.5	.9	1.0
1948	Alemán	1.4	1.6	.5	.7
1949	Alemán	1.5	1.7	.9	1.5
1950	Alemán	1.4	1.5	1.3	1.7
1951	Alemán	1.5	1.5	1.3	2.0
1952	Alemán	1.8	2.0	1.2	2.1
1953	Ruiz Cortines	1.9	2.1	1.3	1.9
1954	Ruiz Cortines	1.9	2.2	1.3	2.4
1955	Ruiz Cortines	1.8	2.0	1.2	2.1
1956	Ruiz Cortines	1.8	2.2	1.2	2.2
1957	Ruiz Cortines	2.2	2.8	1.7	3.2
1958	Ruiz Cortines	2.5	3.2	1.6	3.3
1959	López Mateos	2.7	3.7	1.5	3.1
1960	López Mateos	2.5	3.5	1.0	2.7
1961	López Mateos	1.4	2.0	1.3	3.4
1962	López Mateos	1.2	1.8	2.0	5.0
1963	López Mateos	1.8	2.9	2.4	5.6

[a] Slash indicates latter person administered actual funds.
[b] In pesos per capita of 1950.
SOURCE: See Appendix B.

1869–1870, 6.3 and 4.0 per cent, projected and actual respectively. Projected expenditure had decreased by 1900 to about 1 per cent and it remained at that point until 1925. Actual allotments ran double that figure after 1917, even under Carranza. In spite of financial problems, Carranza paid out .5 pesos per capita (in 1950 prices) in 1918, more than anyone since the Revolution started. During the depression of the early 1930's the projected percentage of the budget devoted to pensions increased to about 3 per cent in order to maintain the rate of pesos per capita to which the retired bureaucracy had become accustomed during the late 1920's. In fact, the actual pesos-per-capita expenditure went up to 2 pesos per capita during those trying years of economic recession. Cárdenas reduced pensions, in percentage and in per-capita terms; 1 per cent and 1 peso per capita became the standard toward the end of Cárdenas's term.

During World War II pensioners fared badly, at least on paper. Avila Camacho cut appropriations for them to .1 per cent of the budget in 1944, probably an all-time low. Actual results followed the Cárdenas standard, though pensions were reduced to .6 pesos per capita the following year.

Alemán and Ruiz Cortines changed this pattern, for, as gossip went, the only friends the government had were in the bureaucracy. Whether or not this was true, projected and actual pesos per capita were increased to about 2 pesos per capita after 1950. At any rate, the fact that these governments reduced administrative expense to a relative minimum while increasing pension allocations is surprising.

The ideology of balanced revolution has spurred a considerable actual increase in per-capita expenditure for pensions—3 to 5 pesos has been the figure since 1957. Apparently López Mateos decided to upgrade government service, for the fact that pensions may now provide a semblance of a good living standard during years of retirement could attract a better grade of people into government service. This argument could be used for the period since 1950. Or one may simply note that the lower realms of the bureaucracy are finally sharing honestly in government financial activity due to the greater amount of money which the executive has to spend. The figures do not reveal motives in this case.

MINOR ADMINISTRATIVE EXPENSE

Remaining administrative activity has generally played a minor role in the federal budget. Agencies which have had comparatively little percentage of federal funds include the Interior Department, Ministry of Foreign Relations, Attorney General's Office, and Ministry of the Presidency (Office of the Presidency until 1959). General Expenses, as treated here, have covered expenditure for the Department of General Supply (1919–1924), the Department of Press and Publicity (1937–1939), and the Ministry of National Resources (1947–present). Unclassified expenditure has been low in percentage, as have been the expenses of the legislature and the judiciary.

Though the budgetary categories in Table 5-6 have not been important in federal outlay, several interesting observations can be made. Actually the legislature always has received a larger percentage of the budget than the judiciary, despite the fact that the courts function throughout the country all year long. This situation calls attention to the low position of the judiciary in Mexican life. In the past it has been a political arm;[12] and except in run-of-the-mill business, it is still subject to political pressure.[13]

The predicament of federal judges attempting to justify prison sentences of up to sixteen years for those labor leaders who led strikes in the early years of López Mateos's government was ludicrous. In order to break threats to the official party's captured labor movement, López Mateos charged dissident elements with "social dissolution," a law originally passed during World War II to jail Nazi elements. The real charge against the strikers was that they were Communists. Filomeno Mata, a famous newspaperman from a famous family which had led the protest in the press against Porfirio Díaz, noted upon his release from jail:

The Great Dictator [Porfirio Díaz] never left anyone without a reply, but you, Mr. President, did not deign to answer me nor even to deny me the solicited audience.

The horrendous process against the railroad [strikers] and members of political parties . . . has culminated with the most cruel and inhuman sentences that any judge might execute, evading the spirit and the letter of the law, violating rights and guarantees, altering the truth, twistedly interpreting the facts and justifiable circumstances of the acts . . . which [are] totally legal in the light of the provisions of the Fundamental Charter of the Republic. . . .[14]

I was not set free as an act of justice. I was thrown into the street in order to die outside the jail, even if on the sidewalk, because the Government does not want a dead politician, but political prisoners.[15]

Mata may well be a Communist and he may well have illegally threatened the official party's power, but he was not tried on these charges, and his effective protest, along with those of others, con-

[12] Gruening, *Mexico and Its Heritage*, 497–512.

[13] For an indictment of López Mateos's judiciary, see Filomeno Mata, "Carta Abierta a los Periodistas y Escritores y a la Opinión Pública," *Política*, Sept. 1, 1963, D-E. A neutral account of how the judiciary operates administratively is provided by Tucker, *The Mexican Government Today*, Chapter 8.

[14] Filomeno Mata, "Por la Libertad de los Presos Políticos; Carta Abierta . . . al C. Presidente de la República, *Política*, Jan. 1, 1964, 12–13.

[15] *Política*, Nov. 1, 1963.

TABLE 5-6

Minor Administrative Allocations in Percentage Terms

Year	Legislature		Presidency		Judiciary		Foreign Relations	
	Projected	Actual	Projected	Actual	Projected	Actual	Projected	Actual
1869–1970	4.1	4.0	.3	.2	1.4	1.5	.8	.7
1900–1901	1.7	1.6	.3	.2	.9	.8	1.0	1.5
1910–1911	1.6	1.7	.3	.2	.6	.6	1.8	2.4
1911–1912	1.4	1.4	.2	.3	.6	.6	2.0	2.3
1912–1913	1.2	1.6	.2	.3	.6	.6	1.9	1.9
1913–1914	1.6	..	.2	..	.5	..	1.6	..
1914–1915	1.6	..	.3	..	.6	..	1.9	..
1917	1.5	2.3	.2	.4	.5	.6	1.2	1.0
1918	1.6	2.5	.6	.6	.8	1.1	1.9	2.2
1919	1.5	1.2	.6	1.0	.8	1.8	1.7	3.6
1920	1.8	2.9	.5	.6	1.0	1.6	2.2	3.2
1921	2.0	2.8	.5	.8	1.0	1.0	2.2	2.9
1922	1.7	2.6	.6	.8	.7	1.0	2.2	2.3
1923	2.0	3.2	.5	.6	.8	1.0	1.9	2.1
1924	2.3	2.8	.5	.9	.9	1.0	1.8	2.0
1925	2.9	3.8	.5	.6	1.1	1.0	1.9	1.7
1926	3.6	3.3	.6	.6	1.4	1.1	1.9	1.8
1927	2.9	2.5	.5	.8	1.2	1.2	1.9	1.9
1928	2.1	2.1	.5	1.4	1.2	1.1	2.3	2.0
1929	2.2	2.2	.5	.6	1.3	1.3	2.2	2.2
1930	2.2	1.9	.4	.5	2.3	1.3	2.2	2.3
1931	1.6	2.2	.7	.8	2.2	1.6	2.0	2.3
1932	1.8	2.1	.7	.8	1.3	1.3	2.2	2.1
1933	2.2	2.6	.7	.7	1.3	1.2	2.0	1.9
1934	2.0	2.2	.8	.7	1.2	1.1	1.9	1.7
1935	1.8	1.9	.5	.5	1.1	1.0	1.5	1.5
1936	1.8	1.6	.5	.4	1.4	1.0	1.7	1.3

TABLE 5-6 (continued)

Minor Administrative Allocations in Percentage Terms

Year	Legislature		Presidency		Judiciary		Foreign Relations	
	Projected	Actual	Projected	Actual	Projected	Actual	Projected	Actual
1937	1.8	1.3	.5	.3	1.2	.8	1.4	1.1
1938	1.3	1.3	.4	.4	1.0	.8	1.0	.8
1939	1.2	1.5	.3	.3	.9	.7	1.0	1.4
1940	1.2	1.7	.3	.3	.9	1.1	.9	.6
1941	1.1	2.2	.3	.3	.8	.6	.9	.8
1942	1.2	1.4	.3	.2	.9	.6	.9	.6
1943	1.0	1.1	.2	.1	.7	.4	.8	.5
1944	.8	.9	.2	.1	.5	.3	.5	.5
1945	.9	1.2	.1	.3	.6	.4	.6	.5
1946	1.0	1.3	.1	.6	.6	.4	.6	.6
1947	.8	1.0	.1	.6	.4	.4	1.5	1.0
1948	.6	.9	.1	.5	.3	.3	1.1	.9
1949	.7	.7	.1	.1	.3	.2	1.3	.9
1950	.7	.9	.2	.1	.4	.3	1.5	1.1
1951	.6	.8	.1	.3	.5	.3	1.5	.9
1952	.5	.5	.1	.2	.5	.3	1.3	.8
1953	.6	.6	.1	.2	.5	.4	1.3	.9
1954	.6	.4	.1	.2	.5	.3	1.2	.9
1955	.5	.4	.1	.2	.5	.3	1.4	.9
1956	.5	.5	.1	.2	.5	.3	1.3	.9
1957	.4	.5	.1	.2	.4	.3	1.2	.8
1958	.4	.5	.1	.2	.4	.3	1.1	.8
1959	.5	.4	.2	.5	.5	.3	1.1	.8
1960	.5	.3	.2	.9	.4	.2	1.1	.6
1961	.5	.3	.2	.4	.5	.2	1.1	.6
1962	.5	.4	.2	.6	.4	.3	1.1	.8
1963	.5	.4	.2	.8	.4	.3	1.1	.8

TABLE 5-6 (continued)

Minor Administrative Allocations in Percentage Terms

Year	Interior		Attorney General		General Administration		Erogaciones Adicionales	
	Projected	Actual	Projected	Actual	Projected	Actual	Projected	Actual
1869–1970	5.6	5.4	1.4	1.6	—	34.7	—	—
1900–1901	7.1	7.0	1.2	1.2	—	—	—	—
1910–1911	10.7	9.8	1.6	2.1	—	—	—	—
1911–1912	12.3	12.5	1.6	1.7	—	—	—	—
1912–1913	11.2	11.3	1.7	1.7	—	—	—	—
1913–1914	12.1	..	1.4	..	—	—	—	—
1914–1915	8.6	..	1.4	..	—	—	—	—
1917	2.2	1.2	.2	.2	—	—	—	—
1918	.7	.8	.3	.4	—	.2	—	—
1919	.7	2.3	.3	.5	.6	.1	—	—
1920	.9	1.9	.5	.6	.5	.4	—	—
1921	.8	1.2	.5	.5	.2	.1	—	—
1922	2.1	1.8	.4	.5	.1	.1	—	—
1923	2.4	1.8	.3	.5	.1	.1	—	—
1924	1.8	1.7	.3	.4	.1	.1	—	—
1925	1.2	1.2	.3	.3	—	—	—	—
1926	1.2	1.1	.3	.3	—	—	—	—
1927	1.1	1.0	.4	.4	—	—	—	—
1928	1.1	1.0	.4	.2	—	—	—	—
1929	.9	.8	.4	.4	—	—	—	—
1930	1.1	1.0	.5	.5	—	—	—	—
1931	.9	1.1	.5	.6	—	—	—	—
1932	1.0	1.2	.6	.5	—	—	—	—
1933	1.1	1.0	.6	.5	—	—	—	—
1934	1.2	1.0	.5	.5	—	—	—	—
1935	1.0	1.1	.4	.4	—	—	—	—
1936	1.4	1.1	.5	.3	—	—	—	—

TABLE 5-6 (continued)

Minor Administrative Allocations in Percentage Terms

Year	Interior		Attorney General		General Administration		Erogaciones Adicionales	
	Projected	Actual	Projected	Actual	Projected	Actual	Projected	Actual
1937	1.2	.9	.4	.3	—	.5	—	—
1938	1.7	1.0	.3	.3	.6	.7	—	—
1939	1.3	1.2	.3	.2	.4	.5	—	—
1940	1.3	1.0	.3	.2	—	—	—	—
1941	1.6	1.4	.3	.2	—	—	—	—
1942	1.7	1.9	.3	.2	—	—	—	—
1943	1.3	1.1	.2	.2	—	—	—	—
1944	1.1	.9	.2	.1	—	—	—	—
1945	1.2	.8	.2	.2	—	—	—	—
1946	1.1	.6	.2	.2	—	—	—	—
1947	.7	.5	.2	.1	.3	.3	.1	1.0
1948	.6	.5	.2	.1	.3	.3	.2	.9
1949	.6	.5	.2	.1	.3	.2	.1	.3
1950	.6	.6	.2	.1	.2	.2	.1	1.8
1951	.7	.6	.1	.1	.2	.2	—	1.7
1952	.6	.6	.2	.1	.2	.2	.1	4.5
1953	.6	.5	.1	.1	.2	.2	.2	.5
1954	.7	.5	.2	.1	.2	.2	.2	1.2
1955	.7	.5	.2	.1	.2	.3	.2	1.9
1956	.6	.4	.2	.1	.2	.4	.1	2.0
1957	.6	.5	.1	.1	.1	.2	.2	1.8
1958	.6	.4	.2	.1	.2	.2	.1	3.0
1959	.4	.3	.2	.1	.3	.7	.2	2.1
1960	.6	.3	.2	.1	.6	.9	.2	2.2
1961	.6	.3	.2	.1	.7	.2	1.1	2.0
1962	.5	.4	.2	.1	.8	.9	2.1	2.4
1963	.6	.4	.2	.1	1.1	1.0	1.7	2.9

SOURCE: See Appendix B.

demned the Mexican judiciary for sentencing political prisoners under a vague law. After fifty years of Revolution, the judiciary is still under the thumb of the executive.

The comparative amount of actual pesos per capita which the presidency, judiciary, and legislature have received in sample years is quite revealing. Under Madero, in 1911–1912 the legislature received .5 pesos per capita, the judiciary received .2 pesos, and the presidency was allotted .1 pesos. In 1931 comparative allotment of funds was, respectively, 1.2, .9, and .4 pesos. In 1940 the figures were 1.5, 1.0, and .3 pesos. Alemán did not really reduce the legislature by 1949 (it received 1.2 pesos per capita) but the judiciary had fallen to .3 pesos, and the presidency had risen to .8 pesos. Under López Mateos, in 1963 the totals were .9, .7, and 1.9 pesos per capita. The presidency received 2.5 pesos per capita in 1960 as part of the expanded role of central government planning and co-ordination of direct and indirect public expenditure.[16] Also the presidency published some valuable statiscal studies in addition to reams of propaganda.[17]

Though the ideology of different phases of the Revolution has allotted different amounts to administrative categories of the budget, total administration has received increased pesos per capita, especially since the 1950's. Even the category which receives the least percentage of the budget is relatively wealthy compared to days gone by. The Attorney General's office, for example, received 2.3 pesos per capita in 1953, almost as much as the highly heralded agricultural credit received in 1938 under Cárdenas. But let us turn to economic expenditure in order to compare it more fully to administrative outlay.

[16] For a discussion of the Ministry of the Presidency's role in state planning see Miguel Wionczek, "Planeación Formal Incompleta: El Caso de México," in Everett E. Hagen (ed.), *Planeación del Desarrollo Económico,* tr. by F. Rosenzweig (México, D. F.: Fondo de Cultura Económica, 1964), 189–229.

[17] See, for example, *50 Años en Cifras,* and México, Secretaría de la Presidencia, *México Inversión Pública Federal, 1925–1963.*

6

Economic Expenditure

The expenditure considered here represents all the federal funds including capital investment allocated to agencies or budgetary categories which deal directly with the economic life of the nation. Funds spent on price supports, for example, may be classified as a social expenditure as well as an economic expenditure, but since they primarily promote economic stability, they are classified as an economic expenditure for the purpose of this work. Consistency is the important factor here.

Year-by-year economic budgetary policy of the Revolution is presented in Table 6-1. The emergence of the active state is most clearly represented by the increase of actual economic expenditure in 1936. Though economic outlay had risen to 32.5 per cent in 1925 when Calles founded the Bank of Mexico, a marked step up from the percentage of 18.4 actual outlay in 1924, this rate was not maintained. Ortiz Rubio approached it in 1930 and 1932, but it was down to 23.2 during the year of 1934 immediately before Cárdenas took over budgeting for 1935. Cárdenas actually disbursed 31.6 per cent of the budget on the economy in 1935, and in the following year he reached 42.6 per cent. Cárdenas had planned to spend but 30.6 per cent on the economy in 1936, and projections caught up to his actual percentage of disbursements in only one year, 1938. Presidents from Cárdenas to Ruiz Cortines consistently underestimated their projected emphasis on economic development. Apparently they budgeted their projected funds to cover all aspects of government, and pumped most new income into economic expenditure. López Mateos reversed this trend; he spent less than projected in 1961 and 1962.

TABLE 6-I

Economic Expenditure: Percentage Share and Pesos
Per Capita Since 1910

Year	President[a]	Per Cent Projected	Pesos[b]	Per Cent Actual	Pesos[b]
1869–1870	Juárez	19.1	...	5.0	...
1900–1901	Díaz	14.3	4.2	15.3	4.5
1910–1911	Díaz	19.1	6.6	16.7	5.7
1911–1912	Madero	19.1	6.9	17.6	5.9
1912–1913	Madero/Huerta	15.8	6.1	15.2	5.9
1913–1914	Huerta	13.7	...	...	...
1914–1915	Huerta	17.0	...	...	...
1917	Carranza	12.8	...	12.7	...
1918	Carranza	16.6	5.1	17.4	3.1
1919	Carranza	15.7	6.5	18.8	2.3
1920	Carranza/De la Huerta	15.1	6.3	17.2	4.4
1921	Obregón	14.5	7.7	16.9	8.1
1922	Obregón	25.9	24.7	18.0	10.2
1923	Obregón	20.1	16.0	18.3	9.8
1924	Obregón	14.3	10.0	18.4	11.9
1925	Calles	14.4	9.2	32.5	21.5
1926	Calles	20.0	13.4	21.5	15.4
1927	Calles	25.1	17.7	22.2	15.3
1928	Calles	26.3	17.3	23.1	15.1
1929	Portes Gil	24.8	15.9	23.2	14.3
1930	Portes Gil/Ortiz Rubio	26.6	16.9	29.3	17.6
1931	Ortiz Rubio	27.1	19.4	26.7	14.5
1932	Ortiz Rubio	30.3	16.7	28.4	15.6
1933	Rodríguez	21.1	10.9	20.3	12.0
1934	Rodríguez	22.8	12.6	23.2	14.0
1935	Cárdenas	28.9	17.7	31.6	21.1
1936	Cárdenas	30.6	18.0	42.6	35.6
1937	Cárdenas	26.9	15.3	41.9	34.2
1938	Cárdenas	37.1	24.9	37.0	29.9
1939	Cárdenas	31.8	21.7	38.2	34.1
1940	Cárdenas	27.8	18.7	34.1	31.0
1941	Avila Camacho	23.9	16.2	37.0	34.8
1942	Avila Camacho	22.8	15.4	29.4	30.0
1943	Avila Camacho	29.2	20.5	39.0	41.7
1944	Avila Camacho	32.2	26.9	43.2	47.6
1945	Avila Camacho	38.6	26.0	41.4	43.7

TABLE 6-1 (continued)

Economic Expenditure: Percentage Share and Pesos Per Capita Since 1910

Year	President[a]	Per Cent Pro- jected	Pesos[b]	Per Cent Actual	Pesos[b]
1946	Avila Camacho	37.7	25.3	45.4	44.9
1947	Alemán	40.6	36.0	45.8	52.3
1948	Alemán	43.0	48.2	49.5	66.9
1949	Alemán	36.9	42.1	56.7	94.9
1950	Alemán	38.2	40.7	49.2	66.1
1951	Alemán	37.4	37.6	53.3	80.7
1952	Alemán	39.2	43.2	56.9	101.3
1953	Ruiz Cortines	37.9	41.3	54.0	77.7
1954	Ruiz Cortines	43.1	49.1	57.9	108.2
1955	Ruiz Cortines	44.2	49.8	50.5	89.0
1956	Ruiz Cortines	46.6	56.6	52.4	97.6
1957	Ruiz Cortines	45.6	57.2	50.5	94.6
1958	Ruiz Cortines	45.4	58.6	51.0	104.1
1959	López Mateos	40.9	56.4	44.8	93.2
1960	López Mateos	40.1	55.5	42.1	114.4
1961	López Mateos	39.2	56.0	31.8	83.8
1962	López Mateos	36.8	56.0	35.1	87.8
1963	López Mateos	37.2	59.2	41.3	96.6

[a] Slash indicates latter person administered actual funds.
[b] In pesos per capita of 1950.
SOURCE: See Appendix B.

In 1936 Cárdenas actually spent 35.6 pesos per capita on economic expense. This was treble the amount spent in 1924, twelve years earlier. Twelve years later this amount had nearly doubled when it reached 66.9 pesos per capita in 1948 under Alemán. The following year Alemán increased this outlay to 94.9 pesos, a figure which became a high for actual expenditure. No president, before or after Ruiz Cortines in 1958, had ever planned to spend more than about 60 pesos per capita.

The highest percentages actually dedicated to economic life came under Ruiz Cortines and Alemán: 57.9 in 1954 and 56.9 in 1952. López Mateos cut these figures back to 31.8 by 1961 and

TABLE 6-2

Agriculture and Irrigation

Year	President[a]	Per Cent Projected	Pesos[b]	Per Cent Actual	Pesos[b]
1869–1870	Juárez	.7	...	1.7	...
1900–1901	Díaz	1.6	.5	1.9	5.6
1910–1911	Díaz	3.8	1.3	3.3	1.1
1911–1912	Madero	3.9	1.4	3.5	1.1
1912–1913	Madero/Huerta	3.7	1.4	3.2	1.1
1913–1914	Huerta	3.1	...	...	...
1914–1915	Huerta	1.7	...	...	...
1917	Carranza	2.2	...	2.2	...
1918	Carranza	3.7	1.1	2.4	1.1
1919	Carranza	3.0	1.2	2.9	3.5
1920	Carranza/De la Huerta	2.4	1.0	3.0	.8
1921	Obregón	2.1	1.1	4.1	2.0
1922	Obregón	10.1	9.6	4.5	2.6
1923	Obregón	6.1	4.9	5.0	2.7
1924	Obregón	3.6	2.5	5.4	3.5
1925	Calles	3.5	2.2	4.3	2.9
1926	Calles	5.0	3.3	8.6	6.1
1927	Calles	10.8	7.6	9.0	6.2
1928	Calles	10.8	7.1	10.8	7.0
1929	Portes Gil	8.1	5.2	7.3	4.5
1930	Portes Gil/Ortiz Rubio	7.7	4.9	8.5	5.1
1931	Ortiz Rubio	7.1	5.1	6.7	3.6
1932	Ortiz Rubio	7.5	4.1	7.0	3.8
1933	Rodríguez	6.1	3.1	5.7	3.4
1934	Rodríguez	6.1	3.4	5.5	3.3
1935	Cárdenas	5.8	3.5	4.7	3.1
1936	Cárdenas	6.0	3.5	7.4	6.2
1937	Cárdenas	5.5	3.1	8.4	6.9
1938	Cárdenas	9.8	6.6	7.8	6.3
1939	Cárdenas	9.1	6.2	8.3	7.4
1940	Cárdenas	7.2	4.9	6.6	6.0
1941	Avila Camacho	4.7	3.2	3.3	3.1
1942	Avila Camacho	3.7	2.5	2.2	2.2
1943	Avila Camacho	13.4	9.4	8.4	9.0
1944	Avila Camacho	9.7	8.1	8.1	8.9
1945	Avila Camacho	17.3	11.2	10.1	10.7
1946	Avila Camacho	18.5	12.4	11.7	11.6

TABLE 6-2 (continued)

Agriculture and Irrigation

Year	President[a]	Per Cent Projected	Pesos[b]	Per Cent Actual	Pesos[b]
1947	Alemán	15.2	13.4	12.5	14.3
1948	Alemán	11.6	13.0	9.7	13.1
1949	Alemán	10.9	12.7	7.6	13.0
1950	Alemán	10.3	10.8	8.5	11.4
1951	Alemán	11.4	11.5	8.1	12.3
1952	Alemán	11.3	12.4	10.3	18.3
1953	Ruiz Cortines	10.9	11.8	11.1	15.9
1954	Ruiz Cortines	12.2	13.9	10.1	18.8
1955	Ruiz Cortines	9.5	10.7	8.7	15.3
1956	Ruiz Cortines	13.4	16.2	7.5	13.9
1957	Ruiz Cortines	12.4	15.5	7.3	13.7
1958	Ruiz Cortines	10.7	13.8	6.7	13.7
1959	López Mateos	9.9	13.7	6.3	13.2
1960	López Mateos	8.6	11.9	4.8	13.0
1961	López Mateos	8.9	12.7	4.8	12.6
1962	López Mateos	7.7	11.7	6.7	16.7
1963	López Mateos	7.7	12.2	8.0	18.7

[a] Slash indicates latter person administered actual funds.
[b] In pesos per capita of 1950.
SOURCE: See Appendix B.

raised economic emphasis only to 41.3 thereafter. Mexico has come a long way in state intervention in the economy since the days when Juárez actually spent only 5 per cent on this category. After 1947, even projected expenditure, which has never fluctuated in percentage terms like actual figures, has generally been more than double what Juárez and Díaz planned to spend. Components of these totals offer some fascinating revelations.

AGRICULTURE AND IRRIGATION

Since Mexico had a predominantly agrarian economy during the first sixty years of this century, expenditure for agriculture and irrigation has been vital to national development. Irrigation work sponsored by the federal government was begun in 1926, and the National Irrigation Commission was raised to cabinet rank as the Ministry of Hydraulic Resources under Alemán in 1947. Prior to that time irrigation expenditure was included in the Ministry of Agriculture, therefore, total outlay for these two related items is combined in Table 6-2. Funds for potable water and sewage disposal have been deducted from expenditure of the Ministry of Hydraulic Resources as they constitute a social expense.

The watershed in Mexican governmental policy does not fall in either the Alemán or the Cárdenas periods as often has been thought. Budgetary emphasis on agriculture and irrigation came in the later Calles period. In 1927 and 1928 Calles projected 10.8 per cent of the budget for this type of economic development. Such projections were far above previous plans for the countryside, except for the 10.1 per cent which Obregón had hoped to spend in 1922. Harsh realities of policy-making in Mexico in the early 1920's stopped Obregón from this kind of development, but by the late 1920's Calles could carry out his own plans for economic growth. The rebellion of 1927 shaved 1.8 per cent off Calles's projections, but in 1928 no obstacles barred his way to spending the amount budgeted. Calles doubled the percentage which Obregón had spent, and he tripled Madero's actual percentage of disbursement for agriculture and irrigation. Calles placed his emphasis on development of the land rather than distribution of the land, and he set one pattern that has held to this day. Contrariwise, presidents who have emphasized land distribution generally have placed less importance on funds dedicated for agricultural and irrigation improvements.

The troubled political period from 1928 to 1934 generally followed the above characterization. Portes Gil gave away land at a rapid rate, as we will see in Part II, and therefore he reduced the percentage of the federal purse channeled into agriculture and irrigation. During the depression Ortiz Rubio did not distribute much land, but he did actually spend 8.5 per cent of the budget for agricultural development. Interim President Rodríguez was an exception, for he was too busy drafting a new agrarian code and steering Mexico through new elections to irrigate or to distribute much land, and at any rate he was not a devotee of great state intervention in economic affairs, despite his public pronouncements. Rodríguez was willing to emphasize social expenditure, but mainly he was an administrative president.

Cárdenas made a slow start at supporting the Ministry of Agriculture and its National Irrigation Commission, but from 1937 to 1939 he actually did devote about 8 per cent of the budget to these agencies, up to 2 per cent less than he had projected in 1938. Cárdenas's interest waned in his last year and the stage was prepared for diminution during the first two years of Avila Camacho's regime when the actual percentage fell to 3.3 and 2.2 per cent.

As the dream of land distribution began to fade before the prospect of economic development, Avila Camacho increased actual expenditure for irrigation to about 8 per cent in 1943 and 1944. Projections rose in 1945–1946 and reached the high for Mexico's history before or since, 18.5 per cent in 1946, though only about 11 per cent was actually spent during these two years.

Miguel Alemán turned away from land reform to increase actual outlay for agriculture and irrigation to 12.5 per cent during his first year of office, and he maintained this rate at about 8 to 11 per cent for most of the rest of his presidency. His protégé, Ruiz Cortines, maintained this percentage until 1955 when a decline in agriculture and irrigation emphasis occurred. By 1961 actual outlay fell to 4.8 per cent.

Though Calles began irrigation programs of importance and pushed agricultural development, the size of federal income meant that he would actually spend only 7 pesos per capita. This figure was not surpassed until 1939, and after 1943 the Ministry of Agriculture received such a great share of its funds solely for irrigation that a separate ministry was created in 1947. In 1947 some 11.4 pesos were actually expended for irrigation and 2.9 pesos went to agriculture. Since 1926, irrigation has received the yearly emphasis presented in Table 6-3. These figures are extracted from Table 6-2.

The Ministry of Irrigation has actually received much more than the Ministry of Agriculture since 1947 (the latter figures may be obtained by subtracting the figures presented in Table 6-3 from those in Table 6-2). This has been the pattern since 1934, for apparently all governments have been willing to spend only small amounts on agricultural research and dissemination of ideas and techniques throughout Mexico. Though there has been much talk

TABLE 6-3

Expenditure for Irrigation, 1926–1963 (included in Table 6-2)

A.

Funds Expended by the National Irrigation Commission, 1926–1946

Year	Per Cent Projected	Pesos[a]	Per Cent Actual	Pesos[a]
1926	3.3	2.2	1.6	1.1
1927	6.3	4.4	4.6	3.2
1928	6.9	4.5	6.9	4.5
1929	4.1	2.6	3.5	2.2
1930	3.7	2.3	4.4	2.6
1931	3.8	2.7	2.3	1.2
1932	3.4	1.9	3.1	1.7
1933	2.6	1.3	2.5	1.5
1934[c]	3.5	1.9	3.0	1.8
1935	3.0	1.8	2.8	1.9
1936	3.0	1.8	4.9	4.1
1937	2.8	1.6	6.2	5.1
1938	7.2	4.8	5.1	4.1
1939[d]	6.1	4.2	5.6	5.0
1940	4.5	3.0	4.5[b]	4.1[b]
1941	1.7	1.2	1.0[b]	.9[b]
1942	...[e]	...[e]	...[e]	...[e]
1943	9.9	7.0	6.3	6.7
1944	7.3	6.1	6.1[b]	6.7[b]
1945	14.4	9.7	7.9[b]	8.3[b]
1946	15.8	10.6	9.7[b]	9.6[b]

[a] In pesos of 1950 per capita.

[b] Actual expenditure may not be exact since the projected budget does not provide an accurate key to changes in actual accounts.

[c] Tamayo (see source below) quotes figures given by Emilio Alanís Patiño, but gives no citation.

[d] Figures do not include works in the Valley of Mexico.

[e] Figures not included in *Presupuesto* and not clear in *Cuenta Pública*.

SOURCES: Jorge L. Tamayo, "Inversiones Gubernamentales en Regadío," *Revista de Economía* 9:1 (1946) 37–41, gives data from the *Cuenta Pública* for 1926–1940 and 1943; Appendix B is the source for 1940–1946. Cf. Adolfo Orive Alba, *La Política de Irrigación en México* (México, D. F.: Fondo de Cultura Económica, 1960), especially Chapter 16 and p. 161.

TABLE 6-3 (continued)

Expenditure for Irrigation, 1926–1963 (included in Table 6-2)

B.

Funds Expended by the Ministry of Irrigation, 1947–1963

Year	Per Cent Projected	Pesos[a]	Per Cent Actual	Pesos[a]
1947	12.9	11.4	10.0	11.4
1948	9.8	10.9	8.2	11.1
1949	9.2	10.7	6.5	11.1
1950	8.7	9.4	7.3	9.8
1951	9.9	9.9	6.9	10.5
1952	9.8	10.8	9.2	9.6
1953	9.4	10.2	9.8	14.1
1954	10.1	11.5	8.8	16.4
1955	7.5	8.5	7.2	12.7
1956	11.3	13.7	6.1	11.3
1957	10.1	12.7	5.7	10.7
1958	8.1	10.4	5.2	10.6
1959	7.4	10.2	4.5	9.4
1960	6.4	8.8	3.6	9.8
1961	6.6	9.5	3.6	9.3
1962	5.5	8.4	5.5	13.7
1963	5.7	9.1	6.7	15.7

[a] In pesos per capita of 1950.

SOURCE: See Table 6-2.

of agricultural education, few centers have actually been set up and equipped with adequate support and personnel.

Irrigation funds were greatly increased over projected amounts from 1953 to 1955 and during 1962–1963. The Ministry of Irrigation has generally received almost the amount allotted to it, except during the years 1956 and 1957. The giant outlay of federal funds for irrigation has given rise to many complaints that public contracts were inefficient and expensive, especially during the corrupt Alemán government. However, one writer has recently attacked López Mateos's irrigation policy, noting that one new hectare of irrigated land cost only 3,797.75 pesos under Ruiz Cortines, but 27,693.46 pesos during the six year period 1958–1964.[1] Even allowing for inflation or geography, this is quite an increase, if the figures are accurate.

Irrigation, agriculture, and modernization of the Mexican countryside are all aspects of federal policy which have been united in regional development projects. The Balsas River Commission under the direction of Lázaro Cárdenas, for example, covers eight states of western and southwestern Mexico. Cárdenas is working to provide electrification, education, transportation, and general development of the region following his successful decade of developing the Tepalcatepec River, an affluent of the Balsas River.[2]

AGRICULTURE CREDIT

Cárdenas has long been active in contributing to the development of Mexico's economy. In 1935 he established agricultural credit in the Mexican budget to provide the peasant with the means to improve his crops and get them to market without having to lose his profit to the speculator. Agricultural credit means funds for seeds, tools, equipment, and transportation, and it stimulates change in a country which has been agriculturally traditional and subsistence-oriented. Either the hacienda produced for nearby markets with a great waste of land, or it produced for itself on a subsistence basis. The poor peasant, of course, has usually been able to do little more than feed himself and grow a small amount for barter. Cárdenas tried to break the old system when he distributed land, and he was aware that agricultural credit would have to be made available or else the peasant who received the land would not be able to work it. Cárdenas has been criticized for not making enough credit available to the countryside, but given the limited budgets he had from 1934 to 1940 in comparison with those of the following two decades, he worked miracles. However much has been said about the need for agricultural credit, Cárdenas established and sustained it as a standard until López Mateos arrived on the political scene.

[1] Héctor Hugo del Cueto, *Informe Semanal de los Negocios*, Aug. 12, 1964, cited by Valentín Campa, "La Política Fiscal de López Mateos," *Política*, Nov. 1, 1964.
[2] Irrigation programs are described in Aldolfo Orive Alba, "Las Obras de Irrigación en México" in *México Cincuenta Años de Revolución*, I. *La Economía*, 337–383, and Cline, *Mexico; Revolution to Evolution, 1940–1960*, Chapter 7.

Prior to Cárdenas little action was taken to supply credit to the farmer. In 1926 Calles founded the National Bank of Agricultural Credit to supply credit to the collective farmer (*ejidatario*) and to the small private farmer. This bank was organized to sell stock to the federal, state, and local governments, and to private banks and individuals looking for investment opportunities. Since the bank loaned to peasants who had little or nothing with which to guarantee loans, and since the *ejidatario* can not mortgage inalienable community land, investors preferred to make their own loans at higher rates to safer risks. The federal government had to supply nearly all of the bank's capital. It has not been possible to identify this expenditure in the budgetary accounts, but an official connected with the program has written that between 1926 and 1928 the government invested in shares at the average rate of 2 per cent of the actual budget per year.[3] An ex-Treasury Minister has noted that most of the government purchases came during the first year.[4] It is significant to note that the government did not keep up this rate, and since no permanent provision was provided in the budget for agricultural credit, it died out along with the bank.

The next phase of agricultural credit came during the Ortiz Rubio period. As credit and currency contracted in Mexico during the world depression in 1931 and 1932, Ortiz Rubio authorized about 2 per cent of his budgets for a reorganized National Bank of Agricultural Credit. The actual allotment was .1 per cent of the budget in 1931 and 4.1 per cent the following year. Political crisis and the sluggish action of interim President Rodríguez in undertaking anything except in planning brought an end to credit during 1933 and 1934. Legal reorganization of agricultural credit in January, 1934, had no practical effects that year. A contemporary friend of agrarian Mexico protested that the failure of the government to extend aid to the small and collective farmer during these years was due to the government's lack of commitment to help the poor peasant who was not a good risk. Eyler Simpson described the real problems of Mexico when he noted:

[3] Manuel Gómez Morín, *El Crédito Agrícola en México* (Madrid: Espasa-Calpe, 1928), 169.
[4] Alberto J. Pani, *La Política Hacendaria y la Revolución* (México, D. F.: Editorial Cultura, 1926), 89.

The problem of ejido credit in Mexico is not primarily a question of laws, formal institutional organization, or even as has been indicated, of money: the problem resides in precisely the ejidatario himself. Until the government is ready to recognize this and to back up recognition by a willingness to dedicate as a legitimate part of the banking system the time, money, and personnel necessary for the difficult task of modifying age-old psychological attitudes, it must inevitably continue to see its efforts to organize the ejidatarios vitiated. In sum, the problem of ejido credit, in its most fundamental aspects, is not a banking problem; it is a problem in education. Progress in its solution for a number of years must be measured not in terms of profits and pecuniary gains, but in changed attitudes and values, in the growth of initiative, responsibility, and the cooperative spirit.[5]

General Lázaro Cárdenas came into the presidency determined to back the *ejidatario* as well as the small farmer with credit and patience. In 1935 he allocated and spent 7.3 per cent of his budget for agricultural credit, and increased the actual percentage to 9.5 per cent the following year. Even though he did not maintain this high percentage, he did set a standard thereafter of 3 to 4 per cent of actual disbursements for this category of national affairs. The 4.7 to 4.9 per cent he projected after 1938 became the standard figure for budgetary planning until 1942.

Table 6-4 shows the effect of increasing population and monetary inflation on the pattern set by Cárdenas. The actual percentage of the budget expended for agricultural credit held up through the war years of 1942–1943, and then faded toward the end of Avila Camacho's term. In 1948 this type of credit was abruptly abandoned. Though 30 million pesos were allotted, only 5,944,000 were actually spent, reducing agricultural credit to .2 per cent of the budget. As we shall see shortly, Alemán de-emphasized several categories of economic expenditure, including this one, to pump money into federal investments. Agricultural credit recovered only slightly from this blow, and Alemán left office with only .5 per cent of the budget actually dedicated to farm credit. Ruiz Cortines spent more than projected on credit to farmers by increasing this category to 1.3 per cent during his first year. With this effort behind him, he lapsed into the traditional presidential

---

[5] Simpson, *The Ejido*, 410–411. See Chapters 22 and 23 for detailed case studies of the problems of *ejidatario* organization compounded by political considerations and bureaucratic inefficiency. This book covers the latter 1920's and pre-Cárdenas 1930's.

TABLE 6-4

Federal Support of Agricultural Credit

Year	Per Cent Projected	Amount[a]	Pesos[b]	Per Cent Actual	Amount[a]	Pesos[b]
1931	2.0	6,000	1.4	.1	200	.1
1932	1.9	4,000	1.1	4.1	8,594	2.3
1933	– – –	– – –	– – –	– – –	– – –	– – –
1934	– – –	– – –	– – –	– – –	– – –	– – –
1935	7.3	20,000	4.5	7.2	21,750	4.8
1936	7.1	20,000	4.2	9.5	38,550	7.9
1937	6.0	20,000	3.4	3.3	15,627	2.7
1938	4.8	20,000	3.2	3.6	18,000	2.9
1939	4.9	22,000	3.3	3.8	22,000	3.4
1940	4.7	21,000	3.2	3.4	20,600	3.1
1941	4.5	22,000	3.1	4.3	29,458	4.0
1942	4.5	25,000	3.0	2.9	24,250	3.0
1943	3.4	23,940	2.4	2.3	24,940	2.5
1944	2.2	23,940	1.8	1.6	23,940	1.8
1945	2.4	23,940	1.6	1.5	23,940	1.6
1946	2.1	25,000	1.4	1.4	25,000	1.4
1947	1.8	30,000	1.6	1.4	30,000	1.6
1948	1.3	30,000	1.5	.2	5,944	.3
1949	1.2	30,000	1.4	.9	33,937	1.5
1950	1.1	30,000	1.2	.8	29,168	1.1
1951	1.0	30,000	1.0	.6	30,000	.9
1952	.8	30,000	.9	.5	29,899	.9
1953	.7	30,000	.8	1.3	71,337	1.9
1954	.6	30,000	.7	.4	29,554	.7
1955	.5	30,000	.6	.9	80,000	1.6
1956	.8	50,000	1.0	.8	80,000	1.5
1957	.7	50,000	.9	.7	80,000	1.3
1958	.6	50,000	.8	.6	80,000	1.2
1959	.8	78,099	1.1	.6	80,000	1.2
1960	.8	77,437	1.1	.4	80,000	1.1
1961	1.2	135,000	1.7	.7	135,000	1.8
1962	.6	80,000	.9	2.1	428,395	5.2
1963	.6	80,000	1.0	2.2	447,315	5.1

[a] Total amount in thousands of current pesos.

[b] In pesos of 1950 per capita.

SOURCE: This table is based upon federal allocations to the Banco Nacional de Crédito Ejidal and the Banco Nacional de Crédito Agrícola y Ganadero. It does not necessarily reflect the amount these banks loan each year as the banks have private as well as state and local government resources. See also Appendix B.

solution to the problem. The problem of agricultural credit was ignored until the ideology of balanced revolution brought aid to the poverty-stricken countryside. In 1962 President López Mateos increased the projected percentage for farm credits from .6 to an actual 2.1 per cent. He did the same thing in 1963 when he pumped new, unbudgeted funds into this category. All figures on agricultural credit presented here are separated from the investments category of the Mexican budget 1935–1948 and from unclassified expenditure thereafter.

Until Ruiz Cortines briefly attempted to compensate for population increase and inflation by increasing the standard amount of pesos which Cárdenas had projected, agrarian credit deteriorated year by year. Not until López Mateos dramatically increased the actual amount, however, was the traditional pattern changed. Whereas Cárdenas actually expended about 5 to 8 pesos per capita between 1935 and 1936, the amount fell to about 3 pesos per capita in his last four years. Avila Camacho raised funds to 4 pesos per capita after the election of 1940, but they gradually declined to 1.4 pesos per capita when he left office. Alemán reduced actual per capita expenditure to .3 pesos in 1948. He somewhat redeemed himself in the eyes of the countryside after 1949 by restoring agricultural credit to about 1 to 1.5 pesos per capita, and this amount was maintained as Ruiz Cortines increased government shares to the farm credit banks. López Mateos's per-capita expenditure reached 5.2 pesos in 1962, the high figure since 1936. Projections remained under 1 peso per capita.

The allocation of 5 pesos per capita for agricultural credit is still far below Mexico's needs. In a country where so much land has been distributed into inalienable communal ownership, the federal government which distributed the land must bear the burden of providing credit. Credit must be low in interest and any rate up to 8 per cent a year is low in Mexico where it is often possible to earn up to 8 per cent a month on one's investment. Since 1962, money has been made available for agricultural credit to Mexico under the Alliance for Progress. However, these funds are restricted by the Agency for International Development of the United States Government for loans to small, individual landholders.[6] Twenty million dollars were loaned to Nacional Finan-

[6] *El Día,* June 15, 1965.

ciera in 1962 and again in 1965 for loans to noncommunal small farmers through the private banking system of Mexico; these amounts do not show up in the federal budget.

Since more money has always been available to small, individual farmers than to *ejidatarios* (though never enough), and since even the National Agricultural Bank tended to loan to noncommunal groups, Cárdenas established a separate Ejidal Bank in 1939. Table 6-5 presents the Ejidal Bank's share of federal funds

TABLE 6-5

Ejidal Bank Share of Federal Agricultural Credit Allocations

Year	Per Cent Projected	Pesos[a]	Per Cent Actual	Pesos[a]
1939	90.9	3.0	90.9	3.1
1940	95.2	3.0	97.1	3.0
1941	90.9	2.8	84.9	3.4
1942	80.0	2.4	82.5	2.5
1943	83.5	2.0	80.2	2.0
1944	83.5	1.5	83.5	1.5
1945	83.5	1.3	83.5	1.3
1946	80.0	1.1	80.0	1.1
1947	66.7	1.1	66.7	1.1
1948	66.7	1.0	66.4	.2
1949	66.7	.9	72.7	1.1
1950	66.7	.8	69.1	.8
1951	66.7	.7	66.7	.6
1952	66.7	.6	66.9	.6
1953	66.7	.5	29.8	.6
1954	66.7	.5	66.1	.5
1955	66.7	.4	62.5	1.0
1956	70.0	.7	62.5	.9
1957	70.0	.6	62.5	.8
1958	70.0	.6	62.5	.8
1959	64.0	.7	62.5	.8
1960	64.6	.7	62.5	.7
1961	77.8	1.3	77.8	1.4
1962	62.5	.6	93.1	4.8
1963	62.5	.6	93.2	4.8

[a] In 1950 pesos per capita.
SOURCE: Table 6-4.

allotted for agricultural credit after 1939. This bank has, from its inception, actually received the bulk of governmental funds. The National Bank of Agricultural and Livestock Credit actually received less than 10 per cent of governmental funds under Cárdenas, but it gradually increased to more than 30 per cent by 1951. In 1953 Ruiz Cortines spent more than 70 per cent of the government's rural credit allowance on this bank which is now completely devoted to the small, individual farmer. However, in the following year this figure returned to its normal balance of more than 30 per cent. As agricultural credit to the private sector was made available by the Alliance for Progress after 1961, the government has increased the Ejidal Bank's share to more than 90 per cent of government disbursements to the two agricultural credit banks.[7]

Projected budgets were quite consistent in allocating the share of funds to the Ejidal Bank which the bank actually received until the period 1953–1960, when the bank received a smaller share than planned. Table 6-5 shows that after 1962 López Mateos channeled 30 per cent more to *ejido* credit than planned. Projected percentage of *ejidal* credit as a share of government agricultural credit remained stable at 66.7 per cent from 1947 to 1955 and it remained at 70 per cent for three more years.

The difference in presidential policy among Cárdenas, Alemán, and López Mateos is especially striking in this discussion of agricultural credit. It is easy to understand why Cárdenas and López Mateos are the heroes for the agricultural sector of society, for they not only distributed the greatest amount of land, but, relatively speaking, they provided credit to make the land workable. Alemán is understandably the hero of the modern sector of society which has given up trying to make small, inefficient, and poor lands feed the country. The Alemán approach to irrigation, public works, and industrialization has been unpopular to the peasant, but as Mexico urbanizes Alemán may turn from villain to hero for an increasingly large proportion of Mexican society.

---

[7] Díaz Ordaz has recently created a new Banco Nacional Agropecuario (Farm Bank) with an initial government investment of 500,000,000 pesos. Theoretically, this bank will not supplant the existing agricultural credit banks. See *El Día*, March 6, 1965,

COMMUNICATIONS AND PUBLIC WORKS

The Ministry of Communications and Public Works was a key post in the Mexican government during the nineteenth century when control of communications determined who would control the government. This has been no less true in twentieth-century Mexico with its new methods of communication by railway, paved road, airplane, telephone, and telegraph. The minister who watches over the travel of men and the transmission of ideas is in an important position to advise Mexico's president how to meet the threat of armed rebellion. Diminished threat of revolt, growth of federal funds dedicated to public works, as well as complexity of governmental operation and specialization, determined that in 1959 the ministry be divided into two parts to form a Ministry of Communications and Transportation and a Ministry of Public Works. Figures in Table 6-6 examine the combined expenditure of these two ministries in order to present historically consistent data.

Expenditure for communications and public works has played a major role in federal budgetary policy to integrate the Mexican nation. Yet the percentages of expenditure devoted to linking different parts of the country together and providing a national infrastructure have at times seemed low. Mexico's problem has been how to make a small budget effective in many ways. Porfirio Díaz set the pattern for Madero's government and the standard for subsequent regimes until the rise of the active state. Under Ortiz Rubio in 1930 and 1931 the Ministry came to life to invigorate the economy in time of crisis. Road construction, for example, organized by Calles in 1925, really got under way when Juan Andreu Almazán became Minister of Communications and Public Works in the Ortiz Rubio cabinet. Díaz's standard was surpassed by several per cent in 1930–1931 and actual expenditure of this ministry reached 9 to 10 pesos per capita, double that of the 1900–1910 period. The political problems caused by Ortiz Rubio's forced withdrawal from the presidency in 1932 meant that the drive behind the integration of the nation would lessen until Cárdenas became president.

TABLE 6-6

Communications and Public Works

Year	President[a]	Per Cent Projected	Pesos[b]	Per Cent Actual	Pesos[b]
1869–1870	Juárez	14.6	. . .	2.8	. . .
1900–1901	Díaz	12.7	3.7	13.4	4.0
1910–1911	Díaz	15.3	5.3	13.4	4.6
1911–1912	Madero	15.2	5.5	14.1	4.7
1912–1913	Madero/Huerta	12.1	4.7	12.0	4.6
1913–1914	Huerta	10.6	. . .	. . .	. . .
1914–1915	Huerta	13.9	. . .	. . .	. . .
1917	Carranza	9.2	. . .	9.4	. . .
1918	Carranza	11.4	3.5	13.6	2.5
1919	Carranza	11.5	4.8	12.8	1.5
1920	Carranza/De la Huerta	10.9	4.5	12.5	3.2
1921	Obregón	10.5	5.6	11.2	5.3
1922	Obregón	14.6	13.9	11.8	6.7
1923	Obregón	12.0	9.6	11.2	6.0
1924	Obregón	9.0	6.3	11.0	7.1
1925	Calles	8.9	5.7	7.8	5.2
1926	Calles	12.7	8.5	10.8	7.7
1927	Calles	12.1	8.5	10.5	7.2
1928	Calles	12.5	8.2	9.0	5.9
1929	Portes Gil	12.8	8.2	12.3	7.6
1930	Portes Gil/Ortiz Rubio	15.1	9.6	16.7	10.1
1931	Ortiz Rubio	15.1	10.8	16.7	9.1
1932	Ortiz Rubio	15.1	8.3	14.5	7.9
1933	Rodríguez	12.2	6.3	12.4	7.3
1934	Rodríguez	12.5	6.9	12.3	7.4
1935	Cárdenas	11.6	7.1	12.0	8.0
1936	Cárdenas	12.4	7.3	15.2	12.7
1937	Cárdenas	10.9	6.2	18.2	14.9
1938	Cárdenas	17.5	11.7	14.0	11.3
1939	Cárdenas	13.2	9.0	10.4	9.3
1940	Cárdenas	11.4	7.7	10.1	9.2
1941	Avila Camacho	10.8	7.3	8.2	7.7
1942	Avila Camacho	11.0	7.4	7.8	8.0
1943	Avila Camacho	9.5	6.7	8.9	9.5
1944	Avila Camacho	18.2	15.2	14.1	15.5
1945	Avila Camacho	16.0	10.8	10.1	10.7
1946	Avila Camacho	14.9	10.0	9.5	9.4

TABLE 6-6 (continued)

Communications and Public Works

Year	President[a]	Per Cent Pro-jected	Pesos[b]	Per Cent Actual	Pesos[b]
1947	Alemán	18.0	16.0	13.6	15.5
1948	Alemán	18.1	20.3	14.4	19.5
1949	Alemán	17.4	19.9	12.0	20.1
1950	Alemán	17.6	18.7	13.2	17.7
1951	Alemán	17.3	17.4	11.6	17.6
1952	Alemán	17.4	19.2	12.6	22.4
1953	Ruiz Cortines	17.7	19.3	13.0	18.7
1954	Ruiz Cortines	20.0	22.8	11.3	21.1
1955	Ruiz Cortines	16.7	18.8	11.7	20.6
1956	Ruiz Cortines	16.1	19.5	10.0	18.6
1957	Ruiz Cortines	18.5	23.2	11.9	22.3
1958	Ruiz Cortines	19.5	25.2	11.1	22.7
1959	López Mateos	17.2	23.7	10.5	21.9
1960	López Mateos	17.4	24.1	9.3	25.3
1961	López Mateos	16.3	23.3	8.6	22.7
1962	López Mateos	16.4	25.0	9.2	23.0
1963	López Mateos	13.1	20.8	8.9	20.8

[a] Slash indicates latter person administered actual funds.
[b] In pesos per capita of 1950.
SOURCE: Appendix B.

Cárdenas did not immediately give the Minister of Communication and Public Works (SCOP) great importance, relatively speaking, as he was interested in the prospects of state planning in the Ministry of National Economy. He placed his key man, Francisco J. Múgica, in the chief post of this latter ministry at the outset of his regime in order to work out a program of national economic integration. In the midst of the Cárdenas-Calles struggle, Cárdenas reorganized his cabinet, transferring Múgica to SCOP where he could control this sensitive political post as well as get down to the practical job of solving national integration. The results of this move showed up in 1937 when an all time high share of the federal purse was actually expended by SCOP,

18.2 per cent. Múgica's ministry reached its highest affluence in per-capita expenditure that year when it actually spent 14.9 pesos.

Expropriation of the oil in 1938 and onset of wartime economy shortly thereafter meant that SCOP's share of the budget was decreased, actually going as low as 7.8 percent in 1942, 8 pesos per capita. Public works projects such as road construction were practically halted from 1939 to 1942, as Appendix L shows. This dip in fortunes of SCOP ended with Miguel Alemán's accession to the presidency. About 14 per cent of the budget was spent by SCOP in 1947–1948 (a greater percentage was allotted), and actual expenditure per capita reached 22.4 pesos in 1952. This figure was topped in 1960 by López Mateos who gave the Ministry of Communications and the Ministry of Public Works a combined per-capita outlay of 25.3 pesos, slightly more than what had been planned for that year. Table 6-7 summarizes the share of expend-

TABLE 6-7

Public Works' Share of Federal Outlay for
Communications and Public Works

Year	Per Cent Projected	Per Cent Actual
1955	62.1	56.5
1956	56.1	50.1
1957	56.8	52.5
1958	61.1	49.5
1959	65.1	61.9
1960	63.8	62.4
1961	58.3	59.3
1962	60.4	51.1
1963	51.1	50.6

SOURCE: Table 6-6.

iture on communications and public works which has been spent on public works since 1955 when such funds were clearly presented in the budget. The Ministry of Public Works has received about 50 to 60 per cent of total disbursements for the two ministries which replaced SCOP in 1959.

INVESTMENTS

Federal investments in railroads, electrical power, stocks, bonds, trust funds, and credits to state and local government were not important until 1949. Juárez had projected 3.8 per cent of his budget for purchase of shares in the railway from Veracruz to the capital, but he was actually unable to spend any funds for this purpose. Calles's creation of the Bank of Mexico in 1925 meant a large financial investment of 18.5 per cent which had not been projected. The real import of federal investments dates from Alemán's term. In 1949 President Alemán projected 5.4 per cent of the budget to cover expenditure for the new category of investments which had been founded in 1947, but he actually spent 24.1 per cent of federal disbursements on this category. Much of investment went for transfers to stimulate industry and agriculture.

Alemán and his advisers believed that government and business should work together with the co-operation of labor to industrialize Mexico. Sanford Mosk has aptly noted that what Alemán and his followers have advocated is not state intervention in the ordinary sense of the term, for they "assign the government a prominent role . . . , but they want the government to arrive at its decisions on the basis of information and advice supplied by the interested industrialist groups. What they propose is business intervention in government rather than government intervention in business." [8] Co-operation with the private sector through state participation in mixed public and private enterprise, discussed in Chapter 4, has accounted for the destiny of much of the investment in Table 6-8.

Investments have never been projected at more than 12 per cent of the budget, but they were well over that amount from 1949 to 1960, reaching from 20 to almost 25 per cent six times (1949, 1951, 1952, 1954, 1958, 1960). During this period per-capita expenditure for investments reached 54.6 pesos in 1960, and it was more than 30 pesos in all but two years (1950 and 1953). Under López Mateos investments decreased after 1960, falling below 10 per cent and 25 pesos per capita of federal outlay. Investments have been related to the unclassified share of the budget devoted to economic expenditure.

[8] Mosk, *Industrial Revolution in Mexico,* 29.

TABLE 6-8

Investments

Year	Per Cent Projected	Pesos[a]	Per Cent Actual	Pesos[a]
1869–1870	3.8	...	– – –	– – –
1925	– – –	– – –	18.5	12.3
1926	– – –	– – –	– – –	– – –
1927	– – –	– – –	.7	.5
1928	.5	.3	.7	.5
1929	.9	.6	.9	.6
1930	.2	.1	.5	.3
1931	– – –	– – –	– – –	– – –
1932	2.8	1.5	– – –	– – –
1933	– – –	– – –	– – –	– – –
1934	– – –	– – –	.1	.1
1935	.1	.1	– – –	– – –
1936	– – –	– – –	.8	.7
1937	– – –	– – –	– – –	– – –
1938	.7	.5	1.5	1.2
1939	.5	.3	.3	.3
1940	.2	.1	.2	.2
1941	– – –	– – –	.8	.8
1942	.2	.1	1.0	1.0
1943	– – –	– – –	1.5	1.6
1944	– – –	– – –	3.1	3.4
1945	– – –	– – –	3.4	3.6
1946	– – –	– – –	2.0	2.0
1947	.2	.2	2.5	2.9
1948	2.8	3.1	5.6	7.6
1949	5.4	6.2	24.1	40.3
1950	7.1	7.6	13.2	17.7
1951	5.7	5.7	23.2	35.1
1952	6.1	6.7	24.8	44.1
1953	6.1	6.6	17.4	25.0
1954	8.4	9.6	20.2	37.7
1955	11.8	13.3	17.3	30.5
1956	12.0	14.6	19.7	36.7
1957	9.0	11.3	17.5	32.8
1958	7.7	9.9	20.3	41.5
1959	6.5	9.0	15.8	32.9
1960	7.3	10.1	20.1	54.6
1961	7.4	10.6	6.6	17.4
1962	6.5	9.9	5.9	14.7
1963	9.0	14.3	9.7	22.7

[a] In pesos per capita of 1950.
SOURCE: See Appendix B.

UNCLASSIFIED ECONOMIC EXPENDITURE

Transfers to industry and commerce, subsidies to decentralized agencies, and price supports are provided with funds under the title of *erogaciones adicionales* in the budget. The economic share of unclassified expenditure (Table 6-9) overlaps with investments,

TABLE 6-9

Unclassified Share of Economic Expenditure

Year	Per Cent Projected	Pesos[a]	Per Cent Actual	Pesos[a]
1869–1870	– – –	– – –	.5	. . .
1938	– – –	– – –	.5	.4
1939	– – –	– – –	7.9	7.0
1940	– – –	– – –	5.6	5.1
1941	– – –	– – –	11.7	11.0
1942	– – –	– – –	7.1	7.2
1943	– – –	– – –	12.6	13.5
1944	– – –	– – –	11.9	13.1
1945	.4	.3	12.0	12.7
1946	– – –	– – –	15.7	15.5
1947	3.7	3.3	14.4	16.4
1948	6.6	7.4	14.9	20.1
1949	.7	.8	11.2	18.7
1950	.7	.7	12.4	16.7
1951	.7	.7	8.9	13.5
1952	2.4	2.6	7.9	14.1
1953	1.3	1.4	10.4	15.0
1954	.8	.9	15.2	28.4
1955	4.5	5.1	11.1	19.6
1956	3.2	3.9	13.6	25.3
1957	3.9	4.9	12.3	23.0
1958	5.9	7.6	11.6	23.7
1959	5.1	7.0	10.5	21.9
1960	4.2	5.8	6.6	17.9
1961	3.5	5.0	8.6	22.7
1962	3.8	5.8	10.1	25.2
1963	5.0	8.0	11.1	26.0

[a] In pesos per capita of 1950
SOURCE: See Appendix B

and many items could logically appear under one head or the other. The category of *erogaciones adicionales* was established in the budget in 1947, and prior to that time such items as agricultural credit were included in investments instead of here. Other items such as transfers to stimulate economic production were included in Treasury Department allocations.

Cárdenas had begun a modest transfer of funds to producers of certain agricultural products in order to develop henequen, banana, sugar, and paper production, for example, and this program was greatly expanded to include the development of commerce and industry under Avila Camacho. Alemán continued the post-1940 trajectory. He announced in his Program of Government:

Within the program of economic development of the country, the plan of industrialization constitutes the most important chapter, since upon its execution depend the fundamental objectives towards which the historic development of our country has oriented: the autonomous national economy and the material and cultural elevation of the great mass of the people.

The entire country demands industrialization. In order to accomplish it, it is indispensable to: 1) realize a review of industries existing before the war; 2) complete the necessary study of industries which were created by the state of emergency and [examine] the possibilities of their subsistence; 3) study and develop industries which are necessary for the development of the country and which have not been initiated here.[9]

Actual expenditure for this category has always been far ahead of projections, both in percentages and in pesos per capita. Since Avila Camacho, it has remained more than 10 per cent of actual expenditure except for four years (1951, 1952, 1960, and 1961). In monetary terms, actual outlay has remained about 20 pesos per capita since 1954 almost without exception.

MINOR ECONOMIC EXPENDITURE

Three categories of the Mexican budget are included in Table 6-10, in order to resume the activities of governmental agencies which have not had great importance in budgetary consideration. These agencies are the Ministry of Industry and Commerce (Min-

[9] Alemán, "Programa de Gobierno."

TABLE 6-10

Minor Economic Outlay in Percentage Terms

	Industry and Commerce		Agrarian Department		Tourism	
Year	Projected	Actual	Projected	Actual	Projected	Actual
1914–1915	1.4	...	--	--	--	--
1917	1.4	1.1	--	--	--	--
1918	1.5	1.4	--	--	--	--
1919	1.2	3.1	--	--	--	--
1920	1.8	1.7	--	--	--	--
1921	1.9	1.6	--	--	--	--
1922	1.2	1.7	--	--	--	--
1923	2.0	2.1	--	--	--	--
1924	1.7	2.0	--	--	--	--
1925	2.0	1.9	--	--	--	--
1926	2.3	2.1	--	--	--	--
1927	2.2	2.0	--	--	--	--
1928	2.5	2.6	--	--	--	--
1929	3.0	2.7	--	--	--	--
1930	3.6	3.6	--	--	--	--
1931	2.9	3.2	--	--	--	--
1932	3.0	2.8	--	--	--	--
1933	2.8	2.2	--	--	--	--
1934	2.4	3.7	1.8	1.6	--	--
1935	2.1	5.3	2.0	2.4	--	--
1936	2.3	7.6	2.8	2.1	--	--
1937	1.8	10.1	2.7	1.9	--	--
1938	2.0	7.7	2.3	1.9	--	--
1939	1.9	5.9	2.2	1.6	--	--
1940	2.3	6.8	2.0	1.4	--	--
1941	2.2	7.4	1.7	1.3	--	--
1942	1.8	7.3	1.6	1.1	--	--
1943	1.5	4.4	1.4	.9	--	--
1944	1.1	3.6	1.0	.8	--	--
1945	1.4	3.6	1.1	.7	--	--
1946	1.2	4.4	1.0	.7	--	--
1947	.9	.7	.8	.7	--	--
1948	2.0	4.2	.6	.5	--	--
1949	.7	.5	.6	.4	--	--
1950	.8	.7	.6	.4	--	--
1951	.8	.6	.5	.3	--	--
1952	.7	.5	.5	.3	--	--
1953	.7	.5	.5	.3	--	--
1954	.7	.4	.4	.3	--	--
1955	.7	.5	.5	.3	--	--
1956	.7	.5	.4	.3	--	--
1957	.7	.5	.4	.3	--	--
1958	.6	.4	.4	.3	--	--
1959	.8	.5	.5	.4	.1	.2
1960	1.0	.5	.6	.3	.2	.1
1961	.9	.5	.7	.4	.3	1.6
1962	.8	.5	.7	.4	.3	.2
1963	.8	.6	.7	.5	.3	.3

SOURCE: See Appendix B.

istry of National Economy), the Agrarian Department, and the Department of Tourism.

The Ministry of Development (Fomento) was the nineteenth-century Mexican governmental unit charged with regulating and developing agricultural economy, but it contained a small branch which dealt with industrial and commercial affairs. A branch of labor was added after the revolution by Madero. Given Porfirio Díaz's concept of the state as a protector of capital, there was no need to regulate or stimulate industry or commerce. Mexico was primarily agricultural and it was felt that an independent Ministry of Industry, Commerce, and Labor was not necessary until new persons came to power after 1910. The upheaval of 1910 made Mexicans in general aware of the importance of business in national life. General Victoriano Huerta divided the Ministry of Development into Agriculture, already discussed, and a ministry to deal with industrial and commercial affairs. The new ministry was conceived mainly for an administrative role, and its action represented the passive concept of the state which prevailed until the world depression of 1929.

The economic crisis in Mexico had several effects on ministerial action. President Ortiz Rubio increased federal emphasis on stimulation of the economy when he actually allocated an increased percentage of the projected and actual budget to the Ministry of Industry, Commerce, and Labor in 1930. This did not seem to be enough to resolve the economic problem of 1930–1933, however, nor did it allay the fears of the populace. In order to restore confidence of the business community and to maintain the confidence of the people in the Revolution, larger steps had to be taken. On September 21, 1932, twenty days after taking office, President Rodríguez announced the reorganization of the Mexican executive power to enable him to combat the crisis actively. During the fall and winter of 1932 Mexican newspapers covered with interest and acclaim the conversion of the Ministry of Industry, Commerce, and Labor to a Ministry of National Economy and an independent Labor Department. The first minister of national economy, Primo Villa Michel, took office January 2, 1933. He told the country of the purpose of his agency:

The Ministry of National Economy is intended to fill a need of coordination of the activities . . . in the economic life of the country which until today have not had a definite and unified orientation. . . .

The present crisis has come to underline the urgent need of an adequate orientation of our political economy as a means to obtain balanced development of the diverse factors which form the economic structure of our country. The imperious need to obtain national equilibrium demands action technically oriented to amplify the field and capacity of our interior markets and assure our exterior markets. The Ministry of National Economy offers to be, then, an aid to the Federal Government in the politics of state interventionism in economic and social affairs which almost all countries follow.[10]

State planning of how to co-ordinate rural and urban economic development came into vogue under Rodríguez, but it did not receive a significant emphasis in the budget until General Lázaro Cárdenas became president in December of 1934. With Francisco J. Múgica as Minister of the National Economy, economic planning received 5.3 per cent of actual expenditure in 1935. Though Múgica was transferred to the Ministry of Communications and Public Works to control that key post in the Cárdenas-Calles struggle over political power, the Ministry of National Economy gained in stature until by 1937 it actually received 10.1 per cent of the budget, a great increase over projections. This governmental emphasis was maintained through 1943.

Francisco Javier Gaxiola, Jr., Minister of National Economy under Avila Camacho, recently noted that state planning during the period 1933–1958 was virtually impossible, as was co-ordination of government agencies, for the Ministry of National Economy shared its functions with the prestigious Ministry of the Treasury. Without the authority to act, and without the direct power of the president, the Ministry ceased to have much power after World War II, and it was phased out of budgetary considerations. The ministry existed until 1958 after which its name was changed to the Ministry of Commerce and Industry once again, for its real function lay in regulating and developing the country's business affairs.[11] Significantly, the Ministry of the Presidency, created in 1959, has taken over government planning and co-ordination of programs.[12]

The Agrarian Department was established in 1934 definitively

[10] *El Universal*, Jan. 3, 1933.
[11] Francisco Javier Gaxiola, Jr., Oral History Interviews with James and Edna Wilkie, April 20, 1964, Mexico City.
[12] See Chapter 5, note 16.

to end the hacienda system through the distribution of Mexico's land to the rural population. This Department has always been small and has never received a percentage of the budget which would have allowed it to distribute lands with proper survey. The Department has concentrated on breaking up the land into small holdings without necessarily worrying about the accuracy of titles, and much confusion and struggle over land holdings has resulted. In the 1960's it is still trying to remedy this cause of strife in the countryside by resurveying programs, but this will be a long process.

At the time of the creation of the Tourist Department in 1959, the total value of Mexico's eight principal export commodities came to only 69 per cent of Mexico's income from tourism.[13] The Department has had to compete with the president of its own advisory board for importance in government circles, however, for Miguel Alemán was named president of the National Tourist Council. Alemán spends his time abroad spreading good will. He is followed by a large coterie of assistants, and he enjoys special diplomatic treatment as he is Mexico's roving plenipotentiary ambassador. Though the Tourism Department has not had a great percentage of the federal budget to spend, it actually did have 4.6 pesos per capita available in 1961, its peak year, and that was almost exactly the same amount that Madero spent on communications and public works in 1911–1912. Economic expenditure has indeed come a long way since Madero's upheaval.

President López Mateos, a master of propaganda who increased to a new high "slick paper" publications lauding the government, after 1960 classified economic development of Mexico in his yearly State of the Nation Address under the title of "A Better Standard of Life." [14] The balanced revolution he developed is not phrased in Marxist terms, but it is not treated in capitalistic terms either. Its terminology reflects the ideology of mixed capitalism, though it is more frank about the state's active role since the 1930's. In fact, the casual observer might believe that the government really should get credit for everything that has happened in Mexico. The

[13] José Rogelio Alvarez, "El Turismo," in *México Cincuenta Años de Revolución,* I. *La Economía,* 295–299, p. 295.
[14] López Mateos, *5 Informes de Gobierno* and "Informe . . . 1964," *El Día,* Sept. 2, 1964.

president of Mexico appears to be a benevolent despot of an earlier age, except that his propaganda machine is more powerful, his resources are greater, and he is limited to a non-hereditary kingship of only six years. However, the official party can only continue to hold political power as long as it fulfills its many promises to revolutionize the Mexican way of life.

7

Social Expenditure

The rise of the active state in Mexican public affairs has been slow in regard to social expenditure. We have treated some of the stereotypes surrounding the ideology of social revolution, and we should note here that they should not be confused with social expenditure. Any government may spend funds on education, public health, welfare, sanitary engineering, and labor without advocating social revolution. In fact, Cárdenas's social revolution was undertaken with economic expenditure more than with social expenditure. However, since Cárdenas believed in educating the proletariat to understand its rights, he pushed the budget for education to a high point in Mexican history, and he expended the highest amount on social improvement until López Mateos undertook balanced revolution after 1959. It seems that social costs are hard to justify within the Mexican Revolution, even though the nation is still far from social integration. Perhaps this is due to an innate conservatism in all men. Social expenditure occasions indirect social change that challenges the very nature of the structure of society, be it traditional or be it revolutionary. The results cannot be easily measured, and they may be quite controversial. Contrariwise, economic expenditure is seen to pull the nation together and provide opportunity and change without disrupting the fabric of society. We shall treat the ramifications of these theories in Part II when we attempt to measure social change in Mexico since 1910, but here it is necessary to point out how social expenditure has clearly reflected the different ideological emphases in periods of political, social, economic, and balanced revolution.

Projected social expenditure, limited to education and modest public health welfare and assistance programs reached 9 per cent by the time the Revolution broke out in 1910. Projections held at this figure until the Carranza period when they collapsed. Plans for expanded social expenditure ranged from 10 to 16 per cent during the 1920's and early 1930's. Rodríguez raised the figure to 17.7 per cent in 1933, but the big jump came under Cárdenas. From 1934 to 1940 social budgeting increased to the 20–26 percentage range. Cárdenas reached 25.9 per cent in 1940, and his successor maintained the same high projections throughout the war. Under Avila Camacho projections were from 22 to 26 per cent, the high coming in 1942. Alemán sliced planned emphasis on social expenditure from 21 per cent in 1947 to 17 per cent by 1952. Ruiz Cortines reversed his mentor's pattern, increasing the budget from 18.5 per cent in 1953 to 23.2 per cent by 1958. López Mateos then used the projected budget as the fulcrum of his ideology of balanced revolution. Social expenditure increased from one quarter to one third of the planned outlay.

Prior to 1935 twentieth-century projected and actual budgets were close, as Table 7-1 reveals. From 1922 to 1923 Obregón overestimated social emphasis by 3 to 6 per cent, but during the military rebellion which disrupted finances in 1924, there was little disparity between plans and execution of disbursements.

Cárdenas's plans for social expenditure were greater than his ability to carry them out. Only in 1938 did his plans come close to reality, and the other five years he was from 3 to 5 per cent lower than he had hoped. Nevertheless, social expenditure actually reached the greatest emphasis in Mexican history in 1938, and this figure of 19.9 per cent of the budget held as the record until 1962. Avila Camacho maintained Cardenas's pattern at almost the same rate. The war years of 1943–1944 marked the only fall to 15 per cent and slightly below.

The ideology of economic revolution de-emphasized social expenditure in favor of economic expenditure, and in 1949 actual social expenditure fell to 11.9 per cent, over 6 per cent behind plans and the low since 1928. Social emphasis went down to 11.2 in 1952, the lowest since 1927. It is no wonder that the cry was raised that Alemán had abandoned the goals of the revolution, for he appeared to have forgotten the masses. Ruiz Cortines main-

TABLE 7-1

*Social Expenditure: Percentage Share and Pesos
Per Capita Since 1910*

Year	President[a]	Per Cent Projected	Pesos[b]	Per Cent Actual	Pesos[b]
1869–1870	Juárez	2.7	...	1.6	...
1900–1901	Díaz	3.8	1.1	4.1	1.2
1910–1911	Díaz	9.0	3.1	9.2	3.1
1911–1912	Madero	9.4	3.4	9.9	3.3
1912–1913	Madero/Huerta	9.2	3.6	8.9	3.4
1913–1914	Huerta	11.6	...	...	...
1914–1915	Huerta	8.6	...	...	...
1917	Carranza	2.9	...	1.7	...
1918	Carranza	2.2	.7	2.1	.4
1919	Carranza	1.9	.8	2.1	.3
1920	Carranza/De la Huerta	2.1	.9	2.3	.6
1921	Obregón	6.1	3.2	5.9	2.8
1922	Obregón	14.9	14.2	10.9	6.2
1923	Obregón	16.8	13.4	11.1	6.0
1924	Obregón	10.2	7.1	11.0	7.1
1925	Calles	8.5	5.4	8.7	5.8
1926	Calles	10.2	6.8	9.7	6.9
1927	Calles	10.9	7.7	10.3	7.1
1928	Calles	11.9	7.8	11.7	7.6
1929	Portes Gil	12.1	7.8	12.9	7.9
1930	Portes Gil/Ortiz Rubio	14.3	9.1	14.6	8.8
1931	Ortiz Rubio	14.7	10.5	17.0	9.2
1932	Ortiz Rubio	15.7	8.7	15.8	8.7
1933	Rodríguez	17.7	9.1	15.7	9.2
1934	Rodríguez	16.4	9.1	15.0	9.0
1935	Cárdenas	20.5	12.5	17.3	11.6
1936	Cárdenas	22.2	13.1	16.9	14.1
1937	Cárdenas	23.2	13.2	17.4	14.2
1938	Cárdenas	22.0	14.8	19.9	16.1
1939	Cárdenas	24.4	16.7	18.4	16.4
1940	Cárdenas	25.9	17.5	19.7	17.9
1941	Avila Camacho	25.3	17.2	18.5	17.4
1942	Avila Camacho	26.2	17.7	17.4	17.7
1943	Avila Camacho	22.4	15.8	15.3	16.4
1944	Avila Camacho	16.9	14.1	14.5	16.0
1945	Avila Camacho	25.6	17.3	17.0	18.0

TABLE 7-1 (continued)

Social Expenditure: Percentage Share and Pesos
Per Capita Since 1910

Year	President[a]	Per Cent Pro- jected	Pesos[b]	Per Cent Actual	Pesos[b]
1946	Avila Camacho	24.3	16.3	16.0	15.8
1947	Alemán	21.5	19.1	15.9	18.1
1948	Alemán	17.9	20.1	13.8	18.7
1949	Alemán	18.3	20.9	11.9	19.9
1950	Alemán	18.2	19.4	14.4	19.3
1951	Alemán	18.5	18.6	12.5	18.9
1952	Alemán	16.9	18.6	11.2	19.9
1953	Ruiz Cortines	18.5	20.2	14.1	20.3
1954	Ruiz Cortines	19.4	22.1	12.7	23.7
1955	Ruiz Cortines	19.7	22.2	12.8	22.6
1956	Ruiz Cortines	20.0	24.3	15.5	28.9
1957	Ruiz Cortines	21.6	27.1	15.2	28.3
1958	Ruiz Cortines	23.2	30.0	16.4	33.5
1959	López Mateos	26.1	36.0	17.4	36.2
1960	López Mateos	29.9	41.4	16.4	44.6
1961	López Mateos	30.7	43.9	18.7	49.3
1962	López Mateos	33.6	51.1	20.9	52.2
1963	López Mateos	33.7	53.6	22.6	52.8

[a] Slash indicates latter person administered actual funds.
[b] In pesos per capita of 1950.
SOURCE: See Appendix B.

tained a slightly higher rate, but he did not go higher than 15.2 per cent in his last year.

López Mateos's ideology of balanced revolution did not get under way until 1961 when social outlay actually approached Cárdenas's record. By 1963 social emphasis was at 22.6 per cent and approaching one quarter of the federal budget. It was 11 per cent under projections, but it was still high.

Higher also was actual per-capita disbursement. During the period of violent political revolution the amount was low or nil. The period of ideology of peaceful political revolution saw a rise to 8 pesos per capita. During the Cárdenas era, a new standard

TABLE 7-2

Educational Outlay

Year	Presidenta	Per Cent Projected	Pesosb	Per Cent Actual	Pesosb
1869–1870	Juárez	2.7	...	1.6	...
1900–1901	Díaz	3.4	1.0	3.7	1.1
1910–1911	Díaz	6.8	2.3	7.2	2.5
1911–1912	Madero	7.3	2.6	7.8	2.6
1912–1913	Madero/Huerta	7.3	2.8	6.9	2.7
1913–1914	Huerta	9.9	...	...	...
1914–1915	Huerta	6.9	...	...	...
1917	Carranza	1.4	...	1.1	...
1918	Carranza	1.2	.4	1.3	.2
1919	Carranza	.9	.4	1.2	.1
1920	Carranza/De la Huerta	1.1	.5	1.3	.3
1921	Obregón	3.9	2.1	4.0	1.9
1922	Obregón	13.0	12.4	8.9	5.1
1923	Obregón	15.0	11.9	9.3	5.0
1924	Obregón	8.6	6.0	9.3	6.0
1925	Calles	7.3	4.7	7.1	4.7
1926	Calles	8.5	5.7	7.7	5.5
1927	Calles	8.3	5.9	8.0	5.5
1928	Calles	9.3	6.1	9.3	6.1
1929	Portes Gil	9.6	6.2	10.0	6.2
1930	Portes Gil/Ortiz Rubio	11.3	7.2	11.5	6.9
1931	Ortiz Rubio	11.8	8.4	13.8	7.5
1932	Ortiz Rubio	12.7	7.0	12.9	7.1
1933	Rodríguez	14.7	7.6	12.7	7.5
1934	Rodríguez	12.8	7.1	11.8	7.1
1935	Cárdenas	16.2	9.9	12.6	8.4
1936	Cárdenas	17.0	10.0	12.8	10.7
1937	Cárdenas	18.1	10.3	13.6	11.1
1938	Cárdenas	16.3	10.9	13.0	10.5
1939	Cárdenas	15.3	10.4	11.7	10.4
1940	Cárdenas	16.5	11.1	12.4	11.3
1941	Avila Camacho	15.8	10.7	11.2	10.5
1942	Avila Camacho	16.4	11.1	10.2	10.4
1943	Avila Camacho	13.7	9.6	8.8	9.4
1944	Avila Camacho	10.8	9.0	8.9	9.8
1945	Avila Camacho	17.0	11.5	10.8	11.4
1946	Avila Camacho	17.3	11.6	11.2	11.1

TABLE 7-2 (continued)

Educational Outlay

Year	President[a]	Per Cent Pro- jected	Pesos[b]	Per Cent Actual	Pesos[b]
1947	Alemán	13.3	11.8	10.1	11.5
1948	Alemán	10.7	12.0	8.5	11.5
1949	Alemán	11.0	12.6	7.5	12.6
1950	Alemán	11.4	12.1	9.1	12.2
1951	Alemán	11.5	11.6	7.8	11.8
1952	Alemán	10.7	11.8	7.1	12.6
1953	Ruiz Cortines	11.5	12.5	9.3	13.4
1954	Ruiz Cortines	12.6	14.4	8.7	16.3
1955	Ruiz Cortines	12.5	14.1	8.2	14.4
1956	Ruiz Cortines	12.5	15.2	8.8	16.4
1957	Ruiz Cortines	13.6	17.1	9.1	17.0
1958	Ruiz Cortines	13.7	17.7	9.6	19.6
1959	López Mateos	15.8	21.8	10.6	22.1
1960	López Mateos	18.4	25.4	9.7	26.4
1961	López Mateos	19.1	27.3	10.8	28.5
1962	López Mateos	20.9	31.8	12.4	30.1
1963	López Mateos	21.8	34.7	14.2	33.2

[a] Slash indicates latter person administered actual funds.
[b] In pesos per capita of 1950.
SOURCE: See Appendix B.

was set at 16 to 17 pesos per capita, and this had changed slightly upwards by 1952. Under Ruiz Cortines jumps to higher amounts came in 1954, 1956, and 1958. Truly dramatic rises in social expenditure per capita came in 1960 and 1962 during López Mateos's term. Actual expenditure per capita has usually been close to projected figures, and often more than projected. Even when Alemán reduced social expenditure to 11.2 per cent in 1952, more pesos per capita were allotted for social costs than were planned.

EDUCATION

Table 7-2 presents the figures for educational disbursement. This is the total of funds allotted to education including physical education during the Cárdenas years.[1] Cárdenas believed that physical education was a key to developing the potentialities of the masses, and football games, bicycle races, marching, and physical activity were made a vital part of the educational process by separating funds into a special category administered outside the Ministry of Education.

Education was not a function of the federal government until Obregón founded a full-fledged Ministry of Education under José Vasconcelos in 1921. Therefore, projected and actual expenditure was very low until the last decade of Díaz's government. Education's role in national policy doubled from 1900 to Díaz's fall, but it only reached 7.2 per cent of actual disbursements and 2.5 pesos per capita. Madero slightly increased the projected and actual totals while he was alive, and Huerta raised the amount to 9.9 per cent of the budget in 1913–1914 even though he had expended only 6.9 per cent of the budget which Madero began in 1912–1913. Under Carranza federal education all but died out completely, for no reconstruction was carried out after the terrible ravages of war; educational expenditure rose only slightly above 1 per cent of projected and actual budgets. In 1921 there was some recovery, but not until 1922 was federal activity really renewed with vigor. As the federal government began to take over the destitute state governments' responsibility for educational activity, budgetary requirements increased.[2] Obregón's hopes of raising the educational percentage to 15 in 1923 did not become a reality though a high of 9.3 per cent was reached. Under Calles education was held at between 7.1 and 9.3 per cent of federal projections and actual budgets. Portes Gil did not upset this pattern during his fourteen months as interim president, though he did project a higher figure which guided Ortiz Rubio in 1930. Throughout the depression from 1930 to 1932, and during the two years immediately afterward, projections and actual expenditure ran between 11.3 and 13.8 per cent, the latter figure constituting actual outlay in 1931. Per-capita cost held at a consistent high between 7.1 and 7.5 pesos.

[1] Cf. José E. Iturriaga, *La Estructura Social y Cultural de México* (México, D. F.: Fondo de Cultura Económica, 1951), 172, for a chart on projected budgetary percentages which is often in great error, especially in the late 1930's, perhaps due to the variety of sources he uses.

[2] On rural education see Ramón Ruiz, *Mexico, The Challenge of Poverty and Illiteracy* (San Marino: The Huntington Library, 1963).

The Six-Year Plan projected increases of 1 per cent per year for education's share of the budget, 1934–1940, beginning with a base of 15 per cent and rising to 20 per cent.[3] Cárdenas was never able to keep up with this plan. He scheduled 18.1 per cent of the budget for education in 1937, the high for the Revolution until 1960, but he managed to spend only 13.6 per cent of the budget on this category. Per capita expenditure reached a new high of 11.1 pesos in 1937, more than Cárdenas had earmarked.

The official party did not make the mistake of stipulating what percentage of federal funds it would spend on education during the course of the Second Six-Year Plan, 1940–1946.[4] Avila Camacho planned to expend relatively high amounts of the budget for education, the totals reaching 17 per cent in 1945 and 1946, but his high was actually only 11.2 per cent in 1941 and 1946. He maintained per capita expenditure at the Cárdenas level.

The Alemán regime de-emphasized education's actual percentage of the budget. The public felt this and criticized Alemán for rejecting the revolutionary principle of education for the masses. Avila Camacho had an excuse for reducing actual educational expenditure during the war years 1943 and 1944 to slightly under 9 per cent of federal outlay, but Alemán never allocated more than 9 per cent after his first year in office. In Alemán's last year actual expenditure fell to 7.1 per cent of the budget, a post-1925 low. Alemán did not totally conceal his intentions, for he reduced projections to 10.7 by his second year in office, 1948. Nevertheless, he allocated about the same amount of pesos per capita as he had projected each year, and the Ministry of Education had over 12 pesos per capita to spend during three years, a new high for Mexican history.

The government of Ruiz Cortines did not much change the pattern set by Alemán. Projections increased only gradually; actual expenditure did not. However, outlay per capita rose to almost 20 pesos by 1958, the year Ruiz Cortines left office.

López Mateos instituted a different policy during his first year of office 1959. Projected budgets increased to 18.4 per cent of the budget in 1960, a new high for educational outlay since Cárdenas. By 1963 this percentage had risen to 21.8 per cent. The difference

[3] Gilberto Bosques, *The National Revolutionary Party of Mexico and the Six-Year Plan* (México, D. F.: P[artido] N[acional] R[evolucionario], 1937), 184.
[4] Partido de la Revolución Mexicana, *Segundo Plan Sexenal, 1941–1946*.

in actual percentage due to the increasing amount of funds available to the government was considerable, for education did not receive a share in the new funds. Actual outlay constituted only 9.7 to 14.2 per cent of the budget. If López Mateos had not promised in his budget message to spend greater amounts, he would be a hero for raising actual disbursements to 14.2 per cent in 1963 —as it is, his feat somehow looks unexceptional.[5] Though the percentage emphasis does not look great, increasing total federal outlay has resulted in a greatly expanded projected and actual expenditure per capita. In 1963 this total reached 33.2 pesos. Comparatively speaking, the Ministry of Education is quite wealthy in relation to its earlier days, and it has doubled the funds per capita that it had as late as 1956.

PUBLIC HEALTH, WELFARE, AND ASSISTANCE

Public health, welfare, and assistance were a minor part of the functions of the Interior Ministry until 1917. Carranza established a separate Public Health Department. Under Cárdenas a separate agency for public assistance was created. These two agencies, Public Health and Assistance, were joined to form one min-

[5] An example of the López Mateos governmental use of social propaganda based on budget projections rather than on realities is seen in the speech given by Sr. Bravo Ahuja at the inauguration of the Centro Nacional de Enseñanza Superior in Mexico City; see *El Día*, Nov. 7, 1964. Also, a book recently published by the Ministry of Education extolling the virtues of López Mateos's high budgets for education gives only projected financial outlay (*La Obra Educativa en el Sexenio 1958-1964*). This book resulted in an interesting debate between Pablo Latapí, Manuel Germán Parra, and Jorge Efrén Domínguez Ramírez over whether or not the government should spend more than 25 per cent of the budget on education. When Parra pointed out that the projection of 25 per cent compared to actual expenditure was meaningless he was roundly castigated. For a summary of the issues and citations on the debate published in Mexico City's press, see Jorge Domínguez Ramírez, "Comentarios al Artículo: 'Educación y Presupuestos' del Doctor Manuel Germán Parra," *El Día*, March 3, 1965. It is important to note that the government projections change from year to year and from president to president and debate could best center on actual policies as well as on plans which may or may not be carried out. The famous Plan de Once Años which López Mateos set in motion will apparently be de-emphasized by Díaz Ordaz who has projected a plan to stamp out illiteracy in his term. Compare México, Departamento de Muestreo, *Fundamento Estadístico del "Plan de Once Años de Educación Primaria"* (México, D. F.: Talleres Gráficos de la Nación, 1961), with Díaz Ordaz's plans outlined in *El Día*, March 3, 1965. Each president must not only have his own plans, but may tire of them before six years are over, as did López Mateos—the Plan de Once Años was announced with great fanfare and gradually was not mentioned by the end of López Mateos's term.

istry under Avila Camacho. Welfare funds were included in the Interior Department and in Public Health and Assistance until the new ministry was organized to handle all such national affairs. These funds are included in Table 7-3.

The need for a public health program was dramatized in 1916 by the publication of Alberto J. Pani's *Hygiene in Mexico*. Pani indicted the neglect of national health under Díaz on the premise that "there exists a precise and direct proportion between the sum of civilization acquired by a country and the degree of perfection reached in its administration and stewardship of public health." [6] Pani traced high mortality rates to very bad health conditions in Mexico City.

The creation of an agency to assist the public and offer federal welfare funds was influenced by the publication in 1930 of a book by Ramón Beteta and Eyler N. Simpson. This book, *Mendicancy in Mexico,* called attention to the number of beggars on the streets in Mexico City.[7] Earlier writers had made the *léperos* infamous, but Beteta and Simpson took the sympathetic view that these people had to be helped. They suggested that public health is intimately related to public welfare and that imprisonment of beggars does not solve the problem of poverty in society. This work caught up the spirit of the 1930's in Mexico, for it turned away from an impersonal treatment of statistics to case histories of people living in terrible misery.

Despite Mexico's great need for social development, social aid programs and public health have never occupied a significant share in budgetary considerations. The highest amount ever projected for this activity came in Cárdenas's last year of office and during Avila Camacho's first three years in the presidency. Avila Camacho projected 8.8 per cent of the budget in 1942, but the greatest emphasis actually given was 6.5 per cent in 1941. Prior to this, Porfirio Díaz had set the pattern for social expenditure and Madero followed it. During the Carranza period social expenditure of this nature was practically abandoned due to the war conditions in the country—conditions that increased the need for

[6] Alberto J. Pani, *Hygiene in Mexico, A Study of Sanitary and Educational Problems* (New York: Putnam's Sons, 1917). Quote is given by Gruening, *Mexico and Its Heritage,* 533, from the Spanish edition of 1916.

[7] [Ramón Beteta and Eyler N. Simpson], *La Mendicidad en México* (México, D. F.: Beneficencia Pública del Distrito Federal, 1930).

TABLE 7-3

Public Health, Welfare, and Assistance Funds

Year	President[a]	Per Cent Projected	Pesos[b]	Per Cent Actual	Pesos[b]
1869–1870	Juárez	– – –	– – –	– – –	– – –
1900–1901	Díaz	.4	.1	.4	.1
1910–1911	Díaz	2.2	.8	2.0	.7
1911–1912	Madero	2.1	.8	2.1	.7
1912–1913	Madero/Huerta	1.9	.7	2.0	.8
1913–1914	Huerta	1.7	…	…	…
1914–1915	Huerta	1.7	…	…	…
1917	Carranza	1.5	…	.6	…
1918	Carranza	1.0	.3	.8	.1
1919	Carranza	1.0	.4	.9	.1
1920	Carranza/De la Huerta	1.0	.4	1.0	.3
1921	Obregón	1.0	.5	1.1	.5
1922	Obregón	1.0	1.0	1.3	.7
1923	Obregón	1.1	.9	1.2	.6
1924	Obregón	.9	.6	1.2	.8
1925	Calles	1.2	.8	1.6	1.1
1926	Calles	1.7	1.1	2.0	1.4
1927	Calles	2.6	1.8	2.3	1.6
1928	Calles	2.6	1.7	2.4	1.6
1929	Portes Gil	2.5	1.6	2.9	1.8
1930	Portes Gil/Ortiz Rubio	3.0	1.9	3.1	1.9
1931	Ortiz Rubio	2.9	2.1	3.2	1.7
1932	Ortiz Rubio	3.0	1.7	2.9	1.6
1933	Rodríguez	3.0	1.6	2.6	1.5
1934	Rodríguez	3.1	1.7	2.7	1.6
1935	Cárdenas	3.8	2.3	3.5	2.3
1936	Cárdenas	4.5	2.6	3.6	3.0
1937	Cárdenas	4.5	2.6	3.3	2.7
1938	Cárdenas	4.6	3.1	6.1	4.9
1939	Cárdenas	7.9	5.4	5.8	5.2
1940	Cárdenas	8.2	5.5	6.4	5.8
1941	Avila Camacho	8.3	5.6	6.5	6.1
1942	Avila Camacho	8.8	5.9	6.4	6.5
1943	Avila Camacho	7.8	5.5	5.8	6.2
1944	Avila Camacho	5.3	4.4	4.7	5.2
1945	Avila Camacho	6.5	4.4	4.9	5.2
1946	Avila Camacho	4.8	3.2	3.4	3.4

TABLE 7-3 (continued)

Public Health, Welfare, and Assistance Funds

Year	President[a]	Per Cent Projected	Pesos[b]	Per Cent Actual	Pesos[b]
1947	Alemán	6.3	5.6	4.9	5.6
1948	Alemán	5.0	5.6	4.1	5.5
1949	Alemán	4.9	5.6	3.3	5.5
1950	Alemán	4.7	5.0	3.8	5.1
1951	Alemán	4.5	4.5	3.1	4.7
1952	Alemán	3.8	4.2	2.5	4.5
1953	Ruiz Cortines	4.3	4.7	3.2	4.6
1954	Ruiz Cortines	4.1	4.7	2.7	5.0
1955	Ruiz Cortines	4.1	4.6	2.8	4.9
1956	Ruiz Cortines	4.2	5.1	2.9	5.4
1957	Ruiz Cortines	4.5	5.6	3.3	6.2
1958	Ruiz Cortines	4.5	5.8	3.3	6.7
1959	López Mateos	5.1	7.0	3.4	7.1
1960	López Mateos	5.2	7.2	3.5	9.5
1961	López Mateos	4.9	7.0	3.9	10.3
1962	López Mateos	4.6	7.0	4.0	10.0
1963	López Mateos	4.4	7.0	3.3	7.7

[a] Slash indicates latter person administered actual funds.
[b] In pesos per capita of 1950.
SOURCE: See Appendix B.

programs of social action. Not until 1926 did this expenditure recover to pre-1910 levels. Under Cárdenas percentage outlay for public health, welfare, and assistance finally achieved some stature within government programming. Expenditure actually went as high as 5.8 pesos per capita in 1940, double that of 1936.

After Avila Camacho's term, the ideology of economic revolution turned away from this type of social aid. Alemán cut back projections to 3.8 per cent in 1952, a post-1935 low, and the actual percentage ran only 2.5 per cent, the low since Calles left office. Ruiz Cortines maintained this pattern with only slight increases. The ideology of balanced revolution of López Mateos did not offer any change in the share of the budget dedicated to public health and social aid. Only increasing finances allowed this ministry to improve the position of the people, and this came after 1959. Between 1951 and 1955 actual expenditure per capita was 1 to 2 pesos under the Cárdenas-Avila Camacho effort of 1940–1942. López Mateos's per-capita expenditure was projected only slightly above the 1940–1942 standard; however, he actually made more funds available to this agency and about 10 pesos per capita were spent from 1960 to 1962, a dramatic increase.

EXPENDITURE ON POTABLE WATER AND SEWAGE DISPOSAL SYSTEMS

With the creation of the Ministry of Hydraulic Resources in 1947, a small amount of the budget was projected to develop sanitary engineering programs throughout the republic. Actual allocations,

TABLE 7-4

Expenditure on Potable Water and Sewage Disposal Systems, 1947–1963

Year	Per Cent Projected	Pesos[a]	Per Cent Actual	Pesos[a]
1947	.3	.3	– – –	– – –
1948	.4	.5	.3	.4
1949	.4	.5	.3	.5
1950	.4	.4	.3	.4
1951	.6	.6	.4	.6
1952	.7	.8	.5	.9
1953	.7	.8	.4	.6
1954	.6	.7	.3	.6
1955	1.1	1.2	.4	.7
1956	1.2	1.5	.4	.7
1957	1.1	1.4	.5	.9
1958	1.2	1.6	.5	1.0
1959	1.1	1.5	.5	1.0
1960	1.0	1.4	.4	1.1
1961	1.0	1.4	.4	1.1
1962	.8	1.2	.4	1.0
1963	.5	.8	.4	.9

[a] In pesos per capita of 1950.
SOURCE: Appendix B.

however, were not made available until the following year and the amount was minimal. The expenditure for potable water and sewage systems has always had little importance in Mexico and might have been included in the table of minor social expenditure except for the fact that this item is importantly related to the Poverty Index developed in Part II.

We may view presidential policy as follows. Alemán gave sanitary engineering formal budgetary standing, but he did not stimulate its growth. Ruiz Cortines approximately doubled the percentage projected, but the actual share never rose above .5 per cent. In terms of pesos per capita, sanitary engineering was to have reached one peso in 1955, but it did not do so in practice until 1958. Despite the propaganda campaign launched by López Mateos regarding the development of the potable water and sewage disposal systems, the Ruiz Cortines program of expenditure was barely maintained, and it lost ground slightly in percentage actually allocated. The figures given in Table 7-4 are included in the expenditure of the Ministry of Hydraulic Resources but have been separated in this study in order to distinguish between social and economic functions of the Ministry.

THE CREATION OF A LABOR DEPARTMENT

As we saw in the last chapter, the establishment of the Ministry of National Economy marked the transition from the passive state to the active state, and the creation of an independent labor department was part of this program. President Rodríguez sent the initiative for reorganization of his cabinet to Congress in 1932 with the following message:

Universal industrial development and parallel development of social activities have had strong repercussions in all sectors of collective life and have determined its complete transformation. The actual conditions of uncertainty in the world have come to confirm the theory already known that political, juridical, and social phenomena can not be explained in a satisfactory form if the characteristics which imprint economic phenomena are ignored.

State intervention, one of the most debated modern institutions, has come to impose itself gradually but surely in all countries. The modern state has abandoned its purely political conformation in order to intervene decidedly in the collective economic life. In order to do this [the State] has transformed its structural organization and created specialized agencies for a better division of labor.

The Executive must follow a socio-economic political policy founded on a technical base . . . [in order to adjust] a growing number of cases in which the interests of Capital and Labor find themselves in conflict. And since the conflicts between Capital and Labor merit immediate resolution . . . Mexico, like almost all of the advanced nations of the world, requires the establishment of a Department of Labor, an auxiliary agency directly responsible to the Federal Executive.[8]

The Mexican Department of Labor has never disbursed large amounts of money. It regulates labor conditions and conflicts, and establishes policy. Juan de Dios Bojórquez, the constitutionalist of 1917, was the first Minister of Labor and he gave the department the necessary leadership for combating the depression of the early 1930's. Cárdenas's Minister of Labor, Silvano Barba González, used this agency to encourage strikes by handing down decisions favoring labor over capital. The Minister of Labor from 1952 to 1958 was Adolfo López Mateos, and he used the agency to prevent strikes through active conciliation of opposing interests. (The pattern of strikes since 1920 is taken up in Part II.) Since the Department of Labor has not played a large role in budgetary operations, it is not analyzed separately in percentage and per-capita terms, but is included in Table 7-5 which examines minor social expenditure as a percentage of the budget.

INDIAN AFFAIRS

Cárdenas was vitally interested in integrating the Indian into the national social and economic life. To this end, he established a Department of Indian Affairs to organize the teaching of Spanish and to help the Indian adapt to modern life. Cárdenas's goal was not to change the Indian's way of life completely, but to introduce him to the methods and goals of twentieth-century civilization while encouraging him to maintain the best of his own life and values. Cárdenas summed up this view in 1940:

The formula of "incorporating the Indian into civilization" still retains vestiges of old systems which tried to hide de facto inequality because that incorporation has been generally understood to have the

[8] *Excelsior*, Sept. 21, 1932.

TABLE 7-5

Minor Social Expenditure in Percentage Terms

Year	Labor Department		Indian Affairs		*Erogaciones Adicionales*	
	Projected	Actual	Projected	Actual	Projected	Actual
1921	– –	– –	– –	– –	1.2	.8
1922	– –	– –	– –	– –	.9	.7
1923	– –	– –	– –	– –	.7	.6
1924	– –	– –	– –	– –	.7	.5
1933	– –	.4	– –	– –	– – –	– – –
1934	.5	.5	– –	– –	– – –	– – –
1935	.5	.5	– –	.7	– – –	– – –
1936	.5	.4	.2	.1	– – –	– – –
1937	.5	.4	.1	.1	– – –	– – –
1938	.5	.4	.6	.4	– – –	– – –
1939	.5	.4	.7	.5	– – –	– – –
1940	.5	.4	.7	.5	– – –	– – –
1941	.6	.4	.6	.4	– – –	– – –
1942	.5	.4	.5	.4	– – –	– – –
1943	.5	.4	.4	.3	– – –	– – –
1944	.5	.6	.3	.3	– – –	– – –
1945	.5	.4	.4	.2	1.2	.7
1946	.4	.3	.4	.2	1.4	.9
1947	.3	.3	– –	– –	1.3	.6
1948	.2	.2	– –	– –	1.6	.7
1949	.2	.1	– –	– –	1.8	.7
1950	.2	.2	– –	– –	1.5	1.0
1951	.2	.2	– –	– –	1.7	1.0
1952	.2	.1	– –	– –	1.5	1.0
1953	.2	.2	– –	– –	1.8	1.0
1954	.3	.2	– –	– –	1.8	.8
1955	.3	.2	– –	– –	1.7	1.2
1956	.3	.2	– –	– –	1.8	3.2
1957	.4	.3	– –	– –	2.0	2.0
1958	.4	.2	– –	– –	3.4	2.8
1959	.4	.2	– –	– –	3.7	2.7
1960	.4	.2	– –	– –	4.9	2.6
1961	.4	.2	– –	– –	5.3	3.4
1962	.3	.2	– –	– –	7.0	3.9
1963	.3	.3	– –	– –	6.7	4.4

SOURCE: See Appendix B.

purpose of de-Indianization . . . , that is to say, of ending primitive culture by stamping out regional dialects, traditions, customs and even the most profound sentiments of man rooted to his land. Actually, no one now attempts a resurrection of the pre-Cortesian Indian systems or of stagnant life incompatible with the currents of modern life. What must be sustained is the incorporation of the Indian into universal culture, that is to say, to full development of all his potentialities and natural faculties of race [and] the improvement of his conditions of life, adding to his resources of subsistence and labor all the implements of technology of science, and of universal art, but always on the basis of racial personality and respect of conscience. . . .[9]

The Department of Indian Affairs was abolished in order to establish an Institute of Indian Affairs in 1948. The Instituto Nacional Indigenista was created in accord with the resolution of the First Inter-American Indianist Congress, held in Mexico in 1940, where Cárdenas spoke the above words. The new Institute is a decentralized agency which is not under the control of direct federal expenditure. This Institute builds roads, supplies potable water to Indian villages, teaches sports and hygiene, and works to improve the life of the Indian. The Institute takes a different course than Cárdenas took. It claims that the Indian problem in Mexico is not racial since Mexico is a country of mixed bloods. The Institute notes that when the Indian leaves his community he ceases to be an Indian, for the modern culture he accepts is more important than blood in determining his way of life. But the Institute is in agreement with Cárdenas that the Indian way of life should not be crushed out of existence. The purpose of the Institute is to allow the Indian to live with the best values of his past and to retain his arts and crafts while enjoying a higher standard of living.[10]

The Department of Indian Affairs existed only about a dozen years, and it was unimportant in budgetary operations. Plans were made to spend only as much as .7 per cent on it during 1939 and 1940, but in actuality only .5 was spent. These totals are resumed in Table 7-5 which shows that the agency had decreasing importance after 1943. Since the establishment of the National Indigenous Institute as a decentralized agency, figures are not presented

[9] Cárdenas, *Cárdenas Habla,* 271.
[10] Instituto Nacional Indigenista, "Realidades y Proyectos, 16 Años de Trabajo," *Memoria* 10 (1964) 11–13.

as they are not available in the budget. However, according to the most recent résumé of the Institute's work, an even smaller amount has been available for Indian affairs than when the Department of Indian Affairs functioned. If we included this total in the projected budget it would usually amount to .1 per cent. Until 1951 it would not have amounted to that, and since 1962 it would have been about .2 per cent of the budget.[11]

UNCLASSIFIED SOCIAL EXPENDITURE

The share of *erogaciones adicionales* devoted to social budgeting has not been large. Recently it grew somewhat, as Table 7-5 shows. Unclassified expenditures have mainly paid for government contributions to the Mexican Social Security Institute. This Institute, founded in 1943, is a decentralized agency which administers social insurance as a national public service. The program provides coverage for sickness, accidents, maternity, old age, invalidity, and death. Most of the aid is in form of medical service, though monetary aid is part of the program which covers employed persons and their dependents. The Institute collects contributions from employers and employees, invests the funds, and administers all aspects of the insurance.[12]

The best way to see what the role of *erogaciones* has been since it was founded in 1948 is to present the totals allotted to the Mexican Social Security Institute. Funds were first allocated for the Institute in 1944 as part of the public debt, and they became part of *erogaciones adicionales* when the government decided that pensions and medical payments were not really part of Mexico's debt structure. (The figures in Table 7-6 are included in the *erogaciones adicionales* in the previous table.)

The Social Security Institute has always received less in percentage emphasis than promised by the executive. Until the presidency of López Mateos, projected and actual per cent has been less than 3 per cent. The ideology of balanced revolution planned to devote more importance to social security as early as 1958 under Ruiz Cortines, but actual importance did not come until 1962 and 1963 when 2.7 and 3.3 per cent of the budget went to

[11] *Ibid.*, 17.
[12] Consult Tucker, *The Mexican Government Today*, Chapter 23.

TABLE 7-6

Federal Allocations to the Mexican Social Security Institute
(included in Table 7-5)

Year	Per Cent Projected	Pesos[a]	Per Cent Actual	Pesos[a]
1945	1.2	.8	.7	.7
1946	1.4	.9	.9	.9
1947	1.3	1.2	.6	.7
1948	1.6	1.8	.7	.9
1949	1.6	1.9	.5	.9
1950	1.5	1.6	1.0	1.3
1951	1.5	1.5	.8	1.2
1952	1.5	1.7	1.0	1.8
1953	1.7	1.9	1.0	1.4
1954	1.8	2.1	.8	1.5
1955	1.6	1.8	.9	1.6
1956	1.7	2.1	1.1	2.0
1957	1.9	2.4	1.6	3.0
1958	2.7	3.5	1.7	3.5
1959	3.1	4.3	1.9	4.0
1960	3.5	4.8	1.8	4.9
1961	3.6	5.1	2.1	5.5
1962	4.5	6.9	2.7	6.7
1963	4.3	6.8	3.3	7.7

[a] In pesos per capita of 1950.
SOURCE: Table 7-5.

social security; about 4.5 per cent had been projected. The Mexican Social Security Institute had limited funds per capita to work with until 1957. During Ruiz Cortines's last two years, 3 pesos per capita were made available to the Institute. López Mateos more than doubled this figure. Thus after years of poverty and unimportance, social security has risen to prominence, becoming a key item in the propaganda for the ideology of balanced revolution.

With the big budgets which the Mexican government has come to enjoy since the 1940's, the ideology of balanced revolution may be implemented. It is obvious that the greatest amount of funds per capita in Mexican history is available for budgeting. Even if percentages are not allotted equally between social, administrative, and economic expenditure, there is a chance that the goal of the Revolution to eliminate poverty in material and non-material life will be realized.

PART II

SOCIAL CHANGE

We have examined four ideological periods in the
Mexican Revolution since 1910 which have set out to
eliminate poverty and raise the standard of living for
the masses. Mexico's presidents have taken different
actions to integrate the Mexican nation, working
within the ideological context of a given period. We
have examined these actions as tests of political ideology in order to assess the real differences among the
periods which have guided revolutionary thought and
actual programs, and now we must assess the results of
policy.

What has been the effect of federal expenditure on
the goal of social change for the masses? In the context of political policy represented by projected and
actual expenditure, what social results have occurred
since 1910? In asking these questions it is necessary to
reiterate that no assumption is made that federal expenditure directly brings about social change. Governmental handling of the budget only creates an atmosphere in which the private sector and foreign interests
can contribute to economic development to a greater
or lesser degree. Since the government has been the
major force in Mexican life since 1910, especially since
the rise of the active state, its policies have been pre-
dominant in effecting social change.

The social results of the Mexican Revolution have
always been measured indirectly. Thus, for example,
analysts of the Mexican experience have tended to examine the Mexican Revolution with the following assumptions. If the ideology of political revolution were
successful, Mexico would have free elections. If the
ideology of social revolution works out, the people
would have the right to strike, and the amount of land

distributed would measure the psychological social gains of the masses. If there were an economic revolution, it would mean a change in the class structure. The Mexican government has preferred to point to the statistics of economic development, which are impressive, in order to imply that social change has kept up with the material advances of the country. The assumption is that if the country is economically integrated, it must be socially integrated. All these approaches are indirect. They do not tell us whether the ordinary Mexican is any better off than he was before 1910. The task which follows, then, is directly to measure social change in the Mexican Revolution.

8

Indirect Analysis of Social Change

Let us begin analysis of social change with a résumé of existing approaches to the study of the Mexican Revolution. Since these approaches have not always been stated with a historical view, it has been necessary to gather statistics from many sources in order to present a coherent examination of traditional methods. We will take up presidential election results, strike data, land distribution, economic growth, and changing class structure as criteria for inferring social change.

PRESIDENTIAL ELECTION RESULTS

To what degree has political democracy become a reality? Table 8-1 presents the percentages by which the official party has won presidential elections since 1910. It is obvious that the official party, which controls election procedures and counts the votes, has always won elections for the presidency by what is generally considered to be an overwhelming landslide. When Lyndon B. Johnson won 61 per cent of the votes in the United States presidential election of 1964, his triumph was considered to be one of the most powerful political victories for a national executive in the country's history. In Mexico any official party candidate who received such a low figure would have considered himself morally defeated.

Mexican presidents have been elected with over 84 per cent of the vote or more in all but two cases. In 1946 and 1952 the official party polled only 77.9 and 74.3 per cent of the vote. Apparently Mexico's leaders felt that they were so unpopular that they had to allow the opposition at least a show of influence, especially

TABLE 8-1

*Presidential Election Victory Percentages Won by
the Official Party of the Revolution*

Election Year	Per Cent	Legal Votes Cast	Votes for Official Party
1911	99.3	20,145	19,997
1917	97.1	821,062	797,305
1920	95.8	1,181,550	1,131,751
1924	84.1	1,593,233	1,340,634
1928	100.0	1,670,453	1,670,453
1929	93.6	2,082,306	1,948,848
1934	98.2	2,265,971	2,225,000
1940	93.9	2,637,582	2,476,641
1946	77.9	2,293,547	1,786,901
1952	74.3	3,651,201	2,713,419
1958	90.6	7,475,057	6,769,754
1964	89.0	9,402,783	8,368,466

SOURCE: México, Cámara de Diputados, *Diario de los Debates*, Nov. 2, 1911; April 26, 1917; Oct. 26, 1920; Sept. 27, 1924; Nov. 28, 1929; Sept. 12, 1934, 1940, 1946, 1952; Sept. 10, 1958; *Dictamen*, published in *El Día*, Sept. 9, 1964. The official party was not formally established until 1929, but it existed in a *de facto* sense beginning with Madero's victory. The Family has had many squabbles, and the founding of the official party did not end them. Only since Avila Camacho's term has the Family been relatively harmonious.

after the election of 1940 which may have actually been a defeat for the official party. Marte R. Gómez, a cabinet official, who took office under Avila Camacho after the contested election of 1940, has admitted that the official party lost in the Federal District but won throughout Mexico.[1] This is a rare statement, for the official party has never admitted losing the Federal District in any election, and the official figures gave Avila Camacho a 72 per cent victory in the capital in 1940.

There has never been any question that the official party manipulates the vote. Ernest Gruening detailed the electoral corruption in Mexico from 1910 through the 1920's, and Frank Brandenburg has described electoral realities as late as 1964.[2] Francisco I. Madero won perhaps the most honest election in Mexico's history

[1] Marte R. Gómez, Oral History Interviews with James and Edna Wilkie, May 15, 1964, Mexico City. Gómez was Minister of Agriculture under Avila Camacho.
[2] Brandenburg, *The Making of Modern Mexico*, Chapter 6.

in 1911, but only 20,145 votes were cast and the newspapers were full of accounts of violence and turbulence. The election for vice-president was especially bitter, and many persons charged that Madero rigged the election in order to choose his man for the post. The year before, Madero had lost to Porfirio Díaz who received 98.9 per cent of the vote.[3] No election was heatedly contested until that of 1924 when Calles came into the presidency with only 84.1 per cent of the vote. Obregón won re-election handily for no one dared to contest him in 1928—he won 100 per cent of the votes. Pascual Ortiz Rubio, who had not been in Mexico for years, as he had been kept out of politics with diplomatic assignments, won the 1929 election against the popular José Vasconcelos with 93.6 per cent of the tally. It is little wonder that Vasconcelos left Mexico embittered and angry at the way his support had literally been stolen. Cárdenas won the 1934 election with a 98.2 per cent figure. After this record, it is surprising to see the victory figure slip below 80 per cent in 1946 and 1952. Strong opposition existed in those two years, however, and the official party had to admit that its position was weakening. Many foreign observers felt that democracy was finally coming to Mexico, but this did not prove to be the case.

Though the official party has won by huge majorities, this does not mean the presidential elections are entirely corrupt. Indeed, the party is a highly efficient organ which has organized in every corner of Mexico. Anyone having political ambition or hoping to obtain a large government public works contract knows that he will not fare well unless he is a party member. The peasant leagues, the labor unions, the military, and the bureaucracy belong to the party, and they actively seek to vote en bloc. It is highly probable that the official party would win the presidential elections even if it did not manipulate the vote tally for propaganda purposes. Honest elections, however, would open the way to party losses at lower governmental levels and could mean the loss of the presidency if absolute confidence in the official party were diminished. The official party is strong because the populace has no other effective party to which it can turn.[4]

[3] México, Cámara de Diputados, *Diario de los Debates*, Sept. 27, 1910.
[4] For the major study on the failure of Mexican political democracy see Alberto J. Pani, *Una Encuesta Sobre la Cuestión Democrática de México* (México, D. F.: Editorial Cultura, 1948).

It is significant that the only opposition party of note, the National Action Party (PAN) founded in 1939 under the leadership of Manuel Gómez Morín, and identified with Catholic interests, was able to win 7.8 per cent of the vote in 1952 and increase this figure to 9.4 per cent in 1958. It won 11.0 per cent in 1964, and has managed to increase its influence. The PAN claims that it is defrauded of votes in each election, but the fact that the government has had to concede an increasing percentage of the vote to this party (which has never been in power and does not have any patronage to dispense) is quite an important development in Mexican electoral history. Of course there are the charges that PAN is an agent of the government and receives a subsidy, but such complaints may be dismissed. True, the official party is happy to see *some* opposition, but it is not willing to build a political party that has long-range influence. PAN plays the healthy role that a third party in the United States plays, for though it is not able to win the presidency, it acts as a critic of the party in power.

The official party's decision to revert to overwhelming presidental victories in 1958 brought an election return of more than 90 per cent of the vote. Adolfo López Mateos toured the country and sought support from the populace on the basis of having kept peace on the labor front in time of rising prices and labor tension. He triumphed at the polls, but, according to many critics, morally lost the election on the picket line. An important sector of Mexican labor rose up in strike against the government in 1958.

THE RIGHT TO STRIKE

The right of labor to strike was consecrated in the Constitution of 1917, therefore, if labor has gained anything in the Mexican Revolution it should have gained the right to strike. This right has an impact on the masses which can not definitely be measured, for it is psychological. If laborers feel that they can redress their grievances by calling a halt to work, then they do not feel that they are held captive to supply cheap, degraded service. Even though the laborer may be used by his union leaders for political ends, theoretically he still has pride in his work and in his position which he does not have when he is forced by government to work in a disadvantageous wage position. Of course practice often may differ from theory, but we cannot resolve this question here. It is possible, however, to examine the statistical rate of strikes to see under which presidents the laborer has gained psychological rights as well as an increased paycheck.

There is no doubt that the strike in Mexico is related to political affairs. Theoretically there are political strikes and economic strikes, but in a country like Mexico where the government has assumed responsibility for ordering the affairs of the nation, whether under the active or the passive state, great numbers of strikes must be for or against the government. There is as yet little middle ground, especially in the major industries, and in transportation, communications, and education. The cycle of strikes reveals that some presidents have severely limited this right in practice, distinguishing between "Revolution with disorder" and "Revolution with order." Proponents of economic revolution, like Calles, Alemán, and Ruiz Cortines have tried to prevent the strike as a disrupter of the economy, whereas Cárdenas came to real power on the basis of the political strike against capital. López Mateos appeared to have a more balanced labor policy, for he crushed the political strikes but did not break the most economically oriented strikes.

Table 8-2 reveals the straits the Revolution was in during the Calles epoch, 1924–1933. After an auspicious beginning for labor once Carranza was removed from the political scene, the 1920's wound up with few strikes and small numbers of strikers.[5] Table 8-2 is a convenient way of looking at the peaks and depressions in the labor movement which correspond to the political philosophy of Mexico's presidents. In the transition from Carranza to Obregón, labor was in a good position to make demands, especially with Obregón's desire to foster social change. Though Calles talked much about the rights of labor, he kept it well in hand as one of his means of support. Calles believed in "Revolution with order," hence strikes and strikers were considered disruptive of national development, and his philosophy clashed directly with Cárdenas's ideology of social revolution. When in 1935 some 145,-212 strikers, the peak to that time, paralyzed Mexico for months, a confrontation between Calles and Cárdenas was inevitable.

By 1940, however, Cárdenas found himself in a strange position.

[5] There are no statistics on strikes and strikers in Mexico prior to 1920.

TABLE 8-2

Strikes and Strikers, 1920–1963

Year	Strikes	Strikers
1920	173	88,536
1921	310	100,380
1922	197	71,382
1923	146	61,403
1924	136	23,988
1925	51	9,861
1926	23	2,977
1927	16	1,005
1928	7	498
1929	14	3,473
1930	15	3,718
1931	11	227
1932[a]	56	3,574
1933[a]	13	1,084
1934	202	14,685
1935	642	145,212
1936	674	113,885
1937	576	61,732
1938	319	13,435
1939	303	14,486
1940	357	19,784
1941	142	2,748
1942	98	13,643
1943	766	81,557
1944	887	165,744
1945	220	48,055
1946	207	10,202
1947	130	10,678
1948	88	26,424
1949	90	15,380
1950	82	13,166
1951	144	13,553
1952	113	18,298
1953	167	38,552
1954	93	25,759
1955	135	10,710
1956	159	7,573
1957	193	7,137
1958	740	60,611
1959	379	62,770
1960	377	63,567
1961	373	33,184
1962	725	80,989
1963	504	26,035

[a] Incomplete data.

SOURCE: *Anuario Estadístico, 1940,* 376; *1943–1945,* 480; *1953,* 396; and *1962–1964,* 305.

In a speech which noted that the state was now a major employer, he told labor that "the moment has arrived when it must be understood that the weakening of solidarity . . . that exists between the Mexican proletariat and the Revolutionary Regime will provoke a grave crisis for our institutions and the downfall of labor." The labor movement would have to exercise more restraint, he said, for Mexico's economic problems, especially after the expropriation of the oil, could not tolerate the stress of labor demands which threatened the Revolution itself.[6]

The year 1941 marked a diminution of the labor problem to pre-Cárdenas levels, but the wage-price squeeze caught up with Avila Camacho during the war, and labor pressed its demands and brought strikes and strikers to a new high in 1944. During the heyday of economic revolution under Alemán and Ruiz Cortines, however, labor was shackled; from 1946 to 1952 there were few strikes and strikers in Mexico, even though the pressure of falling real wages was tremendous. A comparison of minimum wages in Table 8-3 to the strike pattern is quite revealing. When real minimum wages reached their lowest point during 1944–1945, Avila Camacho, with Cárdenas as his Minister of Defense, could not prevent an outbreak of strikes. However, when real minimum wages fell again in 1950–1951, Alemán kept firm control and did not allow labor trouble to disrupt his economic revolution. Ruiz Cortines greatly increased wages in 1952–1953, but minimum levels were actually falling again when strikes hit López Mateos at the propitious moment of presidential transition. López Mateos was spurred to action and he increased real wages to the highest point since 1934–1935. The rash of strikes in the latter years, Cárdenas's first year in office, came when the real minimum wage was relatively high, compared to later years. Strike figures for Cárdenas and López Mateos, then, when compared to the real minimum wage index, show that strikes under these presidents were politically as well as economically motivated. Both these periods of strike activity came after repression of labor had reached notorious levels, and when strikes were possible.

If the reader questions whether or not a close relationship has existed between governmental policy and the number of strikes and strikers in Mexico, he should consult Appendix G. A tenta-

[6] *El Nacional*, July 25, 1940.

tive comparison of data from 1927 to 1961 shows that there were many more strikes and strikers as a percentage of the total population in the United States than in Mexico (data for the United States are not available prior to 1927 and for Mexico after 1961). It is interesting to note that in 1936 the index of strikers was exactly the same in both countries. Labor in Mexico did indeed appear to take a revolutionary stance under Cárdenas during the mid-1930's because its action in all other years was so limited, especially in comparison to what was happening in the United States. Calles, Ortiz Rubio, Rodríguez, Avila Camacho, Alemán, and Ruiz Cortines were each able to keep the index of strikers below one tenth of the 1936 figure for two years or more. It was no wonder that strikers took advantage of the presidential change in 1958. In comparison to the United States there had not been a significant number of strikers as a percentage of the total population since 1944, and for three straight years from 1955 to 1957 the index had been at a post-1941 low. The role of labor had not been so restricted since the pre-Cárdenas era.

The number of strikes compared to the population of the United States and Mexico also permits us to compare vastly different bases for analysis. Except for the years 1935, 1936, 1943, 1944, and 1958, the ratio of strikes to population in the United States exceeded the ratio in Mexico, often greatly.

In calling attention to the data in Appendix G some comments and qualifications are in order. In both countries rural laborers generally have been unorganized for calling strikes, and we are dealing with a predominately urban scale. Since the population which has been active economically from year to year is unknown for Mexico, data are compared to total population. This is actually a better basis for comparison because of the large proportion of poverty-striken persons in Mexico who are not counted as economically active. Due to the different bases of economic development it is not possible to say with any exactness whether or not an equal percentage of strikers in each country is equally damaging to the economy. A case could be made both ways, but since we do not know qualitative comparisons (kinds of strikes and duration, for example), it is dangerous to go very far with analysis. The magnitude of difference between labor action in the United States and Mexico, however, indicates in very broad terms that

Mexican labor organizations generally have been captive unions. This conclusion tends to corroborate scholarly nonquantitative analysis of labor's position in Mexico.

It is clear that strikes generally were not caused when the real minimum wage collapsed under the failure of the government to raise the legal minimum wage in times of inflation. As Table 8-3

TABLE 8-3

Urban Minimum Wage Index, 1934–1935 to 1962–1963
(1940–1941 = 100)

Biennium	Average Minimum Wage Index	Wholesale Price Index, Mexico City	Real Minimum Wage Index
1934–1935	75.7	69.4	109.1
1936–1937	86.2	87.4	98.6
1938–1939	96.1	93.6	102.7
1940–1941	100.0	100.0	100.0
1942–1943	100.0	132.6	75.4
1944–1945	125.0	186.9	66.9
1946–1947	163.2	223.3	73.1
1948–1949	198.0	251.0	78.9
1950–1951	220.4	336.2	65.6
1952–1953	352.0	337.0	104.5
1954–1955	466.0	468.5	99.5
1956–1957	517.1	527.8	98.0
1958–1959	538.8	560.0	96.2
1960–1961	619.1	597.2	103.7
1962–1963	856.6	616.9	138.9

Source: *50 Años en Cifras*, 112; Price Index, Table 1-8.

shows, only in 1944 when the real minimum wage index was at its low was there a corresponding high in indices of strikes and strikers.

In sum, the right to strike and the minimum wage have not been guarantees to social change; they have been involved with politics. One American investigator has written that inflation in Mexico during the 1940's and early 1950's was not deliberately brought about by the government, but that it was due to rising

TABLE 8-4

Execution of Definitive Presidential Resolutions Distributing Land Since 1915

President	Date Term Ends	Approx. Months	Total Hectares Executed	Average Per Month	Index	Total as a Per Cent of Mexico's Surface[a]	Cumulative Total	Per Cent of Mexico's Surface[a]
Carranza	May 21, 1920	66.5	167,936	2,525	2	.1	167,936	.1
De la Huerta[b]	Nov. 30, 1920	6.0	33,696	5,616	5	– – –	201,632	.1
Obregón	Nov. 30, 1924	48.0	1,100,117	22,919	19	.6	1,301,749	.7
Calles	Nov. 29, 1928	48.0	2,972,876	61,935	51	1.5	4,274,625	2.2
Portes Gil	Feb. 4, 1930	14.1	1,707,750	121,117	100	.9	5,982,375	3.0
Ortiz Rubio	Sept. 3, 1932	30.8	944,538	30,667	25	.5	6,926,913	3.5
Rodríguez	Nov. 29, 1934	27.0	790,694	29,285	24	.4	7,717,607	3.9
Cárdenas	Nov. 29, 1940	72.0	17,906,429	248,700	205	9.1	25,624,036	13.0
Avila Camacho	Nov. 30, 1946	72.0	5,944,449	82,562	68	3.0	31,568,485	16.1
Alemán	Nov. 30, 1952	72.0	4,844,123	67,279	56	2.5	36,412,608	18.6
Ruiz Cortines	Nov. 30, 1958	72.0	4,936,668	68,565	56	2.5	41,349,276	21.0
López Mateos	Nov. 30, 1964	72.0	11,361,370	157,797	130	5.8	52,710,646	26.8

[a] Mexico's total continental surface (excluding islands) is 196,718,300 hectares (*Anuario Estadístico, 1964–1965*, 13).

[b] In regard to the source below, data for De la Huerta given in the *Memoria* are subtracted from revisions on Obregón which include figures on De la Huerta.

SOURCE: México, Departamento de Asuntos Agrarios y Colonización, revised data for period from 1915 to August 31, 1966 (departmental records, Table B-3), based upon México, Departamento Agrario, *Memoria, 1945–1946*, Part II (Statistics).

costs. He notes, however, that government policy of maintaining legal minimum wage levels far behind rising prices did not contribute to increased capital formation, as excess profits tended to go into relatively nonproductive commercial and urban real estate ventures or into luxury buying instead of into industrialization and investment in capital goods.[7]

LAND DISTRIBUTION

Though the revolutionary governments have clouded the labor movement in Mexico by making it a political consideration, they have a better record in aiding the peasants. True, laborers have received more benefits of social security and higher wages than the peasant, but a large number of peasants have received their own plot of land. To people rooted to the soil, including urban intellectuals who generally have an idealistic and romantic attachment to Mexico's agrarian past, the psychological impact of land distribution has been the most important single factor in judging the results of the Revolution.

Land distribution programs of Mexico's presidents since the rearrangement of legal land holding was undertaken in 1915 already have been described. Here it is necessary only to summarize the rate of change in land tenure during the various periods of the Revolution in order to comment on its effects. Table 8-4 shows figures of the land actually granted instead of the presidential resolutions to grant lands, for the latter may not be implemented in the same term. Thus we can see what presidents did rather than what they set in motion. Between 1915 and 1964 the Revolution has distributed 52,710,646 hectares of land, or 26.8 per cent of Mexico's surface. This compares to 57,778,102 hectares of *latifundia*, covering 29.4 per cent of Mexico, which were created by the Liberal governments between 1853 and 1911.[8] It is clear from

[7] Barry N. Seigel, "Inflation and Economic Development: Studies in the Mexican Experience, Ph.D. thesis in economics, University of California, Berkeley, 1957, published as *Inflación y Desarrollo; las Experiencias de México* (México, D. F.: Centro de Estudios Monetarios Latinoamericanos, 1960); private saving as a percentage of the GNP passed the 1939 level in the years 1948, 1949, 1950, 1952, 1954, and 1955, but only by 1 or 2 per cent, and generally savings were 1 or 2 per cent lower than in 1939 (p. 119 of the thesis).

[8] Wilkie, "Mexican Latifundia and Land Reform." Land surface of 100 per cent is for the continental total only (islands excluded).

the index for average distribution per month in office that Lázaro Cárdenas has the record for rearrangement of land tenure in the Revolution, followed by Adolfo López Mateos and then by Emilio Portes Gil. The low index number is held by Venustiano Carranza.

Several times during the course of revolutionary distribution of land, the government has declared that all the land available for grants has been distributed. Calles encouraged Ortiz Rubio to bring the program to an end in 1930, as we have seen, and Silvano Barba González, Avila Camacho's chief of the Agrarian Department and a leading *cardenista,* noted in 1945 that

Cárdenas's velocity of land distribution could not last forever: first, because applications for lands diminish as agrarian needs of the people are satisfied; second, because the technical labors directed towards the localization of affectable lands are rendered more difficult, delayed and laborious as land distribution advances, which in turn delays the agrarian proceedings; and third, because the volume of affectable lands diminishes by the day and naturally will run out when all rural property has been distributed.[9]

Yet over 21,000,000 hectares have been found for distribution since 1945.

If the government has resolved several times to bring land distribution to an end, how can we account for the startling revival of the program under Lázaro Cárdenas and López Mateos? Population figures shed light on this problem. In spite of the relative decrease of agriculturally employed persons in the total population (Table 8-5), the absolute number has gained tremendously, especially since 1940 as modern health techniques have lowered death rates. An increase in rural population was not foreseen by the proponents of land distribution, for the problem of the 1920's seemed to be one of filling Mexico's empty spaces; this was the old nineteenth-century problem of opening Mexico to make it great and it was given renewed vigor by events in Europe. Gilberto Loyo, Mexico's famous demographer, wrote in 1931 at the University of Rome that a nation's greatness lay in an expanded population.[10] Since the devastating effects of civil war in Mexico

[9] México, Departamento Agrario, *Memoria 1945–1946,* no pagination.

[10] Gilberto Loyo, *Las Deficiencias Cuantitativas de la Población de México y una Política Demográfica Nacional* (México: P[artido] N[acional] R[evolucionario], 1934, 3rd ed.)

TABLE 8-5

Increase of Agriculturally Employed Population

| | | Agriculturally Employed[a] | | Per Cent Change in Absolute Number | |
Year	Total Population	Per Cent of Total Population	Absolute Number	Increase Per Period	Increase Per Year
1910	15,160,369	23.7	3,596,157	– –	– –
1921	14,334,780	24.3	3,490,039	−3.0	−.3
1930	16,552,722	21.9	3,626,871	3.9	.4
1940	19,653,552	19.5	3,830,871	5.6	.6
1950	25,791,017	18.7	4,823,901	25.9	2.6
1960	34,923,129	17.6	6,144,930	27.4	2.7

[a] Agriculture includes ranching, hunting, fishing, and forestry.
SOURCE: *Resumen del Censo, 1910–1960.*

—the agriculturally employed population dropped 3 per cent between 1910 and 1920 and gained only 3.9 per cent between 1920 and 1930—Loyo's argument seemed convincing. Apparently, there was no reason why every man could not have his own plot. And it was logical for Cárdenas to attempt to break the strength of *latifundia* in Mexico. Agrarian reform had been postponed too long, for when Cárdenas came into office only 3.9 per cent of Mexico's surface had been distributed.

When Cárdenas left office at the end of 1940 the situation in Mexico was different. Land had been distributed at a great rate and the old desires of the Revolution had been satisfied. The threat of a world war and the need to consolidate the gains of the Cárdenas period 1934–1940 dictated a more moderate course. Population employed in the countryside had not increased notably during the 1930's—it was still under 4 million—and land distribution fell progressively lower under Avila Camacho, Alemán, and Ruiz Cortines. Demographic increase, however, gradually created a new tension. As Table 8-5 shows, the percentage of population working in agricultural pursuits shot up during the 1940's to 4.8 million persons and continued to grow more rapidly during the 1950's. Incredibly, by 1960 some 6.1 million persons were trying to make a living from the land. The average plot of 12 to 25 hectares given out during the 1930's was now over-crowded with eligible young laborers. These new workers could work only part-time on the family plot or perhaps go to the United States to work as *braceros*. Obviously the pressure of population in Mexico was building up on the land. This explains, in part, why López Mateos was spurred to approach Cárdenas's record of giving out land. Note, however, that López Mateos concentrated on distributing land that other presidents had already resolved to give away. He could look "revolutionary" at a time when dissatisfaction with economic revolution was rife, yet he would not upset the nation by resolving to distribute more land. López Mateos sought other solutions in executing land distribution, for he emphasized the confirmation of titles as a significant part of his program. He left a huge problem to his successor Gustavo Díaz Ordaz, 1964–1970, for either Díaz Ordaz will have to resolve to give away lands and then act rapidly to execute his resolutions or he may well stand condemned by the Mexican populace as anti-revolutionary. Apparently Díaz Ordaz has chosen his course carefully, however, and he will distribute the great private preserves of livestock ranching land created under Alemán. Yet his Chief of the Agrarian Department has pointed out that even with distribution of this land, Mexico must realize that there is now not enough land for each person to own an economically viable plot.[11]

It is possible to look at distribution of land as a political necessity, for unless a relatively high percentage of the population employed agriculturally has received benefits from the Revolution, trouble may be expected in the countryside, and Mexico has been a country where the bulk of the economically active population has been employed in agriculture (Table 8-6).

Regarding the percentage of the agriculturally employed population which has received benefits, it is reasonable to supppose that since landholding rights are inalienable, and since they revert to the communal village for redistribution if they are given up or if the recipient dies without heirs, a growing pool of recipient shares can be determined by adding the new recipients

[11] Aguirre speech of April 24, 1965.

TABLE 8-6

Per Cent of Economically Active Population
Employed in Agriculture [a]

Year	Per Cent	Year	Per Cent
1910	68.3	1940	63.4
1921	68.8	1950	58.3
1930	67.7	1960	54.1

[a] Over twelve years old.

SOURCE: Decennial census data are adjusted here for consistency (servants are included for 1910, 1921, 1940, consistent with present policy).

of land in each presidential term to the total recipients who have gone before. Thus by 1934 a total of 783,330 persons had received some benefit from the government's land program, either by a land grant or by a confirmation of title. This total remained fixed even though original recipients may not then have held the land, for persons without land would have been awarded the privilege relinquished by the original titleholder. The total of 783,330 was 21.1 per cent of the population employed agriculturally in 1934. Since the actual structure of employment except in census years is unknown, it is assumed that between census years it changes proportionately to the rates given in Table 8-5. When Cárdenas left office in 1940, a census year, 41.6 per cent of the population employed in agriculture had seen revolutionary promises redeemed. This is a very high total, and it helps us to understand why the government's talk of the Revolution is credible to the masses of Mexicans. Table 8-7 brings together these assumptions and presents an estimate of the per cent of agriculturally employed population which has received some benefit from the Revolution at the end of each presidential term. Of course, this estimate is only approximate, for in later years some lands have been sold and some noncommunal lands have been distributed. Presumably, these exceptions have been minor and do not alter the calculations.

A comparison of the average hectares granted to each recipient in Table 8-7 with the average hectares granted by Porfirio Díaz

TABLE 8-7

Recipients of Land by Presidential Term Since 1915

Year Term Ends	President	Recipients		(A) Cumulative Number of Recipients	(B) Agriculturally Employed Population	"A" as Per Cent of "B"
		Number	Average Hectares			
1920	Carranza	46,398	3.6	46,398	3,490,039[a]	1.3
1920	De la Huerta	6,330	5.3	52,728	3,490,039[a]	1.5
1924	Obregón	128,468	8.6	181,196	*3,545,880	5.1
1928	Calles	297,428	10.6	478,624	*3,601,720	13.3
1930	Portes Gil	171,577	10.0	650,201	3,626,871	17.9
1932	Ortiz Rubio	64,573	14.6	714,774	*3,670,393	19.5
1934	Rodríguez	68,556	11.5	783,330	*3,713,915	21.1
1940	Cárdenas	811,157	22.1	1,594,487	3,830,871	41.6
1946	Avila Camacho	157,536	37.7	1,752,023	*4,428,487	39.6
1952	Alemán	97,391	49.7	1,849,414	*5,084,392	36.4
1958	Ruiz Cortines	231,888	21.1	2,081,302	*5,865,865	35.5
1964	López Mateos	304,498	37.3	2,385,800	*6,808,582[b]	35.0

[a] Data for the census of 1921. [b] Increase calculated at same rate as for 1950's

SOURCE: Tables 8-4 and 8-5.

and Francisco I. Madero, in Table 3-1, reveals the great change in agrarian philosophy after Madero's death. During civil war between 1913 and 1915 it became clear that the land would have to be distributed in small plots to the common man. The average-sized holding distributed by the federal government always has been less than 50 hectares of land. The average here is meaningless except to show the relative programs of each president, for plots distributed in irrigated areas will be very small, perhaps from 1 to 5 hectares, and land given out in arid parts of the republic for pasture will require hundreds of hectares in order to be economically productive. Thus as presidential averages rise, we may be seeing mainly less usable land granted to peasants. In the last years, too, presidents have tried to give larger plots which will contribute to feeding the country instead of limiting the recipient to subsistence agriculture.

Presidential interest in resolving the agrarian problem can also be treated by examining the amount of credit made available to the countryside, for land without credit has often been more of a burden for the people than a positive economic gain. Cárdenas firmly established agricultural credit in the federal budget in 1935, but, as we have seen, inflation and disinterest took their toll of the standard which he projected until López Mateos renewed agricultural credit with an attempt to solve Mexico's rural credit problem.

In the final analysis we cannot say that the peasants who have received land live any better materially than they did without land. But we do know that, psychologically, the old patterns of master and man have come to an end. Many peasants have come to hold their own land. Land distribution has penetrated every corner of the republic and there is a spirit of hope in all peasants who have not yet received land that they too will be the lucky ones someday to own a plot, even if it is bad land.

ECONOMIC MODERNIZATION

Economic growth in Mexico has been so successful since 1940 that many revolutionists have claimed that it is a fair index of what has happened to social life in the nation; if the economy is booming, conditions must be better for the masses than when

TABLE 8-8

Representative Indices of Economic Growth During Eras of Political, Social, and Economic Revolution
(1940 = 100)

Sector	Political		Social		Economic	
	1910	1920	1930	1940	1950	1960
Volume of Manufacturing	41	32	62	100	217	465
Volume of Cement Production	12	9	47	100	286	636
Volume of Steel Production	46	29^d	69	100	262	1034
Volume of Zinc Extraction	2	14	124	100	195	233
Volume of Crude Oil Production	8	435^d	89	100	166	245
Generation of Electrical Energy	*12	*13	58	100	175	421
Volume of Agricultural Production	121	74	78	100	177	318
Livestock Census	71^a	...	85	100	131	179
Road Network (all types)	– –	– –	14	100	216	454
Motor Vehicles (autos, buses, trucks)	...	31^e	60	100	208	551
Railroad Tonnage Transported	...	39^d	70	100	144	241
Resources of Credit Institutions	47^b	36^f	33	100	804	3143
Monetary Circulation	40^c	...	34^g	100	573	1648
Value of Exports	27^c	89	48	100	452	962
Value of Imports	29^c	59	52	100	658	2217
Real Income Per Capita	...	...	63	100	159	187
Population	77	73^d	84	100	131	178

a 1902   b 1907   c 1909–1910   d 1921   e 1924   f 1926   g 1931

Source: 50 Años en Cifras.

growth is slow, jobs are few, and money is not changing hands. Table 8-8, based upon official presentation of statistics, shows the growth in various sectors of the economy since 1940 in comparison to earlier periods of ideological revolution. It is obvious that the great economic changes in Mexico have come since 1940. Cárdenas's last year in office marks the watershed of economic growth, for in the next eighteen years all the indices reached high levels which were running ahead of population growth, including agricultural production which had fallen drastically to 1930 and still had not regained its 1910 level in 1940. Production of crude oil was at its peak in 1921, but it fell off through the 1920's as foreign interests declined to risk capital investment which was threatened by nationalization. Oil was nationalized in 1938, but production has never approached the boom figure of 1921. It is interesting to note that by 1930 railway length reached its maximum, but transportation of tonnage, though at a record high, had not yet really begun to grow.[12]

The proponents of economic revolution can point to the record of economic growth with pride, for Mexico has never produced such a volume of goods and services so quickly as it did during the years from 1940 to 1960. Yet, as we noted in Chapter 4, the ideology of economic revolution did not abandon the countryside. We may also point out that the ideology of social revolution did not abandon industrialization. Complexity in the results of Mexican revolutionary programs may be seen in comparing the growth of manufacturing and irrigation. During the decade of the 1930's the index of manufacturing production presented in Table 8-8 went up 61.3 per cent, a gain over the 52.0 per cent increase during the twenty years of political revolution, 1910–1930. Though the gain of the 1930's was not as high as the increase of 365 per cent which had come during the twenty years of economic revolution, the struggle for social justice during the 1930's did not sacrifice the growth of manufacturing production (see Table 10-8).

Nor did economic revolution sacrifice agrarian policy entirely, for irrigation was undertaken on a large scale to open lands for expansion and to improve lands already occupied, many of which had no water. Table 8-9 brings together data on the politics of

[12] New railway lines have been added to the system, but old lines have been retired, and thus over-all length of the system has not changed much since 1930.

TABLE 8-9

Land Irrigation by Presidential Term Since 1926

President	Date Term Ends	Approximate Months[a]	Total Hectares Irrigated (In Thousands)	Average Per Month	Cumulative Hectares Irrigated (In Thousands)
Calles	Nov. 30, 1928	36	2	– – –	2
Portes Gil	Feb. 4, 1930	12	6	1	8
Ortiz Rubio	Sept. 1, 1932	36	50	1	58
Rodríguez	Nov. 30, 1934	24	91	4	149
Cárdenas	Nov. 30, 1940	72	118	2	267
Avila Camacho	Nov. 30, 1946	72	549	8	816
Alemán	Nov. 30, 1952	72	626	9	1442
Ruiz Cortines	Nov. 30, 1958	72	770	11	2212
López Mateos	Nov. 30, 1964	72	365	5	2577

[a] Hectares are calculated on yearly bases which do not coincide exactly with dates of presidential terms (except for the presidency of López Mateos). The only big discrepancy is for 1932 when Ortiz Rubio left office September 1. Ortiz Rubio is credited with all hectares for that year on the assumption that his successor would largely execute plans already drawn up during the previous eight months. Exact dates of presidential terms are found in Appendix C.

SOURCES: Adolfo Orive Alba, "Las Obras de Irrigación," in *México Cincuenta Años de Revolución*, 335–383 (México, D. F.: Fondo de Cultura Económica, 1960, 4 vols.), I. *La Economía*, 354; *50 Años en Cifras*, 49; Presidential Message 1964, *El Día*, Sept. 2, 1964.

land irrigation since Calles undertook the program in 1926. Since irrigation works are long-term projects, they often overlap presidential periods, and one president may inaugurate the work of another; this was especially true during the confused period 1928–1934. Nevertheless, we can compare land irrigation to land distribution in Table 8-4 to understand each period in the Revolution. Until economic revolution got under way, emphasis on land irrigation was played down. During times of great distribution of land immediately before and after economic revolution, 1940–1960, land irrigation gave way directly to land distribution.

The relation of water to land shows up more clearly in presidential grants of waters, for there is no possible confusion about who signed resolutions. Table 8-10 portrays an aspect of the agrarian problem often neglected by students of Mexico; land distribution is only one side of the agrarian picture since water is the key to making the land productive. Ruiz Cortines is the undisputed leader in alloting grants and accessions to waters. Avila Camacho follows and Alemán is third. Portes Gil rates high, which is surprising due to both his short time in office and his emphasis on land distribution. The other great distributors of land, Cárdenas and López Mateos, neglected this aspect of the agrarian problem. Thus revolutionary policy has been quite complex in its execution.

Despite attempts of the government to use water policy to bring agricultural output into some balance with other Mexican economic output, industrial activity has been increasing at a much more rapid rate than agricultural production. After alternating periods of emphasis on land distribution and on water policy to solve Mexico's agrarian problems, the agricultural problem is still Mexico's main headache. Though some authors have recently taken the view that Mexico has enjoyed a "balanced boom" since 1940,[13] the historical view does not reveal any balance in economic development.

As Table 8-11 shows, primary activities which are agriculturally based have consistently contributed less than one quarter of the Gross National Product while secondary activities, industrially

[13] Cline, *Mexico; Revolution to Evolution, 1940–1964*, Chapter 27, and Pedro C. M. Teichert, *Economic Policy Revolution and Industrialization in Latin America* (U. of Miss., 1959), Chapter 12.

TABLE 8-10

Resolutions of Grants and Accessions to Waters by Presidential Term Since 1915 [a]

President	Date Term Ends	Months	Cubic Meters	Average Per Month	Index
Carranza	May 21, 1920	66.5	22,435,012	337,369	2
De la Huerta	Nov. 30, 1920	6.0	- - -	- - -	- - -
Obregón	Nov. 30, 1924	48.0	88,137,812	1,836,204	8
Calles	Nov. 30, 1928	48.0	486,841,846	10,142,538	45
Portes Gil	Feb. 4, 1930	14.1	315,244,029	22,357,733	100
Ortiz Rubio	Sept. 1, 1932	30.8	261,840,183	8,501,305	38
Rodríguez	Nov. 30, 1934	27.0	139,288,492	5,158,833	23
Cárdenas	Nov. 30, 1940	72.0	631,126,735	8,765,649	39
Avila Camacho	Nov. 30, 1946	72.0	2,269,695,645	31,523,551	141
Alemán	Nov. 30, 1952	72.0	1,752,386,943	24,338,708	109
Ruiz Cortines	Nov. 30, 1958	72.0	3,146,289,523	43,698,466	196
López Mateos	Nov. 30, 1964	72.0	1,007,400,368	13,991,672	63
Total			10,120,686,588		

[a] Grants are made by the President of Mexico; accessions are made by the Agrarian Department.
SOURCE: Departamento de Asuntos Agrarios y Colonización (unrevised figures).

based, have gained, especially at the expense of output in tertiary activities. An Index of Per Capita Contribution to Gross National Product reveals that, since the Revolution, the per-capita share of primary activities has approached the average per-capita contribution of all sectors at a very slow rate. Secondary activities remained well over 50 per cent higher than the average until 1940 and then went up to over double the average. Only tertiary activities have markedly approached the average. It is obvious that since the 1940's there has been an increasing lack of balance between sectors in the Mexican economy. Since more than half the economically employed population works in agriculture, as the Mexican president points out in presenting the statistics in Table 8-11, the primary source of activity has not pulled its share in national economic development.

SOCIAL CLASS CHANGES

The successes of economic development and the emergence of a modern urbanized sector of Mexican society have stimulated several investigators to examine the rise of the middle class in Mexico.[14] Howard F. Cline has concluded that the class changes in Table 8-12 have taken place.

According to these estimates, the Revolution in classes and occupational structure has come since 1940, slowly but steadily. The population belonging to the popular class has changed more slowly than the upper and middle classes in percentage terms, though the absolute decrease from a larger base has been greater.

Calculations of the Mexican government based on income rather than occupation do not present such a sanguine view, for by these standards the middle class constituted only 16.9 per cent of the population in 1960, about double the percentage of 1900. The popular class has been reduced from 91.1 per cent to only 82.4 per cent of the population in the same time span.[15] These figures would seem to understate the amount of opportunity and

[14] Nathan L. Whetten, "The Rise of a Middle Class in Mexico," in Vol. 2 *Materiales para el Estudio de la Clase Media en América Latina* (Washington, D. C.: Unión Panamericana, 1950-1951), 6 vols.; John J. Johnson, *Political Change in Latin America: The Emergence of the Middle Sectors* (Stanford: Stanford University Press, 1958).

[15] *50 Años en Cifras*, 154.

TABLE 8-II

Gross National Product by Sectors of Origin and Per Capita Contribution

A. Per Cent by Sector of Origin

	1910	1921	1930	1940	1950	1960
Primary Activities[a]	27.4	25.3	19.7	20.5	23.8	23.0
Secondary Activities[b]	20.0	21.5	25.4	24.9	32.5	36.1
Tertiary Activities[c]	52.6	53.2	54.9	54.6	43.7	40.9
Total	100.0	100.0	100.0	100.0	100.0	100.0

B. Index of Per-Capita Contribution
(Average = 100)

	1910	1921	1930	1940	1950	1960
Primary Activities[a]	38.2	33.7	29.0	32.4	40.8	43.6
Secondary Activities[b]	153.6	165.4	182.9	159.9	203.8	216.0
Tertiary Activities[c]	348.7	450.6	298.1	258.1	169.8	134.1

[a] Agriculture (includes ranching, hunting, and fishing).
[b] Includes mining, construction, petroleum, and manufacturing.
[c] Includes public and private services and unspecified activities.
SOURCE: *50 Años en Cifras*, 34–37.

social change, however, and in light of the following chapters Cline's estimations offer a more reasonable view.

TABLE 8-12

Classes and Occupational Structure, 1895–1960

	1895	1940	1950	1956	*1960
Total	100.0	100.0	100.0	100.0	100.0
Upper Class[a]	1.5	2.9	2.0	5.0	6.5
Middle Class[b]	7.8	12.6	25.0	30.0	33.5
Transitional[c]	– – –	6.5	20.0	20.0	20.0
Popular[d]	90.7	78.0	53.0	45.0	40.0

[a] Managerial and professional.

[b] Professional, Technical, Office Workers, Small Tradesmen, Artisans.

[c] Small Tradesmen, Semi-skilled Artisans, Miners, Petroleum Labor, Service Employees.

[d] Service Employees, Manual and Day Laborers, Agriculturists, Unknown.

SOURCE: Cline, *Mexico; Revolution to Evolution, 1940–1960*, Chapter 11. Cline's work is based upon and expands Iturriaga's study of *La Estructura Social*.

All the foregoing approaches to examination of social change in the Mexican Revolution have a problem in that they imply change for the masses and do not directly attempt to measure it. Since the Revolution was undertaken to raise the standard of living for the poverty-stricken masses and socially to integrate the Mexican nation, the question persists: What social change has actually taken place for the masses?

9

An Index of Poverty

The purpose of this chapter is to present an index which will allow us quantitatively to compare poverty levels and the rate of social change in each federal entity since 1910. A definition of poverty is established here by a discussion of the seven items included in the Poverty Index. Complete statistics for each item are given, but detailed interpretation is reserved until the index is presented. Regional analysis is undertaken on the basis of the Poverty Index in order to offer a comprehensible interpretation of the social results of the Revolution.

DEFINITION OF POVERTY

Poverty can be discussed in many different meanings and contexts. In the rich nations one may speak of intellectual and spiritual poverty in addition to a poverty of monetary income which falls below an arbitrary standard of living. In underdeveloped countries, it is hard to speak of these types of poverty when large numbers of the population can not, for example, read or write, speak the national language, or obtain proper diet and medical care. If persons live in isolated villages and are ill-clothed and ill-shod, it is difficult to talk of intellectual and spiritual poverty, for day-to-day adversity is the primary fact which governs life. There are, of course, many romanticists who actually believe that the life of the Mexican peasant is an idyllic one and should not be upset for the dubious advantages of modern civilization, but these people have never lived in the Mexican countryside. All revolutionists have talked in terms of raising the standard of living of the people. None has proposed to let the masses remain stagnant in a traditional agricultural paradise where they can pluck their guitars, drink pulque or tequila, and fall into a timely siesta to accommodate the passing tourist looking for the picturesque old Mexico of Porfirio Díaz.

If Mexico is to become a modern, integrated nation, the people must lead a better life. The success of the Revolution can and must be evaluated in social as well as economic terms. It is necessary to note that this study is not proposing any method of change, or even suggesting that spiritual poverty might not result from amelioration of the hardships in the old way of life which we define. The poverty treated in this study can not begin to compare with poverty in a developed country, for it deals with some basic deprivations of life.

The characteristics of poverty chosen for the Index are the only census items for standard of living that can be traced back with historical continuity. From 1910 to 1940 only three items were gathered by census takers which would reveal the immediate social position of the populace. After a decade of social revolution in the 1930's, the 1940 census was concerned with specifically checking to see what the social conditions of the people were. Therefore, since 1940 we have seven items with which to work. In 1960, with the shift to renewed interest in the social conditions of the masses, the López Mateos government included a new item in the census which attempts to measure directly the nation's dietary pattern. The new item asks whether or not persons more than one year old eat regularly at least of the following foods yielding nonvegetable protein: meat, fish, milk, and eggs. This item is, of course, of no use here, for it will take several censuses to see what changes take place, and what the item really means.

Analysis of social change during the period 1910–1960 is based on the assumption that all of the seven items under consideration represent relative degrees of nonmodern standards of living. The items cover the persons actually stating in the census that they (1) are illiterate, (2) speak only an Indian language, (3) live in a community with less than 2500 persons, (4) go barefoot, (5) wear sandals, (6) regularly eat tortillas instead of wheat bread and (7) are without sewage disposal. These characteristics of poverty carry equal weight in the Index, since, for example, who is to say that illiteracy is more of a problem than only speaking an Indian language. In either case the individual is denied access to many benefits of modern culture.

Lest we grow indignant that the above items are based on American standards applied somehow dishonestly to Mexico in the hope of corrupting her to follow our path, we should note that Mexican anthropologists have attempted since at least as early as 1916 to modernize Mexican society while maintaining the best of traditional values. Mexico's most famous anthropologist, Manuel Gamio, has written that the Spanish language must be spread to every corner of Mexico in order to integrate the nation, and the tortilla and the sandal must give at least some ground to the progress that man has laboriously worked out to improve human health and comfort.[1] Three of the above items (4–6) were included in the 1940 census on the assumption that an analysis of poverty would reveal the number of Indians in the populace. As we will see, these items did not have as much to do with Indian culture as with the general culture of poverty.

There are problems in developing analyses of poverty and perhaps a few should be noted before we continue our discussion. Any definition of poverty must be somewhat abstract, and it must override individual variations. It is important to recognize, however, that though an individual may exhibit one or more of the characteristics in the Poverty Index and still not be considered poor by his neighbors, the sum of poverty characteristics has a great deal to do with the collective well-being of the nation.

If we view the items included in the Poverty Index as characteristics which tend to reveal the relative health of society at a given historical time, then the Index will make sense. If we view the items on an individual level we face such inconsistencies as pointed out by Oscar Lewis in his study of *Life in a Mexican Village: Tepoztlán Restudied* (Urbana: University of Illinois, 1951, Chapter IX). Lewis's statistical calculations of standards of living showed that the eating of tortillas correlated positively with economic position: wealthy people preferred bread. On the other hand, the wearing of shoes did not correlate with wealth, but with

[1] Manuel Gamio, *Forjando Patria* (México, D. F.: Editorial Porrúa, 1960, 182. This edition contains an article published in *América Indígena* (Jan., 1945) on "Las Características Culturales y los Censos Indígenas" which discusses the deficiencies in traditional ways of life. See also *Hacia un México Nuevo* (México, D. F.: n.p., 1935), 31–52.

age: the older generation desired to go barefoot or wear sandals. Nevertheless, we may note that regardless of how individuals lived in Tepoztlán in the 1940's when Lewis studied them, by 1950 the census showed that in the state of Morelos (in which Tepoztlán is located) a dramatic decline had taken place in the percentage of the population regularly eating tortillas and going barefoot. The former figure decreased spectacularly again by 1960. The percentage of the population wearing sandals went up slightly between 1940 and 1950 before falling somewhat below the 1940 figure by 1960. As we turn to a discussion of each item in the Index, let us keep in mind its collective nature. It is designed to reveal trends in social change and not individual conditions of poverty.

ILLITERACY

The role of illiteracy as a major factor in the culture of poverty does not need exegesis, and we can include it at the outset as a basic problem which the Revolution has tried to resolve. The population answering that it was illiterate (could not read and write) in the census years is presented in Table 9-1. Since the standard minimum age for tabulating illiteracy was ten from 1910 to 1930 and six thereafter, some adjustments have been made in the figures of the first two censuses in order to arrive at comparable figures. All those in the six-to-ten age group in 1910 are added to the number of persons in the illiterate category; this involves a double counting of the persons ten years old, but this is a minimal error. Though ten-year-olds are not double counted in 1921, five-year-olds are included. The Mexican Dirección General de Estadística converted the 1930 census to compare it to later censuses by adding all those in the age group six to nine to the number of persons illiterate. There is a slight discrepancy, then, between the comparative totals for 1910–1921 and 1930–1960, but the difference is not large, and we get a relatively clear picture of the historical problem of illiteracy in Mexico.

Table 9-1 is historically quite reliable since the entities which have the highest percentage of illiterate population today had the highest percentage in 1910. More than 40 per cent of the people in the Federal District could not read and write on the eve of the

TABLE 9-1

Illiteracy in Mexico

A. Total

	1910	1921[b]	1930	1940	1950	1960
Number[a]	c	d	e	f	g	h
Per Cent	76.9	71.2	66.6	58.0	42.5	37.8
Per Cent Change		−7.4	−6.5	−12.9	−26.7	−11.1

B. Per Cent in Federal Entities

	1910	1921	1930	1940	1950	1960
Aguascalientes	70.1	60.3	59.0	44.6	30.8	27.1
Baja California	*51.8	35.9	31.7	21.7	18.7	18.9
Baja Calif. Terr.	*59.0	52.9	46.1	37.8	22.6	20.5
Campeche	64.9	65.1	62.1	50.0	37.7	31.9
Chiapas	89.2	86.3	81.3	78.8	63.9	60.7
Chihuahua	67.3	72.9	51.4	38.9	26.9	25.1
Coahuila	64.2	57.5	52.5	38.0	25.5	19.6
Colima	61.1	59.3	53.1	41.9	32.4	31.4
Distrito Federal	43.3	35.0	32.9	26.0	18.2	16.6
Durango	78.6	68.9	62.0	50.1	31.0	24.8
Guanajuato	82.9	80.3	76.2	71.2	54.3	48.9
Guerrero	90.2	84.4	84.5	80.8	66.5	62.8
Hidalgo	80.6	80.1	77.2	72.4	58.0	56.0
Jalisco	71.2	65.0	62.4	52.5	38.1	34.8
México	80.6	72.6	75.8	69.1	50.9	42.6
Michoacán	83.5	82.0	73.9	70.1	53.0	49.1

Morelos	72.5	*70.0[i]	67.7	55.9	40.4	39.2
Nayarit	74.5	65.2	62.9	51.0	37.3	34.1
Nuevo León	61.5	51.2	47.1	31.8	21.3	19.3
Oaxaca	88.8	85.9	82.6	79.8	61.2	59.1
Puebla	82.4	77.0	74.1	68.2	54.0	49.8
Querétaro	81.5	84.4	80.3	76.9	61.8	57.1
Quintana Roo	61.4	*57.4[i]	54.5	45.9	37.0	35.5
San Luis Potosí	81.0	84.2	73.7	66.4	50.7	46.7
Sinaloa	75.2	68.7	63.4	52.0	41.6	34.0
Sonora	61.4	55.1	49.0	38.0	26.9	23.8
Tabasco	80.7	78.9	72.5	64.7	41.9	38.3
Tamaulipas	68.4	52.6	49.7	35.3	25.6	22.7
Tlaxcala	74.2	73.9	67.1	59.7	44.1	38.5
Veracruz	80.5	75.4	72.0	64.1	50.5	45.3
Yucatán	74.7	63.6	57.5	50.0	35.2	34.3
Zacatecas	77.3	73.6	66.4	58.9	40.5	36.3

a Over six years old.
b Over five years old.

c 9,964,697   d 8,812,995   e 9,017,540   f 9,411,075   g 8,942,399   h 10,573,163

i Morelos is adjusted to 70 per cent, as 61.9 per cent in the census seemed too low after the ten years of war centered there. The adjustment is an estimate, as little change was possible in 1921 compared to 1910. The census figure for Quintana Roo is also too low and has been adjusted.

SOURCES: for 1910: *Anuario Estadístico, 1938*, 42–49, *Resumen del Censo, 1910*, I, 15–28, 99, 108–431 and III, 5–27; for 1921: *Resumen del Censo, 1930*, 47 and volumes by entity; for 1930: México, Dirección General de Estadística, *Compendio Estadístico, 1953*, 61–66, including note on conversion; for 1940: *Ibid., 1956–1957*, 37–38; for 1950: *Resumen del Censo, 1950*, 82–83 (1.5 per cent of the population did not respond to this item); for 1960: *Anuario Estadístico, 1960–1961*, 32–33. Cf. Iturriaga, *La Estructura Social*, 165.

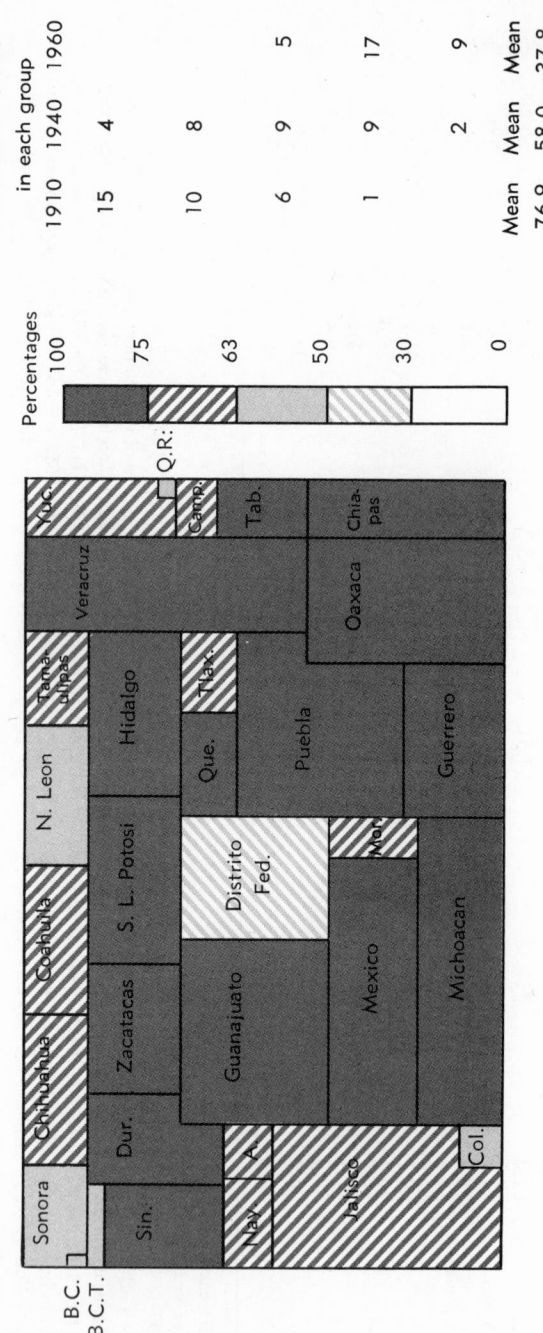

Number of States
in each group

	1910	1940	1960
	15	4	
	10	8	
	6	9	5
	1	9	17
		2	9
	Mean	Mean	Mean
	76.9	58.0	37.8

Percentages

100

75

63

50

30

0

Q.R.:

Graphic Population Map, 1910
by Richard W. Wilkie

— Equals a population
of 50,000

FIG. 3. Percentage of Illiteracy in Mexico, 1910 (by entity).

Source: Table 9-1

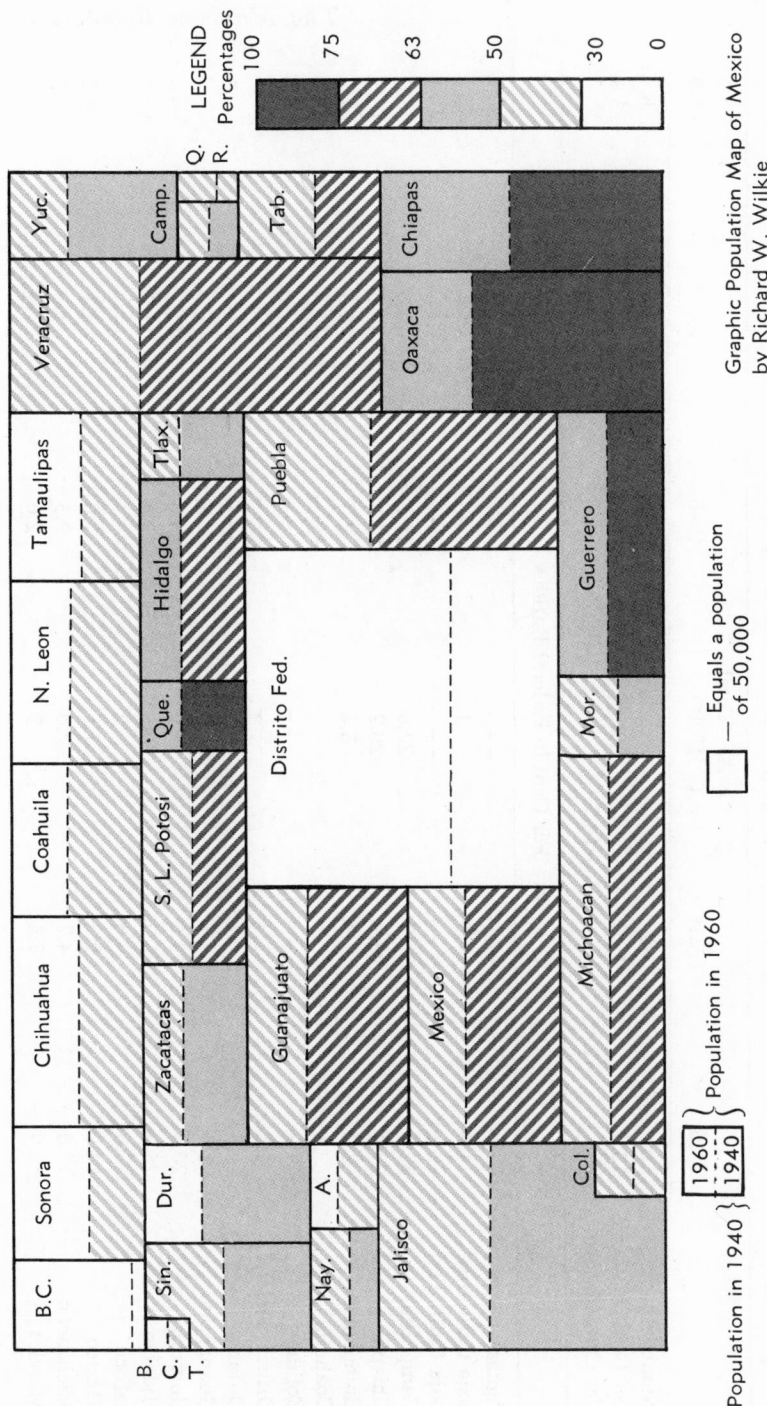

FIG. 4. Percentage of Illiteracy in Mexico, 1940 and 1960 (by entity).

Graphic Population Map of Mexico
by Richard W. Wilkie

LEGEND
Percentages

100

75

63

50

30

0

— Equals a population
of 50,000

Population in 1960

1960
1940

Population in 1940 Population in 1960

Source: Table 9-1

TABLE 9-2

Population Speaking Only an Indian Language

A. Total

	1910	1921[b]	1930	1940	1950[b]	1960
Number[a]	c	d	e	f	g	h
Per Cent	13.0	10.2	8.5	7.4	4.9	3.8
Per Cent Change	−21.5	−16.7	−12.9	−33.8	−22.5	

B. Per Cent in Federal Entities

	1910	1921	1930	1940	1950	1960
Aguascalientes	—	—	—	—	—	—
Baja California	1.4	.9	.1	—	—	—
Baja Calif. Terr.	—	—	—	—	—	—
Campeche	32.6	27.2	22.6	16.3	10.0	6.0
Chiapas	27.4	23.9	20.2	21.3	17.0	15.5
Chihuahua	8.2	6.9	3.3	2.3	1.3	1.1
Coahuila	.1	.1	—	—	—	—
Colima	—	—	—	—	—	—
Distrito Federal	1.5	.4	—	—	—	—
Durango	.8	.7	.5	.1	—	.2
Guanajuato	1.4	1.1	—	—	—	—
Guerrero	20.4	19.6	14.8	14.0	11.3	10.0
Hidalgo	26.3	25.9	20.5	18.6	13.2	12.2
Jalisco	.3	.3	.2	—	—	.1
México	14.2	9.2	7.5	7.0	4.1	2.3
Michoacán	5.0	4.7	2.0	2.3	1.5	.8
Morelos	9.0	7.4	.9	2.0	.4	.2

Nayarit	7.5	3.5	.8	1.3	1.5	1.6
Nuevo León	—	—	—	—	—	—
Oaxaca	48.8	46.2	34.3	31.7	21.8	20.4
Puebla	17.1	17.6	18.2	14.8	9.8	8.0
Querétaro	7.1	6.0	2.9	2.0	1.6	1.5
Quintana Roo	*29.6ⁱ	*24.7ⁱ	20.5	16.6	15.4	15.1
San Luis Potosí	10.1	9.7	7.6	8.8	5.7	4.7
Sinaloa	2.1	1.4	.3	.3	.2	.1
Sonora	5.5	4.0	2.2	1.9	.8	.3
Tabasco	6.4	5.9	2.2	1.3	.7	.5
Tamaulipas	—	—	—	—	—	—
Tlaxcala	13.6	13.1	5.6	3.8	1.8	.8
Veracruz	17.5	14.5	10.1	9.1	6.4	5.1
Yucatán	58.9	45.4	33.7	27.4	16.3	12.6
Zacatecas	—	—	—	—	—	—

a Over five years old. In 1910 the total population was classified according to native tongue. We have taken ages up to five years out of the total speaking an Indian language on the assumption that the children who were counted as speaking an Indian language made up the same percentage as the total for all Indian-language speakers, 13 per cent. Thus 13 per cent of the age group under five (2,633,168) gives 342,312 which should not be included in the total of 1,960,306 Indian speakers of all ages. By subtracting 342,312 from the latter total and by subtracting the age group under five (2,633,168) from the total population in 1910 we get 1,617,994 Indian-language speakers out of a population of 12,527,201 persons more than five years old. No possibility was allowed in the census of 1910 for Indian-Spanish speakers since the number was probably negligible, so we use Indian speakers; in 1930 the distinction is made between Indian-Spanish speakers and Indian speakers and we use the latter from 1930 on.

b Derived.

c 1,617,994   d 1,261,059   e 1,185,162   f 1,237,018   g 1,069,231   h 1,104,955

i The official figures for Quintana Roo are too low for 1910 (13 per cent) and 1921 (19.2 per cent). An adjustment has been made which is proportional to the figure for Campeche as Campeche and Quintana Roo had similar percentages in 1930.

SOURCE: For 1910: *Anuario Estadístico, 1940,* 68; for 1921: derived; for 1930: *Resumen del Censo, 1930,* 122–123; for 1940: Whetten, *Rural Mexico,* 582, and *Compendio Estadístico, 1947,* 25; for 1950: derived; for 1960: *Resumen del Censo, 1960,* 651–652, 649.

Revolution, and in 1960 this figure was 16.6 per cent. We do not need to analyze all this data, since it speaks for itself; but it is important to note that while the percentage of illiteracy has decreased considerably, the absolute population which is illiterate has gained steadily since 1930. By 1950 there were more people unable to read and write in Mexico than there were in 1910. The greatest percentage decrease came in the decade 1940–1950.

INDIAN LANGUAGE

The integration of the Mexican nation and elimination of poverty require that the populace which speaks only an Indian language be taught to speak Spanish. The inability to speak Spanish has relegated a large number of persons to an inferior position in society and has limited their opportunity to participate in national markets and culture. The Indian who can not speak Spanish finds it very difficult indeed to defend himself against persons who wish to take his land. He often will find himself abused by agents of federal, state, and local government, and since he can not speak the language, his recourse is limited, especially because it will be most difficult to take his case to court.

The population speaking only an Indian tongue is used for the purposes of this study since persons who speak both Indian and Spanish may be considered in the process of modernization and in more ample contact with the modern world than those who can not speak Spanish. The population which only speaks Indian is presented in Table 9-2. There are two problems with this item. In 1921 and 1950 the results generally do not make sense compared to the data which were gathered or processed on a sounder basis in 1910, 1930, 1940 and 1960. Apparently error crept into the results of this item in the 1950 census because the Statistical Agency had some of its funds diverted to meet the official party's expenses of an approaching presidential campaign.[2] If we were to believe the 1950 data, only-Indian-speakers went down as a per cent of the population in Quintana Roo, for example, from 16.6 in 1940 to 6.1 in 1950, thereafter rebounding to 15.1 in 1960.[3] In order to remedy this defect in the national total for

[2] Ramón Beteta, Oral History Interviews with James and Edna Wilkie, Dec. 17, 1964, Mexico City.
[3] *Resumen del Censo, 1950,* 82–83.

1950, the change in Indian-speakers is assumed as approximately proportional to decrease in illiteracy between 1940 and 1960. In this manner, we get 4.9 per cent of the total population speaking only an Indian language instead of 3.7 per cent as the census reports for this item. Theoretically, the increase in population could have brought about a small relative increase of only Indian-speakers in 1960, as the director of Mexico's Statistical Agency, Albino Zertuche, suggested in 1964. However, the nature of the changes in only-Indian-speakers from 1940 to 1960 indicates that the census needs adjustment for this item. The changes are too abrupt in such entities as Quintana Roo to point to population growth.[4]

The 1921 census needs adjustment for the percentage of the population speaking only an Indian language, too. Even though civil war disrupted the nation from 1910 to 1921 and many Indians began to speak Spanish, the figure given is much too low for credibility, and thus the result for 1921 is derived in the same fashion as for 1950.[5]

Whereas illiteracy has always been a significant factor holding back the social development of all federal entities in Mexico, the percentage of the population which only speaks an Indian language has been limited in importance to about half of the political divisions of the republic. Oaxaca has consistently had the highest percentage of persons only speaking an Indian language, almost half of the population over five years old in 1910 and about one fifth of the population in 1960.

VILLAGE MEXICO

Persons living in communities with a population under 2500 have been included in the Poverty Index to show the relative, historical isolation of the Mexican populace. If an individual, for example, lives in the isolation of those thousands of little communities which number less than 2500 persons, it is most difficult for him to enjoy medical care, communications, variety of even basic tools, or a market which would allow him to earn a fair return for his

[4] Zertuche's statement is in *El Día*, June 4, 1964. A check of the census analysis by entity reveals that the results given in the *Resumen del Censo* are correct and no arithmetical error is involved.

[5] The 1921 census gives 5.7 per cent of the population as not speaking Spanish, *Resumen del Censo, 1930*, 122.

work. The census considers 2500 as the cut-off for rural population in Mexico, but this figure is much too low; as one authority
has pointed out, towns of 10,000 may often be classified as rural
as we use the term in developed areas.[6] Of course, due to Mexico's
geography and history, communities of under 2500 and even under 10,000 generally do not enjoy the advantages of small-town
life as we know it in the United States where the community
hospital, water supply, and school are served by excellent communications and a nearby service city.

The differentiation between rural and urban life is not so important here as examination of the opportunity of the rural masses
to enjoy access to modern life. Frank Tannenbaum, a friend of
agricultural Mexico, has recommended:

If Mexico were wise, Mexican industry would be accepted as a supple-
ment to an agricultural economy, and the emphasis would be upon
the marvelous energy and cohesive powers of the rural community. It
would use the community to the fullest extent and invigorate it by
bringing to it the skills and techniques modern science has made possible for the little place. Mexico, I am convinced, can reach its fullest
cultural and economic development only by adopting a policy inher-
ent in its very genius: that of enriching the local community. Any
plan that would destroy the vitality of the Mexican rural community
is bound to prove tragic in its consequences and repeat the slums of
an earlier industrialization without holding out the promise of the
increased output that will give employment and sustenance to the
fifty or sixty million people who will have to be fed by the end of
the century. . . .[7]

Tannenbaum's controversial [8] recommendation is based upon the
pessimistic view that Mexico's population will outrun food supply, and his analysis of the problems of village Mexico is powerful.

During the years from 1931 to 1933 Frank Tannenbaum obtained the co-operation of the Mexican Ministry of Education and
the Mexican Statistical Agency to analyze the access of village
Mexico to modern technology. He gathered descriptive data on
3611 rural villages representing every state and territory and one
half of all the counties (*municipios*) of Mexico. These villages

[6] Whetten, *Rural Mexico,* Chapter 2.
[7] Tannenbaum, *Mexico, The Struggle for Peace and Bread* (New York: Knopf,
1950), 245–246.
[8] See Manuel Germán Parra, *La Industrialización de México* (México, D. F.: Imprenta Universitaria, 1954) .

had 17 per cent of the population of Mexico in 1930 and their size was an average of 520 persons, compared to the average village size of 300 persons. These villages, which were larger than average and which had larger material resources, were very poor indeed. Upon publishing the study in 1946, Tannenbaum noted that village Mexico was substantially unchanged since his study was undertaken, and that rural Mexico is timeless.[9] Though change has come rapidly to rural Mexico since 1940, Tannenbaum's analysis of the early 1930's is still valid to show the kinds of deprivation that haunt village Mexico today. The percentages are no longer as high, but the basic problems persist. Table 9-3

TABLE 9-3

Tannenbaum's Analysis of Village Mexico, 1931–1933

Villages Without	Per Cent	Villages Without	Per Cent
Tractors	96.5	Herb Doctor	72.6
Steel Plows	54.3	Priest	93.7
Trains	93.1	Carpenter	49.9
Human Carriers	54.2	Plumber	96.3
Telephones	88.4	Tailor	89.3
Telegraph	95.8	Shoemaker	83.4
Post Offices	80.9	Tinsmith	90.1
Doctor	97.8	Weaver	84.2
Lawyer	99.2	Potter	83.3
Engineer	98.9	Markets	93.1
Druggist	97.0	Stores	51.0
Midwife	85.4	Phonograph	41.5

SOURCE: Tannenbaum, "Technology and Race in Mexico," Table 2-6.

gives the results of some of his samples. The penetration of trucks and buses into the hinterlands of Mexico, along with the transistor radio and the public address system, has forever shattered the quiet of the countryside, but Mexico is a long way from eradicating primitive living conditions.

[9] Frank Tannenbaum, "Technology and Race in Mexico," in L. W. Shannon (ed.), *Underdeveloped Areas* (New York: Harper, 1957), 160–166.

TABLE 9-4
Persons Living in Communities Under 2500 Population

A. Total

	1910	1921[a]	1930	1940	1950	1960
Number	b	c	d	e	f	g
Per Cent	71.3	69.0	66.5	64.9	57.4	49.3
Per Cent Change		-3.2	-3.6	-2.4	-11.6	-14.1

B. Per Cent in Federal Entities

	1910	1921[a]	1930	1940	1950	1960
Aguascalientes	89.0	50.2	45.3	42.6	45.1	40.1
Baja California	100.0	71.2	45.7	49.5	35.5	22.3
Baja Calif. Terr.	87.0	72.7	63.9	64.2	67.1	63.7
Campeche	43.0	53.9	54.9	50.4	42.6	36.8
Chiapas	81.5	79.0	82.5	83.9	76.9	75.6
Chihuahua	74.1	71.8	67.0	63.3	55.9	42.9
Coahuila	57.2	49.3	47.9	49.4	42.6	33.3
Colima	64.1	56.8	55.8	54.9	39.9	38.2
Distrito Federal	12.7	11.3	7.7	6.2	5.5	4.2
Durango	79.5	75.3	76.7	75.9	71.3	64.5
Guanajuato	69.4	66.9	65.9	64.9	58.4	53.6
Guerrero	84.6	86.3	84.8	85.4	78.3	74.3
Hidalgo	89.3	85.5	83.0	81.8	78.8	77.6
Jalisco	71.5	63.7	60.6	58.8	52.1	41.5
México	73.1	82.6	79.5	77.3	73.6	61.4

	1910[b]	1921[c]	1930[d]	1940[e]	1950[f]	1960[g]
Michoacán	74.7	75.0	73.7	71.1	68.0	59.4
Morelos	58.3	77.8	74.9	72.1	56.6	46.8
Nayarit	76.1	68.8	65.0	69.8	65.9	57.4
Nuevo León	66.1	62.3	58.8	56.1	44.1	29.6
Oaxaca	74.7	79.4	81.9	84.7	79.3	75.6
Puebla	72.5	74.2	72.2	72.2	66.8	60.8
Querétaro	78.9	77.8	80.2	80.7	75.8	71.9
Quintana Roo	100.0	100.0	73.7	75.1	73.1	68.6
San Luis Potosí	71.4	75.0	72.6	74.7	69.6	66.4
Sinaloa	84.2	77.1	77.1	78.2	72.1	61.8
Sonora	47.4	67.6	63.3	67.3	54.7	42.4
Tabasco	86.0	82.4	82.7	82.0	78.1	73.4
Tamaulipas	76.3	56.0	57.2	54.5	47.0	40.2
Tlaxcala	79.0	77.5	72.4	70.4	61.2	56.1
Veracruz	71.7	73.7	71.5	71.2	66.7	60.4
Yucatán	68.6	54.2	51.9	51.3	44.8	40.2
Zacatecas	76.4	80.2	76.0	75.3	75.0	72.8

a Census data given for under 2,000 in 1921 is adjusted in *Resumen del Censo, 1930,* 40 to show population under 2,500.
b 10,812,028   c 9,869,276   d 11,012,091   e 12,757,441   f 14,807,534   g 17,218,011

SOURCE: for 1910: *Resumen del Censo, 1910,* I, 24–25, 33; for 1921: *Resumen del Censo, 1930,* 40; for 1930: *Ibid.;* for 1940: Whetten, *Rural Mexico,* 579; for 1950: Julio Durán Ochoa, *Población* (México, D. F.: Fondo de Cultura Económica, 1955), 37 (there was no complementary rural population included in the 1950 census); for 1960: Jorge L. Tamayo, *Geografía General de México* (México, D. F.: Instituto Mexicano de Investigaciones Económicas, 1962, 4 vols.), III, 402.

By moving into larger villages, much of the population has gained the advantages of size which can provide a school, or a better school, electricity, "potable water" (the term is used advisedly since even in Mexico City the water is not potable with consistent certainty), medical care, and the patterns of complex modern life. Table 9-4 shows the decrease in the populace living in villages with less than 2500 population, the lowest figure traceable back into time with consistency.

It is apparent that Mexico in the 1960's is still very much village Mexico. The total population which lives in groups under 2500 is just below 50 per cent. Only 13 of the federal entities have a percentage smaller than this national average. This is some change since 1930 when only four entities (Aguascalientes, Baja California, Coahuila, Federal District) had less than half of their population living in villages. Not until the post-1940 period did the rate of decrease in the percentage of population living in villages under 2500 begin to gain speed, especially after 1950.

The above trend in the decrease of village life need not mean that Mexico has become more urban, for only part of the population is moving to the big city.[10] Regarding the trend to the big city, it is important to note that there is a strong possibility for urbanization without social breakdown. Oscar Lewis has followed families into Mexico City from Tepoztlán in the state of Morelos, a town slightly larger (3230 in 1940) than the 2500 figure under discussion. He has found that family life remains strong, there are smaller numbers of divorces, fewer abandoned children, and less personality disorganization in comparison to the process of urbanization in the United States. He accounts for this on the basis that Mexico City has close ties with rural areas (certainly there is a great amount of visiting back and forth between country and city relatives), and is essentially conservative in tradition. Mexico City is not highly industrialized, a fact which alleviates some social breakdown. Another important characteristic would appear to be that Mexican peasants live in well-organized villages that are more similar to cities and towns than like the open-country settlement pattern of the United States.[11]

[10] Professor Harley L. Browning, department of sociology, University of Texas, is preparing a manuscript on the topic of "Urbanization in Mexico."

[11] Oscar Lewis, "Urbanization Without Breakdown: A Case Study," *Scientific Monthly* 75:1 (1952) 31–41.

A second investigator has corroborated Lewis's findings by examining the urbanization process among Mixtec Indian migrants to Mexico City from Tilantongo, Oaxaca.[12] Douglas Butterworth finds that a high degree of mental health is enjoyed by the migrants. There is an increase in identification with the Mexican nation without a decrease in identification to Tilantongo, and marriage is contracted almost exclusively with women from the village (even after years of absence). There is a diminution of drinking, and a unanimous agreement that life in Mexico City is better than it was in Tilantongo. Migrants point out that they have "lost the fear" of the human and natural "bad elements" which they had in Oaxaca.

Oscar Lewis has analyzed extensively the restricted life in Tepoztlán. There is great interpersonal tension, distrust, and fear of neighbors and authorities. The populace is governed by superstition. Creativity and artistic expression are constricted. There is a relative lack of concern for the future, and a lack of ambition for self-improvement.[13] Since it is difficult to change life in such a psychological atmosphere, it is little wonder that the more adventuresome persons migrate to cities to find greater economic, social, and cultural opportunity.

Though the relative share of population living in villages with less than 2500 persons has fallen to slightly less than half of the population of Mexico, the absolute increase in the amount of people living in these villages has risen to 17,218,011 in 1960 from 10,812,028 in 1910. Mexico has a large task of modernizing village Mexico, and it will be very expensive to duplicate, in

[12] Douglas S. Butterworth, "A Study of the Urbanization Process Among Mixtec Migrants from Tilantongo in Mexico City," *América Indígena* 22 (1962) 259–274. The population of Tilantongo has ranged from 2700 to 3700 during the period from 1930 to 1960.

[13] Oscar Lewis, *Tepoztlán, Village in Mexico* (New York: Holt, Rinehart and Winston, 1960), and *Life in a Mexican Village: Tepoztlán Restudied* (Urbana: University of Illinois Press, 1951). See also his *Pedro Martínez, A Mexican Peasant and His Family* (New York: Random House, 1964) and *The Children of Sánchez, Autobiography of a Mexican Family*, New York: Random House, 1961) for portraits of rural and urban life. The Mexican novelist Juan Rulfo presents a contemporary pitcure of superstition and fear in a small Indian village in *Pedro Páramo*, tr. by L. Kemp (New York: Grove, 1959). Ricardo Pozas's *Juan the Chamula; An Ethnological Re-Creation of the Life of a Mexican Indian*, tr. by L. Kemp (Berkeley: University of California Press, 1962) develops the story of a Chamula Indian who leaves Chiapas, fights in the Revolution, and then returns home to accept village life.

many small places, the expensive advantages of modern technology. Rapid urbanization is already straining the public services of the government in larger centers, let alone in the isolated areas of Mexico.

BAREFOOT POPULATION

The percentage of population that is barefoot in Mexico indicates several things. We may deduce that barefoot population is probably ill-clothed. We know that the persons who go barefoot in the highlands suffer from mud and cold which cracks and hardens the skin on their feet into blisters and callosity. In the tropics the barefoot population is open to disease and infection. Barefoot persons generally do not have the arch and body support conducive to sustained work.

Table 9-5 reveals the population which reported in the census that it was barefoot. As has been pointed out, only illiteracy, Indian language, and population under 2500 are available prior to 1940, hence this and the following items cover only three censuses. More than one quarter of Mexico's populace was barefoot in 1940, and twenty years later 14.3 per cent still had no foot protection. An increase in 1960 in the barefoot population in entities which were relatively low in 1950 indicates the migration of poor persons to these areas that offer more opportunity. States which gained were Baja California, Coahuila, Colima, and Nayarit. Slight gains in barefoot population were registered in Chihuahua, Durango, and Jalisco, but this may have been related to an increase in poverty rather than the migration of poverty-stricken peoples.

POPULATION WEARING SANDALS

The number of persons who wear sandals (*sandalias* or *huaraches*) gives us an important view of ill-shod population. Theoretically sandals offer more protection than does going barefoot. This is partially true in the tropics where diseases that enter through the foot can be avoided to a greater degree with sandals, but sandals do not provide protection from the weather nor are they apt to be healthful for arch and foot support. In the tropics and in the highlands they are not efficient for sustained work. In the high-

TABLE 9-5

Barefoot Population

	1940[b]		1950		1960
		A. Total			
Number[a]	5,233,244		4,768,827		4,828,177
Per Cent	26.6		19.1		14.3
Per Cent Change		−28.2		−25.1	

B. Per Cent in Federal Entities

Aguascalientes	4.3	6.0	3.9
Baja California	.6	.5	2.4
Baja Calif. Terr.	10.6	10.2	4.9
Campeche	32.1	19.0	10.3
Chiapas	74.6	64.7	54.5
Chihuahua	5.2	4.3	4.6
Coahuila	2.3	2.5	3.4
Colima	2.1	2.2	3.8
Distrito Federal	6.4	3.1	2.9
Durango	3.5	3.4	4.0
Guanajuato	10.8	6.8	4.4
Guerrero	52.8	34.3	25.7
Hidalgo	42.0	35.8	25.8
Jalisco	5.1	3.1	3.9
México	47.4	35.8	20.0
Michoacán	15.6	10.0	7.6
Morelos	31.3	15.7	11.1
Nayarit	5.7	2.8	4.8
Nuevo León	3.1	4.5	3.6
Oaxaca	63.5	44.9	38.1
Puebla	50.4	39.5	30.0
Querétaro	12.2	7.8	5.7
Quintana Roo	29.2	14.6	4.9
San Luis Potosí	18.2	13.9	13.1
Sinaloa	6.6	6.4	4.1
Sonora	3.5	2.9	3.0
Tabasco	75.7	60.1	51.2
Tamaulipas	4.5	3.5	3.1
Tlaxcala	61.7	51.7	37.9
Veracruz	44.8	35.3	26.4
Yucatán	14.8	4.3	4.4
Zacatecas	4.3	3.0	3.7

[a] Over one year old. Census of 1940 included total population for this item, presumably on the assumption that the children would soon follow their parents' pattern.

[b] Includes under one-year-olds.

Source: for 1940: *Resumen del Censo, 1940,* 1, 34, 39, 71–72; for 1950: *Resumen del Censo, 1950,* 75, 87–88; *Resumen del Censo, 1960,* 274–279 (cf. calculation, p. 280, which includes whole population instead of population over those one year old).

TABLE 9-6

Population Regularly Wearing Sandals

	A. Total		
	1940[b]	1950	1960
Number[a]	4,629,959	6,640,673	7,912,170
Per Cent	23.6	26.6	23.4
Per Cent Change		+12.7	−12.0

	B. Per Cent in Federal Entities		
Aguascalientes	20.4	23.5	17.6
Baja California	.2	.4	1.0
Baja Calif. Terr.	12.1	12.7	10.9
Campeche	14.3	20.1	22.3
Chiapas	9.8	17.2	20.9
Chihuahua	10.6	10.6	9.6
Coahuila	8.3	8.3	7.0
Colima	53.0	59.1	52.0
Distrito Federal	2.2	1.6	2.5
Durango	27.2	28.4	25.4
Guanajuato	36.7	40.0	34.0
Guerrero	30.5	46.7	50.5
Hidalgo	32.1	35.4	36.9
Jalisco	39.9	43.7	36.3
México	25.6	29.4	22.9
Michoacán	33.2	37.0	34.8
Morelos	28.0	30.4	26.9
Nayarit	54.8	53.6	47.1
Nuevo León	9.2	10.6	7.4
Oaxaca	29.5	44.8	44.3
Puebla	26.8	31.3	33.4
Querétaro	60.7	64.5	52.5
Quintana Roo	7.4	17.6	29.6
San Luis Potosí	34.6	39.0	32.4
Sinaloa	33.3	37.9	36.9
Sonora	6.1	7.8	7.7
Tabasco	6.4	14.2	13.2
Tamaulipas	8.4	9.5	8.1
Tlaxcala	12.4	15.2	17.9
Veracruz	12.4	17.1	11.2
Yucatán	26.6	32.6	36.0
Zacatecas	34.6	40.8	35.2

[a] Over one year old. See Table 9-5, Note a.
[b] Includes those under one year old.
SOURCE: See Table 9-5.

lands the sandals may often figuratively grow to the foot and seem to become part of it.

Figures for the population wearing sandals are presented in Table 9-6. The percentage here has not decreased nearly as rapidly as the percentage of barefoot population, and it increased by about 10 per cent during the 1940's. In Yucatán, for example, the decade of the 1940's witnessed a dramatic decrease in the barefoot population from 14.8 per cent to 4.3 per cent. In the same period, users of sandals increased from 26.6 per cent to 32.6 per cent of the Yucatecans. The same phenomenon is true for Quintana Roo in the 1950's. Of course, persons who wear sandals occasionally for relaxation or comfort are not included in the table.

Although a decrease in barefoot population and an increase in sandal wearers might be construed as indicating a decrease in poverty characteristics, this shift actually only reflects a change within the culture of poverty. In this vein, analysis of sandal usage may give us an indication of transition which is necessary before some elements of the poverty-stricken strata of society accept the modern dress which the shoe represents. Evidently at least part of the barefoot population shifts to sandals before obtaining shoes. Such a generalization holds true in Guerrero, Oaxaca, Chiapas, and Tabasco, for example, where the barefoot population decreased and sandal wearers increased, but it does not for such entities as Querétaro, Chihuahua, and Nayarit, where sandal wearers as well as barefoot population decreased. The fact is that the census does not lend itself to definite analysis about transition among the ill-shod, and we must be content with the most tentative kind of speculation in this regard.

DEFICIENT DIETARY COMPLEX

The population regularly eating tortillas (baked, unleavened corn cakes) instead of wheat bread is included in the Poverty Index to indicate substandard dietary patterns since 1910. The tortilla is representative of the traditional diet; wheat bread is characteristic of the modern complex of foods. We should note that most Mexicans eat tortillas, and that even the wealthy population serves them at the table along with wheat bread.[14] However, bread has

[14] Tortillas made of wheat, banana, *yuca, garbanzo,* etc., are available in some

long been a symbol of modern civilization in Mexico, as Francisco Bulnes noted in 1899 when he distinguished between the corn-eaters (backward Indians) and the wheat-eaters (modern non-Indians). Bulnes, engineer, congressman, and publicist of the Porfirio Díaz group, did not believe that the corn-eaters are inherently unprogressive. He felt that wheat-eaters receive in the diet the minerals that they need while the consumers of corn (and rice) suffer deficiencies. Thus for Bulnes the lack of phosphorus, for example, explained the corn-eaters' apparent low mental powers and "sleepy, brutish appearance, as profoundly conservative as the mountains and as eminently melancholy as the graveyard." [15]

The traditional corn complex of foods encompasses beans, chilies, *atole* (a gruel of corn), and coffee. This is the basic diet, and it will be supplemented by regional dishes and drinks.[16] The traditional complex of foods is notorious for being deficient in animal protein, fats, vitamins, and minerals, and for supplying an overabundance of carbohydrates and vegetable protein. This complex tends to cause acidosis, high blood pressure, anemia, inadequate growth, lack of energy, weak resistance, and premature old age. In addition, the high calcium content of tortillas may not be readily absorbed into the system due to the above shortages.[17]

It is important to note that abuse of the so-called civilized complex of foods may cause these same problems, but this is a matter of personal habit in modern society and not a stricture placed on the populace by a complex of deficient foods and the demands of traditional cultural pattern. Whereas the population of the United States tends to consume an overabundance of calories daily, the population in Mexico receives an underallowance of from 10 to

---

regions of Mexico, but the tortilla complex of foods is not upset by the consumption of these regional breads.

[15] Francisco Bulnes is quoted in William Rex Crawford, *A Century of Latin-American Thought* (Cambridge: Harvard University Press, 1944), 254.

[16] Interview with José Quintín Olascoaga, Nov. 3, 1964; Dr. Olascoaga was head of the nutrition department of the *Instituto Nacional de Cardiología* in Mexico City until his recent retirement.

[17] Nathaniel and Sylvia Weyl, *The Reconquest of Mexico; the Years of Lázaro Cárdenas* (London: Oxford University Press, 1939), 332, cite Juan M. González on "Mortalidad Infantil," *El Universal*, July 14, 1931. See especially Dr. José Quintín Olascoaga's comments on p. 70 in his book: Salvador Lira López, Ramón Fernández y Fernández and Olascoaga, *La Pobreza Rural de México* (México, D. F.: n.p., 1945). Olascoaga's 4-volume study of nutrition in Mexico is superb: *Dietética* (México, D. F.: Imprenta de Libros, 1950–1963). Whetten, *Rural Mexico*, 308–315, and Simpson, *The Ejido*, 263–268 also take up the dietary problem.

30 per cent or more, depending upon the type of work done and the season. If a person's home and dress is inadequate along with diet, caloric deficiencies will increase above these amounts.[18] One eminent Mexican authority feels that the traditional diet need not be suppressed, for if it is integrated with the modern high-protein complex of foods—meat, fish, fowl, milk, and eggs—represented by wheat bread which is our census measurement of type of diet, then tastes need not undergo a drastic anti-traditional change.[19]

Apparently, however, the traditional diet is beginning to undergo rapid change, especially since 1950. According to Table 9-7, in twenty years the percentage eating the tortilla has decreased from more than half to less than one third of the population. Rapid change has come in the territory of Baja California, Chiapas, Durango, Guanajuato, Guerrero, Hidalgo, Michoacán, Morelos, Nayarit, Nuevo León, Oaxaca, Puebla, Quintana Roo, San Luis Potosí, Sinaloa, Sonora, Tabasco, Veracruz, and Zacatecas. Until Baja California captured the lowest figure in 1960, the traditional diet was least important in the Federal District in 1950.

Migration into Mexico City has slowed the rate of assimilation to the modern complex of foods since 1950. Though, as Butterworth points out, tortillas are still preferred by migrants from Tilantongo, "the diet of migrants is without exception much improved over that of residents of Tilantongo. Food is generally cited as the material evidence of the improved standard of living of the migrants. Whereas in Tilantongo the normal diet is limited to tortillas and salt, beans being eaten only once or twice a week and meat weekly or semimonthly, in Mexico City beans are eaten daily [and] meat is eaten at least once a week by even the poorest family." [20] Significantly, only 5.6 per cent of the populace in the Federal District reported that it eats only tortillas in 1960.

A changing dietary pattern does not mean, however, that much of the country does not still live by the traditional complex of foods. The tortilla is still favored over wheat bread by 66 per cent of the population of Zacatecas, 60.8 per cent of Querétaro, 59.5 per cent of Tlaxcala, 57.1 per cent of San Luis Potosí, 54.1 per

[18] Francisco de P. Miranda, *La Alimentación en México* (México, D. F.: Instituto Nacional de Nutriología, 1947).

[19] Interview with José Quintín Olascoaga, Nov. 3, 1964.

[20] Butterworth, "A Study of the Urbanization Process," 269.

TABLE 9-7

Population Regularly Eating Tortillas Instead of Wheat Bread

	A. Total		
	1940[b]	1950	1960
Number[a]	10,795,582	11,383,923	10,618,726
Per Cent	54.9	45.6	31.4
Per Cent Change		−16.9	−31.2

B. Per Cent in Federal Entities			
Aguascalientes	52.3	57.4	43.8
Baja California	5.0	6.9	5.0
Baja Calif. Terr.	44.2	27.8	15.6
Campeche	13.8	14.2	11.2
Chiapas	62.5	58.7	35.3
Chihuahua	47.9	35.8	26.4
Coahuila	42.5	25.5	19.7
Colima	28.3	32.6	22.2
Distrito Federal	12.4	6.3	5.6
Durango	62.7	62.0	49.8
Guanajuato	75.5	70.6	54.1
Guerrero	78.9	64.9	49.7
Hidalgo	69.1	62.9	48.5
Jalisco	59.7	54.8	36.1
México	70.0	61.2	41.1
Michoacán	70.5	55.5	42.2
Morelos	32.8	21.6	12.7
Nayarit	37.5	36.1	26.8
Nuevo León	30.2	26.6	14.4
Oaxaca	60.2	56.4	34.7
Puebla	68.8	59.3	46.8
Querétaro	78.0	71.9	60.8
Quintana Roo	70.0	40.4	18.8
San Luis Potosí	74.8	69.6	57.1
Sinaloa	66.3	46.5	24.9
Sonora	26.8	13.8	7.9
Tabasco	62.2	55.9	36.3
Tamaulipas	42.8	29.9	20.5
Tlaxcala	75.2	69.9	59.5
Veracruz	44.2	40.2	23.1
Yucatán	5.7	7.0	7.9
Zacatecas	80.3	76.9	66.2

[a] Over one year old. See Table 9-5, Note a.

[b] Includes those under one year old.

SOURCE: for 1940: *Resumen del Censo, 1940*, 34, 71, and Whetten, *Rural Mexico*, 306 and 609; for 1950: *Compendio Estadístico, 1953*, 68; for 1960: *Resumen del Censo, 1960*, 274–279 (cf. 280–281 for calculations including population under one year old).

cent of Guanajuato, and almost half of the people in Durango, Guerrero, Hidalgo and Puebla.

The foregoing three items included in the Poverty Index are not always related to Indian culture, for as Woodrow Borah pointed out in 1954, Indian culture is related to the general culture of rural poverty in Mexico.[21] The census items which were intended to measure the amount of Indian culture in the republic established clearly that poverty does not necessarily have anything to do with such culture. Over half of the population of Aguascalientes ate tortillas in 1940, and the percentage of the population which spoke only an Indian language was nil. The same pattern was true for the population wearing sandals in Colima. Over three quarters of the population of Tabasco was barefoot, but only about 2 per cent of the people were limited to the Indian language.[22]

POPULATION WITHOUT SEWAGE DISPOSAL

Finally, sewage disposal is included in the Poverty Index, for the unresolved problem of not getting rid of waste creates disease which cripples man's ability to work and to enjoy life. In the countryside, the problem of sewage disposal is acute, for if outhouses are used they tend to be located at the rear of dwellings near the kitchen, and a ground for fly-breeding close to the larder is most unhealthful. The farmer who defecates in the fields not only does himself a disservice in contaminating his own vegetables, but he also contaminates much fresh produce for market. Thus the boiling and soaking of vegetables are necessary but not widely practiced.

Though modern medicines cut the death rate caused by diarrhea, intestinal parasites, and other gastroenteric illnesses to 25.1 per cent of all known deaths from disease in 1960 (the figure was 36.1 per cent as late as 1951),[23] the lack of sewage disposal persists. The hours of disability and unhappiness which persons un-

[21] Woodrow Borah, "Race and Class in Mexico," *Pacific Historical Review* 23 (1954) 331–342.
[22] Cf. Whetten, *Rural Mexico*, Chapter 15, on "Indian-Colonial" levels of living.
[23] *Compendio Estadístico 1962*, 38, and *1953*, 95. Old age, accident, diverse and unknown causes of death have been excluded from total deaths for the purposes of this calculation.

TABLE 9-8

Population Without Sewage Disposal Within Building

	A. Total		
	1939	1950[a]	1960
Number	17,160,573	20,555,441	24,966,849
Per Cent	86.5	79.7	71.5
Per Cent Change		−7.9	−10.3

B. Per Cent in Federal Entities			
Aguascalientes	87.0	76.7	57.4
Baja California	81.0	76.2	70.1
Baja Calif. Terr.	98.2	89.6	79.9
Campeche	95.5	87.5	80.4
Chiapas	97.4	88.2	86.3
Chihuahua	89.5	82.0	67.0
Coahuila	89.8	82.2	70.3
Colima	84.5	70.7	68.5
Distrito Federal	25.4	27.0	30.2
Durango	92.8	88.8	82.5
Guanajuato	94.0	85.3	78.2
Guerrero	98.6	92.5	88.7
Hidalgo	92.3	87.2	85.2
Jalisco	90.3	82.0	67.2
México	95.2	93.3	86.5
Michoacán	93.0	89.7	80.0
Morelos	87.4	78.4	71.2
Nayarit	93.8	90.3	82.2
Nuevo León	83.4	72.4	55.7
Oaxaca	97.2	93.6	90.9
Puebla	86.8	83.8	80.2
Querétaro	91.9	86.5	81.8
Quintana Roo	98.6	97.0	93.3
San Luis Potosí	92.5	86.4	82.2
Sinaloa	94.8	90.0	81.2
Sonora	92.5	82.6	70.8
Tabasco	92.5	88.4	83.3
Tamaulipas	82.7	74.8	66.6
Tlaxcala	94.2	90.0	87.4
Veracruz	90.0	85.0	77.5
Yucatán	92.7	86.0	80.5
Zacatecas	98.1	97.1	90.1

[a] Derived.

SOURCE: México, Dirección General de Estadística, *Censo de Edificios, Resumen, 1939*, 20–21 (Table 6) and Whetten, *Rural Mexico*, 297; *Resumen del Censo, 1960*, 629.

dergo who suffer from such diseases cannot be calculated. Mexican authorities in the Federal District have installed tanks in the public markets for the disinfection of vegetable produce, but the tanks go unused.[24] The problem caused by the fertilization of vegetables with human waste is not seriously combated at all.

Table 9-8 presents the percentage of the population without sewage disposal since 1939. No data were available for 1950, so it is assumed that the population without sewage disposal decreased in approximate proportion to urbanization. The percentage for the entire country decreased in 1960 over 1940 except in the Federal District where extremely rapid urbanization put strain on sewage disposal facilities to increase the totals. In 1940 some 25.4 per cent of the persons in the Federal District did not have sewage disposal and by 1960 this had increased to 30.2 per cent. All in all this is not a serious increase for the rapid rate of urbanization which the Federal District has undergone. Whereas the population of the Federal District grew by 177.1 per cent from 1,757,530 in 1940 to 4,870,876 in 1960, the percentage without sewage disposal increased by only 18.9 per cent.[25]

The population in Mexico City has standards which are considerably higher than the country in general, for more than 70 per cent of Mexico's populace does not have sewage disposal. In only two other entities is the percentage without sewage disposal less than 60 per cent of the population, Nuevo León and Aguascalientes. The figure was over 90 per cent for Zacatecas, Quintana Roo, and Oaxaca in 1960. In 1940 some 22 of Mexico's 32 states had a figure of 90 per cent or more, the high being 98.6 in Guerrero and Quintana Roo.

In sum, the items used in the Poverty Index are useful devices for measuring social modernization in Mexico. They are not perfect, for some adjustments have necessarily been made in the statistics, and the early censuses may not be completely reliable. On the other hand, problems in all censuses may not be as serious as many have thought.[26] Certainly we are better off with the sample

[24] Carmen de la Vega, "La Desinfección de Verduras en los Mercados Abatiría las Muertes por Males Intestinales," *El Día,* Jan. 17, 1965.

[25] Population figures for the Federal District are from *Resumen del Censo, 1960,* 3.

[26] In regard to census reliability, O. Andrew Collver examined the reliability of *Birth Rates in Latin America: New Estimates of Historical Trends and Fluctuations* (Berkeley: University of California Institute of International Studies, 1965),

in the census than with the isolated comments of a few travelers, who subjectively have weighed many of these same factors to come up with their interpretation of Mexico. The major problems in the items are in the censuses of 1920 and 1950, but reasonable adjustments have been made, and the assumption that three items 1910–1930 are representative of seven items 1940–1960 is not affected. On the whole the Index items appear to offer relatively reliable and consistent measurement of poverty.

REGIONAL POVERTY INDEX AND LEVEL

The above mass of data is intelligible for our purpose of assessing the social outcome of federal expenditure if an index is formulated to present a coherent view of regional change. Given the relatively equal nonmodern characteristics of each of the seven items discussed above, an arithmetical average of percentages yields an abstract total figure for the level of poverty in each federal entity by decade. Since the averages in the poverty level consist of three items from 1910 to 1930 which are included in the seven items from 1940 to 1960, and since the three items behave nationally on the same pattern as do the seven for the years from 1940 to 1960, we may say that the three items from 1910 to 1930 are representative of the seven had they been recorded prior to 1940. The three-item total averages since 1940 differ from the seven-item total by only 2.6 per cent in 1940, 4.5 in 1950, and 2.8 in 1960.[27] Thus the Poverty Index is calculated from the averages (1940 = 100) on the assumption that we have a reasonably accurate seven-item representation for the period 1910 to 1960.

The construction of an index involves problems concerning the nature of relationships which we seek to examine. Statistical analysis provides no simple rules about the construction of indices, in the same manner that the historical method provides no elimi-

---

189, and found that from one point of view the Mexican censuses since 1895 all fall within the rate of calculated growth (1.6 per cent in 1900 and −1.9 per cent in 1940). This is one of several analyses he makes.

[27] These differences do not necessarily hold true for each entity within the country as a whole, but this does not upset the assumption that the three items are representative of the seven (1910–1930), for the differences are usually less and only infrequently slightly more. The maximum difference in 1940 was 9.3 in Tlaxcala and only six other entities have a difference of as much as from 5.1 to 6.8.

nation of interpretation, and there are many possible ways to look at the same group of numbers; the definition of point of view is the important element.

Since the definition of poverty developed in this study is one in which social deprivation is considered in a collective rather than an individual sense, we are interested in the rate of change in total undifferentiated characteristics. Therefore, the Poverty Index in Table 9-9 is calculated from the arithmetical averages discussed above. If we had been primarily interested in poverty as an individual phenomenon, it would have been more suitable to discuss an alternative index which maintains the relation of separate characteristics for each census year.[28]

Table 9-9 presents the Poverty Index's rate of change during fifty years of the Mexican Revolution. Prior to 1940 the Index decreased most rapidly in Baja California, Aguascalientes, the Federal District, Tamaulipas and Yucatán (in order). The slowest rate of change came in Querétaro, Sonora, Morelos, Chiapas, Oaxaca, Guerrero, and San Luis Potosí. Since 1940 the fastest rate of change came in Nuevo León, Sonora, Coahuila, and Morelos; the slowest in Zacatecas and Hidalgo. The over-all pattern from 1910 to 1960 repeats that of 1910–1940, except that the least amount of change in the range of the Index came in Querétaro and Zacatecas. The index of the rate of change is only part of the story, for we must also take into account the varying levels of poverty.

The poverty level, based upon the arithmetic average of poverty characteristics for each federal entity, is presented in Table 9-10. The averages show the relative position of each political unit in regard to the level of poverty from 1910 to 1960. The averages are meaningless except to show comparatively the level of poverty characteristics.

By comparing Tables 9-9 and 9-10 we may examine the rate of social change as it is related to differing levels of poverty. The entity with one of the highest levels of poverty in 1910, but which

[28] For comparative purposes, Appendix H offers an alternative method which is calculated to reflect the decrease in poverty as influenced by categories within the total index. It is significant to note that the alternative method is in basic over-all agreement with our Index concerning trend of social change, though rates by federal entity show quite different patterns due to the nature of relationships which are measured.

TABLE 9-9

Poverty Index

(three- and seven-item arithmetic averages for 1940 = 100)

Federal Entity	1910	1921	1930	1940	1950	1960
Total	123.7	115.4	108.7	100.0	85.7	72.0
Aguascalientes	182.5	126.7	119.6	100.0	95.3	75.6
Baja California	215.6	151.7	108.8	100.0	87.5	75.8
Baja Calif. Terr.	143.2	123.1	107.8	100.0	86.1	73.2
Campeche	120.4	125.3	119.6	100.0	84.8	73.0
Chiapas	107.7	102.8	100.0	100.0	90.3	81.4
Chihuahua	143.2	145.1	116.5	100.0	84.1	68.6
Coahuila	139.0	122.3	114.9	100.0	81.0	66.6
Colima	129.3	119.9	112.5	100.0	89.5	81.6
Distrito Federal	178.6	145.0	126.1	100.0	78.5	78.9
Durango	126.1	115.0	110.5	100.0	91.3	80.5
Guanajuato	112.8	108.9	104.3	100.0	89.3	77.4
Guerrero	108.3	105.6	102.2	100.0	89.5	82.0
Hidalgo	113.5	110.8	104.6	100.0	90.9	83.8
Jalisco	128.5	115.9	110.7	100.0	89.4	71.8
México	109.5	107.2	106.1	100.0	88.9	70.7
Michoacán	113.7	112.7	104.3	100.0	88.5	77.0
Morelos	107.5	119.4	110.4	100.0	78.7	67.2
Nayarit	124.3	112.6	105.4	100.0	91.6	80.9
Nuevo León	145.2	129.1	120.5	100.0	84.0	60.8
Oaxaca	108.2	107.8	101.3	100.0	90.0	81.3
Puebla	110.8	108.8	106.0	100.0	88.8	79.6
Querétaro	105.0	105.4	102.4	100.0	91.9	82.3
Quintana Roo	138.8	132.3	108.1	100.0	86.1	77.5
San Luis Potosí	108.4	112.7	102.7	100.0	90.5	81.8
Sinaloa	123.8	112.8	107.9	100.0	88.9	73.0
Sonora	106.6	118.2	106.8	100.0	80.3	66.0
Tabasco	117.0	113.0	106.4	100.0	88.2	77.0
Tamaulipas	161.1	120.9	119.0	100.0	83.4	70.6
Tlaxcala	125.3	123.6	109.0	100.0	88.5	79.0
Veracruz	117.5	113.3	106.4	100.0	89.7	74.2
Yucatán	157.1	126.8	111.2	100.0	84.2	77.6
Zacatecas	114.5	114.6	106.1	100.0	94.8	90.2

SOURCES: Calculated from Tables 9-1, 9-2, and 9-4 to 9-8.

changed fastest from 1910 to 1940, was Aguascalientes. The greatest social change since 1940 in relation to high poverty level came in the state of Mexico. Nuevo León exhibits the greatest social change since 1940 among the low poverty level states. While from 1910 to 1940 there were 22 entities with high or medium poverty levels and slow change, from 1940 to 1960 some 20 entities exhibited medium change for the same levels of poverty. The range in rate of change was less after 1940 which leads one to conclude that more balanced social development was becoming possible. In the low poverty group, Sonora moved from a slow rate of change to a fast rate after 1940, and the Federal District and Baja California slowed to a medium rate of change.

Seven regions are identified according to poverty level in Table 9-10, the Federal District being separated into its own zone since it does not fit into any pattern of development, as does the rest of Mexico. The geo-social regions hold together very well, even when tested by rates of change in Table 9-9. The exceptions are Hidalgo and Zacatecas which did not move with their East Central region into a rate of medium change after 1940. Tlaxcala in East Central Mexico offers an example of a state that could have been included in another region of poverty; its rate of change prior to 1940 and its level of poverty after 1921 might have placed it in the West Central area. Rate of change after 1940 and level of poverty in 1910, however, require that Tlaxcala be counted with the East Central region, which, in any case, is where it falls in purely geographic terms.

Historically, the regions in Table 9-10 have maintained the same relation to each other in terms of poverty level. The poorest region has been the South. The East Central has followed, but not closely. The only change in the relation of the regions came in 1930 when the West Central replaced the Gulf as the third poorest region in the country. The Gulf area took over the West Central's old position of fourth poorest region. The West occupies the fifth place in the hierarchy of poverty, but in 1910 it was equal to the West Center's average, and in 1950 and 1960 it was very close to the average of the Gulf position. Poverty in the North has been far below the latter levels, and the Federal District greatly below the North.

TABLE 9-10

Poverty Level (in Percentages)[a]

Federal Entity	1910	1921	1930	1940	1950	1960
Total Mexico	56.9	53.1	50.0	46.0	39.4	33.1
North[b]	*46.6*	*41.1*	*36.2*	*31.5*	*26.2*	*21.3*
Baja Calif.	48.7	34.3	24.6	22.6	19.8	17.1
Chihuahua	52.7	53.4	42.9	36.8	30.9	25.2
Coahuila	45.7	40.2	37.8	32.9	26.6	21.9
Nuevo León	44.3	39.4	36.8	30.5	25.6	18.5
Sonora	35.9	39.8	36.0	33.7	27.1	22.2
Tamaulipas	52.5	39.4	38.8	32.6	27.2	23.0
West[b]	*56.9*	*49.1*	*46.1*	*41.8*	*37.7*	*32.0*
Aguascalientes	65.5	45.5	42.9	35.9	34.2	27.1
Baja Calif. Terr.	54.7	47.0	41.2	38.2	32.9	28.0
Colima	48.9	45.3	42.5	37.8	33.8	30.8
Durango	56.2	51.3	49.3	44.6	40.7	35.9
Jalisco	56.4	50.9	48.6	43.9	39.2	31.5
Nayarit	58.1	50.4	47.2	44.8	41.0	36.2
Sinaloa	58.7	53.5	51.1	47.4	42.1	34.6
West Central[b]	*55.9*	*56.3*	*53.5*	*50.4*	*43.7*	*36.9*
Guanajuato	57.0	55.0	52.7	50.5	45.1	39.1
México	61.2	59.9	59.3	55.9	49.7	39.5
Michoacán	57.8	57.3	53.0	50.8	45.0	39.1
Morelos	47.5	52.8	48.8	44.2	34.8	29.7
East Central[b]	*61.7*	*61.5*	*57.5*	*54.7*	*49.7*	*45.0*
Hidalgo	66.2	64.6	61.0	58.3	53.0	48.9
Puebla	61.4	60.3	58.7	55.4	49.9	44.1
Querétaro	60.4	60.6	58.9	57.5	52.8	47.3
San Luis Potosí	57.3	59.6	54.3	52.9	47.9	43.3
Tlaxcala	67.5	66.6	58.8	53.9	47.7	42.6
Zacatecas	57.5	57.5	53.3	50.2	47.6	43.5
South[b]	*67.7*	*66.0*	*63.4*	*62.6*	*56.3*	*51.1*
Chiapas	65.8	62.8	61.1	61.1	55.2	49.7
Guerrero	68.2	66.5	64.4	63.0	56.4	51.7
Oaxaca	69.0	68.8	64.6	63.8	57.4	51.9
Gulf[b]	*59.2*	*55.8*	*50.4*	*45.9*	*39.8*	*35.0*
Campeche	46.8	48.7	46.5	38.9	33.0	28.4
Quintana Roo	68.0	64.8	53.0	49.0	42.2	38.0
Tabasco	64.4	62.2	58.5	55.0	48.5	42.4
Veracruz	56.4	54.4	51.1	48.0	43.1	35.6
Yucatán	60.3	48.7	42.7	38.4	32.3	30.8
D. F.	*20.0*	*16.2*	*14.1*	*11.2*	*8.8*	*8.8*

[a] Arithmetic averages (adjusted 1910–1930).

[b] Average regardless of size, see 243f.

SOURCE: Table 9-9. Averages are calculated by multiplying the rate of change in Table 9-9 times the seven-item average for 1940 in this table.

TABLE 9-11

Regional Geo-Social Poverty Index and Per Cent Change

Region	A. Index (1940 = 100)					
	1910	1921	1930	1940	1950	1960
Total	123.7	115.4	108.7	100	85.7	72.0
North	147.9	130.5	114.9	100	83.2	67.6
West	136.1	117.5	110.3	100	90.2	76.6
West Central	110.9	111.7	106.1	100	86.7	73.2
East Central	112.8	112.4	105.1	100	90.9	82.3
South	108.1	105.4	101.3	100	89.9	81.6
Gulf	129.0	121.6	109.8	100	86.7	76.3
Federal District	178.6	144.6	125.9	100	78.6	78.6

	B. Per Cent Change				
Total	− 6.7	− 5.8	− 8.0	−14.3	−16.0
North	−11.8	−12.0	−13.0	−16.8	−18.8
West	−13.7	− 6.1	− 9.3	− 9.8	−15.1
West Central	.7	− 5.0	− 5.8	−13.3	−15.6
East Central	− .4	− 6.5	− 4.9	− 9.1	− 9.5
South	− 2.5	− 3.9	− 1.3	−10.1	− 9.2
Gulf	− 5.7	− 9.7	− 8.9	−13.3	−12.0
Federal District	−19.0	−12.9	−20.6	−21.4	− − −

SOURCE: Calculated from Table 9-10.

The regional index of change is suggested in Table 9-11. Prior to 1940 the Federal District was the zone which underwent the most rapid decrease in poverty level. The North made the next most rapid decrease. The West and the Gulf showed a similar rate of change. The West Central region changed only slightly faster than the South which remained stagnant. Since 1940 the North has taken over the leadership in most rapidly decreasing the poverty level. There was no change in the Federal District's Poverty Index during the 1950's, but the level of poverty was still by far the lowest in Mexico. The West Central region changed at about the same rate as the country's total change. The West and the Gulf saw decrease in the rate of poverty at the same rate as did the East Central and the South, though the latter two changed far slower than the former two.

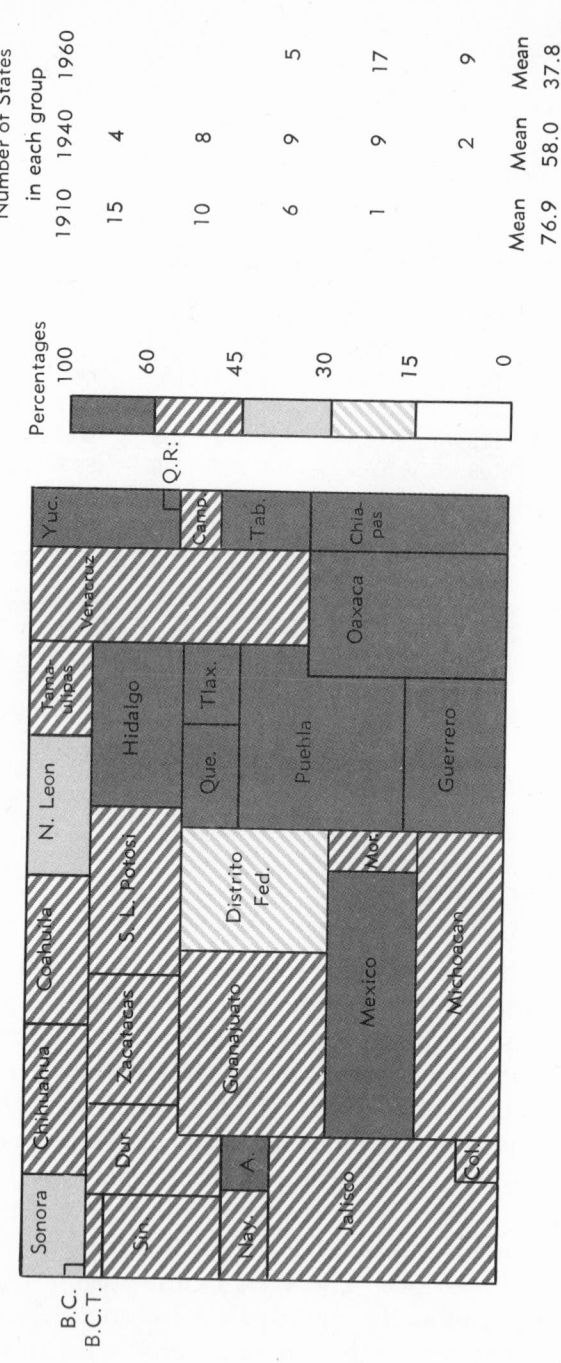

Fig. 5. Poverty Level in Mexico, 1910.

Source: Table 9-10

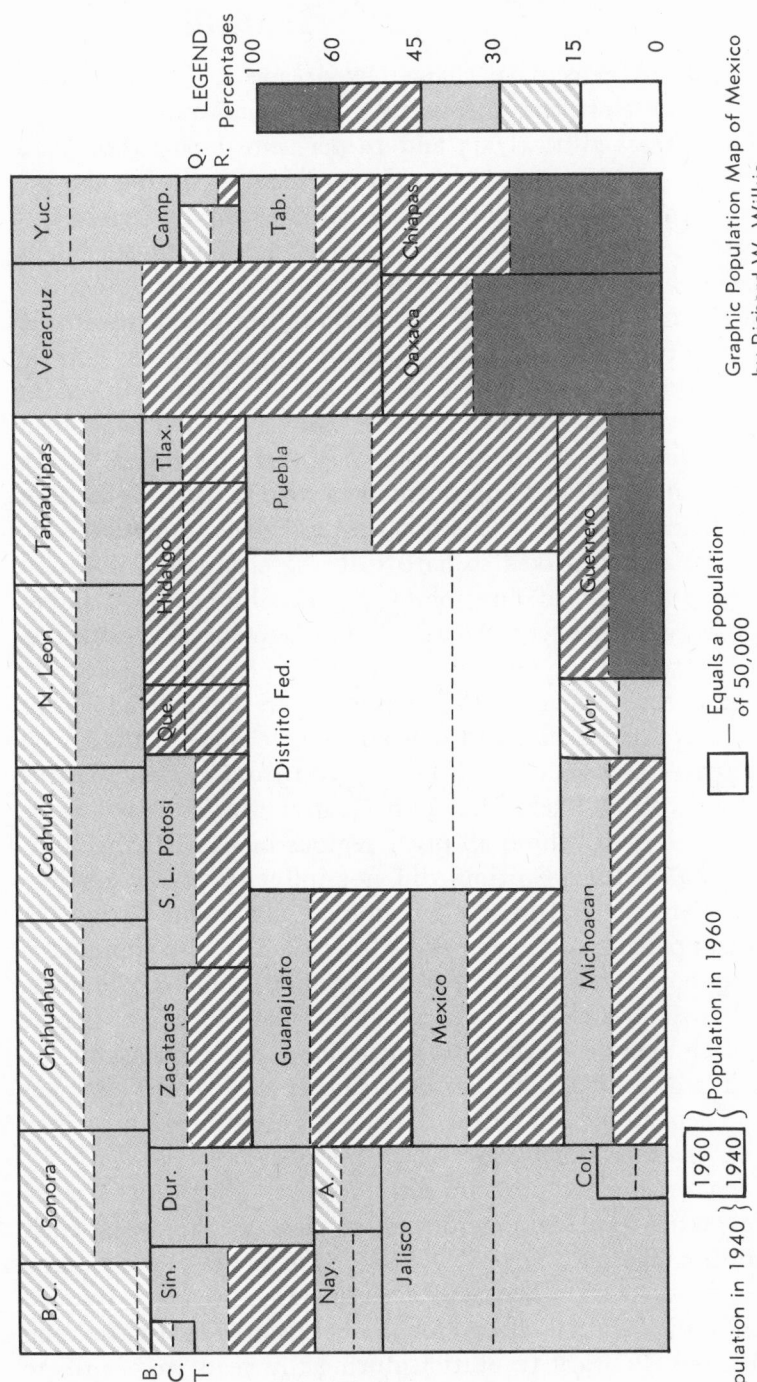

LEGEND
Percentages

100

60

45

30

15

0

Q.
R.

Graphic Population Map of Mexico
by Richard W. Wilkie

— Equals a population
of 50,000

Population in 1960

1960
1940 } Population in 1940

FIG. 6. Poverty Level in Mexico, 1940 and 1960.

Source: Table 9-10

In regard to percentage change by decade in Table 9-11, it seems that the North has consistently seen a high rate of change, and that it reached nearly 17 and 19 per cent during the 1950's and 1960's. The North made its slowest changes during the period from 1910 to 1921. There was a gain during the 1920's, and this increased slightly during the Cárdenas era. The North might have been expected to have made the greatest decreases in the poverty level when the control of the federal government was in the hands of northerners up to 1934, but this apparently was not the case. Nor did the West Central region which contains Michoacán receive most benefits when its native son Lázaro Cárdenas held the presidency. In fact the decrease in poverty registered during the 1930's in the West Central area was low. If social revolution did not succeed in Cárdenas's homeground, it is understandable why Cárdenas has worked so hard to bring economic revolution to the area as regional director of the Tepalcatepec and Balsas River basin development project. This judgment of social revolution is made on the assumption that little decrease in poverty could have come during the depression years immediately prior to Cárdenas's presidency, and that all social change of the 1930's came during Cárdenas's term from 1934 to 1940. President Manuel Avila Camacho of Puebla left East Central Mexico much as he found it. It lagged behind all other regions in social change during the 1940's. Ruiz Cortines did not influence social development in Veracruz and his Gulf region to any extent during the 1950's, compared to other regions. Only Alemán, also from Veracruz, may have significantly helped his region from 1946 to 1952. Thus the rule has generally held that the plans for social change which each president has entertained have not emphasized the president's own area. This is ironic since presidential policy has usually been influenced by the experience each president gained as governor of his home state.

Cárdenas's agrarian program did not help agricultural Mexico to live better, but his sponsorship of class warfare apparently brought the greatest change in Mexico before 1940 to the Federal District. The 1920's, when agrarian reform was dying, witnessed the beginning of social change for the backward East Central and Gulf regions. Political revolution during the years from 1910 to 1921 saw little social change in the area of combat: West Central

TABLE 9-12

Regional Geo-Social Shares of Population

Region	1910	1921	1930	1940	1950	1960
Total Population	15,160,369	14,334,780	16,552,722	19,653,552	25,791,017	34,923,129
Total Per Cent	100.0	100.0	100.0	100.0	100.0[a]	100.0
North[b]	11.1	12.0	12.4	13.4	14.7	15.8
West[b]	16.0	15.8	14.9	14.8	14.1	14.1
West Central	21.3	19.5	19.1	18.0	17.1	16.8
East Central	21.6	20.0	20.0	19.2	17.7	15.9
South	13.7	13.7	13.7	13.3	12.6	11.9
Gulf	11.6	12.7	12.5	12.4	11.9	11.6
Federal District	4.7	6.3	7.4	8.9	11.8	13.9

[a] Includes .1 per cent complementary population.
[b] See Table 9-1, Note i.
SOURCE: Appendix K.

and East Central Mexico. We may surmise that war did not free the populace to live better, as was expected, but destroyed the means by which they could seek a better life, especially in the West Central region where the Poverty Index went up. This conclusion is borne out by the increase in poverty level in the two northern states of Sonora and Chihuahua, other great battlefields of the period from 1910 to 1921. The era of emphasis on industrialization and increased agricultural production during the 1940's opened the door to social change in all regions, especially to the South and East Central portions of the country which had seen little change during the 1930's. The West did not show signs of increased change until the 1950's.

The seven regions discussed here have the population shown in Table 9-12. The West Central region, most populous in 1910, today has the greatest percentage of persons in Mexico, but only slightly more than the North, which has gained considerably since 1940. Like the East Central area, the West Central region has declined in the share of population, but at a more steady rate since 1910. Also, the South has decreased in percentage terms since 1940, and the West prior to 1940. The Gulf region has the same percentage of the population as it did in 1910; it gained until the 1930's and then fell off slightly. The Federal District has grown the most, of course, for it is the center of business, industry, and opportunity

TABLE 9-13

Regional Shares of Mexico's Area[a]

Region	Share
Square Hectares	1,967,183
Total Per Cent	100.0
North	40.7
West	18.8
West Central	6.0
East Central	10.6
South	11.7
Gulf	12.1
Federal District	.1

[a] Insular territory excluded (5,364 square hectares).
SOURCE: *Compendio Estadístico, 1960–1961*, 13.

for all of Mexico. It is evident that the population is moving out of the poor central and southern regions to find a better life in the North and in the Federal District.

Table 9-13 presents a summary of territory in each of the above regions. The North, which will soon undoubtedly have the most population, is Mexico's largest region. The Federal District, which will probably challenge the North for population leadership, has .1 per cent of the country's area. Like the Federal District, the East and West Central regions of Mexico have greater percentage of population than percentage of land, but this problem does not remotely compare to the rapid urbanization of the Federal District. Mexico's poorest region, the South, has 11.7 per cent of the territory, and when this amount is added to the poverty-stricken East Central region which has 10.6 per cent of the territory, almost one quarter of Mexico's land area lies in the zone of poverty.

THE STANDARD VIEW OF REGIONAL MEXICO

It is important to note that, had the standard census regions been used to show regional poverty, the range in poverty level within each region would have been so great that social change would be obscured. The census view is based upon a geo-economic conception of regional Mexico, but if social regions are at such variance with standard regions, it would appear that the census regions should be re-examined. In order to group states together which have approximately the same level or standard of poverty in historical continuity, it has been necessary to formulate a new concept of social regions in Mexico.

Table 9-14 compares the range of poverty level in geo-economic (census) regions and in geo-social regions for the years 1910, 1940, and 1960. It is significant that the census regions show a startling lack of homogeneity, especially in the central region which includes the Federal District, for the range in the poverty level is consistently high; in only 4 cases out of 15 does the range fall below 20 points. The social regions projected in this study, however, have a range which is consistently low; in only 4 cases out of 18 is it above 15 points. In 8 cases the range is under 10 points. Whereas in the census regions the total average for all Mexico is always over 20 points in range, social regions show an average of

TABLE 9-14

*Geo-Social Regions and Geo-Economic Regions
Compared in Selected Years*

| A.   Range in Poverty Level Examined in Geo-Economic Regions | | | |
Region	1910	1940	1960
Pacific North	22.8	22.5	19.1
North	13.2	22.4	25.0
Center	33.2	47.1	40.1
South Pacific	20.1	26.0	21.1
Gulf	21.2	16.6	14.0

| B.   Range in Poverty Level Examined in Geo-Social Regions | | | |
Region			
North	16.8	14.2	8.1
West	16.6	11.5	9.1
West Central	13.7	11.7	9.8
East Central	10.7	8.1	6.3
South	3.2	2.7	2.2
Gulf	21.2	16.6	14.0
Federal District	– – –	– – –	– – –

SOURCE: See Table 9-10.

13.6, 10.8, and 8.3 in the years under consideration. It is clear
that the social regions allow us to see the integration of regions
in a manner that is quite impossible when the census regions are
used for analysis. In 1910 the northern border had a wide diver-
sity in the poverty level, and this persisted through 1940. By 1960
the North was clearly a homogeneous region. This pattern has
been also true for the West and West Central regions as the range
in the Poverty Index has decreased. The Gulf region still has
some distance to go before it will be a truly well-knit region. In
1910 and 1921 Quintana Roo could not strictly be considered part
of the Gulf poverty pattern, but since 1930 Tabasco has been the
state which does not fit well into the regional group.

Since the standard geo-economic view of Mexico is used as the
major approach to Mexican statistical analysis,[29] Appendix I presents the Poverty Index in that form in order that scholars who

---

[29] See, for example, Whetten, *Rural Mexico,* and Simpson, *The Ejido.*

use the census analysis may use the social data offered here. Several other regional analyses have recently been prepared.[30] Howard Cline organizes regions in a historical context based on "aboriginal base, physical habitat, colonial and recent backgrounds, economic interests, demography, urbanization, and 'ethos.' "[31] His regions have no relation to the social regions offered here. Paul Lamartine Yates has published a study of regional Mexico which is really a study of the economic development per capita of selected federal entities. It is fine for Yates as an economist to tell us that in 1958 there were 20.2 motor vehicles for every 1000 Mexicans, but this does not tell us how well each Mexican has lived, comparatively, during fifty years of Revolution.[32] The social regions given in the analysis of the Poverty Index in the present study overcome the problems of per-capita analysis, and offer a new view of poverty in Mexico during the twentieth century.

[30] See [Fernando Zamora], *Diagnóstico Económico Regional 1958* (México, D. F.: Secretaría de la Economía Nacional, 1959) and México, Comisión Nacional de los Salarios Mínimos, *Descripciones Geográficas Económicas de las Zonas, Memoria de los Trabajos de 1963* (3 vols.). These works break down zones without regard to the boundaries of federal entities. The basis is geographic and economic.

[31] Cline, *Mexico, Revolution to Evolution*, Chapter 5.

[32] Paul Lamartine Yates, *El Desarrollo Regional de México* (México, D. F.: Banco de México, 1961), 97, 105; per-capita social welfare index is presented on 98–99.

10

Federal Policy and Social Change

In Part 1 we analyzed the nature of federal expenditure in the Mexican Revolution, and we have in the previous chapter directly examined the amount and rate of social change during ideological periods of political, social, and economic revolution. We are now able to bring these two different types of analyses together in order to present a tentative view of process in the Mexican Revolution. We shall discuss the limitation in attempting to relate federal expenditure directly to regional social change, and then turn to an analysis of the relationship of budgetary policy and decrease in the Poverty Index. The rate of social and economic change in periods of the Revolution is discussed in relation to ideology, and an analysis of revolutionary programs follows in which the strengths and weaknesses of the official party's policy are taken up.

ANALYSIS OF EXPENDITURE AND SOCIAL CHANGE

The reader is reminded that since there is apparently no historical record of the federal entities in which gross federal expenditure has been spent, it is not possible to link total federal expenditure directly to regional analysis. However, we have some partial direct data which reveal recent trends. In 1964 the Mexican Public Investment Agency, directed by José P. González Blanco, attempted to overcome this lack of basic data for developmental programming, and it published a geographical analysis of public investment (including expenditure by decentralized agencies) for five years of the López Mateos term. This study reveals that a few states received most of the government's capital investment funds at a time when balanced revolution was the keynote. Evidently the concept of balanced development still did not take into account balanced regional growth. Federal investments were largely directed to entities which do not lie within regions of high poverty. The relationship of this aspect of federal expenditure to the geo-social regions of poverty is presented in Table 10-1. In line with

TABLE 10-I

Projected Federal Capital Investment Compared to Population by Region, 1959–1963

Federal Entity	A. Investment	B. Population (1960)	C. Difference of A to B	D. Ratio A/B	
Total Mexico (Per Cent)	100.0	100.0	– – –	– – –	
North	16.5	15.8	.7	1.0	1
Baja California	2.3	1.5	.8	1.5	1
Chihuahua	5.8	3.5	2.3	1.7	1
Coahuila	1.7	2.6	– .9	.7	1
Nuevo León	1.8	3.1	– 1.3	.6	1
Sonora	2.7	2.2	.5	1.2	1
Tamaulipas	2.2	2.9	– .7	.8	1
West	15.6	14.1	1.5	1.1	1
Aguascalientes	.4	.7	– .3	.6	1
Baja Calif. Terr.	.5	.2	.3	2.5	1
Colima	1.0	.5	.5	2.0	1
Durango	2.1	2.2	– .1	1.0	1
Jalisco	2.8	7.0	– 4.2	.4	1
Nayarit	.7	1.1	– .4	.6	1
Sinaloa	8.1	2.4	5.7	3.4	1
West Central	8.1	16.8	– 8.7	.5	1
Guanajuato	1.6	5.0	– 3.4	.3	1
México	3.5	5.4	– 1.9	.7	1
Michoacán	2.4	5.3	– 2.9	.5	1
Morelos	.6	1.1	– .5	.6	1
East Central	7.6	15.8	– 8.2	.5	1
Hidalgo	1.2	2.8	– 1.6	.4	1
Puebla	1.0	5.7	– 4.7	.2	1
Querétaro	.6	1.0	– .4	.6	1
San Luis Potosí	2.9	3.0	– .1	1.0	1
Tlaxcala	.5	1.0	– .5	.5	1
Zacatecas	1.4	2.3	– .9	.6	1
South	11.9	11.9	– – –	1.0	1
Chiapas	4.6	3.5	.9	1.3	1
Guerrero	2.6	3.4	– .8	.8	1
Oaxaca	4.7	5.0	– .3	.9	1
Gulf	9.3	11.6	– 2.3	.8	1
Campeche	1.2	.5	.7	2.4	1
Quintana Roo	.7	.1	.6	7.0	1
Tabasco	2.2	1.4	.8	1.6	1
Veracruz	3.7	7.8	– 4.1	.5	1
Yucatán	1.5	1.8	– .3	.8	1
Federal District	31.0	14.0	17.0	2.2	1

SOURCES: México, Secretaría de la Presidencia, *México Inversión Pública Federal, 1925–1963*, Chapter 2; *Resumen del Censo, 1960*.

TABLE 10-2

Number of Poverty Characteristics Compared to Federal Capital Investment and Total Population, 1960

Federal Entity	Characteristics of Poverty		Investment (1959–1963)		Population	
	A. Number (in Thousands)ᵃ	B. Per Cent	C. Per Cent	D. Difference of C to B	E. Per Cent	F. Difference of E to B
Total Mexico	*11,560*	*100.0*	*100.0*	*— —*	*100.0*	*— —*
North	*1,207*	*10.4*	*16.5*	*6.1*	*15.8*	*5.4*
Baja California	89	.8	2.3	1.5	1.5	.7
Chihuahua	309	2.7	5.8	3.1	3.5	.8
Coahuila	199	1.7	1.7	— —	2.6	.9
Nuevo León	200	1.7	1.8	.1	3.1	1.4
Sonora	174	1.5	2.7	1.2	2.2	.7
Tamaulipas	236	2.0	2.2	.2	2.9	.9
West	*1,614*	*14.0*	*15.6*	*1.6*	*14.1*	*.7*
Aguascalientes	66	.6	.4	— .2	.7	.1
Baja Calif. Terr.	23	.2	.5	.3	.2	— —
Colima	51	.4	1.0	.6	.5	.1
Durango	273	2.4	2.1	— .3	2.2	— .2
Jalisco	770	6.7	2.8	— 3.9	7.0	— .3
Nayarit	141	1.2	.7	— .5	1.1	— .1
Sinaloa	290	2.5	8.1	5.6	2.4	— .1
West Central	*2,268*	*19.7*	*8.7*	*— 17.6*	*16.8*	*— 2.9*
Guanajuato	679	5.9	1.6	— 4.3	5.0	— .9
México	750	6.5	3.5	— 3.0	5.4	— 1.1
Michoacán	724	6.3	2.4	— 3.9	5.3	— 1.0
Morelos	115	1.0	.6	.4	1.1	.1

East Central	2,483	21.5	7.6	—13.9	15.8	—5.7
Hidalgo	487	4.2	1.2	—3.0	2.8	—1.4
Puebla	870	7.5	1.0	—6.5	5.7	—1.8
Querétaro	168	1.4	.6	—.8	1.0	—.4
San Luis Potosí	454	4.0	2.9	1.1	3.0	—1.0
Tlaxcala	148	1.3	.5	.8	1.0	—.3
Zacatecas	356	3.1	1.4	1.7	2.3	—.8
South	*2,772*	*18.3*	*11.9*	*—6.4*	*11.9*	*6.4*
Chiapas	602	5.2	4.6	—.6	3.5	—1.7
Guerrero	614	5.3	2.6	—2.7	3.4	—1.9
Oaxaca	896	7.8	4.7	—3.1	5.0	—2.8
Gulf	*1,437*	*12.4*	*9.3*	*—3.7*	*17.6*	*—.8*
Campeche	48	.4	1.2	.8	.5	.1
Quintana Roo	19	.2	.7	.5	.1	.1
Tabasco	210	1.8	2.2	.4	1.4	.4
Verzcruz	971	8.4	3.7	—4.7	7.8	—.6
Yucatán	189	1.6	1.5	—.1	1.8	.2
Federal District	429	3.7	37.0	27.3	14.0	10.3

^a Calculated by multiplying the poverty level for 1960 (Table 9-10) times the population by entity (detail does not add to total due to rounding).

Sources: Table 9-10, Table 10-1, and Appendix K.

the purpose of our analysis, figures examined here are limited to direct investments by the federal government; expenditure by decentralized agencies and mixed public and private enterprises have been excluded.

Table 10-1 offers several interesting observations. The region which received the greatest percentage of federal investment in relation to its population was the Federal District. It greatly outdistanced all other regions and entities during the period from 1959 to 1963, receiving 31 per cent of investment for 14 per cent of the population of Mexico. This amount was 16.3 per cent greater in relation to population than the northern region received (Column C), and the North was the Federal District's nearest competitor for investment funds. The North shared 16.5 per cent of investment, and like the South, had a balance in percentage of investment to population. The poorest geo-social region, the South, received more federal investment than did East Central Mexico, the next poorest region. Apparently, the government determined to do something about the southern region of poverty, but its action was limited in relation to development in other regions. The neglected region under López Mateos was the East Central Area. Puebla received an astoundingly low 1 per cent of investment for 5.7 per cent of Mexico's population—a difference of 4.7 per cent. In contrast, Quintana Roo received .7 per cent investment for .1 per cent of the population in an attempt to open a relatively unpopulated area. The government hoped to encourage immigration into the territory from overpopulated central states, but meager investment paid little dividends. In short, the Federal District absorbed investment disproportionate to population and left the rest of the country (except Sinaloa and Chihuahua) with serious development problems.

We may also examine federal investment from 1959 to 1963 as to how it affected the number of poverty characteristics which remained in 1960. Previously we have examined the level of poverty in each entity and region (Table 9-10), but since each area varies in size we must show the areas which have the greatest amount of poverty in relation to total poverty in Mexico. Table 10-2 portrays the number of characteristics of poverty as they were distributed after five decades of Revolution. Where Table 9-10 showed us that the characteristics of poverty within the Federal

District came to 8.8 per cent in 1960, for example, Table 10-2 reveals that there were some 429,000 poverty characteristics, 3.7 per cent of all such characteristics in the republic in 1960. Sonora, which had a poverty level of 22.2 per cent in Table 9-10, shows 174,000 characteristics of poverty in Table 10-2, 1.5 per cent of Mexico's poverty characteristics.

It is clear in Table 10-2 that several very poor states were neglected by the government. Veracruz had the largest number of poverty characteristics in 1960 (columns A and B), but it also had the largest percentage of population in Mexico (column E). Nevertheless, Veracruz received only 3.7 per cent of federal investments from 1959 to 1963 (column C). This discrepancy does not look so serious when it is compared to Puebla's problem. With 7.5 per cent of Mexico's poverty characteristics, Puebla received only 1 per cent of investment in 1960, the most serious negative relationship between investment and poverty for any individual entity (column D).

In terms of regions, the plight of the West Central area is outstanding as it had 19.7 per cent of the country's poverty characteristics after fifty years of Revolution, yet the region only received as much federal investment, 8.1 per cent, as the state of Sinaloa which had 2.5 per cent of the characteristics of poverty. The West Central region did not do so badly as the East Central region in obtaining funds, however, for as column D shows, the East Central area received the least funds in relation to population, a difference of 13.9 per cent. The South, in contrast, only received 6.4 per cent less than it should have if population and investment were in balance. The North and West (especially Colima) had a positive relationship of poverty and investment, but again the Federal District, which had 3.7 per cent of the poverty characteristics and 31 per cent of investment, came out best with a 27.3 per cent difference. This relationship is even more striking than the positive difference of 17 per cent of investment to population given in Table 10-1.

In analyzing federal investment from 1959 through 1963, Table 10-2 shows the problems which face a poor state like Oaxaca and the advantages enjoyed by a rich state such as Baja California, for example. Oaxaca, with 5 per cent of the republic's population and 7.8 per cent of the characteristics of poverty, not only received

TABLE 10-3

Federal Expenditure for Irrigation and Water Resources by Region, 1926–1958[a]

Federal Entity	Per Cent
Total Mexico	*100.0*
North	*36.9*
Baja California	8.5
Chihuahua	2.6
Coahuila	* .3[b]
Nuevo León	* .3[b]
Sonora	13.2
Tamaulipas	12.0
West	*21.6*
Aguascalientes	.2
Baja Calif. Terr.	– – –
Colima	– – –
Durango	2.4
Jalisco	3.1
Nayarit	1.2
Sinaloa	14.7
West Central	*9.4*
Guanajuato	2.5
México	.2
Michoacán	6.7
Morelos	– – –
East Central	*7.6*
Hidalgo	.9
Puebla	* 5.6[c]
Querétaro	.3
San Luis Potosí	.1
Tlaxcala	– – –
Zacatecas	.7
South	*11.3*
Chiapas	* .4[d]
Guerrero	.3
Oaxaca	*10.6[c]

TABLE 10-3 (continued)

*Federal Expenditure for Irrigation and Water Resources
by Region, 1926–1958*[a]

Federal Entity	Per Cent
Gulf	*8.9*
Campeche	– – –
Quintana Roo	– – –
Tabasco	* .2[d]
Veracruz	* 8.7[c]
Yucatán	– – –
Federal District	*4.3*

[a] Total actual expenditure from 1926 through 1958 was 5,152,521,000 pesos. This amount includes financing of the large irrigation projects and the following hydraulic resource commissions: Valle de México, Papaloapán, Tepalcatepec, Grijalva, Fuerte, and Yaqui. Small irrigation projects, sanitary engineering, and commission studies are excluded from these figures.

[b] Amount divided equally between two states by author as source unclear.

[c] Amount divided between three states (Puebla, 11.9; Oaxaca, 49.5; Veracruz, 38.6) on basis of share in area of Papaloapán Commission's jurisdiction. See Cline, *Mexico, Revolution to Evolution: 1940–1960*, p. 75.

[d] See Note b above.

SOURCE: México, Secretaría de Recursos Hidráulicos, *Informe . . . , 1958–1959.*

about three times less investment in relation to population than Baja California (which had 1.5 per cent of the population and .8 per cent of the poverty characteristics), but also did not enjoy the stimulus of northern border activity which the latter state could boast. State government in Oaxaca, always poor in comparison to the federal government, found itself with almost the entire burden of social and economic development.

Since we do not have figures for total federal capital investment by entity prior to 1959, we must use a different type of gauge to examine regional balance in expenditure before López Mateos's term. Table 10-3 presents cumulative federal expenditure for irrigation and water resources by region from 1926 through 1958. This table includes total expenditure of the National Irrigation Commission until 1946 and the Ministry of Hydraulic Resources since 1947, with some exceptions as noted. Of the 5,152,521,000 pesos expended in more than thirty years, 62.4 per cent was for large irrigation programs and the remainder was dedicated to the work of intra- and interstate water control commissions. The commissions have sponsored economic development and also have stimulated social change. Six commissions were in actual operation from 1947 to 1958.

It is evident from the data that expenditure has been concentrated in a few areas. The North has gained much of its position of wealth because it received almost 37 per cent of all federal water control funds up to 1958. In contrast, the East Central region received only 7.6 per cent. The Gulf region, comprising five states, received 8.9 per cent, Veracruz gaining almost all of the funds. Of course the dry North needed more funds for irrigation than the wet Gulf states, but the latter desperately needed flood control. While the harnessing of the Papaloapán River was a step in aiding the wet states, the state of Tabasco, for example, did not benefit from this development in Veracruz. (The Grijalva and Usumacinta Commission is presently beginning to remedy this neglect of Tabasco). Entities which received no funds for water resources from 1926 through 1958 include the following: Colima, Baja California Territory, Morelos, Tlaxcala, Campeche, Quintana Roo, and Yucatán. Due to the number of small, uneconomical *ejidal* holdings in much of Mexico, it is perhaps understandable that the government channeled funds into the North, especially in light of alarmed foreign predictions that Mexico was going to starve as her population expanded during the 1940's and 1950's. Mexico's limited finances precluded rapid development in all areas but the North, and to a lesser degree the West. As government action expands in the 1960's it should be able to develop water resources in seveial of the poorer areas at the same time, and if the Revolution is going to achieve balanced development, it must begin to expend funds where results may appear meager.

There are difficult problems in trying to develop regions in which over-population and *minifundio* prevail as investment does not gain much productivity. It is impossible for the government to redistribute land given in the name of the Revolution to the peasantry, even if it be in *minifundio*, as redistribution would destroy one of the foremost ideals of the Revolution. The government, therefore, undoubtedly has invested funds in regions where social and economic improvement are possible on the theory that internal migration will resolve some of the problems of poverty as people move from the poor areas to the regions which offer opportunity. Since it is generally the imaginative people who migrate, however, a selection process has been at work which deprives the poorest areas of the very persons who in the long run might bring about a change in high poverty levels.

While balanced revolution in geographic terms was obviously not stimulated by governmental capital investments between 1959 and 1963, López Mateos apparently hoped that private activity would somewhat obviate regional economic and social imbalances. This latter policy was rooted in the granting of tax incentives to companies which would locate outside such a highly developed area as the Federal District. Whether this contradictory policy of federal and private investment would work out remains to be seen. As long as the government tends to neglect infrastructural development of the poorer regions, thus contributing to regional imbalances, it would seem improbable that much private industry would locate far from the confines of developed areas.

The lack of geographic balance in federal expenditure during the Mexican Revolution has most seriously manifested itself socially in the fact that almost one half or more of Mexico's population has continued to live in isolated rural communities (49.3 per cent in 1960). An economic manifestation of imbalance has been the low contribution to the Gross National Product by the agricultural sector of society. Problems of economic and social imbalance were presented historically in Tables 8-11 and 9-4, respectively. Perhaps we can understand the lack of balance better if we examine actual federal budgetary outlay in several categories (agriculture, irrigation, agrarian action) and relate it to expenditure per agriculturally employed worker in Table 10-4. Again, this is only a partial analysis because we are not considering such things as road construction which opens new areas to markets. It is at best a rough manner of gauging government policy in relation to the rural segment of the population which has tended to live poorly during Mexico's history. Census data on agricultural employment is limited to the six census years that are not necessarily representative of yearly quantities of pesos expended; they are representative, however, of the breaks in budgetary policy. Since we do not have figures on federal expenditure by entity, analysis is limited to the pattern for Mexico as a whole.

In spite of increasing expenditure per agricultural worker, the percentage of the budget devoted to the agricultural sector has not been very large. This corroborates historically the data revealed in Tables 10-1 and 10-2 for the years from 1959 to 1963. The largest percentage of the population has received the least consideration from the Mexican Revolution. This may be economically sound, but it is not really revolution made in the name of the masses. The high percentage of the federal budget devoted to resolving the problems of the countryside was much more oriented toward people instead of things in 1940 under Cárdenas than in 1950 under Alemán. Cárdenas emphasized land distribution; Alemán emphasized investment in irrigation.

The meaning of the Mexican Revolution's land policies has recently been examined in a new way by Professor Clark W. Reynolds. He points out in a manuscript in preparation for Yale University's Economic Growth Center that the trend to urbanization was lowest during the 1930's because Cárdenas gave the rural workers a reason to hope that they might benefit from land distribution. With the relative slowdown in distribution during the 1940's and 1950's, the rural population began to migrate to urban areas (as we saw in Table 9-4). Professor Reynolds points out that the above pattern of urbanization during the pre-1940 period was beneficial to the Revolution in an ironic way. It prevented the urban labor market from being flooded during the 1930's when industrialization was beginning to grow, and since 1940 it has provided a steady source of workers who can be assimilated into the expanding market without driving wage rates down. In short, Mexico in the twentieth century has not had a great urban mass complicating developmental problems. Thus, different programs of land distribution in eras of social and economic revolution have been successful for the very reason that their respective critics have deemed them failures. This is a challenging new evaluation of process in the Mexican Revolution which will certainly require that the postulates of land policy be re-examined.

Some additional observations about Table 10-4 are in order in light of our discussion above. Since expenditure, qualitatively speaking, has shifted away from providing benefits to people in

TABLE 10-4

Federal Agricultural Outlay[a] *Per Agricultural Worker, 1910–1960*

Year	Per Cent of Budget	Pesos Per Worker[b]	Pesos Per Capita of Rural Population[b]
1910	3.3	4.7	1.6
1921	4.1	8.0	2.8
1930	8.5	23.4	7.7
1940	11.4	53.2	16.0
1950	10.0	71.8	23.4
1960	5.9	91.1	32.5

[a] Includes actual expenditure for the Ministries of Agriculture and Irrigation, the Agrarian Department, and agricultural credit.

[b] In pesos per capita of 1950.

SOURCES: See Tables 1-8, 6-2, 6-4, 6-10, 8-5, and 9-4.

order to stimulate agricultural production, we have one important reason why the Revolution has been pronounced dead by many analysts;[1] a close study of government outlay shows why their subjective view of the Revolution has developed. Even though outlay has increased, over-all government impact on the agricultural population has decreased in percentage terms. Actually, in terms of expenditure per agricultural worker, the period of economic revolution has greatly aided the countryside. As Tables 10-1 and 10-2 show, however, the government has invested selectively in certain areas. This pattern of expenditure has influenced the fact that per-capita contribution of agriculture to the Gross National Product has remained less than half of the national average (see Table 8-11). Professor Reynolds's interpretation of the role of agrarian policy, however, suggests that the social success or failure of the Mexican Revolution cannot really be judged in terms of agricultural policy or per-capita expenditure for the agriculturally employed population. In any case, since we do not have the necessary data to examine per-capita federal expenditure by states and regions, it is necessary to turn to a different type of analysis.

[1] See Stanley R. Ross, *Is the Mexican Revolution Dead?* (New York; Knopf, 1966), Chapters 2 and 3.

TABLE 10-5

Decrease in the Poverty Index During Eras of Political, Social, and Economic Revolution

	Political		Social		Economic	
	1910	1921	1930	1940	1950	1960
Index (1940 = 100)	123.7	115.4	108.7	100.0	85.7	72.0
Per Cent Change		−6.7	−5.8	−8.0	−14.3	−16.0

SOURCE: See Tables 9-9 and 9-11.

DECREASE IN THE POVERTY INDEX

In relating federal expenditure to decrease in the Poverty Index on the assumption that government policy creates the climate in which the private sector will operate, a concept which we have already discussed, it is important to add a clarification. Since it is the effect of ideology in each period of the Revolution which interests us, it is our purpose to relate political, social, and economic revolution to analysis of social change. This approach uses federal expenditure to characterize ideology, not to figure the cost of social change for the masses. It is the style of spending of whole budgets, as we have seen, which shapes the atmosphere in Mexico at any given time. It is not specific types of expenditure—social, economic, administrative—which decrease the Poverty Index. It would, in fact, be grossly unfair to impute a decline in poverty characteristics in the Index solely to social expenditure, for the principles of economic revolution postulate the concept that economic expenditure will in the long run do more for the masses than direct social expenditure. As we saw above, discussion of per-capita social change may be quite informative, but it is extremely limited by the nature of the data as well as by our understanding of its meaning. We found that in attempting to investigate outlay per agricultural worker we were unable to take into account or to identify all of the expenditure which might affect him. Since it is our purpose here to avoid this type of problem and to relate to social change the total influence of the politics of modernization, it is preferable to avoid calculating costs of social change.

In order to develop the relationship of social change and different ideological periods in the Mexican Revolutions, the rate of decrease in the Poverty Index is expressed in Table 10-5. The decrease in the Index indicates, as we have seen, that social revolution did not yield the greatest amount of social change. The period of violence from 1910 to 1921 did not give a better life to the masses, and the 1920's shows little advance in comparison to other periods. Only since 1940 has social change for the masses become relatively rapid, and even then it may be debated whether or not a rate of 14 to 16 per cent can be considered revolutionary. Given the nature of poverty which existed in Mexico for centu-

TABLE 10-6

Increase in Index of Gross Domestic Product Per Capita by Decade (Preliminary Figures in Constant Prices)

	1910	1920–1921	1930	1940	1950	1960
Index (1940 = 100)	77.4	71.2	81.2	100.0	143.3	191.6
Per Cent Change	3.3	12.0	23.2	43.3	33.7	

SOURCE: Clark W. Reynolds, "The Structure and Growth of the Mexican Economy, 1900–1960," manuscript in preparation for the Yale University Economic Growth Center.

ries, however, the decrease in the Poverty Index since 1940 is very impressive. Thus, the level of characteristics of poverty which have prevented or slowed modernization has declined significantly. Looking at Mexican life styles in collective terms, conditions of social deprivation have decreased in the face of economic modernization. Those who claim that Mexico needs another violent revolution to change the low standard of living for the masses once and for all should note that civil war gravely damaged the Mexican economy from 1910 to 1921, and it is the development of the Mexican economy since 1940 that has begun, finally, to decrease poverty levels. Violent revolution may have been necessary in 1910 to break traditional patterns, but new violence could only disrupt the emerging modern society.[2] There are no easy solutions to bring about either social or economic development.

ECONOMIC CHANGE

A major independent statistical analysis has recently been made of Mexican economy since 1900 by Clark W. Reynolds of Yale University's Economic Growth Center. A concise measure of his conclusions is found in an index for rate of growth of the Gross Domestic Product (GDP) Per Capita (Table 10-6). The great increase in percentage change has come since 1940. Growth almost halted, predictably, during the period from 1910 to 1920 and gained slowly during the 1920's. Unpredictably, increase in the GDP per capita almost doubled during the 1930's, compared to the 1920's. Apparently, depression and social unrest were not as

[2] Though we are examining the decline in the level of total undifferentiated poverty characteristics, we should recall that the Poverty Index can be viewed with alternative figures in which ratios of change by category of poverty are maintained for each census year (see Appendix H). The rate of change in the alternative index reveals that life styles of poverty in individual terms have decreased with the same pattern developed in Table 10-5. The alternative data, however, show greater social change in all periods, especially the epoch of violent revolution. Though change is calculated at the rate of 12.2 per cent from 1910 to 1921 and about 9.5 per cent during the 1920's and 1930's, the most significant change has come in the post-1940 era; percentage decrease in poverty was 16 per cent in the 1940's and 17.5 per cent in the 1950's. Since the alternative index indicates greater social change from 1910 to 1921 than we have discussed, it might be presumed that violent revolution is conducive to the immediate social change for the masses. While we are not arguing in favor of violent revolution or against it (or that it is or is not a necessary stage for rapid social change), it appears from that data in both indexes of change that the solid decreases in poverty have come since 1940 during the era of economic revolution.

TABLE 10-7

A Comparison of Social and Economic Modernization in the Mexican Revolution

Per Cent	1910's	1920's	1930's	1940's	1950's
(A) Poverty Index	− 6.7	− 5.8	− 8.0	−14.3	−16.0
(B) Gross Domestic Product Per Capita	+ 3.3	+12.0	+23.2	+43.3	+33.7
(C) Ratio B/A	.5/1	2.1/1	2.9/1	3.0/1	2.1/1

SOURCE: See Tables 10-5 and 10-6.

disruptive of the economy as has been believed. During the 1940's the rate of growth for the decade was about 87 per cent higher than the rate of the 1930's. Though the rate of economic change during the 1950's fell about one quarter to a midpoint between growth during the 1930's and 1940's, the Index was at an historical high point.

The pattern of economic growth in the 1950's is explained by Dwight S. Brothers and Leopoldo Solís M. as follows. The government during the 1950's provided a sufficient check on low-priority expenditure and on consumption to permit adequate financing of selected large-scale structural programs. At the same time, this control prevented excess demand which would upset monetary stability. The two writers conclude that the rapid economic growth of the 1960's is based upon stabilization policies of the latter 1950's, which were widely criticized at the time as restricting the pace of economic development.[3] We may add that selective federal investment, which emerged during the 1940's, has been a major cause in regional social development imbalances discussed above.

SOCIAL AND ECONOMIC CHANGE COMPARED

Social modernization—decrease in the Poverty Index—has been much slower than economic modernization since the 1930's. Table 10-7 shows the relationship. Economic growth lagged behind social change by a ratio of one-half to one during civil war, and it grew at about twice the rate of improvement for the masses in the 1920's. During the twenty-year period from 1930 to 1950 economic growth exceeded social change by three to one, falling off to two to one in the latter stage of economic revolution. Conclusively, then, we can not infer from the rate of economic growth the amount of social change for the masses, though we do not know if this conclusion holds true for any but the poorest class.

Since the Revolution has been organized to benefit the masses, either directly as in social revolution, or indirectly, as in political and economic revolution, and since nation-building is dependent upon both social and economic gains, our analysis shows that ap-

[3] Dwight S. Brothers and Leopoldo Solís M., *Mexican Financial Development* [1940–1960] (Austin: University of Texas Press, 1966), 141, 180.

parently the results of each type of revolution have been incon-
sistent with its own immediate goals. It should be obvious that
political revolution never achieved a political democracy, and
from 1910 to 1929 it did not contribute much to its secondary
goals of either social or economic gain. Social revolution yielded

TABLE 10-8

Manufacturing Production, 1910–1945

			A.		
			Index		
			(1929 = 100)		
Year	Volume	Value	Year	Volume	Value
1910	69.1	43.5	1928	94.4	85.5
1911	65.3	42.7	1929	100.0	100.0
1912	53.0	33.2	1930	105.3	87.5
1913	61.4	39.9	1931	125.2	75.9
1914	45.8	34.0	1932	90.8	66.6
1915	54.9	44.0	1933	84.1	59.2
1916	50.5	42.4	1934	125.4	118.1
1917	46.0	40.7	1935	122.0	108.6
1918	43.7	64.8	1936	140.5	128.9
1919	55.3	66.4	1937	147.2	150.3
1920	53.6	63.4	1938	151.5	165.9
1921	52.7	53.5	1939	160.5	184.9
1922	71.8	57.9	1940	165.3	202.5
1923	81.5	76.7	1941	179.8	232.2
1924	85.6	91.1	1942	200.0	284.5
1925	87.6	89.0	1943	202.0	356.6
1926	99.4	97.4	1944	212.2	400.6
1927	90.1	84.3	1945	222.9	463.6

| | B. | |
| | Percentage Change in Index | |
Years	Volume	Value
1920–1925	63.4	40.4
1925–1930	20.2	−1.7
1930–1935	16.0	24.1
1935–1940	35.5	86.5
1940–1945	34.8	128.9

SOURCE: Sanford A. Mosk, *Industrial Revolution in Mexico* (Berkeley: University of
California Press, 1950), 120.

more economic change than social change, and it is no wonder that by 1940 Mexicans who had not received psychological or material benefits from land grants or the right to strike were ready to join the opposition—social change in a decade of social revolution had obviously not lived up to propaganda. Economic revolution sponsored by the government not only brought about its primary goal of rapid economic change, but it also fostered more rapid social modernization than any other type of program.

Cárdenas's social revolution did not harm capitalism (in spite of the fact that the private sector was supposedly frightened to death of his "communism"), and this is incontrovertibly shown in Table 10-8, given by Sanford Mosk. Mosk sees *Industrial Revolution in Mexico* as commencing in the early 1940's, but his yearly figures show that the basis for rapid industrialization was firmly established by 1940 when Cárdenas left office. In fact, the volume of manufacturing production increased about as fast during the Cárdenas era as it did during the Avila Camacho epoch.

Volume of production in the latter years, however, was over-

TABLE 10-9

Index of United States Direct Investment in Mexico and in Europe, 1929–1960

(1929 = 100)

	Mexico		Europe	
Year	Amount[a]	Index	Amount[a]	Index
1929	683	100	1353	100
1936	480	70	1259	93
1940	358	52	1420	105
1950	415	61	1733	128
1960	795	116	6681	494

[a] Millions of current dollars.

Sources: for Mexico: U.S. Office of Business Economics, *U.S. Investments in Foreign Countries* (Washington, D.C.: Government Printing Office, 1960), 92; *Ibid.*, *U.S. Investments in the Latin American Economy* (Washington, D.C.: Government Printing Office, 1957), 112 and 180; *Statistical Abstract of the United States, 1965*, 858. For Europe: Same as above and U.S. Bureau of Foreign and Domestic Commerce, *American Direct Investments in Foreign Countries—1940* (Washington, D.C.: Government Printing Office, 1942), 5.

shadowed by the great rise in value of manufactured goods during the early 1940's. Nevertheless, we must recognize that the dramatic increase in volume of production under Cárdenas came at a time when United States capital was fleeing Mexico.

Investors from the United States obviously could not have supplied all the capital for industrial growth under Cárdenas. They withdrew capital from Mexico at a faster rate than from Europe, and Europe after 1929 is commonly cited as the classic example of an area which was drastically affected by loss of United States investment. Table 10-9 shows that United States investment in Mexico decreased by about half between 1929 and 1940. The problems of Mexico during the early 1930's stimulated Mexicans into developing an industrial society which, they hoped, would be free from the vagaries of international financial crises. The amount of United States investment in Mexico was valued too high in 1929, but even allowing for this, the impact of the depression on Mexico was quite significant. We may note that Mexico's economy recovered rapidly from destruction caused during the violent era, but after 1925 manufacturing growth slowed considerably. In short, while it is true that economic revolution did not get under way ideologically until after 1940, the "take-off stage" for industrial revolution came during the epoch of social revolution.

Given this comparison of social and economic relationships, it is clear that social change has not kept up with economic revolution. In fact one may question whether or not a rapid social change has ever occurred for the masses in the Mexican Revolution. The greatest decrease in the poverty level over a decade was only 16 per cent and it came during the 1950's. Prior to 1940 change did not even reach an average of 1 per cent a year. After fifty years of Revolution one might note that the Poverty Index has decreased from an average level of 56.9 to 33.1. If we project change into the future at the rate of social change in the 1950's—16 per cent a decade—we find that in another fifty years the Poverty Index would still be at a relatively high average level of nearly 14. Even at the rate of a 2 per cent decrease each year, the index would still be high at about 11.

Of course, this does not mean the Revolution has failed or will fail (we do not know at what rate the Poverty Index will decrease in the future). Social change, it seems, is much slower than economic change. Things are easier to mold than people. Given the amount of social change prior to 1910, the rate since 1910 is actually quite rapid. Perhaps it is appropriate to remind advocates of a new violent upheaval in Mexico of Lenin's reflections on the meaning of "revolution." Lenin, speaking on the fourth anniversary of the Russian Revolution, ruefully pointed out that, even for Communists, revolutions take time:

Borne along on the crest of the wave of enthusiasm . . . we reckoned . . . on being able to organize the state production and the state distribution of products on communist lines in a small peasant country by order of the proletarian state. Experience has proved that we were wrong. It transpires that a number of transitional stages are necessary —state capitalism and socialism—in order to prepare by many years of effort for the transition to communism. . . . We must first set to work in this small-peasant country to build solid little gangways to socialism by way of state capitalism. Otherwise we shall never get to communism: we shall never bring these scores of millions of people to communism. That is what experience, what the objective course of development of the revolution has taught us.[4]

The successes of the Mexican Revolution have been sufficient that Marxist-Leninist thought has not been the cry for new and violent upheaval except by an isolated group of Communist party members. Vicente Lombardo Toledano, Cárdenas's labor leader, has been in the vanguard of up-dating and translating Marxism into a terminology which permits Mexican Marxists to adopt Communist theory to their own concept of co-operation with the Mexican Revolutionary Family. Lombardo's view is based upon the necessary stage of the triumph of capitalism in Mexico, and since Mexican entrepreneurship has been scarce, the "capitalist" has become the Western political or economic imperialist. The "proletariat" is the exploited Mexican people in general, and the "class struggle" is the equivalent of "National Liberation." Once imperialists are driven out, Lombardo says, National Liberation is free to industrialize the new nation and wipe out economic and psychological inferiority. In times of crisis, as during the 1930's and 1940's when the Marxists feared the fascist threat, Lombardo

---

[4] Quoted by Arthur P. Mendel, *Essential Works of Marxism* (New York: Bantam, 1961), 98.

prescribed an alliance with national capitalism in the form of a Popular Front. The Popular Front would defeat the enemy and build a postwar world in which foreign imperialism would be impotent and native capitalism could be attacked.[5] Though Lombardo has withdrawn from the official party, and he is at present the head of his own *Partido Popular Socialista,* he is a venerable member of the Revolutionary Family. Lombardo has predicated his postwar co-operation with the official party, which he helped reorganize in 1938, on the theory that Mexico is not ready for a proletarian revolution, for capitalism is still even more weak in Mexico than it was in Russia in 1917. However, he can not account for the reason Cuba has had a Marxist Revolution when it was worse off than Mexico prior to Castro's triumph.[6] Lombardo's position has meant that he has done ideological battle with the Mexican Communist party, which, he claims, has been unable to see where Moscow is really headed.

The issues of Communist revolution have become so complex since the passing of Stalinism in the late 1950's that Peking has attacked Moscow's policy of "peaceful coexistence" as giving up the true battle and destiny of Marxism-Leninism violently to overthrow capitalism. Lombardo Toledano has opted for Moscow's road to Communism.[7] Another group of Mexican Marxists led by Carlos Fuentes has broken with those Mexican Marxists who insist that proletarian revolution is not only necessary but imminent. This group claims that the sophistication of today's developmental problems vitiates the dogmatic application of nineteenth-century Marxist terminology to the twentieth century, for it is obvious that great social change has and is going on under the sponsorship of the Mexican Revolution.[8] The Mexican Revolution is obviously very complex in its programs and results, and

[5] Vicente Lombardo Toledano, *The C.T.A.L., the War, and the Postwar,* tr. by O. I. Roche (México, D. F.: n.p., 1945). See Lewis S. Feur, *Marx and Engels; Basic Writings in Politics and Philosophy* (Garden City: Doubleday, 1959), xix–xx, for a discussion which captures the essence of underdeveloped-area Marxism.

[6] Vicente Lombardo Toledano, Oral History Interviews with James and Edna Wilkie, Jan. 29, 1965, Mexico City.

[7] See Vicente Lombardo Toledano, *¿Moscú o Pekín? La Via Mexicana Hacia el Socialismo* (México, D. F.: Partido Popular Socialista, 1963).

[8] Carlos Fuentes, Oral History Interviews with James and Edna Wilkie, Aug. 15, 1964; see also Carlos Fuentes *et al.* ["Carta Abierta a Política"], *Política,* Aug. 15, 1964, and "El Dilema de México: Revolución o Retroceso; una Nueva Perspectiva para la Izquierda Nacional," *El Día,* Sept. 3, 1964.

this can be further illustrated and examined in the light of several deficiencies in the ideology of revolutionary budgetary policy.

GOVERNMENT BUDGETING FOR SOCIAL CHANGE

By 1960 there was a clear need for more rapid social improvement than had been the case even during the 1950's, Mexico's years of greatest social change. As the economy advances, the people must advance with it or the national integration which the Mexican Revolution has sought to attain will not be possible. Though social improvements have come in times of expanding economy, the government has apparently given it far too little budgetary importance. Per-capita expenditure for social change has reached an all-time high, but it has ranked much less importantly than economic and administrative expenditure since 1940. The decrease in the Poverty Index has been most rapid while economic development has been emphasized, but it has not been rapid enough to bring a better life to millions of Mexicans. How long will they wait? Propaganda will not feed them, give them jobs, and educate them.

Social integration of the Mexican nation depends heavily upon not only eliminating illiteracy but in raising the standard of education. If López Mateos had expended on education the percentage of the budget which he promised, a beginning could have been made in fulfilling Mexico's educational needs. In 1963, some 51 pesos per capita would have actually been expended for education instead of 33.2 pesos per capita. It is not that López Mateos failed to provide the Ministry of Education with the funds which he promised; rather he did not give education the per cent he projected and which it needs. There are not enough schools for the primary school population, and the quality of public education leaves much to be desired. "Higher education," that is education beyond primary school, is reserved for a small minority. Mexico's statistical agency has estimated that in 1964 illiteracy had fallen to 28.9 per cent of the population over six years old,[9] but the quality of this literacy has been frequently questioned.[10]

[9] México, Dirección General de Estadística, *Revista de Estadística* 27 (1964) 843–850.

[10] See, for example, *Política*, Sept. 1, 1964.

One writer has indicated, for example, that only about 15 per cent of those entering primary school are finally graduated.[11] A journalist has noted that only 20 per cent of those entering the University of Mexico are graduated.[12] Yet in 1964 some 5356 graduates could not find teaching jobs for 1965. The Ministry of Education recommended to the normal schools in 1964 that they "restrict their enrollment in accord with the opportunities of work." The determination of the Ministry was founded in the reality that teachers are not lacking, but the percentage of the federal budget necessary to construct classrooms sufficient to provide primary education for all has not been made available.[13]

The public health problem in Mexico is closely related to education. Modern medicine has cut the high death rate caused by inadequate sanitation and hygiene, but the basic problem of unhealthful living conditions persists mainly because the people have never been taught how to manage food and human waste. If the government would subsidize the sale of commercial fertilizer or give it to the communal and small farmer, while at the same time would undertake a vast educational campaign to teach people the value of health, an immediate rise in the standard of living would be noted. As it is, the communal farmer can not afford to buy commercial fertilizer and he must use human excrement on his crops. The next breakthrough in Mexican living standards must come in health and hygiene, for curative medicine can only alleviate the major illnesses caused by lack of elementary hygienic standards. As one writer pointed out in regard to the United States, the revolution in public health during the period 1900–1917 opened the way to full human productivity.[14]

The low percentage of population affected by federal potable water and sewage disposal programs from 1946 to 1963 is given in Table 10-10. More people have received the benefits of safe drinking water than modern sewage disposal systems. The former figure in the South, for example, is three times greater than the

[11] Héctor Hugo del Cueto, "El Pavoroso Problema Escolar en México," *Revista Nacional*, Dec. 1, 1964.

[12] Elena Poniatowska ["Entrevista con los Doctores Guillermo Haro, Elí de Gortari y José F. Herrán"], *Siempre*, July 1, 1964, ii–xx.

[13] *El Día*, Dec. 11, 1964.

[14] Selma J. Mushkin, "Health as an Investment," in "Investment in Human Beings," ed. by T. W. Schultz, *Journal of Political Economy*, 70 (Oct. 1962) Part 2.

latter. This ratio is standard for all regions except the North and West. It should be noted that the term "potable water" in Mexico cannot generally be compared to the use of the term in highly developed countries. In Mexico, a village with several spigots to

TABLE 10-10

Population Affected by Federal Potable Water and Sewage Disposal Programs, 1946–1963 (Excluding Federal District)

Federal Entity	Per Cent Benefited by Potable Water	Per Cent Benefited by Sewage Disposal
Total Mexico	*40.4*[a]	*20.1*[a]
North	*56.4*[b]	*44.8*[b]
Baja California	71.0	71.0
Chihuahua	56.8	36.5
Coahuila	46.0	22.4
Nuevo León	71.0	63.8
Sonora	41.7	32.5
Tamaulipas	51.9	42.4
West	*49.1*[b]	*24.0*[b]
Aguascalientes	69.0	56.3
Baja Calif. Terr.	40.8	36.3
Colima	72.5	26.5
Durango	34.0	13.5
Jalisco	53.2	3.0
Nayarit	41.1	15.8
Sinaloa	33.0	16.8
West Central	*36.1*[b]	*10.2*[b]
Guanajuato	40.7	26.0
México	25.8	8.7
Michoacán	31.8	6.1
Morelos	46.3	– – –
East Central	*31.1*[b]	*10.4*[b]
Hidalgo	33.3	4.7
Puebla	27.5	2.8
Querétaro	31.8	20.8
San Luis Potosí	29.1	18.0
Tlaxcala	36.6	6.1
Zacatecas	28.0	9.7
South	*21.8*[b]	*7.4*[b]
Chiapas	23.3	14.2
Guerrero	20.7	5.3
Oaxaca	21.4	2.8
Gulf	*34.6*[b]	*12.4*[b]
Campeche	28.3	– – –
Quintana Roo	37.8	– – –
Tabasco	26.5	16.6
Veracruz	34.1	17.7
Yucatán	46.2	27.8

[a] Average figure for 31 entities, regardless of size.

[b] Average for number of entities in region, regardless of size.

SOURCE: México, Secretaría de Recursos Hidráulicos, *Agua Potable y Alcantarillados . . . , 1946–1963*, México, D. F.: Talleres Gráficos de la Nación, 1964.

service the entire community is said to enjoy potable water. Since
the system often is not maintained, it may fall into rapid decay,
a problem which also affects many of Mexico's sewage systems. If
all the people in the country who devote many of their hours to
carrying water from spigot to home were to be released from this
task in order to engage in productive labor, poor standards of
living might change dramatically. Unfortunately, the population
in the poorest regions has not had *any* spigots, and the problem
of productive labor has been submerged in the problem of village
health. In 1963 more than half of the population of most entities
had not benefited from safe drinking water; the figures for population unaffected by modern sewage disposal were even worse.
Since state and local governments have done little to remedy these
problems outside of big towns, the federal government has been
almost entirely responsible for this neglected aspect of social development. Though the government faces many difficult decisions
in allocating funds to do many urgent jobs, this writer would
recommend that funds for sanitary engineering need to take precedence at this point in the Mexican Revolution.

Mexico need not and should not sacrifice economic development for social expenditure. However, unless the ideology of balanced revolution can show compelling reasons for maintaining
high administrative costs, it would seem that the balance which
the Mexican Revolution should seek is not between administrative, economic, and social expenditure, but between social and
economic outlay.

The Mexican government has had an increasing actual budget
with which to develop social and economic growth. Table 10-11
offers a view of expanding governmental operations in periods
of political, social, and economic developmental ideology.

The budget has increased tremendously since the early 1940's,
but so has population. The average of real pesos per capita gives
us a true picture of how federal budgets have actually expanded.
During the period from 1910 to 1920 the federal government had
only 27.3 pesos per capita with which to work. During the 1920's
this increased to double that amount, and in the decade of the
1930's it increased to 69.1 pesos. By the 1940's the average annual
amount which the government actually expended was 112.5 pesos
per capita. During the 1950's this figure reached 175.6 pesos. We

TABLE 10-11

Average Actual Expenditure of the Federal Budget by Decade in Per Capita Pesos of 1950

Decade	Average
1910's	27.3
1920's	58.2
1930's	69.1
1940's	112.5
1950's	175.6

SOURCE: See Table 1-9.

can not, of course, carry this analysis into the 1960's for the decade is only half over and social statistics will not be available for analysis until after the census of 1970.

In spite of immensely greater budgetary resources during the 1950's, the ideology of economic revolution was not able to maintain the rate of economic growth of the 1940's. Decrease in the Poverty Index continued, though perhaps not so rapidly as expanded governmental action might warrant. We may speculate that once the economy has reached a certain level, percentage growth is more expensive to maintain, especially when the development of an internal market has not kept pace with economic output, as Sanford Mosk cautioned in 1950.[15] Or we may say that World War II was a significant factor giving stimulus to the economy, and that when it ended, more government funds were required to yield economic change.

It would seem that the decentralized and mixed public and private agencies would have filled an economic function of progressively relieving the federal government from great direct economic expenditure. The Nacional Financiera, for example, has contracted a number of foreign credits and loans for economic purposes which should have released funds in the federal budget for increased social expenditure. This is mere speculation, however, for we do not really know the historical relation of indirect spending of such agencies as the Nacional Financiera to direct

[15] Mosk, Industrial Revolution in Mexico, Chapter 11.

budgetary outlay. We may have seen the onset of balanced revolutionary planning in the budgets of López Mateos because indirect expenditure did release federal funds for social purposes. On
the other hand, there may have been no such reason for shift in
expenditure.

The formulation of the budget in itself presents great problems
for programming social and economic development in Mexico.
Ever since the 1930's each president has talked about rationalizing
development, but given the nature of budgetary projections which
are totally unrealistic, governmental programming still does not
seem to be very feasible. Representatives to Congress do not really
represent districts, and therefore they are not constantly watching
the formulation of the budget to see how money might be channeled to their home area. The process of siphoning federal funds
into home states derogatively is called "pork barrel" legislation
in the United States, and though it may have undesirable effects
at times, it certainly means that congressmen are aware of budgetary arrangements. In contrast, the congressman in Mexico is in
effect a representative of his party, and therefore he is content to
let the President of Mexico decide how the budget will be allocated. There is no stimulus, therefore, for the president and his
Minister of the Treasury to make realistic projections of income.
Realism in the projected budget would no doubt be unwelcome,
for then each agency would know in advance how much of the
federal purse it might reasonably hope to expend. The present
system allows the executive branch of government great flexibility
in determining what it will do with extra funds. True, some
agencies have budgetary items which are marked for automatic
amplification, but the Minister of the Treasury generally has dis-
cretionary authority to determine the amount of the amplification. At any rate the president generally has the power to author-
ize transfers of amounts within the budget or he can get power
as he needs it from Congress. In 1964 the president did not seek
approval of his allocations of amplifications in the budget until
almost the very end of the fiscal year. A representative of the National Action Party, Guillermo Ruiz Vázquez, summed up the
irony in this situation as follows:

It would really be grave to approve or disapprove an amplification of
the budget which is equal to 40 per cent over the amount originally

authorized for this fiscal year. . . . [Since only 33 days remain in the fiscal year, a vote] would be more an approval of accounts than an authorization to spend an additional 40 per cent of public funds.[16]

Federal income has been increasing rapidly, and Appendix F shows the sources from which federal funds have come in selected years. We may note that the sources of funds for the ideology of political revolution were taxes on imports and industry. Social revolutionists emphasized traditional taxation policy, perhaps because social ferment precluded the restructuring of the tax base. If Cárdenas had been seriously attempting to overthrow capitalism, presumably he would have sought to shift federal income away from its base in import and export taxes. Economic revolution shifted emphasis to income taxes, which affected middle and richer classes. Balanced revolution, seeking to please everybody, turned to internal loans to augment the capacity of the state's expenditure. It can be seen that none of these taxes has really fallen on the masses, except perhaps the stamp tax which lost importance by 1932. Wage-earners could certainly not have been hurt much prior to 1963; López Mateos announced that only 2 per cent of the population paid taxes in 1962, though projected tax reforms would bring this up to 20 per cent.[17]

We have tried to examine Mexican budgetary policy in relation to social and economic goals of the Revolution. It is hoped that, if at times it has appeared that we have neglected the particular historical situation of any government's actions in order to make comparisons, general historical consideration of each period will have minimized such effect. It is a large task to analyze the entire Revolution, but examination of budgetary policy and changing rates of poverty have offered what we hope are useful threads to understand a complex movement. They are not the only themes in the Mexican Revolution, but they are important ones.

[16] *El Día,* Nov. 28, 1964.
[17] *El Universal,* Dec. 12, 1962.

Conclusion

The president of Mexico has great power to use federal funds in almost any way he sees fit in order to carry out his programs. These programs are not generally spelled out to the public, but budgetary analysis reveals what they have been. We find, therefore, a considerable difference between the styles of presidents in the Revolution. Presidents have reflected the ideology of their time by the way they allocated the federal purse for administrative, social, and economic expenditure in order to integrate the Mexican nation.

A political concept of the state dominated Mexican governmental affairs from the fall of the dictator Porfirio Díaz to the rise of Lázaro Cárdenas during the early 1930's. Cárdenas himself seized the opportunity that the crisis in political revolution presented to undertake the social restructure of Mexico. He not only definitively reoriented the economy away from the agricultural hacienda system, he also proposed to change the educational system and swiftly to integrate the Mexican people into a nation, a program which had been delayed since Mexico's independence in 1821. We have seen that his programs had little practical effect on the life of the common man, who remained illiterate, shoeless, isolated, underfed, and without sewage disposal. A large number still could not speak Spanish by the time Cárdenas left office. Even with Cárdenas's Six-Year Plan, Mexico could not be remade in one presidential term. The social drive apparently went out of the Revolution when Cárdenas turned his office over to Manuel Avila Camacho, and many have been led to conclude that the Revolution died in 1940. We have found that social benefits for the masses as well as economic development came at a rapid rate only after 1940.

Strikes, land distribution, and Socialist Education were curtailed as Mexico entered an epoch of ideology dominated by the concept of economic revolution. In a period of industrialization, irrigation, and public works, everyone was sure that immediate benefits to the masses were being postponed until Mexico was economically developed. The group which sponsored economic revolution, led by Alemán, also believed that social benefits would have to be sacrificed in the name of progress. The Poverty Index, however, indicates that the revolution was very much alive, and that Mexico experienced its most rapid social change for the masses between 1940 and 1960. West Central and East Central Mexico benefited more in decrease of poverty from economic impetus, for example, than they ever did from the so-called immediate benefits of social revolution.

We must remember, nevertheless, that because of the reorientation of the economy under Cárdenas, money was channeled by the private sector into the business of urbanization. Whereas Cárdenas had planned to establish a rural Mexico based on the communal farm, he created *minifundios* which have not contributed to the growth of the Mexican economy. Many wealthy landholders, fearing expropriation, invested in the city, at first in real estate, then in business, and finally in light industry. The basis for a new order unintentionally grew out of the social revolution.

Though Mexican workers (who may have gained in psychological terms from land labor policies under Cárdenas) might have lost ground in "indirect benefits" between 1940 and 1960, they could take advantage of the ideology of economic revolution's new opportunities. The Poverty Index began to decline relatively rapidly after 1940. Though inflation was not caused by deliberate government policy, minimum wages were maintained at a low rate to allow for Mexican capital formation, but according to one investigator capital formation did not result from such a policy.[1] Since a low minimum wage policy was not responsible for capital formation and consequent rapid economic development, we must look elsewhere for the drive of economic revolution.

Once the stimulus to the economy provided by World War II

[1] Seigel's study, "Inflation and Economic Development" is discussed in Chapter 8.

was gone, Alemán and Ruiz Cortines expanded state action into the economic life of Mexico to the greatest extent in national history. Agricultural credit and land distribution were ignored, since there was no guarantee that loans could be paid back by *ejidatarios,* and especially since the communal farm appeared to be holding back agricultural production due to its uneconomic organization. Money was taken from social and "unproductive" economic expenditure to be channeled into investments and subsidies of private enterprises developed in conjunction with government planning. Economic growth was the result, and a decrease in the Poverty Index was a major by-product.

Overt governmental neglect of social programs and lower level bureaucrats, however, led to struggle in the official family which resulted in the apparent rejection of the Alemán ideology by Ruiz Cortines; but since Ruiz Cortines had no program of his own, he became more *alemanista* than Alemán. Not until López Mateos did the minimum wage and social expenditure for education again become important in governmental policy.

The Revolution has been governed by the intellectual currents which have been prevalent in different periods. Madero was obsessed with the ideal of political democracy as the solution to social ills. Let each man vote, and government can not oppress him. This was a negative view of the state's role and it lasted until 1930. The goals of social redemption through government action, proposed by the Constitution of 1917, were forgotten in the rush of Mexico's return to normalcy in the 1920's after a decade of civil war. There was no need for an expanded budget, for the government was not responsible for the development of the Mexican nation. In any case, international politics represented by Ambassador Dwight W. Morrow of the United States demanded other courses of action. The budget would have to be balanced, the foreign debt paid, and foreign rights protected.

With the end of the passive state in the depression of the 1930's, the Mexican Revolution from 1910 to 1930 passed from the scene. The old guard of the revolutionists, represented by Plutarco Elías Calles did not leave the political arena without a struggle, however, for there was more than a clash of personalities at stake; there was a concept of government and organization of life which had to be fought out. The clash in policy is best represented by Calles's administrative budgets and Cárdenas's dynamic use of federal funds to bring change into Mexico. Social revolution gained ascendancy from 1934 to 1940, but it began to fade with the expropriation of the foreign-owned oil industry in 1938. The swing to the ideology of economic revolution was completed under Avila Camacho and lasted until the official party recognized in the late 1950's that a change was necessary in order to continue to lead in Mexico.

The ideology of balanced revolution proposed by López Mateos offered to bring the best of political, economic, and social periods into a unified program. López Mateos allowed opposition into the House of Representatives, for the banner of revolutionary democracy had worn unbelievably thin. In fact the only people who have found democracy in Mexico in recent years have been naïve foreign commentators who have given up assessing political democracy and turned to analyzing "social democracy." The Mexicans themselves have not been misled, however, and the lack of political democracy has been continually criticized, especially by the intellectuals. Still, the people are philosophic about the Revolutionary Family, for they have always been governed by one elite group or another. If the official party continues to sponsor national growth and cedes to the demands or desires of pressure groups, complaints will be neither loud nor effective.

The possibility of a sophisticated, balanced revolution has come in the past ten years. Mexico now has enough funds per capita to begin to undertake the massive social expenditure to complement the economic development which must be maintained. The considerable growth of the budget has resulted from increased taxation in Mexico, but it is also dependent upon credit. To this date the governmental debt apparently has been skillfully managed by the ideologists of balanced revolution, but we are back to the problems generated by the 1920's: If debt payment considerations dominate expenditure, what will happen to Mexico's national development? One may argue that devoting a large share of the budget to the public debt—as much as 36.2 per cent in 1961—brings more credits to stimulate expanded governmental activity. We can arrive at no conclusion regarding these views, for the future is unpredictable. We can, however, point up what the government is doing, and later we will be able to evaluate the social results of the style of balanced revolution.

Historically, Obregón and Calles found governmental independence of action more and more limited as they were drawn into the web of debt payments and international finance. Obregón might have attempted to carry out the program of social expenditure which he projected in the early 1920's had he not become involved with the problems of recognition and the assumption of Mexico's pre-revolutionary debt. These presidents, like Madero, had little concept of the active state. Calles was basically an administrator, and he viewed the state's role as one of co-ordination and indirect stimulus. Thus he founded the Bank of Mexico, the National Irrigation Commission, the National Road Commission, and many more agencies to encourage national reconstruction and expansion. Obregón and Calles lived in a world of the passive state in the 1920's, and it was quite different from the world of the active state which López Mateos faced in the 1960's, for foreign capital and foreign governments were not so understanding about the use of international credits and loans.

The presidents of active state intervention have engaged in some, generally limited, deficit spending. Cárdenas inaugurated deficit spending as standard governmental policy in the late 1930's. Avila Camacho increased it during World War II, and though Alemán played it down, subsequent presidents have not worried about balancing the budget.

Alemán thought that his program of state action would be less controversial and problematic than Cárdenas's action, which set out to remake traditional society; but as one looks back on revolutionary process, it is clear that Alemán's policies revamped the basis of Mexican society as much as Cárdenas's programs. In the long run the change in the poverty level of a significant percentage of persons may well constitute a revolution which will finally effectively challenge the old order which has worked against change in the structure of social and economic power. Though Cárdenas distributed much land of Mexico, and broke the hacienda system, the people who received the land have often remained impoverished due to the small size of their holding, inability to find credit, and isolation from markets, supplies, doctors, and schools. Whatever one may think about urbanization in Mexico, it does bring people into larger units where it is more possible for them to enjoy a better standard of living. Cárdenas had come to de-emphasize the political and economic labor strike by the time his presidential period was over, and he had given up his Socialistic Education program in the face of hostile pressure from the Church. As Cárdenas's term concluded there were many protests against his social revolution. In the face of civil war, Cárdenas chose a moderate to follow him in the presidency. He gave up social revolution, perhaps because he saw that people did not live much better than before the depression. Certainly peace was more important to Cárdenas than renewed civil war.

Labor turmoil and population pressure on the land have dictated the turn to balanced revolution since 1960. The advance of the economy and decrease in the Poverty Index during the years of economic revolution led to a crisis in Mexican politics which approached the threat to the official party that arose at the end of Cárdenas's term. The crisis was not reflected directly in the presidential campaign, as it was in 1940, but it showed up in the massive labor revolt against the government and its captive unions. After years of Revolution and promises, the Revolutionary Family must now fulfill the articulate demands of labor and peasant, even if, as in the case of land distribution, the program may no longer be feasible. If the ideology of balanced revolution is to be successful, it must learn from the past which shows that the stereotypes of the Revolution do not hold up.

We have examined presidential policy in eras of political, social, and economic revolution, and it is clear from the social results of the Revolution that certain ideas held dear by different wings within the Revolutionary Family are erroneous. Political revolution destroyed the old institutional order; it did not create a democratic state. Social revolution attacked the old structure of society; it did not bring about a new one, either economically or socially. Economic revolution brought industrialization to a high point; it did not create balanced economic growth or a large internal market. As the balanced revolution undertakes to remedy the failures of earlier phases of the Revolution, the question will be whether Mexico has the resources to permit adequate growth in all sectors of the society and economy at once. Or will a hier-

archy of goals again demand dramatic pushes in one direction and
then another?

Madero was not a real revolutionist. He engineered an overthrow of the presidency, but planned to leave government, society,
and economy to run as they always had with the exception that
democracy would be introduced. The violence which followed his
assassination contributed little to the social growth of Mexico and
destroyed the economy. The programs of the 1920's amounted to
a rejection of social change, for the politics of social redemption
turned to the politics of high finance and luxury for the official
party leaders throughout most of the 1920's and early 1930's. The
regime of Portes Gil was an exception to this pattern.

Cárdenas did not ruin the Mexican economy and he did not
materially help the masses to any great extent, as his enemies and
friends have continued to claim. Though his program for the
rural proletariat did not bear fruit, his policy of aiding the urban
worker brought social change in the Federal District. Industrialization gained steam in the late 1930's, and consequently we
need not give all credit to the post-1940 period for the process
of economic advance. In practice, social revolution did not scare
private capital as much as private investors have claimed. Cárdenas's legacy to the masses was not so much in material improvement, but in the psychological position of importance which he
gave them. Cárdenas revivified the social ideals of the Constitution of 1917, and he brought the masses into politics in organized
groups which could no longer be ignored. The urban and rural
proletariat provided a counterbalance to the power of the military, and the generals lost their power during Cárdenas's term.
Cárdenas was able further to limit the role of the military in national life by serving as Minister of War under Avila Camacho
during World War II. The generals who might have renewed a
bid for prestige were overshadowed by the fame and wisdom of
an ex-president who knew how to ensure that the military would
serve and not dominate government. Cárdenas was the progenitor
of real active state intervention in all phases of national life. He
had to fight the battle such a controversial policy raised, and he
has set the standard for social and economic budgetary policy ever
since. Cárdenas's specific programs were criticized by the Alemán

group, but his policy of government budgeting for national economic integration was accepted.

Alemán undertook indirect social programs which did not sacrifice the masses, as his opponents have claimed. Since decrease of poverty apparently occurred more rapidly after 1940 than during the Cárdenas era, we may say that direct social benefits for the people are not the whole answer for national integration. The people must not wait around for someone to give them something to do, as Cárdenas proposed; they must themselves see that social advance comes from personal initiative to solve their problems.[2] Government action which gives benefits without a basis for opportunity and social advancement can not solve the problems of Mexico. Alemán's policies, however, provided the base for this social advance with too little direct attention to the people. Without education and public health, for example, social integration will not keep up with economic development.

In sum, the Mexican Revolution is not yet complete. Much has been done for the people, but there is still much remaining to do before Mexico is a socially integrated nation. Government policy is of primary importance in directing this work of nation-building, for it has created the climate for over-all development. Prior to 1910 there was very little social improvement. Fifty years later some regions of the country, especially the South, live in severe poverty. The results of the Revolution have been very mixed when tested regionally. With the concrete identification of different periods in the Mexican Revolution, it is clear that social change is a long process, longer than many imagine. Theory of revolutions is often based on the violent stages of governmental change, the assumption being that if social change is to occur it will take place concomitantly with political upheaval. We have shown that the real revolution in Mexican society has come about mainly in times of political stability since 1940. In other words, it took thirty years before the official party of the Revolution was

[2] When talking about this with Cárdenas in the summer of 1962, he was still insistent that if the government gives the people something to do they will work. He rejected the idea that people have always waited for the government, the Church, and the military to give them work, hence they do not actively solve their own problems and this is a basic deterrent to social advance. Interview with Cárdenas, August 25, 1962, while traveling from Uruapan to Apatzingán, Michoacán.

able to introduce the conditions under which relatively rapid social development could take place. This is not so surprising, for
even though it took seven years of violence before a constitution
was written in 1917 which projected the goals of the movement,
much constructive governmental activity remained before an ac-
cumulation of favorable conditions allowed social change.

Several recommendations concerning future scholarship may be
drawn from this work. Since we have shown that presidential
power in Mexico is closely related to the budgetary system which
gives the chief executive great flexibility of operation, the question arises as to whether or not the locus of power in other presidential systems may not stem largely from the same type of arrangement. Certainly this might be a fruitful line of inquiry in
examining developing nations which have a political system that
theoretically operates with checks and balances. Most foreign investigators have simply assumed that the Mexican government
functions with the modicum of checks and balances which its
Constitution provides. Mexican analysts have taken their system
for granted, and in the process we get a great deal of talk about
theory and practice of government in Mexico, but very little understanding about how the system actually works. To develop a
more sophisticated analysis of quantification of ideology than is
presented here, we need to have some studies of budgetary policy
in other developing countries. It is hoped that the method developed in this analysis will aid scholars in carrying out and re-
fining such undertakings.

Students of Mexican history have tended to judge the Mexican
permanent revolution in terms which have ignored the people for
whom the Revolution was theoretically undertaken. The analysis
of social change for the masses presented here will undoubtedly
be controversial. But an attempt to measure the decrease in characteristics of poverty is offered in order to understand a hitherto-
neglected aspect of the revolutionary process. Due to the problems
discussed at length in the last two chapters, the index must by its
nature be tentative and delimited to cover levels of poverty which
probably harm the Mexican in collective terms more than in individual terms. It is difficult, if not impossible, to compress a
series of items into a meaningful Poverty Index; certainly the
result is an abstract one which does not take into account incon-

sistencies or variations, but this is the problem with any conceptual tool of social analysis. It is hoped, however, that in spite of its problems, it will stimulate analysis of different levels of social change.

Finally, we may suggest that the very meaning of the word "revolution" and the very essence of the "revolutionary process" need re-evaluation. If, as we have attempted to show, the revolutionary process may have a series of stages which only begin when the violent stage of upheaval is completed, our findings about revolution in Mexico need to be tested in other societies.

Appendices

The Mexican Government's Functional Classification System

Actividades o Funciones

Grupo

1. *Comunicaciones y Transportes*
   Carreteras
   Ferrocarriles
   Obras Marítimas
   Aeropuertos
   Correos
   Telégrafos
   Telecomunicaciones
   Servicios Generales

2. *Fomento y Conservación de Recursos Naturales Renovables*
   Fomento Agrícola
   Fomento Ganadero
   Fomento Avícola
   Fomento Forestal
   Riego
   Colonización y Reparto Agrario
   Otros Conceptos

3. *Fomento, Promoción y Reglamentación Industrial y Comercial*
   Apoyo a Empresas Comerciales
   Apoyo a Empresas Industriales
   Promoción y Reglamentación del Comercio e Industria
   Energía Eléctrica
   Turismo
   Otros Gastos de Fomento

4. *Servicios Educativos y Culturales*
   Educación Preescolar
   Enseñanza Primaria
   Segunda Enseñanza
   Enseñanza Normal
   Universidades, Escuelas e Institutos de Enseñanza Técnica, Profesional y
       Cultural
   Otras Enseñanzas
   Servicios de Bibliotecas, Hemerotecas y Museos
   Construcciones y Conservaciones Escolares
   Otros Servicios

APPENDIX A (continued)

The Mexican Government's Functional Classification System

Grupo

Actividades o Funciones

5. *Salubridad, Servicios Asistenciales y Hospitalarios*
   Salubridad, Asistencia Médica y Servicios Hospitalarios
   Construcciones Hospitalarias
   Maternidades y Asistencia Infantil
   Asistencia Social
   Diversos Servicios Complementarios

6. *Bienestar y Seguridad Social*
   Servicios Médicos a Empleados Públicos
   Otros Servicios a Empleados Públicos
   Pensiones y Jubilaciones
   Contribución Estatal al Seguro Social
   Ayudas a Núcleos Indígenas
   Otros Gastos Sociales

7. *Ejército, Armada y Servicios Militares*
   Haberes y Otras Remuneraciones
   Servicios Médicos y Hospitalarios
   Servicios Educativos y Sociales
   Pensiones y Jubilaciones
   Gastos de Mantenimiento de las Fuerzas Armadas
   Adquisición y Elaboración de Equipo Bélico
   Construcciones e Instalaciones Militares
   Otras Erogaciones

8. *Administracion General*
   Poder Legislativo
   Dirección Ejecutiva
   Administración de Justicia
   Administración Fiscal
   Relaciones Exteriores
   Ayudas a Estados y Territorios
   Otros Servicios Gubernamentales

9. *Deuda Pública*
   Deuda Pública Interior
   Deuda Pública Exterior
   Deuda Pública Flotante

SOURCE: *Presupuesto, 1963.*

APPENDIX B

Sources of Mexican Budgets by Year

The source for the projected budgets is México, Secretaría de Hacienda y Crédito Público, *Presupuesto General de Egresos*, by year. Actual budgets are from México, Secretaría de Hacienda y Crédito Público, *Cuenta Pública*, by year.

Other sources for the years indicated are:

    A. México, Secretaría de Hacienda y Crédito Público, *Memoria*.

    B. [Moises González Navarro], *Estadísticas Sociales del Porfiriato, 1877–1910*.

    C. México, Dirección General de Estadística, *Anuario Estadístico*.

    D. Gustavo Aguilar, *Los Presupuestos Mexicanos desde los Tiempos de la Colonia hasta Nuestros Días*.

    E. México, Cámara de Diputados, *Diario de los Debates*.

    F. México, Secretaría de Hacienda y Crédito Público, *Boletín de Impuestos*.

    G. *El Día*.

    H. *Excelsior*.

    I. *Novedades*.

    J. *El Popular*.

    K. *El Nacional*.

Year	Other Sources of Projected Budgets	Other Sources of Actual Budgets
1869–1870		
1900–1901		
1910–1911	A, 1910–1911	
1911–1912	A, 1911–1912, 374	
1912–1913		
1913–1914	D	
1914–1915		
1917	A, 1917–1920, I, 222	a
1918		
1919		
1920	A, 1917–1920, I, 292	
1921	D	b
1922	D, 149–150	A, 1920–1923, VI, 169–171
1923	C, 1930, 255	
1924	C, 1930, 255	A, 1923–1925, 68
1925	C, 1930, 255	C, 1930, 521
1926	C, 1930, 255	
1927	C, 1930, 255	C, 1938, 280
1928	C, 1930, 255	*Presupuesto*, 1929, XIV
1929		C, 1938, 280
1930	F, Nov., 1930	C, 1938, 280
1931	F, Nov., 1930	C, 1938, 280
1932		C, 1938, 280

APPENDIX B (continued)

Sources of Mexican Budgets by Year

Year	Other Sources of Projected Budgets	Other Sources of Actual Budgets
1933	K, Dec. 29, 1932	C, 1938, 280
1934	H, Dec. 28, 1933	C, 1938, 280
1935		C, 1938, 280
1936	K, Dec. 28, 1935	
1937	H, Dec. 29, 1936	
1938	K, Dec. 31, 1937	
1939		C, 1940, 742
1940		
1941	K, Dec. 27, 1940	
1942	I, Dec. 27, 1941	
1943	J, Dec. 23, 1944	C, 1943–1945, 763
1944		
1945		
1946		
1947	H, Dec. 27, 1947	C, 1946–1950, 556
1948		
1949	C, 1953, 723	C, 1953, 723
1950	K, Dec. 12, 1951	
1951	*Cuenta Pública*, 1951	
1952	K, Dec. 12, 1951	C, 1953, 723
1953	H, Dec. 16, 1952	
1954	J, Dec. 16, 1953	
1955	C, 1958–1959, 720	C, 1958–1959, 719
1956	C, 1958–1959, 720	C, 1958–1959, 719
1957	C, 1960–1961, 586	E, Oct. 16, 1958
1958	K, Dec. 20, 1957	C, 1960–1961, 586
1959	C, 1960–1961, 586	C, 1960–1961, 586
1960		C, 1960–1961, 586
1961	C, 1960–1961, 586	C, 1960–1961, 586
1962	H, Dec. 15, 1961	
1963	K, Dec. 15, 1962	G, Oct. 30, 1964

[a] 8-month fiscal year to establish calendar year.
[b] 11-month year due to military overthrow of Carranza.

APPENDIX C

Dates of Presidential Terms Since 1910

Executive	Assumption of Office	
Porfirío Díaz	Dec. 1, 1910	
Francisco de la Barra	May 25, 1911	Interim
Francisco I. Madero	Nov. 6, 1911	
Pedro Lascuráin	Feb. 19, 1913	Interim
Victoriano Huerta	Feb. 19, 1913	Interim
Francisco S. Carbajal	July 15–Aug. 13, 1914	Interim
Venustiano Carranza[a]	Aug. 20, 1914	Interim
Venustiano Carranza	May 1, 1917	
Adolfo de la Huerta	May 21, 1920	Interim
Alvaro Obregón	Dec. 1, 1920	
Plutarco Elías Calles	Dec. 1, 1924	
Emilio Portes Gil	Nov. 30, 1928	Interim
Pascual Ortiz Rubio	Feb. 5, 1930	
Abelardo Rodríguez	Sept. 4, 1932	
Lázaro Cárdenas	Nov. 30, 1934	
Manuel Avila Camacho	Nov. 30, 1940	
Miguel Alemán	Dec. 1, 1946	
Adolfo Ruiz Cortines	Dec. 1, 1952	
Adolfo López Mateos	Dec. 1, 1958	
Gustavo Díaz Ordaz	Dec. 1, 1964	

[a] Carranza fought successive presidents of the Convention of Aguascalientes (Eulalio Gutiérrez, Nov. 6, 1914, Roque González Garza, Jan. 16, 1915, and Francisco Lagos Cházaro, June 10, 1915) but they were definitively beaten when they lost control of Mexico City, Aug. 2, 1915.

Sources: *Colección de las Efemérides Publicadas en el Calendario del Más Antiguo Galván* (México, D. F.: Antigua Librería de Murguía, 1950, 2 vols.), Vol. II (1910–1916), and Archivo de la Cámara de Diputados (1917–1964).

APPENDIX D

Key to Shifts of Categories in the Mexican Budget

Categories analyzed in this study have the following sources for items not clear in the Mexican budgetary classification:

A.   PROJECTED BUDGETS

Pensions: Through 1922 included in the Treasury Department as part of the public debt, 1923–1947 in debt (1928–1929 estimated), 1948–present in *erogaciones adicionales*.

Agricultural Credit: 1931–1932 in Treasury Department, 1935–1948 in Investments, 1949–present in *erogaciones adicionales*.

Investments: Through 1947 in the Treasury Department.

Public Debt: Through 1922 in the Treasury Department.

Health, Assistance, and Welfare: 1900–1914 in Interior, latter two in Interior through 1924.

Education: 1869–1870 in Interior and in Attorney General's Department of Justice, 1900–1901 in the latter department.

Communications and Public Works: 1869–1870 in Interior and in Fomento.

Potable Water and Sewage Disposal: 1947–1958 included in Communications and Public Works, 1959–present in Public Works.

Unclassified Social Expenditure: 1921–1924 in Interior, 1938–1946 in Treasury Department, 1945–1946 Instituto Mexicano de Seguro Social classified in public debt.

Foreign Relations: 1917 in Interior.

B.   ACTUAL EXPENDITURE

Sources are the same as above except:

Pensions (1922–1923 and 1931 are also estimated).

Unclassified Social Expenditure (1922 and 1923 are estimated).

APPENDIX E

Military Expenditure in Non-Deflated Pesos

Year	Millions of Pesos		Year	Millions of Pesos	
	Projected	Actual		Projected	Actual
1869–1870	7.0	4.7	1937	80.3	83.1
1900–1901	13.6	14.1	1938	84.4	84.3
1910–1911	21.1	20.6	1939	93.0	91.9
1911–1912	21.3	18.1	1940	110.0	118.3
1912–1913	29.8	28.7	1941	130.0	130.3
1913–1914	43.7	...	1942	145.3	154.3
1914–1915	43.3	...	1943	178.1	195.4
1917	129.0	69.6	1944	196.1	213.1
1918	120.8	60.9	1945	207.8	234.3
1919	134.1	28.1	1946	222.3	252.9
1920	132.5	63.8	1947	279.5	277.3
1921	152.9	120.0	1948	327.8	306.3
1922	156.5	105.7	1949	349.5	330.0
1923	126.5[a]	79.2	1950	355.2	346.3[a]
1924	107.3[a]	117.8[a]	1951	376.1	380.4
1925	92.5[a]	93.5	1952	452.5	467.7
1926	95.0[a]	96.8	1953	507.3	510.6
1927	89.9[a]	99.0	1954	683.6	640.9
1928	97.5[a]	93.1	1955	716.9	709.1
1929	98.0	102.8	1956	820.5	774.7
1930	92.7	86.4	1957	921.0	903.7
1931	81.4	67.7	1958	1,009.5	968.7
1932	54.6	60.9	1959	1,008.9	942.1
1933	55.3	60.5	1960	1,149.5	1,086.1
1934	55.1	60.1	1961	1,174.2	1,113.8
1935	62.0	62.7	1962	1,218.0[b]	1,240.0
1936	69.5	70.4	1963	1,415.1	1,325.1

[a] Calculated from Tables 1-8 and 5-2.
[b] 1217.7 rounded to 1218.0.
SOURCE: Appendix B.

APPENDIX F

Sources of Federal Revenue in Percentage Terms for Selected Years, 1868–1963

Year	Total Revenue (Per Cent)	Major Tax Sources							Loans and Financing	Other Sources
		Import	Export	Commerce and Trade	Industry	Stamps	Income Tax	Public Service		
1868–1869	100.0	27.2	7.0	8.3	– –	7.0	– –	– –	– –	50.5
1898–1899	100.0	44.0	1.8	4.9	1.0	38.5	– –	6.4	– –	.4
1911–1912	100.0	40.1	– –	.8	– –	31.0	– –	7.2	– –	20.9
1912–1913	100.0	43.5	.4	– –	– –	29.5	– –	6.7	– –	19.9
1924	100.0	22.0	7.4	– –	3.9	13.0	1.0	5.8	– –	46.9
1928	100.0	25.0	3.4	– –	15.0	13.1	6.4	19.0	– –	18.1
1929	100.0	26.2	3.8	– –	14.5	11.7	4.9	18.6	– –	20.3
1932	100.0	23.9	1.8	1.6	20.1	13.1	5.0	12.8	– –	21.7
1934	100.0	20.1	2.5	3.7	20.1	4.0	8.9	8.7	– –	32.0
1940	100.0	18.1	11.4	1.7	21.5	9.7	9.8	7.1	– –	20.7
1943	100.0	9.0	19.8	1.4	13.5	7.3	20.0	5.4	– –	23.6
1946	100.0	11.9	12.3	1.3	17.7	10.3	18.5	4.4	– –	23.6
1952	100.0	12.0	13.1	7.5	13.1	.8	24.2	2.8	– –	26.5
1958	100.0	12.0	8.5	5.9	11.3	1.1	21.3	2.7	10.3	26.9
1960	100.0	10.1	5.8	5.7	8.8	1.1	18.8	2.2	33.2	14.3
1963	100.0	10.7	5.9	7.9	11.9	1.3	27.8	2.9	19.9	11.7

SOURCES: México, Secretaría de Hacienda y Crédito Público, *Memoria, 1870*, 760; *1900–1901*, 74. *Cuenta Pública, 1911–1912*, 2. *Memoria, 1911–1913*, 355–356; *1923–1925*, 48. *Anuario Estadístico, 1930*, 512; *1938*, 280–281; *1940*, 741; *1943–1945*, 762; *1946–1950*, 556; *1953*, 723; *1960–1961*, 585; *Cuenta Pública, 1963*.

APPENDIX G

A Comparison of Strikes and Strikers in the United States and Mexico, 1927–1961

Ratio and Indices are Calculated from the Percentage of Strikes and Strikers in the Total Population of the Respective Countries.

(1936 = 100[a])

Year	Ratio of Strikes		Indices of Strikers (1936–100[a])	
	U.S.	Mexico	U.S.	Mexico
1927	6.0	1	45	1
1928	5.0	1	42	1
1929	8.0	1	39	3
1930	5.0	1	24	4
1931	7.0	1	45	– – –
1932	2.3	1	42	3
1933	13.0	1	151	1
1934	1.4	1	189	13
1935	.5	1	143	130
1936	.5	1	100[a]	100[a]
1937	1.2	1	234	53
1938	1.2	1	86	11
1939	1.3	1	145	12
1940	1.1	1	71	16
1941	4.6	1	286	2
1942	4.4	1	101	11
1943	.8	1	234	62
1944	.9	1	248	124
1945	3.8	1	401	35
1946	3.9	1	526	7
1947	4.3	1	244	7
1948	5.8	1	216	18
1949	6.0	1	329	10
1950	10.7	1	257	20
1951	5.2	1	233	9
1952	8.0	1	365	11
1953	5.3	1	243	22
1954	7.0	1	152	14
1955	6.5	1	259	6
1956	4.6	1	183	4
1957	3.5	1	131	4
1958	.9	1	191	30
1959	1.9	1	172	30
1960	1.6	1	119	29
1961	1.8	1	128	15

[a] The percentage of strikers in the total population was exactly the same in the United States and Mexico in 1936.

Sources: Tables 1-9 and 8-2; United States Bureau of the Census, *Historical Statistics of the United States, Colonial Times to 1957 and Revisions* . . . (Washington, D.C., Govt. Printing Office, 1960–), Tables D764-5, and *ibid.*, *Statistical Abstract of the United States*, 1964 (Washington, D.C., Govt. Printing Office, 1964), Table 2.

APPENDIX H

An Alternative Poverty Index[a]

Federal Entity	1910	(1940 = 100) 1921	1930	1940	1950	1960
Total Mexico	139.3	122.3	110.7	100.0	84.0	69.3
Aguascalientes	183.0	126.5	119.2	100.0	103.7	80.2
Baja California	193.6	154.6	119.1	100.0	97.4	79.6
Baja Calif. Terr.	145.9	126.5	110.7	100.0	86.5	67.6
Campeche	138.4	134.7	123.9	100.0	87.9	75.3
Chiapas	113.0	105.3	98.8	100.0	99.9	95.9
Chihuahua	215.5	200.3	127.2	100.0	80.4	69.9
Coahuila	142.3	125.5	117.8	100.0	85.6	79.2
Colima	131.2	122.4	114.1	100.0	94.1	97.1
Distrito Federal	185.6	169.3	125.3	100.0	72.8	75.6
Durango	130.7	118.4	112.3	100.0	91.9	85.0
Guanajuato	111.6	107.8	104.2	100.0	87.0	73.1
Guerrero	118.8	115.2	103.2	100.0	92.7	86.5
Hidalgo	120.6	118.1	106.1	100.0	89.8	82.4
Jalisco	128.5	116.0	110.9	100.0	85.6	73.1
Mexico	138.0	114.5	106.6	100.0	86.2	65.0
Michoacán	147.2	142.3	98.7	100.0	83.9	69.6
Morelos	220.2	201.0	90.0	100.0	69.3	56.7
Nayarit	277.3	165.2	92.7	100.0	88.9	85.9
Nuevo León	137.1	124.0	117.6	100.0	97.3	74.9
Oaxaca	117.8	115.7	102.8	100.0	93.1	84.1
Puebla	112.3	111.5	110.5	100.0	89.0	79.4
Querétaro	186.3	168.7	116.3	100.0	87.3	76.9
Quintana Roo	148.4	135.6	113.5	100.0	102.1	114.0
San Luis Potosí	110.8	112.5	98.2	100.0	87.1	77.6
Sinaloa	126.1	115.3	110.2	100.0	91.3	73.3
Sonora	173.8	152.0	112.9	100.0	78.0	65.6
Tabasco	240.6	225.4	127.4	100.0	100.1	87.1
Tamaulipas	166.8	125.8	122.8	100.0	84.9	71.9
Tlaxcala	198.1	192.9	120.9	100.0	86.1	77.6
Veracruz	139.5	126.8	107.9	100.0	92.1	71.3
Yucatán	166.0	132.8	113.1	100.0	83.5	83.4
Zacatecas	116.3	115.7	106.8	100.0	91.8	86.7

[a] The alternative index is formulated by computing an average of relatives for each of the characteristics of poverty (the items for each federal entity in each census year are calculated relative to 1940 and divided by the total number of items in each census year). Due to the problem of weighting which arises in this numerical computation of ratios, all items with a base of less than 1.0 are counted as 0.0 and excluded from calculations. The weighting problem here occurs by category between censuses in contrast to the problem of weighting in Table 9-9 which occurs within the average for each census. Table 9-9 is not compounded by ratios, however, and it is assumed that the number of items largely cancels errors in numerical weighting.

SOURCE: Same as Table 9-9.

APPENDIX I

Poverty Index and Level Analyzed by Census (Geo-Economic) Regions

	A. Index of Change (1940 = 100)					
	1910	1921	1930	1940	1950	1960
Total Mexico	123.7	115.4	108.7	100.0	85.7	72.0
Pacific North[a]	137.3	121.0	107.2	100.0	87.2	74.1
North[b]	130.6	121.6	111.6	100.0	87.9	75.5
Center[c]	120.0	114.0	107.7	100.0	89.8	77.0
Gulf[d]	129.0	121.6	109.8	100.0	86.7	76.3
South Pacific[e]	111.2	107.6	102.8	100.0	89.8	81.6
(Center without Federal District)	120.0	114.6	108.4	100.0	90.9	77.6
(Federal District)	178.6	145.0	126.1	100.0	78.6	78.6

	B. Poverty Level[f]					
	1910	1921	1930	1940	1950	1960
Total Mexico	56.9	53.1	50.0	46.0	39.4	33.1
Pacific North[a]	51.2	45.1	40.0	37.3	32.5	27.6
North[b]	52.4	48.8	44.8	40.0	35.2	30.2
Center[c]	56.4	53.6	50.6	47.0	41.8	36.2
Gulf[d]	59.2	55.8	50.4	45.9	39.8	35.0
South Pacific[e]	63.0	61.0	58.1	56.5	50.7	46.1
(Center without Federal District)	60.1	57.4	54.3	50.1	45.1	38.9
(Federal District)	20.0	16.2	14.1	11.2	8.8	8.8

[a] Baja California, Baja California Territory, Nayarit, Sinaloa, Sonora.

[b] Chihuahua, Coahuila, Durango, Nuevo León, San Luis Potosí, Tamaulipas, Zacatecas.

[c] Aguascalientes, Federal District, Guanajuato, Hidalgo, Jalisco, México, Michoacán, Morelos, Puebla, Querétaro, Tlaxcala.

[d] Campeche, Quintana Roo, Tabasco, Veracruz, Yucatán.

[e] Colima, Chiapas, Guerrero, Oaxaca.

[f] Calculated from Part A, without regard to size, see 234f.

SOURCE: Tables 9-9 and 9-10.

APPENDIX J

Gross National Investment in Selected Years, 1940–1961

Year	Total Per Cent	Per Cent Private	Per Cent Public
1940	100.0	57.6	42.4
1946	100.0	65.6	34.4
1952	100.0	58.1	41.9
1958	100.0	62.3	37.7
1961	100.0	49.9	50.4

SOURCE: *50 Años en Cifras*, 43.

APPENDIX K

Population of Mexico by Census, 1910–1960

Entidad	1910	1921	1930	1940	1950	1960
Total	15,160,369	14,334,780	16,552,722	19,653,552	25,791,017	34,923,129
Aguascalientes	120,511	107,581	132,900	161,693	188,075	243,363
Baja California	9,760	23,537	48,327	78,907	226,965	520,165
Baja California Territory	42,512	39,294	47,089	51,471	60,864	81,594
Campeche	86,661	76,419	84,630	90,460	122,098	168,219
Chiapas	438,843	421,744	529,983	679,885	907,026	1,210,870
Chihuahua	405,707	401,622	491,792	623,944	846,414	1,226,793
Coahuila	362,092	393,480	436,425	550,717	720,619	907,734
Colima	77,704	91,749	61,923	78,806	112,321	164,450
Distrito Federal	720,753	906,063	1,229,576	1,757,530	3,050,442	4,870,876
Durango	483,175	336,766	404,364	483,829	629,874	760,836
Guanajuato	1,081,651	860,364	987,801	1,046,490	1,328,712	1,735,490
Guerrero	594,278	566,836	641,690	732,910	919,386	1,186,716
Hidalgo	646,551	622,241	677,772	771,818	850,394	994,598
Jalisco	1,208,855	1,191,957	1,255,346	1,418,310	1,746,777	2,443,261
México	989,510	884,617	990,112	1,146,034	1,392,623	1,897,851
Michoacán	991,880	939,849	1,048,381	1,182,003	1,422,717	1,851,876
Morelos	179,594	103,440	132,068	182,711	272,842	386,264
Nayarit	171,173	163,183	167,724	216,698	290,124	389,929
Nuevo León	365,150	336,412	417,491	541,147	740,191	1,078,848
Oaxaca	1,040,398	976,005	1,084,549	1,192,794	1,421,313	1,727,266
Puebla	1,101,600	1,024,955	1,150,425	1,294,620	1,625,830	1,973,837
Querétaro	244,663	220,231	234,058	244,737	286,238	355,045
Quintana Roo	9,109	10,966	10,620	18,752	26,967	50,169
San Luis Potosí	627,800	445,681	579,831	678,779	856,066	1,048,297
Sinaloa	323,642	341,265	395,618	492,821	635,681	838,404
Sonora	265,383	275,127	316,271	364,176	510,607	783,378
Tabasco	187,574	210,437	224,023	285,630	362,716	496,340
Tamaulipas	249,641	286,904	344,039	458,832	718,167	1,024,182
Tlaxcala	184,171	178,570	205,458	224,063	284,551	346,699
Veracruz	1,132,859	1,159,935	1,377,293	1,619,338	2,040,231	2,727,899
Yucatán	339,613	358,221	386,096	418,210	516,899	614,049
Zacatecas	477,556	379,329	459,047	565,437	665,824	817,831
(Complementary census)	--	--	--	--	11,763	--

SOURCE: *Anuario Estadístico, 1960–1961,* 24.

APPENDIX L

Federal Budgetary Outlay for Roads, in Percentage Terms,
1925–1963 (included in Table 6-7)

Year	Per Cent Projected	Per Cent Actual
1925	.5	.5
1926	4.4	4.0
1927	3.6	2.6
1928	3.7	3.7
1929	2.8	2.9
1930	3.9	5.5
1931	4.7	4.9
1932	3.7	.8
1933	1.6	3.3
1934	3.5	3.3
1935	2.9	3.9
1936	3.3	4.4
1937	2.7	4.4
1938	4.1	3.2
1939	1.3	1.0
1940	1.4	1.2
1941	2.2	1.6
1942	1.9	1.5
1943	1.2	3.0
1944	9.8	2.5
1945	4.9	2.8
1946	3.4	2.0
1947	10.4	7.9
1948	11.7	8.8
1949	10.9	7.5
1950	10.6	7.8
1951	10.5	6.7
1952	10.9	6.7
1953	10.8	7.0
1954	11.2	6.0
1955	8.2	6.2
1956	6.2	4.9
1957	8.3	6.0
1958	7.8	5.7
1959	8.6	5.3
1960	8.9	3.6
1961	6.6	3.6
1962	7.4	3.9
1963	5.4	3.8

SOURCE: México, Secretaría de Obras Públicas, *Documentos para la Historia de Carreteras en México . . . 1925–1963*, México, D. F.: Talleres General de Librería Madero, 1964 (3 vols.), Vols. 2 and 3.

APPENDIX M

Estimated Total Federal Debt, 1950–1963[a]

Year	Total[b]	1 Internal (titled)	2 External (titled)	3 External (untitled)
1950	3,686,881	2,078,074	695,154	913,653
1951	3,521,246	1,918,784	766,523	835,939
1952	3,593,730	2,127,724	707,737	758,269
1953	3,492,190	2,134,912	676,678	680,600
1954	6,182,604	4,345,255	949,990	887,359
1955	6,695,032	5,009,563	925,027	760,442
1956	7,146,784	5,611,045	883,974	651,765
1957	7,646,644	6,257,548	845,965	543,131
1958	8,024,951	6,792,449	798,005	434,497
1959	8,373,366	7,276,036	771,456	325,874
1960	12,026,625	11,534,722	274,647	217,256
1961	12,143,362	11,783,203	251,526	108,633
1962	12,232,810	12,002,397	230,413	– – –
1963	12,419,521	12,209,803	209,718	– – –

[a] Figures vary according to source and it appears that the Mexican Treasury Department has changed its mind many times about the amount owed historically. It is difficult to make a full statement about the debt since 1910 due to changing exchange rates and retroactive acceptance of debts, among other factors. The series given here is only a logical one chosen from conflicting sources. This table does not include debts of non-governmental agencies in the public sector unless accepted as federal obligations by the Mexican Congress.

[b] In thousands of non-deflated pesos.

SOURCES: Column 1: *Compendio Estadístico, 1953*, 422–423; *Anuario Estadístico, 1953*, 729; *Compendio Estadístico, 1954*, 395–396; *Ibid., 1955*, 372, 374; *Ibid., 1956–1957*, 460–461; *Ibid., 1958*, 435–436; *Ibid., 1960*, 144–146; *Ibid., 1962*, 205–206; *Anuario Estadístico, 1962–1963*, 540.

Column 2: *Compendio Estadístico, 1960*, 144–146; *Anuario Estadístico, 1962–1963*, 540.

Column 3: *Compendio Estadístico, 1953*, 422–423; *Ibid., 1957*, 460–461; *Ibid., 1958*, 435–436; *Ibid., 1960*, 144–146; *Ibid., 1962*, 205–206; *Anuario Estadístico, 1953*, 729.

Bibliographic Essay

This historical study is based principally on primary sources which hitherto have been unexamined in any systematic way. Corroborative studies or works which take a different view are listed in the Bibliography, which is alphabetically organized in order to provide a key to short forms of citation given in the notes. Many notes serve as a bibliographic guide to aspects of the literature on the Mexican Revolution, and it is not necessary to duplicate such information here.

In regard to sources, Part I utilizes projected accounts and actual expenditure records of the Mexican federal government in the twentieth century. These budgetary data are partially available in several locations in Mexico City. The library of the Ministry of the Treasury is the most complete source, but it is also necessary to use the records of the Contador de la Federación. Material not found in these two places can usually be located in the library of the Bank of Mexico. Projected and actual expenditures are printed in separate volumes, the projected accounts providing the code for understanding actual expenditure by item. The first volume circulates freely; the second is most difficult to find outside of the above locations.

Readers of this study may be interested in a work published which presents budgetary data for the epoch from 1877 to 1911. The study, *Fuerza de Trabajo y Actividad Económica por Sectores; Estadísticas Económicas del Porfiriato* (México, D. F.: n.p., [1965]), prepared by the Seminario de Historia Moderna de Mexico and edited by Fernando Rosenzweig, includes analysis of budgets prior to the Revolution. However, its focus does not really provide a comparable background to the data presented here as it is offered in terms of economic classifications.

A detailed study of the process in Mexican budgetary formulations may be found in Robert E. Scott's "Budget Making in Mexico," *Inter-American Economic Affairs*, 9:2 (1955) 3–20. Parts of Professor Scott's discussion are summarized above, but we have made no attempt to duplicate Scott's sound analysis of how the budget is prepared by the chief executive for submission to Congress.

Examination of the budget gives us an opportunity to identify and trace relationships in politics which previously could not be pinned down with much accuracy. Edwin Lieuwen, for example, has attempted to explain the "Curbing of Militarism in Mexico" in his book on *Arms and Politics in Latin America* (New York: Praeger, 1961). Through an investigation of qualitative rather than quantitative factors in the Mexican Revolution, he has essentially arrived at the conclusions given here. True, he divides the Mexican Revolution into different periods, but he notes that the military now has little influence. Since we have attempted to identify shifts in budgetary policy which have greatly affected the military's role in politics, the analysis given here may be fruitfully compared to Lieuwen's interpretation and guide to sources.

Part II utilizes social statistics to examine historical trends by region. These statistics have often been quoted, but have seldom been organized for long-term analysis. One of the few other studies along this line is Pablo González Casanova's *La Democracia en México* (México, D. F.: Editorial Era, 1965) which was published as this manuscript was being completed. Professor Casanova, Director of the National Political and Social Science School of the National Autonomous University of Mexico, has examined historical statistics in terms of political and social "marginalism." He uses marginalism as a concept to define the position of sectors of society which do not fully participate in the benefits of social organization. González Casanova discusses the number of people who are illiterate, eat tortillas, go barefoot, wear sandals, and speak Indian languages. He ranks Federal entities according to the absolute number of persons who live on the margin of social development, and Veracruz emerges as the most marginal state because it has the largest rural population (Table 30). In developing a concept of political marginalism, however, he also includes, for example, the percentage of the population of eligible voters who did not participate in presidential elections from 1910 to 1958. The professor's definition is not fixed and he adapts it to different contexts as he shifts his focus of inquiry. González Casanova's work should be compared to this study in order to see how another scholar has attempted to analyze the political and social process of the Mexican Revolution in statistical terms.

Questions raised about the meaning of the Mexican Revolution are taken up in Stanley R. Ross's *Is the Mexican Revolution Dead?* (New York: Knopf, 1966). Since Ross answers his question in the affirmative, readers are advised to consult his interpretation (pp. 3–34). Professor Ross has compiled a synthesis of the best of the debate concerning the Revolution. The writings of Luis Cabrera, Daniel Cosío Villegas, Jesús Silva Herzog, Leopoldo Zea, Moisés González Navarro, and others give intellectual views of the Revolution which permit sophisticated discussion. Howard F. Cline's article, "Mexico: A Matured Latin American Revolution, 1910–1960," which is included in Ross's volume, should certainly be read to help answer questions about the definition of the word "revolution."

The literature on the theory of revolution is abundant and Crane Brinton sums much of it up nicely while offering a typology and bibliographic essay in his *Anatomy of Revolution* (New York: Vintage Books, 1958). Brinton only briefly discusses the concept of "permanent" or "institutional revolution," as reflected in the Russian revolution of the twentieth century, but in doing so he largely negates his carefully built comparison of revolutionary stages.

The meaning of the word "poverty" is also subject to controversy, and Robert H. Bremner's enlightening essay, "Poverty in Perspective," has been useful in understanding shifting historical definitions. The essay is in *Change and Continuity in Twentieth-Century America*, edited by John Braeman, Robert H. Bremner, and Everett Walters (Ohio State University Press, 1964).

The pragmatic approach to analyzing poverty, like intellectual analysis, requires that the reader understand the nature of the statistics in the same manner that he should comprehend the bias of writers who have subjectively measured poverty. Since all Mexican budgetary and social statistics which are historically complete have been compiled by the government, it might be argued that the historian who uses quantitative analysis is trapped in a numbers game that leaves him at the mercy of bias which was recorded by a patricular government in a particular historical time. In this sense, it is true that we face limitations; however, independent analysis is possible in the sense that statistics prepared by the government can be examined through rearrangement of the data, and we can probe into contradictions as well as continuities in statistical series. Certainly the statistical series is more complete than random analyses by observers who balance impressions based upon minute numerical samples in order to arrive at personal views. The statistical series represents the efforts of many persons who have probed into Mexican life with system and depth.

The oral history cited in this study provided a bridge between intellectual history and quantitative analysis. In this manner, it was possible to maintain the human element in statistical research. Discussions with Ramón Beteta, for example, were most helpful in clarifying questions about budgetary matters and in analyzing ideological patterns. Interviews were tape recorded in Mexico during 1964 and 1965 as part of "An Oral History of the Mexican Revolution Since 1910." This oral history examines major ideological views of the Revolutionary Family and its enemies. My wife, Edna, and I discussed and debated at great length the processes of the Revolution with more than twenty-five persons. We were particularly interested in finding out how these persons grew up in the Revolution, reacted to it, and then gradually came to determine or influence its course. Some of these interviews have now been published with the following citation: James W. Wilkie y Edna Monzon de Wilkie, *México Visto en el Siglo XX; Entrevistas de Historia Oral: Ramón Beteta, Marte R. Gómez, Manuel Gómez Morin, Vicente Lombardo Toledano, Miguel Palomar y Vizcarra, Emilio Portes Gil, Jesús Silva Herzog* (México, D. F.: Instituto Mexicano de Investigaciones Económicas, 1969).

There is now a well-established tradition of independent analysis of the Mexican Revolution by scholars from the United States. George McCutchen McBride's *The Land Systems of Mexico* (New York: American Geographical Society, 1923) opened an era of intensive investigation by North Americans south of their border. In 1928 Ernest Gruening wrote with wide and penetrating scope

on *Mexico and Its Heritage* (New York: Century). A year later
Frank Tannenbaum explored the ramifications of *The Mex-
ican Agrarian Revolution* (Washington, D. C.: Brookings Insti-
tution), and in 1933, he carried his analysis forward in *Peace by
Revolution, an Interpretation of Mexico* (New York: Columbia
University Press). Tannenbaum's most recent study, *Mexico, the
Struggle for Peace and Bread* (New York: Knopf) was published
in 1950. Eyler Newton Simpson contributed *The Ejido, Mexico's
Way Out* (Chapel Hill: University of North Carolina Press) in
1937; and a study of *Rural Mexico* in the early 1940's by Nathan
L. Whetten (University of Chicago Press) was published in 1948.
In 1950 Sanford A. Mosk shifted the focus of scholarship to *Industrial Revolution in Mexico* (Berkeley and Los Angeles: University of California Press), and shortly thereafter Howard F. Cline
developed a statistical approach to social and economic analysis
of Mexico in his political and diplomatic study of *The United
States and Mexico* (Harvard University Press, 1953). Since the
early 1950's a number of contributions have appeared in this
country which give much detailed insight into the Mexican Revolution, beginning notably with Oscar Lewis's *Life in a Mexican
Village: Tepoztlán Restudied* (Urbana: University of Illinois
Press, 1951). It is hoped that the present work has been able to
draw upon this tradition to answer with some success at least a
few of the questions posed by those who have gone before.

Bibliography

There are literally hundreds of items which could be included in the bibliography of this study; since there are many excellent bibliographies available for the history of twentieth-century Mexico, however, only the items which are cited in the text or which have particular direct bearing to the text are included here. One may consult the following bibliographic sources for a more complete view of published and unpublished material on the Mexican Revolution.

GENERAL BIBLIOGRAPHY

Bernstein, Marvin D. *The Mexican Mining Industry, 1890–1950.* Albany: State University of New York, 1965, 337–394.

Brandenburg, Frank R. *The Making of Modern Mexico.* Englewood Cliffs: Prentice Hall, 1964, 348–367.

Cline, Howard F. "Mexican Community Studies. . . ." *Hispanic American Historical Review* 32 (1952) 212–242.

———. *Mexico, Revolution to Evolution: 1940–1960.* London: Oxford University Press, 1962, 255–370.

González, Luis, G. Monroy, and S. Uribe. *Fuentes de la Historia Contemporánea de México.* México, D. F.: El Colegio de México, 1961. 3 vols.

Hernández, Julia. *Novelistas y Cuentistas de la Revolución.* México, D. F.: Unidad Mexicana de Escritores, 1960.

Ker, Anita M. *Mexican Government Publications . . . 1821–1936.* Washington, D. C.: G.P.O., 1940.

México, Dirección General de Estadística. *Catálago General de las Estadísticas Nacionales.* México, D. F.: Secretaría de Industria y Comercio, 1960.

Phelan, John Leddy. "México y lo Mexicano." *Hispanic American Historical Review* 36 (1956) 309–318.

Potash, Robert A. "Historiography of Mexico Since 1821." *Hispanic American Historical Review* 40 (1960) 383–424.

Ramos, Roberto. *Bibliografía de la Revolución Mexicana*. México, D. F.: Biblioteca del Instituto Nacional de Estudios Históricos de la Revolución Mexicana, 1959 (1st ed. 1931–1940). 3 vols.

Ross, Stanley Robert. "Aportación a la Historiografía de la Revolución Mexicana." *Historia Mexicana* 10 (1960) 282–303.

————. "Bibliography of Sources for Contemporary Mexican History." *Hispanic American Historical Review* 39 (1959) 234–238.

Ross, Stanley Robert, and Bernard E. Bobb. "Historiografía Mexicanista Estados Unidos, 1959–1960." *Historia Mexicana* 11 (1961) 286–313.

Torres-Ríoseco, Arturo. *Bibliografía de la Novela Mejicana*. Cambridge: Harvard University Press, 1933.

SELECT BIBLIOGRAPHY

Adorno, T. W. *et al. The Authoritarian Personality*. New York: Harper, 1950.

Aguilar, Gustavo F. *Los Presupuestos Mexicanos desde los Tiempos de la Colonia hasta Nuestros Días*. México, D. F.: n.p., 1947.

Aguirre, Norberto. "El Problema Ganadero de Chihuahua [discurso de 24 de Abril de 1964]." *El Día*, May 4, 1965.

Aguirre Beltrán, Gonzalo. *El Proceso de Aculturación*. México, D. F.: Universidad Nacional Autónoma de México, 1957.

Albornoz, Alvaro de. *Trayectoria y Ritmo del Crédito Agrícola en México* México, D. F.: Instituto Mexicano de Investigaciones Económicas, 1966.

Alanís Patiño, Emilio. "Zonas y Regiones Económicas de México." *Problemas Agrícolas e Industriales de México* 1 (1946) 49–104 and 2 (1946) 127–142.

Alba, Víctor. *Las Ideas Sociales Contemporáneas en México*. México, D. F.: Fondo de Cultura Económica, 1960.

Alemán, Miguel. "Programa de Gobierno." *El Universal*, Sept. 30, 1945, reprinted in *Política*, Aug. 15, 1964, xxviii–xliv.

Almazán, Juan Andreu. *See* Andreu Almazán

Alvarez, José Rogelio. "El Turismo," in *México Cincuenta Años de Revolución*, I. *La Economía*, 295–299.

Alvarez Amézquita, José, Miguel Bustamante, Antonio López Picazos. *Historia de la Salubridad y de la Asistencia en México*. México, D. F.: Secretaría de Salubridad y Asistencia, 1960. 4 vols.

Anderson, Charles W. "Bankers as Revolutionaries: Politics and Development in Mexico," in William P. Glade and Charles W. Anderson, *The Political Economy of Mexico*. Madison: University of Wisconsin Press, 1963.

Andreu Almazán, Juan. Oral History Interviews with James and Edna Wilkie, Acapulco, Guerrero, 1964.

Anguiano Equihua, Roberto. "El Gasto del Sector Público en México." México, D. F.: Universidad Nacional Autonóma de México, *Licenciatura en Economía*, 1963.

Anuario Estadístico. See México, Dirección General de Estadística.

Avila Camacho y su Ideología. México, D. F.: S. Turanzas del Valle, 1940.

Bach, Federico, and Margarita Reyna. "El Nuevo Indice de Precios al Mayoreo en la Ciudad de México de la Secretaría de la Economía Nacional." *El Trimestre Económico* 10 (1943) 1–63.

Bassols Batalla, Angel. "A New Map of Economic Zones and Regions of Mexico," *Geographia Polonica* 8 (1965) 47–52.

Bennett, Robert L. *The Financial Sector and Economic Development; The Mexican Case.* Baltimore: Johns Hopkins Press, 1965.

Berdejo Alvarado, E. *Niveles de vida de la Población del Distrito Federal.* México, D. F.: n.p., 1960.

Bernstein, Marvin D. *The Mexican Mining Industry, 1890–1950.* Albany: State University of New York, 1965.

Beteta, Ramón. Oral History Interviews with James and Edna Wilkie, Mexico City, 1964.

———. *Pensamiento y Dinámica de la Revolución Mexicana.* México, D. F.: Editorial México Nuevo, 1950.

———. (ed.). *Social and Economic Program of Mexico.* México, D. F.: n.p., 1935.

———. *Tres Años de Política Hacendaria (1947–1948–1949), Perspectiva y Acción.* México, D. F.: Secretaría de Hacienda y Crédito Público, 1951.

[Beteta, Ramón, and E. N. Simpson.] *La Mendicidad en México.* México, D. F.: Beneficencia Pública del Distrito Federal, 1930.

Bett, Virgil M. *Central Banking in Mexico; Monetary Policies and Financial Crises, 1864–1940.* Ann Arbor: University of Michigan Press, 1957.

Blair, Calvin P. "Nacional Financiera: Entrepreneurship in a Mixed Economy," in Vernon (ed.). *Public Policy and Private Enterprise in Mexico,* 191–240.

Bojórquez, Juan de Dios (Pseud. Djed Bórquez). *Crónica del Constituyente.* México, D. F.: Botas, 1938.

Borah, Woodrow. "Race and Class in Mexico." *Pacific Historical Review* 23 (1954) 331–342.

Bosques, Gilberto. *The National Revolutionary Party of Mexico and the Six-Year Plan.* México, D. F.: P[artido] N[acional] R[evolucionario], 1937.

Branch, H. N., comp. *The Mexican Constitution of 1917 Compared with the Constitution of 1857.* Philadelphia: American Academy of Political and Social Science, 1917.

Brandenburg, Frank R. "A Contribution to the Theory of Entrepreneurship and Economic Development: The Case of Mexico." *Inter-*

American Economic Affairs 16:3 (1962) 3–23.

———. *The Making of Modern Mexico*. Englewood Cliffs: Prentice Hall, 1964.

Bremner, Robert H. "Poverty in Perspective," in John Braeman, Robert H. Bremner, and Everett Walters (eds.), *Change and Continuity in Twentieth-Century America*. Columbus: Ohio State University Press, 1964.

Brinton, Crane. *Anatomy of Revolution*. New York: Vintage Books, 1958.

Brothers, Dwight S. and Leopoldo Solís M. *Mexican Financial Development* [1940–1960]. Austin: University of Texas Press, 1966.

Brown, Lyle C. "General Lázaro Cárdenas and Mexican Presidential Politics, 1933–1940; A Study in the Acquisition and Manipulation of Political Power." Unpublished Ph.D. thesis in political science, Austin, University of Texas, 1964.

———. "Mexican Church-State Relations, 1933–1940," *A Journal of Church and State* 6 (1964) 202–222.

Browning, Harley L. "Urbanization in Mexico," manuscript in preparation, department of sociology, University of Texas.

Buck, A. E., and M. A. de Tezanos Pinto. *El Presupuesto en los Gobiernos de Hoy . . . [y] la Legislación . . . de los Paises Latinamericanos*. Buenos Aires: Peuser, 1946.

Butterworth, Douglas S. "A Study of the Urbanization Process Among Mixtec Migrants from Tilantongo in Mexico City." *América Indígena* 22 (1962) 259–274.

Cabrera, Luis. *Veinte Años Despúes*. México, D. F.: Botas, 1938.

Calles, Plutarco Elías. Mexico Before the World; Public Documents and Address of . . . , tr. by R. H. Murray. New York: Academy Press, 1927.

Campa, Valentín. "La Política Fiscal de López Mateos." *Política*, Nov. 1, 1964, 21.

["Campaña Electoral 1957–1958."] *Problemas de México*, July 15, 1958.

Cano, Celerino. "Análisis de la Acción Educativa," in *México Cincuenta Años de Revolución*, vol. IV, *La Cultura*, 23–39.

Cárdenas, Lázaro. *Cárdenas Habla*. México, D. F.: P[artido] R[evolucionario] M[exicano], 1940.

———. *Los Catorce Puntos de la Política Obrera Presidencial*. [México, D. F.]: P[artido] N[acional] R[evolucionario], 1936.

———. Interviews by author Aug. 21 and Sept. 11, 1962, Pátzcuaro, Michoacán.

———. Interview by author Aug. 25, 1962, while traveling from Uruapan to Apatzingán, Michoacán.

Caso, Alfonso. *Indigenismo*. México, D. F.: Instituto Nacional Indigenista, 1958.

Chapa, Telésforo. "Necesidad de Consolidar y Extender un Solo Sistema de Seguridad Social." *El Día,* Jan. 22, 1964.

Chávez Orozco, Luis. *El Presidente López Mateos Visto Por un Historiador.* México, D. F.: Editorial Patria, 1962.

50 Años en Cifras. See México, Secretaría de la Presidencia y Nacional Financiera

Clark, Marjorie Ruth. *Organized Labor in Mexico.* Chapel Hill: University of North Carolina Press, 1934.

Cline, Howard F. "Mexico: A Matured Latin American Revolution." *Annals of American Academy of Political and Social Science* 334 (1961) 84–94.

———. "Mexico; A Maturing Democracy." *Current History* 24 (1953) 136–142.

———. *Mexico, Revolution to Evolution: 1940–1960.* London: Oxford University Press, 1962, 355–370.

———. *The United States and Mexico.* Cambridge: Harvard University Press, 1953.

Colección de las Efemérides Publicadas en el Calendario del Más Antiguo Galván. México, D. F.: Antigua Librería de Murguía, 1950, 2 vols.

Collver, O. Andrew. *Birth Rates in Latin America: New Estimates of Historical Trends and Fluctuations.* Berkeley: University of California Institute of International Studies, 1965.

Combined Mexican Working Party. *The Economic Development of Mexico.* Baltimore: International Bank for Reconstruction and Development and Johns Hopkins Press, 1953.

Compendio Estadístico. See México, Dirección General de Estadística

Confederación de Cámaras Nacionales de Comercio. *Problemas Derivados de la Intervención del Estado en la Economía Nacional.* México, D. F.: n.p., 1946.

Confederación de Cámaras Nacionales de Comercio e Industria. *Análisis Económico Nacional, 1934–1940.* México, D. F.: n.p., 1940.

Cosío Villegas, Daniel. "Mexico's Crisis [1947]" in *American Extremes.* Tr. by Américo Paredes. Austin: University of Texas Press, 1964, 3–27.

Crawford, William Rex. *A Century of Latin-American Thought.* Cambridge: Harvard University Press, 1944.

Cronon, E. David. *Josephus Daniels in Mexico.* Madison: University of Wisconsin Press, 1960.

Cuenta Pública. See Appendix B

Cueto, Héctor Hugo del. "El Pavoroso Problema Escolar en México." *Revista Nacional.* Dec. 1, 1964.

Cumberland, Charles C. *Mexican Revolution: Genesis Under Madero.* Austin: University of Texas Press, 1952.

D'Acosta, Helia. *Alemanismo; Teoría y Práctica del Progreso de México.* México, D. F.: Libros de México, 1925.

Daniels, Josephus. *Shirt-Sleeve Diplomat*. Chapel Hill: University of North Carolina Press, 1947.

Dávila Ibáñez, Eliud Sergio. *Los Ingresos y Egresos del Instituto Mexicano del Seguro Social, 1944–1963*. Monterrery: Instituto Tecnológico y de Estudios Superiores, *Licenciatura en Economía*, 1966.

DeBeers, John S. "El Peso Mexicano, 1941–1949," tr. by M. S. Sarto, *Problemas Agrícolas e Industriales de México* 5.1 (1953).

Diario de los Debates del Congreso Constituyente, 1916–1917. México, D. F.: Talleres Gráficos de la Nación, 1960. 2 vols.

Domínguez Ramírez, Jorge Efrén. "Comentarios al Artículo: 'Educación y Presupuestos' del Doctor Manuel Germán Parra." *El Día*, March 3, 1965.

Dulles, John W. F. *Yesterday in Mexico, A Chronicle of the Revolution, 1919–1936*. Austin: University of Texas Press, 1961.

Durán Ochoa, Julio. *Población*. México, D. F.: Fondo de Cultura Económica, 1955.

Elías Calles, Plutarco. *See* Calles, Plutarco Elías.

Fernández y Fernández, Ramón. "El Crédito Ejidal, Préstamos, Recuperaciones y Cartera." *Trimestre Económico* 25 (1958) 157–188.

———. "Un Indice del Bienestar Público." *Trimestre Económico* 16 (1949) 531–559.

Feur, Lewis S. (ed.) *Marx and Engels; Basic Writings in Politics and Philosophy*. Garden City: Doubleday, 1959.

Flores, Edmundo. *Tratado de Economía Agrícola*. México, D. F.: Fondo de Cultura Económica, 1961.

Flores Zavala, Ernesto. *Elementos de Fianzas Públicas Mexicanas, Los Impuestos*. México, D. F.: Editorial Porrúa, 1963.

Fuentes, Carlos. Oral History Interviews with James and Edna Wilkie, Mexico City, 1964.

Fuentes, Carlos, Fernando Benítez, Víctor Flores Olea, Enrique González Pedrero, Francisco López Cámara. ["Carta Abierta a Política"]. *Política*, Aug. 15, 1964.

———. "El Dilema de México: Revolución o Retroceso; Una Nueva Perspectiva Para la Izquierda Nacional." *El Día*, Sept. 3, 1964.

Galván Duque, Antonio. "Declaraciones del General Calles Sobre Nuestro Problema Agrario." *El Universal*, Dec. 26, 1929.

Gamio, Manuel. *Forjando Patria*. México, D. F.: Editorial Porrúa, 1960.

———. *Hacia un México Nuevo*. México, D. F.: n.p., 1935.

García Treviño, Rodrigo. *Precios Salarios y Mordidas*. México, D. F.: Editorial América, 1953.

Gaxiola, Francisco Javier, Jr. Oral History Interviews with James and Edna Wilkie, Mexico City, 1964.

———. *El Presidente Rodríguez (1932–1934)*. México: Editorial Cultura, 1938.

Glade, William P., Jr. "Las Empresas Gubernamentales Descentraliza-
das," *Problemas Agricolas e Industriales de México* 11.1 (1959).

Glade, William P., Jr., and Charles W. Anderson. *The Political Economy of Mexico.* Madison: University of Wisconsin Press, 1963.

Gómez, Marte R. Oral History Interviews with James and Edna Wilkie, Mexico City, 1964.

————. *La Reforma Agraria de México; Su Crisis Durante el Periódo
1928–1934.* México, D. F.: Manuel Porrúa, 1964.

González Casanova, Pablo. *La Democracia en México.* México, D. F.:
Editorial Era, 1965.

[González Navarro, Moisés.] *Estadísticas Sociales del Porfiriato, 1877–
1910.* México, D. F.: Dirección General de Estadística, 1956.

————. "Social Aspects of the Mexican Revolution," tr. by D. Wood-
ward. *Journal of World History* 8 (1964) 281–289.

González Ramírez, Manuel. *Las Ideas-La Violencia.* Vol. I of *La Revolución Social de México.* México. D. F.: Fondo de Cultura Económica, 1960.

González Roa, Fernando y José Covarrubias. *El Problema Rural de
México.* México, D. F.: Secretaría de Hacienda, 1917.

Goodspeed, Stephen S. "El Papel del Jefe Ejecutivo en México." *Problemas Agrícolas e Industriales de México* 7 (1955) 13–208.

Gruening, Ernest. *Mexico and Its Heritage.* New York: Century, 1928.

Gumpel, Henry J., and Hugo B. Margaín. *Taxation in Mexico.* Boston: Little, Brown, for Harvard U., 1957.

Heilbroner, Robert L. *The Worldly Philosophers; The Lives, Times,
and Ideas of the Great Economic Thinkers.* New York: Simon and
Schuster, 1961.

Instituto Nacional de la Vivienda. *Cinco Encuestas Reales sobre la
Vivienda en el Ejido.* México, D. F.: n.p., 1964.

Instituto Nacional Indigenista. "Realidades y Proyectos, 16 Años de
Trabajo." *Memoria* 10 (1964) 11–113.

Iturriaga, José E. *La Estructura Social y Cultural de México.* México,
D. F.: Fondo de Cultura Económica, 1951.

Izquierdo, Rafael. "Protectionism in Mexico," in Vernon (ed.), *Public
Policy and Private Enterprise in Mexico,* 241–289.

Jaffe, A. J. *People, Jobs and Economic Development; A Case History
of Puerto Rico Supplemented by Recent Mexican Experiences.* Glen-
coe: Free Press, 1959.

Johnson, John J. *Political Change in Latin America: The Emergence
of the Middle Sectors.* Stanford: Stanford University Press, 1958.

Kahl, Joseph A. (ed.) *La Industrialización en América Latina.* México,
D. F.: Fondo de Cultura Económica, 1965.

Kemmerer, Edwin Walter. *Inflation and Revolution, Mexico's Experience of 1912–1917.* Princeton: Princeton University Press, 1940.

Kimmel, Lewis H. *Federal Budget and Fiscal Policy, 1789–1958.* Washington, D. C.: Brookings Institution, 1959.

Kneller, George F. *The Education of the Mexican Nation.* New York: Columbia University Press, 1951.

Laufenburger, Henry. *Fianzas Comparadas; Estados Unidos-Francia-Inglaterra-México-U.R.S.S.* México: Fondo de Cultura Económica, 1951.

León, Luis L. *La Doctrina, la Táctica y la Política de la Revolución.* México, D. F.: El Nacional Revolucionario, [1930].

Lewis, Oscar. *The Children of Sánchez, Autobiography of a Mexican Family.* New York: Random House, 1961.

——. *Life in a Mexican Village: Tepoztlán Restudied.* Urbana: University of Illinois Press, 1951.

——. "México Desde 1940." *Investigación Económica* 18 (1958) 185–256.

——. *Pedro Martínez, A Mexican Peasant and His Family.* New York: Random House, 1964.

——. *Tepoztlán, Village in Mexico.* New York: Holt, Rinehart and Winston, 1960.

——. "Urbanization Without Breakdown: A Case Study." *Scientific Monthly* 75:1 (1952) 31–41.

Lieuwen, Edwin. *Arms and Politics in Latin America.* New York: Praeger, for Council on Foreign Relations, 1961.

Lira López, Salvador, Ramón Fernández y Fernández, and José Quintín Olascoaga. *La Pobreza Rural de México.* México, D. F.: n.p., 1945.

Lombardo Toledano, Vicente. *The C.T.A.L., The War and the Post War,* tr. by O. I. Roche. México, D. F.: n.p., 1945.

——. *El Frente Nacional Democrático [y la Elección Presidencial de 1964].* México, D. F.: Ediciones Lombardo, 1964.

——. *Moscú o Pekín? La Vía Mexicana Hacia el Socialismo.* México, D. F.: Partido Popular Socialista, 1963.

——. Oral History Interviews with James and Edna Wilkie, Mexico City, 1964 and 1965.

Lombardo Toledano, Vicente, and Víctor Manuel Villaseñor. *Un Viaje al Mundo del Porvenir (Seis Conferencias sobre la U. R. S. S.).* México, D. F.: Universidad Obrera, 1936.

López Mateos, Adolfo. *5 Informes de Gobierno.* Naucalpan de Juárez, México: Novaro Editores-Impresores, 1964.

——. "Informe . . . 1964." *El Día,* Sept. 2, 1964.

Loyo, Gilberto. *Las Deficiencias Cuantitativas de la Población de México y una Política Demográfica Nacional.* México D. F.: P[artido] N[acional] R[evolucionario], 1934. 3rd ed.

McBride, George McCutchen. *The Land Systems of Mexico.* New York: American Geographical Society, 1923.

Madero, Francisco I. *La Sucesión Presidencial en 1910.* San Pedro, Coahuila: n.p., 1908.

Mancera Ortiz, Rafael. "El Presupuesto como Estabilizador del Desarrollo Económico." *Trimestre Económico* 20 (1953) 582–598.

Manero, Antonio. *La Revolución Bancaria en México, 1865–1965* . . . México, D. F.: Talleres Gráficos de la Nación, 1957.

María y Campos, Armando de. *Múgica, Crónica Biográfica.* México, D. F.: Compañía de Ediciones Populares, 1939.

Mata, Filomeno. "Carta Abierta a los Periodistas y Escritores y a la Opinión Pública." *Política,* Sept. 1, 1963. D-E.

———. "Por la Libertad de los Presos Políticos; Carta Abierta al C. Presidente de la República." *Política,* Jan. 1, 1964, 12–13.

Mendel, Arthur P. (ed.) *Essential Works of Marxism.* New York: Bantam, 1961.

Mendieta y Núñez, Lucio. *La Administración Pública en México.* México, D. F.: Imprenta Universitaria, 1962.

———. *La Economía del Indio.* México, D. F.: n.p., 1938.

———. *Efectos Sociales de la Reforma Agraria en Tres Comunidades Ejidales de la República Mexicana.* México, D. F.: Universidad Nacional Autónoma de México, 1960.

———. "Ensayo Sociológico sobre la Burocracia Mexicana." *Revista Mexicana de Sociología* 3:3 (1941) 63–111.

———. *El Problema Agrario de México.* México, D. F.: Porrúa, 1964.

———. *Valor Económico y Social de las Razas Indígenas de México.* México, D. F.: Departmento Autónomo de Prensa y Publicidad, 1938.

México, Cámara de Diputados, *Diario de los Debates,* daily by session.

México, Comisión Nacional de los Salarios Mínimos. "Descripciones Geográficas Económicas de las Zonas." *Memoria de los Trabajos de 1963.* 3 vols.

México, Departamento Agrario. *Memoria,* yearly.

———. *Seis Años de Política Agraria del Presidente Adolfo López Mateos, 1958–1964.* México, D. F.: Editora Sol, 1964.

México, Departamento de Muestreo. *Fundamento Estadístico del "Plan de Once Años de Educación Primaria."* México, D. F.: Talleres Gráficos de la Nación, 1961.

México, Dirección General de Estadística. *Anuario Estadístico.* Yearly (or published in alternate years with the *Compendio Estadístico*).

———. *Censo de Edificios, Resumen 1939.*

———. *Censo General de la Población, Resumen 1910, 1921, 1930, 1940, 1950, 1960.* Multi-vols.

———. *Compendio Estadístico.* Yearly (or published in alternate years with the *Anuario Estadístico*).

México, Secretaría de Educación Pública. *Obra Educativa en el Sexenio 1958–1964.* México, D. F.: n.p., 1964.

México, Dirección General de Estadística. *Revista Estadística.* Monthly.

México, Secretaría de Fomento. *Memoria . . . 1901–1904* to *1911–1913.* Yearly.

México, Secretaría de Hacienda y Crédito Público. *Boletín de Impuestos.* Monthly.

———. *Cuenta Pública.* Yearly. *See* Appendix B

———. *Memoria.* Yearly.

———. *Presupuesto General de Egresos de la Federación.* Yearly. *See* Appendix B

México, Secretaría de la Presidencia. *Mexico Inversión Pública Federal, 1925–1963.* México, D. F.: Talleres Gráficos de la Federación, 1964.

México, Secretaría de la Presidencia and Nacional Financiera, S. A. *50 Años de Revolución Mexicana en Cifras.* México, D. F.: Editorial Cultura, 1963.

México. Secretaría de Obras Públicas. *Documentos para la Historia de las Carreteras en México . . . 1925–1963.* México, D. F.: Talleres Gráficos de Librería Madero, 1964, 3 vols.

México. S[ecretaría de] R[ecursos] H[idráulicos]. *Agua Potable y Alcantarillados . . . 1946–1963.* México, D. F.: Talleres Gráficos de la Nación, 1964.

México Cincuenta Años de Revolución. México D. F.: Fondo de Cultura Económica, 1960–1962, 4 vols., I. *La Economía* (1960), II. *La Vida Social* (1961), III. *La Política* (1961), IV. *La Cultura* (1962).

Michaels, Albert L. "Fascism and Sinarquismo: Popular Nationalisms Against the Mexican Revolution," *A Journal of Church and State* 8 (1966) 234–250.

———. "Mexican Politics and Nationalism from Calles to Cárdenas." Unpublished Ph.D. thesis in history, Philadelphia: University of Pennsylvania, 1966.

Miller, Robert R. "Mexico Under Avila Camacho; Major Aspects of the 1940–1946 Administration." Unpublished M. A. thesis in history, Berkeley, University of California, 1951.

Mills, C. Wright. *The Marxists.* New York: Dell, 1962.

Miranda, Francisco de P. *La Alimentación en México.* México, D. F.: Instituto Nacional de Nutriología, 1947.

Molina Enríquez, Andrés. *Los Grandes Problemas Nacionales.* México, D. F.: Imprenta de A. Carranza e hijos, 1909.

Montes de Oca, Luis. "La Intervención del Estado en la Actividad Económica." *Investigación Económica* 3 (1943) 223–264.

Moore, O. Ernest. *Evolución de las Instituciones Financieras de México.* México, D. F.: Centro de Estudios Monetarios Latinoamericanos, 1963.

Mosk, Sanford A. *Industrial Revolution in Mexico.* Berkeley: University of California Press, 1950.

Mushkin, Selma J. "Health as an Investment," in "Investment in Human Beings," ed. by T. W. Schultz. *Journal of Political Economy* 70 (Oct. 1962) Part 2.

Muñoz Cota, José. Oral History Interviews with James and Edna Wilkie, Mexico City, 1963.

Myers, Charles Nash. *Education and National Development in Mexico.* Princeton: Princeton University Press, 1965.

Nacional Financiera, S. A. *La Economía Mexicana en Cifras.* México, D. F.: n.p., 1965.

Navarrete, Ifigenia M. de. *La Distribución del Ingreso y el Desarrollo Económico de México.* México, D. F.: Universidad Nacional Autónoma de México, 1960.

———. *Política Fiscal de México.* México, D. F.: Universidad Nacional Autonóma de México, 1964.

Nelson, Eastin. "A Revolution in Economic Policy: An Hypothesis of Social Dynamics in Latin America." *Southwestern Social Science Quarterly* 34:3 (1953) 3-16.

Nicolson, Harold. *Dwight Morrow.* New York: Harcourt, Brace, 1935.

Niemeyer, E. Victor, Jr. "The Mexican Constitutional Convention of 1916–1917: The Constitutionalizing of a Revolutionary Ideology." Unpublished M. A. thesis in history, Austin, University of Texas, 1951.

Obregón, Alvaro. *Discursos.* . . . México, D. F.: Biblioteca de la Dirección General de Educación Militar, 1932. 2 vols.

Olascoaga, José Quintín. *Dietética.* México, D. F.: Impresora de Libros, 1950–1963. 4 vols.

———. Interview by author, Nov. 3, 1964, Mexico City.

Orive Alba, Adolfo. "Las Obras de Irrigación," in *México Cincuenta Años de Revolución, I. La Economía.* 337–383.

———. *La Política de Irrigación en México.* México, D. F.: Fondo de Cultura Económica, 1960.

Ortiz Mena, Raúl. "Las Nuevas Funciones de las Fianzas Públicas." *Trimestre Económico* 14 (1947) 34–54.

Padgett, Leon Vince. *The Mexican Political System.* Boston: Houghton Mifflin, 1966.

———. "Mexico's One Party System; a Re-evaluation." *American Political Science Review* 51 (1957) 995–1008.

Pani, Alberto J. *Las Conferencias de Bucareli.* México, D. F.: Editorial Jus, 1953.

———. *Una Encuesta sobre Educación Popular.* México, D. F.: Poder Ejecutivo Federal, 1918.

———. *Una Encuesta sobre la Cuestión Democrática de México.* México, D. F.: Editorial Cultura, 1948.

———. *Hygiene in Mexico, A Study of Sanitary and Educational Problems.* New York: Putnam's Sons, 1917.

———. *La Política Hacendaria y la Revolución.* México, D. F.: Editorial Cultura, 1926.

Parra, Manuel Germán (ed.). *Conferencias de Mesa Redonda, 27 de Agosto de 1945–17 de Junio de 1946, Presididas Durante Su Campaña Electoral por el Licenciado Miguel Alemán.* México, D. F.: Cooperativa Talleres Gráficos de la Nación, 1949.

———. *La Industrialización de México,* México, D. F.: Imprenta Universitaria, 1954.

Partido de la Revolución Mexicana. *Segundo Plan Sexenal, 1941–1946.* N.p.: n.d.

Partido Nacional Revolucionario. *Memoria de la Segunda Convención Nacional Ordinaria.* México, D. F.: La Impresora, 1934.

Peña, M. T. de la. *Zacatecas Económico,* México, D. F.: Revista de Estadística, 1948.

Pérez López, Enrique. "El Producto Nacional" in *México Cincuenta Años de Revolución, I. La Economía.* 569–92.

Phipps, Helen. *Some Aspects of the Agrarian Question in Mexico— A Historical Study.* Austin: University of Texas Press, 1925.

Polanyi, Karl. *The Great Transformation; the Political and Economic Origins of our Time.* Boston: Beacon Press, 1963.

Poleman, Thomas. *The Papaloapan Project: Agricultural Development in the Mexican Tropics.* Stanford: Stanford University Press, 1964.

Ponce, Bernardo. *Adolfo Ruiz Cortines.* México, D. F.: Biografías Grandesa, 1952.

Poniatowska, Elena. ["Entrevista con los Doctores Guillermo Haro, Elí de Gortari y José F. Herrán"], *Siempre,* July 1, 1964, ii–xx.

Portes Gil, Emilio. *Autobiografía de la Revolución Mexicana; Un Tratado de Interpretacion Histórica.* México, D. F.: Instituto Mexicano de Cultura, 1964.

———. Oral History Interviews with James and Edna Wilkie, Mexico City, 1964.

———. *Quince Años de Política Mexicana.* México, D. F.: Botas, 1941.

Powell, J. Richard, *The Mexican Petroleum Industry, 1938–1950.* Berkeley: University of California Press, 1956.

Pozas, Ricardo. *Juan the Chamula; An Ethnological Re-Creation of the Life of a Mexican Indian,* tr. by L. Kemp. Berkeley: University of California Press, 1962.

Presupuesto. See Appendix B

Quirk, Robert E. *The Mexican Revolution 1914–1915; The Convention of Aguascalientes.* Bloomington: Indiana University Press, 1960.

Rea Moguel, Alejandro. *México y su Reforma Agraria Integral.* México, D. F.: Antigua Librería Robredo, 1962.

Resumen del Censo. See México, Dirección General de Estadística

Rivera Marín, Guadalupe. "Los Conflictos de Trabajo en México, 1937–1950." *Trimestre Económico* 22 (1955) 181–208.

Reynolds, Clark W. "The Structure and Growth of the Mexican Economy, 1900–1960." Manuscript in preparation for Yale University Economic Growth Center.

[Rosenzweig, Fernando.] *Fuerza de Trabajo y Actividad Económica por Sectores; Estadísticas Económicas del Porfiriato.* México, D. F.: n.p., [1965].

Ross, Stanley R. "Dwight Morrow, Ambassador to Mexico." *Americas* 14 (1958) 272–290.

———. *Francisco I. Madero, Apostle of Mexican Democracy.* New York: Columbia University Press, 1955.

———. *Is the Mexican Revolution Dead?* New York: Knopf, 1966.

Ruiz, Ramón. *Mexico, the Challenge of Poverty and Illiteracy.* San Marino: Huntington Library, 1963.

Rulfo, Juan. *Pedro Páramo,* tr. by L. Kemp. New York: Grove, 1959.

Santillán López, Robert, and Aniceto Rosas Figueroa. *Teoría General de las Fianzas Públicas y el Caso de México.* México, D. F.: Universidad Nacional Autónoma de Mexico, 1962.

Schmitt, Karl M. *Communism in Mexico.* Austin: University of Texas Press, 1965.

Scott, Robert E. "Budget Making in Mexico." *Inter-American Economic Affairs* 9:2 (1955) 3–20.

———. *Mexican Government in Transition.* Urbana: University of Illinois Press, 1959.

Seigel, Barry N. "Inflation and Economic Development: Studies in the Mexican Experience." Ph.D. thesis in economics University of California, Berkeley, 1957, published in Spanish as *Inflación y Desarrollo; las Experiencias de México* (México, D. F.: Centro de Estudios Monetarios Latinoamericanos, 1960).

Servín, Armando. *Las Fianzas Públicas Locales Durante los Ultimos Cincuenta Años (1900–1949).* México, D. F.: Secretaría de Hacienda, 1956.

Shelton, David H. "The Banking System: Money and the Goal of Growth," in Raymond Vernon (ed.), *Public Policy and Private Enterprise in Mexico,* 111–189.

Sherwell, Guillermo Butler. *Mexico's Capacity to Pay; A General Analysis of the Present Economic Position of Mexico.* Washington, D. C.: n.p., 1929.

Sigmund, Paul E., Jr. *The Ideologies of the Developing Nations.* New York: Praeger, 1963.

Silva Herzog, Jesús. *La Expropiación del Petróleo en México.* México, D. F.: Cuadernos Americanos, 1963.

———. *El Agrarismo Mexicano y la Reforma Agraria; Exposición y Crítica.* México, D. F.: Fondo de Cultura Económica, 1959.

———. *La Revolución Mexicana en Crisis.* México, D. F.: Cuadernos Americanos, 1944.

————. *Trayectoria Ideológica de la Revolución Mexicana del Manifiesto del Partido Liberal de 1905 a la Constitución de 1917.* México, D. F.: Cuadernos Americanos, 1963.

Simpson, Eyler N. *The Ejido, Mexico's Way Out.* Chapel Hill: University of North Carolina Press, 1937.

Solís, Leopoldo. "Hacia una Interpretación al Largo Plazo del Desarrollo Económico de México," manuscript prepared for *Estudios Económicos y Demográficos* 1 (1966).

Sturmthal, Adolf. "Economic Development, Income Distribution, and Capital Formation in Mexico," *Journal of Political Economy* 63 (1955) 183–201.

Tamayo, Jorge L. *Geografía General de México.* México, D. F.: Instituto Mexicano de Investigaciones Económicas, 1962. 4 vols.

————. "Inversiones Gubernamentales en Regadío." *Revista de Economía,* Jan. 1946, 37–41.

Tannenbaum, Frank. *The Mexican Agrarian Revolution.* Washington, D. C.: The Brookings Institution, 1929.

————. *Mexico, the Struggle for Peace and Bread.* New York: Knopf, 1950.

————. *Peace by Revolution, an Interpretation of Mexico.* New York: Columbia University Press, 1933.

————. "Personal Government in Mexico." *Foreign Affairs* 27 (1948) 44–57.

————. "The Political Dilemma in Latin America." *Foreign Affairs* 38 (1960) 497–515.

————. "Technology and Race in Mexico," in L. W. Shannon (ed.), *Underdeveloped Areas.* New York: Harper, 1957, 160–166.

Taylor, Philip B. "The Mexican Elections of 1958: Affirmation of Authoritarianism?" *Western Political Science Quarterly* 13 (1960) 722–744.

Teichert, Pedro C. M. *Economic Policy Revolution and Industrialization in Latin America.* U. of Miss. Press, 1959.

Torres Gaitán, Ricardo. *Política Monetaria Mexicana.* México, D. F.: Distribuidora Librería Ariel, 1944.

Tucker, William P. *The Mexican Government Today.* Minneapolis: University of Minnesota Press, 1957.

Turlington, Edgar. *Mexico and Her Foreign Creditors.* New York: Columbia University Press, 1930.

United States. Bureau of the Census. *Historical Statistics of the United States, Colonial Times to 1957 and Revisions. . . .* Washington, D. C.: Government Printing Office, 1960–.

————. *Statistical Abstract of the United States.* Annual.

————. Bureau of Foreign and Domestic Commerce. *American Direct Investments in Foreign Countries—1940.* Washington, D. C.: Government Printing Office, 1942.

————. Office of Business Economics. *U. S. Investments in Foreign*

Countries. Washington, D. C.: Government Printing Office, 1960.

————. *U. S. Investments in the Latin American Economy.* Washington, D. C.: Government Printing Office, 1957.

————. Department of State. Decimal File on Mexico (microfilm).

————. *Foreign Relations.* Multi-vols.

Vasconcelos, José. *El Desastre; Tercera Parte de Ulises Criollo.* México, D. F.: Botas, 1938.

Vega, Carmen de la. "La Desinfección de Verduras en los Mercados Abatiría las Muertes por Males Intestinales." *El Día,* Jan. 17, 1965.

Vernon, Raymond. *The Dilemma of Mexico's Development; The Roles of the Private and Public Sectors.* Cambridge: Harvard University Press, 1963.

———— (ed.). *Public Policy and Private Enterprise in Mexico.* Cambridge: Harvard University Press, 1964.

Vries, Egbert de, *et al. Social Aspects of Economic Development in Latin America.* Tournai: UNESCO, 1963. 2 vols.

Wagley, Charles and Marvin Harris. "The Indians in Mexico," in *Minorities in the New World; Six Case Studies,* 48–86. New York: Columbia University Press, 1958.

Weyl, Nathaniel and Sylvia. *The Reconquest of Mexico; the Years of Lázaro Cárdenas.* London: Oxford University Press, 1939.

Whetten, Nathan L. "The Rise of a Middle Class in Mexico," in Vol. 2 of *Materiales para el Estudio de la Clase Media en América Latina.* Washington, D. C.: Unión Panamericana, 1950–1951, 6 vols.

————. *Rural Mexico.* Chicago: University of Chicago Press, 1948.

Wildavsky, Aaron. *The Politics of the Budgetary Process.* Boston: Little, Brown, 1964.

Wilkie, James W. *The Bolivian Revolution and U.S. Aid Since 1952.* Los Angeles: Latin American Center, University of California, 1969.

————. "Ideological Conflict in the Time of Lázaro Cárdenas." Unpublished M.A. thesis in history, Berkeley, University of California, 1959.

————. "The Meaning of the Cristero Religious War Against the Mexican Revolution." *A Journal of Church and State* 8 (1966) 214–233.

————. Mexican Latifundia and Land Reform: A Statistical View from 1856 to 1964." Manuscript in preparation.

Wilkie, James W., and Albert L. Michaels (eds.). *Insurgent Mexico* (1914) by John Reed. New York: Simon and Schuster, 1969.

————. *Revolution in Mexico: Years of Upheaval 1910–1940.* New York: Knopf, 1969.

Wilkie, James W., and Edna Monzón de Wilkie. *México Visto en el Siglo XX; Entrevistas de Historia Oral: Ramón Beteta, Marte R. Gómez, Manuel Gómez Morín, Vicente Lombardo Toledano, Miguel*

Palomar y Vizcarra, Emilio Portes Gil, Jesús Silva Herzog. México, D. F.: Instituto Mexicano de Investigaciones Económicas, 1969.

Wilkie, Richard W. "Cartography as an Effective Tool in the Study of Social Change: The Mexican Example." Unpublished M.A. thesis in geography, Seattle, University of Washington, 1963.

Wionczek, Miguel. "Electric Power: The Uneasy Partnership," in Raymond Vernon (ed.), *Public Policy and Private Enterprise in Mexico,* 19–110.

Wise, George S. *El México de Alemán,* tr. by O. Novaro. México, D. F.: Editorial Atlante, 1952.

Wollenberg, Charles. *"Tierra y Producción*: Agrarian Reform and the Mexican Revolution, 1940–1964." Unpublished manuscript, 1967.

Yáñez Ruiz, Manuel. *El Problema Fiscal en las Distintas Etapas de Nuestra Organización Política.* México D. F.: Estampillas y Valores, 1958–1961. 6 vols.

Yates, Paul Lamartine. *El Desarrollo Regional de México.* México, D. F.: Banco de México, 1961.

[Zamora, Fernando]. *Diagnóstico Económico Régional 1958.* México, D. F.: Secretaría de La Economía Nacional, 1959.

Index

Tijuana
MEXICALI
110°
Ciudad Juárez
Nogales
30°
BAJA CALIFORNIA
NORTH
SONORA
HERMOSILLO
CHIHUAHUA
CHIHUAHUA
N O R
COAHUIL
Guaymas
Ciudad Obregón
TERRITORY OF BAJA CALIFORNIA
Hidalgo del Parral
Gómez Palacio
Torreón
CULIACÁN
SINALOA
DURANGO
DURANGO
W E S T
La Paz
Tropic of Cancer
WEST
Mazatlán
ZACATECAS
AGUASCALIENTES
NAYARIT
GUADALAJARA
20°
JALISCO
COLIMA
COLIMA
Manzanillo
PACIFIC OCEA
110°